Designs of Destruction

Designs of Destruction

THE MAKING OF MONUMENTS IN THE TWENTIETH CENTURY

Lucia Allais

The University of Chicago Press
Chicago and London

The University of Chicago Press, Chicago 60637
The University of Chicago Press, Ltd., London

Published 2018
Paperback edition 2025
Printed in the United States of America

34 33 32 31 30 29 28 27 26 25   1 2 3 4 5

ISBN-13: 978-0-226-28655-6 (cloth)
ISBN-13: 978-0-226-84007-9 (paper)
ISBN-13: 978-0-226-52261-6 (e-book)
DOI: https://doi.org/10.7208/chicago/9780226522616.001.0001

This publication is made possible in part from the Barr Ferree Foundation Fund for Publications, Department of Art and Archaeology, Princeton University.

Library of Congress Cataloging-in-Publication Data

Names: Allais, Lucia, author.
Title: Designs of destruction : the making of monuments in the twentieth century / Lucia Allais.
Description: Chicago : The University of Chicago Press, 2018. | Includes bibliographical references and index.
Identifiers: LCCN 2018014120 | ISBN 9780226286556 (cloth : alk. paper) | ISBN 9780226522616 (e-book)
Subjects: LCSH: Architecture—Conservation and restoration—International cooperation—History—20th century. | Monuments—Conservation and restoration—International cooperation—History—20th century. | Cultural property—Protection—International cooperation—History—20th century. | World Heritage Committee.
Classification: LCC NA111.5 .A45 2018 | DDC 725/.94—dc23
LC record available at https://lccn.loc.gov/2018014120

⊗ This paper meets the requirements of ANSI/NISO Z39.48-1992 (Permanence of Paper).

For Katie and Louis

Contents

INTRODUCTION

Monument Survival

The architect still labors under the ancient shadow of the obsolete monument: he has still to utilize modern technics and the modern world picture in creating his designs.

Lewis Mumford[1]

Figure 0.1 Monuments cited by Lewis Mumford in "The Death of the Monument" (1937): Giuseppe Sacconi, Altare della Patria (Rome, Italy), 1885. Leo Van Klenze, Walhalla Memorial (Germany), 1830–1842. Henry Bacon, Lincoln Memorial (Washington, DC), 1922. Photo: Vincent Lopez. Library of Congress. Walter Seymour Allward, Canadian National Vimy Memorial (Canada) on July 26, 1937. Image: George Metcalf Archival Collection, Canadian War Museum. Thomas Hastings, Eternal Light Flagstaff (New York, USA), 1924. Photograph: Library of Congress.

In 1937, the American historian Lewis Mumford pronounced "the death of the monument," in a trenchant attempt to settle a question that had vexed architects and critics for almost a decade: could a monument be modern? Mumford answered no, and pointed to memorials that had been built across Europe and North America since the mid-1800s (figure 0.1). With their stepped socles and ribbon colonnades, these buildings "pretended to the august and the monumental" but in fact clung to an architectural mission of a bygone era, to the cult of death, or of personality, with no "touch of the modern spirit in them." In an essay that has become a classic of twentieth-century architectural literature, Mumford wove an elaborate organic metaphor, where empty and ubiquitous monuments were dead matter in an immense world body struggling to outgrow its early phases. Building more such landmarks, he warned, was a misplaced attempt at civilizational "survival." To Mumford and others, the monument simply seemed an obsolete building type—fixed in an era of mobility, permanent in a time of technological change, and singular in a democratic age. "The very idea of a modern monument," Mumford concluded, "is a contradiction in terms."[2]

This book is about an architectural phenomenon that proved Mumford's pronouncement wrong, upsetting every assumption on which he based his hard line between the monument and modernity. Foremost among these was the assumption that new monuments would be built from scratch. Think of buildings that count as monuments today (figure 0.2). There are newly built ones, such as the Memorial to the Murdered Jews of Europe, an undulating grid of concrete blocks designed by the American architect Peter Eisenman in Berlin in 2005 to commemorate the Holocaust. But there are also ready-made ones, such as the Maison des Esclaves, an eighteenth-century slave-owner's house in Gorée, Senegal, where the US president Barack Obama paid a state visit in 2013. Or the ancient Roman amphitheater in Palmyra, Syria, a semicircular stage where a Jihadi organization filmed beheadings after destroying a nearby arch in 2015, and where the Russian military who then occupied the region held a triumphant concert.[3] Just because these last three—house, theater, arch—have existed in some form for hundreds or thousands of years does not mean they are not modern too. They contain a hefty percentage of metal, epoxy, asphalt, and concrete. They accrue more significance every time a political leader stops by. The thousands of yearly visitors they attract are motivated not by a cult of death or personality, but a cult of architectural heritage itself, which is fully enmeshed with contemporary local and global politics.[4] By the contradictory standards Mumford laid out, these are modern monuments: their job is survival and their survival requires precisely the kinds of "technics" he identified as engines of modern life.[5]

More broadly, then: Mumford imagined that architecture's contribution to the modern "world picture" would be purely constructive.[6] But the twentieth century turned out to be the most destructive in human history. Between 1914 and 1970 especially, physical damage to the built environment was enlarged, dispersed, and routinized so far and wide that it became a new architectural category in the public imagination, and an unavoidable datum of global historical thought.[7] Already at the time of Mumford's writing, an accelerating pace of manmade catastrophes in Europe, Africa, Asia, and the Middle East had washed a sinister tint over progressive and imperial narratives of human betterment.[8] Over the course of the next three decades, as tens of millions of lives were upended by mass-death and mass-displacement, landscapes of destruction came to be read as emblems of deep, historical tragedy.[9] Amid this real and imaged tabula rasa, not only did monuments live on. A "monument" became redefined, as any architectural object whose modernity lies not in its style or form, but in its capacity to survive destruction. This global redistribution of significance was informed by efficacy as much as reevaluation. In order to survive, monuments required new classifications, paperwork, information exchanges, as well as new methods for manipulating visual and architectural form. Monument survival itself became a branch of international diplomacy.

This book, then, addresses the remarkable return of the monument to the world stage, by following a movement of internationalists who mobilized, in the middle of the twentieth century, to design the survival of a vast array of architectural monuments. These were bureaucrats, intellectuals, art historians, archaeologists, curators, lawyers, and architects. They professed no less lofty a spiritual creed than Mumford, and likewise claimed to act on a cogent diagnosis of Western civilization's deepest impulses. But rather than await an organic renewal of the built environment, they set out to mitigate its impending erasure by activating a pervasive channel of modern power: bureaucratic organization. If destruction was to be systemic, so too would architectural survival need to be rationalized through administration, paperwork, and pragmatics. Thus, this movement first sought a platform in the "new diplomacy" of the

Figure 0.2 Three twenty-first-century monumental sites: Peter Eisenman, Memorial to the Murdered Jews of Europe, Berlin, Germany (2005). Photo © Barbara Bestor. Maison des Esclaves, Island of Gorée (Sénégal), built around 1776, and a memorial since 1964. Photo © Jean Krausse. Ancient Roman amphitheater at Palmyra (Syria) built in the second century CE.

League of Nations, an institution created in 1919 to regularize, and bureaucratize, international relations.[10] Beginning as a small committee in Geneva, and spreading increasingly wide, they worked to transform thousands of objects once known as "artistic or historic monuments"—from buildings to bridges, shrines to city centers, ruins to colossi—into a new kind of international marker, designated as "cultural" and later "world heritage" site. Monument survival, as this book defines it, is the species of international design by committee that they invented.

The movement coalesced at the first-ever diplomatic event devoted to monuments, the 1931 Athens Conference, and worked throughout the 1930s on a transnational blueprint to protect monuments. After war broke out in 1939, the group developed a branch in the Allied Military Government, producing lists and maps of protected monuments, and perfecting formats of architectural information to suit the visual and epistemic needs of the military.

These documentary procedures became normalized after the war, as monuments advocates established a foothold in the cultural agency of the United Nations, UNESCO. In the 1950s and 1960s, all manners of monument maintenance and preservation were quietly incorporated into international schemes for economic and urban planning, infrastructural development, and nation-building. By the late 1960s, this multilayered expertise machine was called upon to perform new narratives of cultural cooperation, leveraging the spectacular aspects of technology at various monumental sites. These efforts culminated, in 1972, with the signing of the World Heritage Convention, the first international legal instrument devoted to maintaining the modern world as a place of monuments' survival. So self-evident had this idea become, that the Convention took monuments as legal bases for a global imperative of environmental survival as well.[11] The narrative arc of the book is anchored by these two dates, 1931 and 1972.

After 1972, the hard-fought actions of the preceding decades—visiting and listing monuments, clearing their surroundings, debating their material makeup, documenting their evolution in file upon file—became a repertoire of available gestures, offered to any petitioner and backed by law. But in the interim, the features of the monument that Mumford had so confidently declared antiquated had been entirely sublated into their organizational capacity. Instead of being singular, monuments were nodes in a networked plurality; instead of being fixed they facilitated the global circulation of people and images; and instead of being empty and immutable, they could be regularly inhabited, updated, and maintained—*pace* Mumford, kept alive.

The story of monument survival helps fill out the picture of how liberal international ideology created a widespread institutional network of power. In particular, monument survival fulfills what Max Weber identified in 1922 as the features of a modern "bureaucratic authority": the division of projects into repeatable tasks, the autonomy of expertise, the hierarchization of authority, and the reliance on paperwork for historical continuity.[12] Political theorists have expertly applied this Weberian frame to analyze twentieth-century liberal international organizations, showing how institutions such as the UN develop "rules for the world," by creating bureaucracies that are government-like, but detached from the management of a particular territorial domain, such as that of an empire or a nation-state.[13] In the case of monuments, not only the detachment from a given territory but even the absence of a consistent institutional "office" did not prevent expertise about monuments from developing a certain autonomy, jumping to new international ventures when it could, following shifts in the availability of precisely a place from which to exercise this kind of authority over monuments from above, at a time when historical events seemed to drag them ineluctably into chaos from below. In other words, monument survival offered tools that were picked up by successive organizations, independent of immediate political program. This mode of impersonal "passing on," in turn, became evidence to disprove the widespread belief (voiced by Mumford and innumerable others in architectural historiography) that monumental architecture could be associated only with older forms of social authority, such as those of the "patrimonial" or "traditional" state.[14]

This liberal, international project of monument survival was not the only meeting of bureaucracy and monumentality at midcentury. A parallel case is found in what Paul Jaskot has called "the SS monumental building economy," where the use of forced labor in massive building projects allowed the Nazi regime to "integrate cultural goals into punitive processes."[15] Similarly, the Memorials to the Soviet Participants in World War II built across Eastern Europe after 1945 were products of an aesthetic and bureaucratic standardization, "assembled from ready-made parts, planned and manufactured by a relatively small handful of organizations."[16] The liberal counterpart to these two examples operated not through forced labor, or dispersed manufacture. It was a more immaterial form of cultural delegation that made monuments powerful instruments for liberal internationalists. And precisely the two causes Mumford named of monuments' symbolic bankruptcy—their programmatic emptiness and geographic ubiquity—offered entry points into their re-functionalization. As this book shows, international monument survival became a branch of modern design among others through the rationalization of monuments' interior spaces and the management of their infrastructural and urban location. Helping further the agenda of "governing the world," monuments became ends and means of what Mumford called material survival, and which today we more commonly call heritage.[17]

Heritage as Total Fact

The recent literature on heritage is vast and rich in perspectives from anthropology, art history, archaeology, cultural and literary criticism, and now heritage studies.[18] While many authors have eloquently described the ubiquity of heritage, or memory, in modern life, this book addresses architecture's unique role in its globalization in the mid-twentieth century. My aim is to perform a kind of writing back towards literature that has compellingly described heritage as a total social fact, but too often takes architecture for granted as evidence of this totality. Instead, I concern myself with how the opportunity to act architecturally was discovered and integrated into global governance.

To be sure, architecture's capaciousness as a medium has been central to its patrimonial power for much longer than the twentieth century. Certainly monuments have been intended to outlive those who make them since before antiquity. Wars, conquest, and destruction have shaped the valuation of architecture for just as long; the very notion of "art," some classicists suggest, originates in part from the Roman practice of plundering the statuary of enemy cities.[19] But it is modern systems of print communication that arguably turned the monument into a medium for archiving experiences among others, and, eventually, an object of modern governance.[20] Insofar as paperwork has been a motor of epistemic and political modernization since the Enlightenment, then, monuments have been modern for over two hundred years. Certainly the European bourgeois class, feeling increasingly severed from its own past since the French Revolution, has resorted to architectural salvage to invent legitimizing inheritances. In the nineteenth century historic preservation began to progress hand in hand with mechanical reproduction in the visual arts, even as monumental heritage was widely used by late imperial and national governments in their invention of traditions.[21] This book contributes to this broad historical panorama by locating architecture in the international dynamics of heritage modernization during a mid-twentieth-century period when this dynamic was determined overwhelmingly by the pairing of destruction and mass-media.

The committees in this book were all conceived as part of an effort to incorporate media or publicity in international relations, whether through "Intellectual Cooperation" in the 1930s, "morale" during World War II, or the "minds of men" with UNESCO in the postwar.[22] At first, their primary tool for the internationalization of monuments was the list, descended from many other bureaucratic instruments—laws, inventories, charters, edicts, declarations—that had been used to tether monuments to governments since the French Revolution. But eventually they came to involve increasing architectural expertise, management, and design. Still today, World Heritage is primarily a list. But as any group who agitates for "inscription" can attest, listing is not the beginning but an end of monumental politics, the result of numerous spatial and architectural transformations for certain objects to meet certain criteria. The book therefore focuses on the period before the World Heritage Convention was signed, in the tumultuous decades when its principles were worked out on the ground.

Thus this study adds to a growing literature that has probed the significance of destruction in twentieth-century aesthetics, architecture, and art.[23] Rather than focusing on the way destructive transactions unfold around monuments, or that traumatic events heighten their memorial function, I find that destruction (feared or actual) was a normalized circumstance, which made a range of heritage practices practical and desirable (figure 0.3). That is: the projects of monument survival were motivated not by a consistent aesthetic, but by the sheer feasibility of incorporating patrimonial collections into ongoing bureaucratic governance and military strategy. The banality of destruction, not a metaphysic of nostalgia, transformed buildings as diverse as mud huts and classical palaces into modern monuments.

Banality was, of course, the pivotal concept in the political theory of Hannah Arendt, who argued in 1956 that a unified humanity could arise only through a "negative" kind of solidarity, as it was threatened by disappearance.[24] It is possible to detect this negative conceptual motif in monument survival: if, as Arendt argued, human togetherness was the material realization of a lost ideal of interconnectedness, so too did buildings that survived the crescendo of

Figure 0.3 View of the French city of Caen in 1944. © Getty.

destruction acquire a whole new status, as cultural remainders, on an endangered globe. "Monuments" once partitioned into different architectural traditions became seeds of global collection, and places to build a new alliance between architecture and international ideology.

Thus many of the buildings in this book were already famous monuments by the time international experts visited them—the Parthenon, the temples of Abu Simbel, the Cathedral of Saint-Lô, the Bamyian Buddhas, to name but a very few. But innumerable others were local landmarks, thrust into global visibility. The new glue that came to hold politics and architecture together at all these sites was "culture," an international category whose invisibility and apparent self-evidence was precisely its strength. In contrast to other contemporaneous definitions of culture as either lived experience or high art, culture in the international liberal political system was a middling, consensus-building substance that could therefore be attached to inanimate objects: cultural monuments, cultural sites, cultural heritage, cultural property, cultural institutions, cultural affairs.[25] In that sense, Arendt's theory of survival, which called for individual citizens to draw new moral imperatives from the newfound neighborliness of nation-states, is less applicable here.[26] Monument survival offered no such individuation. It owed its success instead to the capacity of culture to "infect everything with sameness," as Theodor Adorno and Max Horkheimer put it in 1946.[27] In the case of monuments it was the material thingliness of architecture that substituted for social cohesion. After all, destruction may have been the century's great unifying political experience, but architecturally speaking, destruction was not one thing. One of the goals of this book, then, is to show the wide variety of state-sponsored and/or internationally-sanctioned techniques and practices of construction and destruction that fueled monuments' survival, and to situate them at the fault line between modernism and historicism.

Other International Styles

In architectural history, the four decades in this book correspond to the period when modern architecture achieved unparalleled international success. Whether one imagines the capital cities designed by the so-called Modern "masters" in India, Brazil, or Bangladesh, the Hilton hotel built on a hilltop in Istanbul, or the skyscrapers with vast fronting plazas of New York's Madison Avenue, midcentury modernism became ubiquitous between 1930 and 1970 in part through a proliferation of ever-larger building commissions from governments, institutions, and corporations. Already in 1971 Henry-Russell Hitchcock, who had helped to coin the phrase International Style in 1931, surveyed the field and confidently asserted that "the brave new world of the 1920s became to a surprising extent the real world of the 1960s and 1970s."[28] Recent studies have shown in great detail that the destructions of the midcentury were "a blessing in disguise" for modern architects, which cleared the slate for them to test out the principles they had been promoting on paper before the war.[29] In this context, midcentury geopolitical instability is credited for giving modernism a mandate for a deep symbolic renewal, whether or not destruction demanded it, and especially to replace classical or traditional architecture as a global idiom.[30] In contrast, historians of architectural preservation usually describe the efforts of preservationists in this period as foiled by the destructive effects of war, modernism, and development.[31] Yet it is precisely by engaging with destructive processes that architectural preservation was transformed from a nationally bound technical specialization, into a highly visible international design expertise. This book charts a third course between the modernists and the preservationists, and questions the easy segmentation of the twentieth century into pre- and post-war, pro- and anti-modern, by locating them in a spectrum of engagements with a broad endangerment sensibility.[32]

My proposal is to loosen the causality between politics and design. The soft and malleable tissue of "culture" that came to connect monumental architecture and international politics could also absorb a multitude of architectural aesthetics. Conversely, the increasing popularity of culture as a channel of international politics helped to disseminate building imperatives and opportunities in manifold ways, giving rise to *other* international styles. The designs in this book's title come out of destruction as historical fact, as byproducts of its intended targets and chosen instruments. Every time a small sketch in the margins of a memorandum prescribes how to deal with architectural remains, should destruction become "necessary," this is a design of destruction.

The book recounts five episodes when the survival of monuments was debated and designed within international organizations. I focus on the connections between monuments and committees, and I explore why certain institutional initiatives gained momentum while others languished, emphasizing how the technical project of planning various monuments' longevity gave transnational jolts to a branch of architectural practice, preservation, that was still relatively nation-bound.[33] Case studies are threaded through a narrative of institutional and intellectual history; only one of the chapters is devoted to a single building complex. More than a story of an emerging canon, the book identifies the means (from graphic formats like lists, maps, and policy memos, to hard materials like stone, iron, and epoxy glue) through which architectural matter was made to convey historical change.

For the remainder of this introduction, I want to prepare the ground for this episodic approach in two ways. Primarily, I will situate the chapters in a broader historical arc of internationalist history from 1919 to 1972, and fill out aspects of this history that are not otherwise covered in the chapters. Second, I will address four architectural discourses that have conceptualized the modernity of the monument: vandalism, the cult of monuments, the new monumentality, and collective memory. Each of these four discourses was already implicated in certain monumental policies by the time this book begins in 1931. They serve here as a foil against which to comprehend the separate, but related, practice of monument survival.

The Politics of Syncopation

The idea that monuments are collective, "belong to no-one, and therefore are the property of all," was articulated in 1793 by the French revolutionary leader Abbé Grégoire, who also coined the term "vandalism" to label the special category of destruction from which he was trying to save them.[34] But Grégoire placed this new class of collective property firmly in the hands of the nation-state. Similar statements about the universality of patrimony emanated from various European intellectuals throughout the nineteenth century, even as new administrations and laws across the continent and its colonies further cemented the bond between monuments and state or imperial bureaucracies.[35] Meanwhile, international *sentiment* for monumental objects grew considerably among learned circles in the second half of the nineteenth century, in "friends of monuments" societies that proliferated locally, fueled by travel and its literature.[36] By the turn of the twentieth century monuments had become one among other motifs in a transnational romantic imagination, which set the terms of various institutional, legal, and commercial agreements to be desired across the globe.[37] But not until the end of World War I did monuments advocates set out to formalize this international project, leveraging this sentiment and legal consciousness to place monuments on the agenda of the League of Nations.

Vivid images of destruction had already played an important role in coalescing international activism around monuments at the turn of the century. A 1905 French petition, for example, argued that the Parthenon should be "prevented from destruction" by calling it "the intellectual patrimony of mankind, an international property" and publishing photographic evidence that its remains had been tampered with. But the petition called for "leaving the monument alone," subject equally "to the slow wearing by time and brutal injuries by man." At this stage buildings were to be defended "from the vandalism of destroyers as much as from the illusions of rebuilders."[38] But after World War I, this view of monumental architecture as suspended equally between human action and natural decay became less tenable, as "barbarism" was increasingly diagnosed as a disease of the masses, a global political unrest that was constantly threatening to devolve into war or revolution.[39]

The League had much to gain from becoming involved in this discourse of "international patrimony." Created in 1919 in the wake of a Great War that had been widely perceived as avoidable, the League was proposed by the American president Woodrow Wilson to prevent another war by reforming international affairs in a "move to institutions."[40] This so-called new diplomacy was designed not to resolve specific geopolitical problems but to stabilize the rhythm of international relations. An ongoing schedule of conferences, held on the idyllic banks of Lake Geneva and publicized to a "world court of public opinion," would force nations into regular dialogue.[41] Regularity was inextricably linked to publicity. In contrast to the earlier diplomatic tradition, with its secret envoys and bilateral pacts, League diplomacy would be public, or at least publicized. This meant doing business "in the presence of and with the press," and developing the League's own media outlets, including its own radio and printing press.[42]

There was not one committee devoted to monuments at the League of Nations. Rather, monuments appeared on the agenda of various subcommissions of the Committee on Intellectual Cooperation (CIC), which is widely understood to have been UNESCO's predecessor.[43] Insofar as it amounted to devoting a branch of international government to disseminating ideas or propaganda, "intellectual cooperation" was a thoroughly modern project and a product of its time. But the CIC often publicized itself as a revival of cosmopolitanisms past, through grandiose appeals to the philosopher-kings of ancient Greece and the European Enlightenment. Worse, the intellectuals leading it often confused their own writerly disposition with the nature of the League as a bureaucracy, which operated through *bureaus*, or writing desks. By the end of the mid-1920s the CIC had gained a reputation as inextricably elitist, and monuments were brought in as part of an evolving struggle to reach an international public more directly.[44]

In 1930 the CIC launched a "League of Minds" whose mandate was specifically to reflect on the problem of civilization's "survival."[45] Proposed by

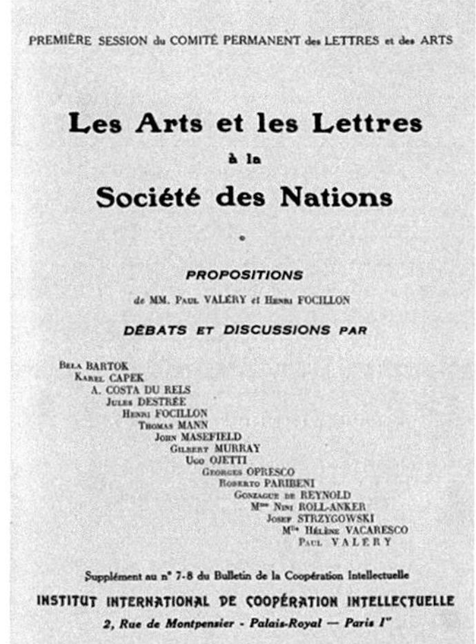

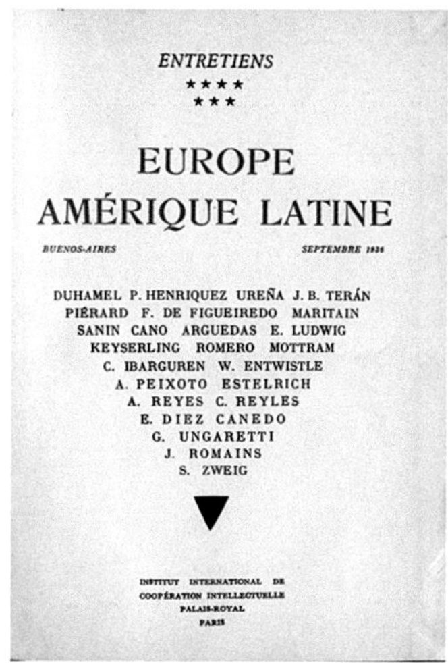

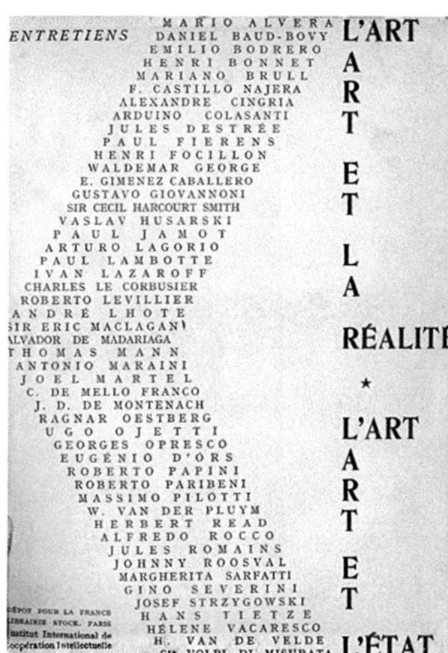

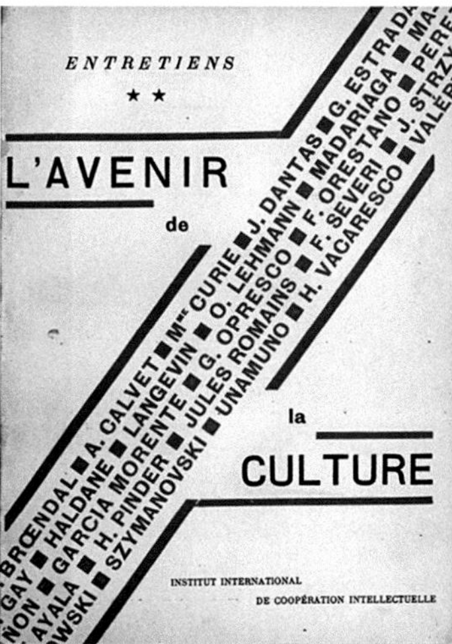

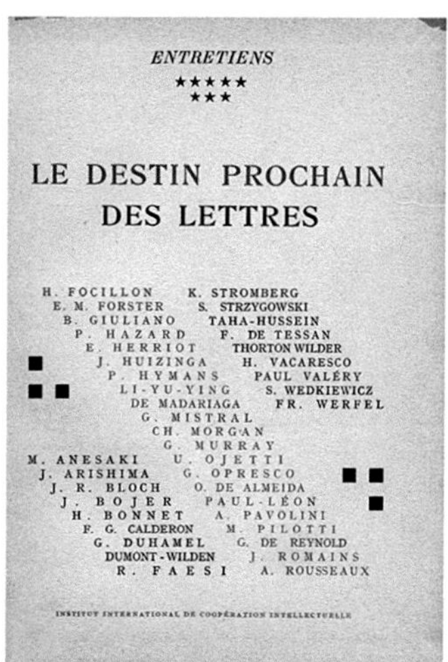

Figure 0.4 Covers of "Conversations" among intellectuals published by the Committee on Intellectual Cooperation of the League of Nations, 1932–1938.

French writer Paul Valéry and French art historian Henri Focillon, this group was to create "a politics of the mind" by mimicking the format of the League itself, staging a series of "conversations" among invited thinkers and publishing the transcripts in French and English, with a limited print run[46] (figure 0.4). As Walter Benjamin noted at the time, Valéry defined modernity as the epoch when longevity ("the will to endure") replaced originality ("the will to stand out").[47] Thus many of the topics Valéry suggested to the League dealt with what he diagnosed as Europe's intellectual "disorder," its urge to negate the past by "destroying, refuting, and deeply modifying it."[48] In the inaugural conversation, Valéry even suggested salvage as a metaphor for the intellectuals' work, asking rhetorically, "what remnants do we want to see float up from the shipwreck of civilization?"[49] The group was never given a platform for much more than musing on this weighty task. But they brought the ominous image of a civilization under threat to the League's reading public and effectively gave the League's more technical groups permission to define an aesthetic object as something that survives a selective destruction. This was enough of a mandate for the League to begin to diversify its specialized work in art, architecture, and archaeology. Four conferences were organized to bring experts from those fields into the diplomatic fold: art conservation (Rome, 1930), monument conservation (Athens 1931), museum architecture (Madrid, 1934), and archaeological digging (Cairo, 1937).

As chapter 1 chronicles in detail, the Athens Conference convened conservators from across Europe and attempted to institute a diplomatic regularity in architectural conservation. Its conclusions were published as a stand-alone volume and became an important legal precedent well into the postwar. The conference itself helped to establish an opportunistic mode of cultural politics in Geneva: intellectual cooperation would work by keeping open two lines of inquiry, the "legal" and the "technical," and waiting for a chance to get on the League's "diplomatic" agenda. But diplomatically, the Athens Conference was a total failure.[50] The schedule of regular meetings it was meant to inaugurate was never launched; the recommendations it delivered to the General Assembly of the League of Nations were never implemented; and an International Committee on Historic Monuments, which was appointed in its wake, never actually met.[51] After the volume proceedings of Athens, the next League publication to address monuments specifically was devoted to practical preparations for war: a *Technical and Legal Manual for the Protection of Monuments and Works of Art in Times of War*.[52] The contrast between these two publications is an index of the worsening of the international climate in the 1930s, marked by Hitler's rise to power, the conflicts in Manchuria and Ethiopia, the Spanish Civil War, the withdrawal of a number of nations from the League, and, eventually, the outbreak of war in September 1939. In fact, what emerges from this period is a pattern where art, archaeological, and architectural objects were consistently used to make of culture a neutralizing, rather than empowering, category of international action.[53]

For example (and it is the crucial one) two projects for legislating the international "protection" of "monuments" circulated between various committees in Paris and Geneva from the mid-1920s to the late 1930s, and were often confused in the paperwork, though they were entirely different.[54] One was an Italian law to regulate the international trade of movable art and archaeological objects, which was supported by other "source" nations (Greece and Egypt, notably), who all spoke of their national collections of art and architecture as "monuments" and of their dispersal as a kind of "destruction."[55] The second was a legal project for an international agreement between states to protect art and architecture from destruction during war. These two projects had opposite fates in the bureaucracy. At first, several draft agreements for trading (and therefore conserving) movable objects between states during peacetime were willingly discussed, whereas until 1936, Geneva repeatedly refused to produce a draft legislation for protecting art or architecture in war, arguing that legislating war went against the logic of "moral disarmament." In the words of the CIC's chairman, Gilbert Murray, "if one has the wisdom to spare monuments of art and architecture during war, one should begin by having the wisdom of not waging war at all."[56] At the heart of this refusal was a fear of having to compare the military value of physical objects and that of human lives. And it is true that the advocates who pressured the League for such a law proposed extensive new legislations that would protect people and things under the single umbrella term "culture."[57] Their expansive definitions of monument protection would have steered the League in a decidedly activist, non-neutral direction—meaning that cultural affairs could have been at the lead of policy more broadly. In this sense, they called the bluff (and the timidity) of the "politics of the mind."

But when the Spanish Civil War broke out in July 1936, and reports of church lootings and acts of violence against art and architecture began to circulate in the international press, the CIC changed its rhetoric.[58] The aforementioned *Technical and Legal Manual*, published in 1938, was the culmination of the about-face that ensued, a document remarkable for recommending a de-emphasis on "moral and educative" work about monuments and focus on their "material protection" instead.[59] Meanwhile, the idea of placing any regulations on the trade of cultural objects had effectively died. As these two projects followed so closely the vissicitudes of events, the "politics of the mind" was revealed to be a politics of willful syncopation. Intellectuals *could* intervene in the League's politics, but only if their intervention appeared off-beat from whatever geopolitical narrative the League was monitoring—a narrative to which it was, in fact, deeply reactive.

One of the legacies of this syncopated model of cultural internationalism is that international laws about immovable monuments function primarily as "customary laws" rather than as binding pacts that are brought to bear in court.[60] Instead of being debated in court, the gap between destruction and protection of monuments still today is negotiated by architectural techniques that are as predictive they are preventive. In the words of this 1938 *Manual*, to "protect" a monument meant "to *meet* the destructive effects of war with defensive measures equally as effective."[61] Thus from the bureaucratic weakness of aesthetic discourse at the League, a preemptive architectural ethos was born. Monuments became physical interfaces for the two opposed forces of building and unbuilding. In what follows, then, I give a history of four projects, one per decade, which were designed to perform this architectural task. This four-part history helps to illustrate how existing aesthetic discourses that had bridged the presumed gap between monuments and modernity, were transformed by the events and ideas that are the subject of this book.

Trajan's Arch, or Vandalism

What was meant by "material protection" can be discerned by looking at the technical half of the League's 1938 manual, which described in great visual and textual detail how to protect immovable architectural objects with scaffolds, sandbags, brick, and other materials, in the event of war. The bulk of the manual was a republication of articles that had appeared since 1936 in the journal of the International Museums Office, *Mouseion*, to publicize the experience of the Spanish Civil War, which itself had built on the earlier experience of World War I.[62] But a new dimension—a new kind of publicity—was added to these practices when they were drawn, photographed, and disseminated by the League as international norms.

Not only did the League advocate the idea that nations *should* prepare monuments for war, but more accurately, it forced into the open the fact that many European nations *had been* preparing them for war. As early as December 1934, the Italian Ministry of Education sent a circular letter to its monuments officials asking them to create "projects" for the protection of monuments in their charge.[63] Similar action was taken by the French monuments service, which established its Civil Defense policy in 1935 by asking each monuments administrator to report how many linear feet of scaffolding and sandbags would be needed to protect every monument in his jurisdiction.[64] The British Civil Defense Service had also been created in 1935, although preparations for monuments did not begin until April 1939. When developing these emergency schemes, nations were tacitly competing as to who could better protect its patrimony. The competition became overt in July 1937, when the French weekly *Nouvelles Littéraires* invited European cultural ministers to respond to a proposal for international monument protection law.[65] Despite sharp divisions about whether such a plan should unfold cooperatively or not (and despite the notable absence of Germany in the discussion), all participating officials began by noting that the time for deliberately destroying monuments had passed, thereby placing themselves unmistakably among the "civilized."

The League's manual was the next entry in this ongoing transnational discourse and it brought the crucial realization that visibility would have to be an integral part of protection. In contrast to movable artworks, architecture could simply not be hidden from the visual field of war. The one point on which all these disparate Civil Defense administrations were unified was that there was no way to protect a monument against a direct hit, given the destructive capacities of aerial bombing. Monuments could be protected only from being byproducts of nearby destruction. And encasing them was a way to *highlight*, rather than dissimulate, monuments. One of the most "material" aspects of material protection, in other words, turned out to be the image it created.

Despite its technical nature, then, this 1938 manual was arguably one of the League's first forays into using visual means of influencing the "world court of public opinion," and as such can be taken as an intervention in the history of vandalism, as an architectural subcategory of iconoclasm. According to the discourse of vandalism, any aesthetic object is rendered modern by being the target of destruction, as long as the destructive act is intentional and is registered aesthetically against the wholeness of an original artifact. World War I was, in this sense, already an "image war," as both sides accused each

ANCONA – Protezione dell'Arco di Traiano.

Figure 0.5 Trajan's Arch in Ancona, photographed before and after its encasement in 1942 by the Italian Ministry of Education, in *Protezione del Patrimonio Italiano* (Firenze: Le Monnier, 1942).

other of wantonly targeting each other's cathedrals, and images and reports of these acts of destruction had been as important as destruction itself.[66] But World War I was also the first conflict where nations had competed to rescue and protect monuments, with several manuals of protection being published at war's end.[67] In that sense, 1918 already showed aspects of what Bruno Latour has called "iconoclash": a further devolving of the phenomenon of iconoclasm, where destruction occurs but its underlying intentions are simply unclear.[68]

The intensification of "material protection," and monument survival more generally, constitute a further step in this devolution of vandalism, where destructive intention and protective action are blurred and the nature of war as a cultural event is entirely redefined. In particular, the League's manual helped to popularize and catalyze a new variation on the peculiar genre of before-and-after photography that, as Ines and Eyal Weizman have recently pointed out, serves as a visual code for destruction as a historical event that lies between images.[69] The manual republished pictures of monuments before and after protection—including pictures of the striking protective outfit, reminiscent of medieval fortifications, that had been built around Madrid's Cibeles Fountain in 1937 by a group of avant-garde architects. The League republished their section drawings, generalizing this practice of constructing iconic sandbag envelopes around urban statuary.[70] In 1942 the Italian government went even further, publishing an album that systematically catalogued its protected monuments through an eerily compelling sequence of before-and-after photographs. Here the effect was almost predictive, since the architecture of the envelope was more modernist than medieval.[71] Trajan's Arch in Ancona, for instance, went from a late classical triumphal arch to an abstract, gridded slab. As the manual explained, because sandbags were in short supply the monument had been encased in a "rigid cage" made of lumber and clad in three layers of *populit* (figure 0.5). This new building material was a proud product of the rationalization of the construction industry under fascism: available in standard-size sheets made from cement-gluing scraps of wood, algae, and other paper products, it was widely used among Italian modern architects for its thinness, and its sound- and fireproofing qualities.[72] The strangely modernist image of this building was further heightened when Ancona was heavily bombed, and the Arch miraculously survived, its mute cage still standing with paper-thinness now fully on show. Facing a vast field of heavy rubble on land, and massive capsized ships in the harbor, this temporary modernism had been intended to anticipate destruction, but it became instead premonitory of reconstruction, evoking the rationalist building idiom of the Italian postwar.

Saint-Lô, or the Cult of Monuments

The outbreak of World War II forced internationalists to rethink their association of destruction with earthly forces, since damage from aerial warfare outperformed even the most fantastic prewar prophecies of destruction from the sky. As chapters 2 and 3 show, the destruction of Europe starting in 1940 was so vast that the philosophical dilemma that had haunted prewar internationalists, the problem of "choosing" between sparing men and sparing monuments, was entirely replaced by a choice of *which* monuments to spare. Chapters 2 and 3 are devoted to the American answer to this conundrum, first in the militarization of architectural knowledge through the making of monuments lists, and secondly in a systematization of protection through the use of monuments maps. Paradoxically, because of the exodus of so many German academics to the United States, this policy was made possible in part by familiarity with a German discourse on *Denkmalschutz* that defined the monument as an object of both administrative protection and art-historical scholarship.

Thus the war rendered newly relevant the work of Viennese art historian Alois Riegl, author of the most original and forward-thinking theory of monumental aesthetics of the twentieth century. Riegl was not only an art historian, but also a lawyer with an internationalist mindset, and in his 1903 text *The Modern Cult of Monuments*, he argued that monuments became modern when they gave rise to a social institution—a cult—which provoked a thoroughgoing relativization of aesthetics.[73] By creating an extensive catalog of monumental values at play in this cult, Riegl hoped both to provide a practical guide for dealing with different constituencies competing to re-make an architectural object, *and* to build a universalist aesthetic theory where monuments were seeds for a communitarian, international empathy. Yet as chapters 2 and 3 of this book show, during the war Riegl's reasoned catalog of qualifiers (monuments "of art," or "of architecture," monuments "to" a particular person or event, intentional and unintentional monuments, commemorative ones versus ones valued for their "newness" or "age" value) was called upon to perform in the service of a militarized logic of "morale." From universal morality to military *morale* there was only a small step, which turned the cult of monuments from an aspect of daily life, into an instrument for normalizing the unprecedented scale of violence, including psychological violence, that was necessary to win a modern war.

The phenomenon of monument survival that I chronicle in this book validates Riegl's theory of modern aesthetic relativity, but questions the way its historical afterlife is usually described. Architecture and heritage literature are rife with commentaries on Riegl's theory, its longevity, and the way it was prophetic of the expansion of monumental values that would occur in later postmodern decades.[74] But what is less often remarked is that the destructions of the midcentury challenged the temporal basis of Riegl's universalism. Riegl's vision of destruction was not catastrophic, despite the deeply Nietzschean resonances of his philosophy. In his own work as a monuments inspector and in his project for a new law, he took "time" as the natural agent of destruction: monuments had a universal age-value because they were all subjected to the continuous, contingent, and uniform action of time. In this book, I show that Riegl's renewed relevance since the 1970s is partly owed to the historical phenomenon of monument survival, and the many material transformations—some inadvertent, many deliberate—that were effected in the interim across so many objects of cultish devotion.

The destructions of World War II transformed and transposed the Rieglian system of monumental values—as is fittingly illustrated by the reconstruction of Notre Dame in Saint-Lô, France. An imposing Gothic structure built incrementally from the fourteenth to the seventeenth centuries, it had partly collapsed after the town was 95% destroyed by Anglo-American bombs in June 1944, then further damaged by retreating German troops. The cathedral's deroofed nave and one remaining tower still dominated the town's skyline, however. It was rebuilt between 1952 and 1974—the inside as an immersive Gothic interior, the outside as a partial ruin, with surviving medieval fragments stitched together by modern stone walls (figure 0.6). The architect of this reconstruction, Yves-Marie Froidevaux, claimed to have captured the "new beauty" born of destruction and produced a purist piety, "a prayer for peace."[75] But with its mangled assemblage of richly sculpted fragments and

Figure 0.6 Yves-Marie Froidevaux, Triptych showing Saint-Lô Cathedral before the war, after the war, and after reconstruction. Image: Médiathèque du Patrimoine. Used with permission.

muted greenish stone, the rebuilt cathedral absorbs almost every one of Riegl's monumental values. It is intentional (as a church); unintentional (inadvertently bombed); historic (authentic fragments were restored); commemorative (as a war memorial); artistic (an "outdoor pulpit" that had attracted praise from no less than Victor Hugo is still intact); it has newness value (through the abstract pattern of the modern wall) and age-value (the new stone was chosen for its weathering properties). Riegl understood these values as projected onto one object by different constituencies; now they inhered in a single architectural project.

There is one modern value that the rebuilt Cathedral relinquished: the value of public time-keeping. Silently lacking from the façade's reconstruction is a square-dialed clock that for centuries had demonstrated the comingling of secular society and religious temporality. Its disappearance is surely a sign that the new architectural piety continues in important ways the metaphysics of Christianity but relies on an enchantment of historical events so that they are remembered outside of lived historical time. (The reconstruction also significantly shrunk the church's seating capacity, reflecting a congregation reduced not only by war but by attrition in church attendance over the centuries.) The continued conflation of the two kinds of cults—the religious and the monumental—was transferred to the city as a whole. It quickly became a popular tourist site known as "the capital of the ruins," and an obligatory pilgrimage destination for anyone wanting to experience what Samuel Beckett (writing in uniform from Saint-Lô in 1944) called "a timeless vision of humanity in ruins."[76]

St. Stephen's, or the New Monumentality

The end of World War II brought a whole new cast of international bureaucrats to the world stage. Many of them took seriously the accusations of elitism that had plagued prewar intellectual cooperation, and sought to learn from the "failure" of the League. They repurposed the blueprint of the "new diplomacy" to fit this second postwar, but designed a new system of "United Nations" to advance international cooperation through specific projects, rather than high diplomacy alone. As political theorist David Mitrany puts it, international governance was to be regular, but also "functional," because "sovereignty cannot be transferred effectively through a formula, only through a function ... by entrusting an authority with a certain task."[77] Accordingly, UN publicity material often supplemented the image of a world parliament with makerly language that depicted it as a set of "workshops for the world."[78] And of the specialized agencies, none was friendlier to architecture than the United Nations Educational, Scientific and Cultural Organization, UNESCO. Created in 1946 to take the place of the CIC, its motto pluralized the prewar politics of the mind by promising to "construct defenses for peace in the minds of men."[79] Its first Director-General, Julian Huxley, wrote enthusiastically about the Tennessee Valley Authority as a model for the functionalization of world politics, because the TVA had not only created a new regional economy but also given rise to a striking array of reinforced concrete constructions including dams, power stations, and an entire associated program of mural art and domestic architecture. The architect, Huxley argued, was "the great humanizer" of the modern period.[80]

Huxley and his staff made for irresistible interlocutors for modern architecture's own internationalist network after 1945. More than an ideal client, UNESCO promised a meeting of aesthetics and international governance that architects had been plotting for decades.[81] Indeed, polemics had continued to proliferate around the word "monument" in the wake of Lewis Mumford's 1937 postmortem with which I began this introduction, and the war only focused these debates.[82] A short manifesto published in 1943, "Nine Points on Monumentality," even made a bold attempt to reclaim monumental construction as a future building program for modern architects.[83] The text's three authors, Sigfried Giedion, Fernand Léger, and Josep-Lluis Sert, were well-known figures of the modern movement in Europe, spending the war years in the United States. In anticipation of an Allied victory and reconstruction, they proposed to reinvent "monumentality" in nine points, binding together new aesthetic goals and new collaborative methods for the avant-garde, and betting also that the "average man" would rise to the occasion as a client and an audience for modernism. "As a rule," they wrote, "those who govern and administer people, brilliant as they may be in their specialized fields, represent the average man of our period in their artistic judgments."[84] Against Mumford's "obsolete monuments," they offered a "new monumentality."

The discourse of the "new monumentality" argued the monument could become modern again if it was re-functionalized—this is why it invoked a "need" for a global aesthetic synthesis, and attached a civic function to monumental sites. On the other hand, the text also dematerialized the monument and continued a line of thinking in Giedion and others that theorized modernism as delivering pure spatial essence, driven by a kind of metaphysics. For a moment in the late 1940s and early 1950s, UNESCO held the promise of being the key client and accelerator for this new monumentality. As this book's Bridge briefly shows, the design of UNESCO's headquarters proved one of its most high-profile engagements with modern architecture. The commission fulfilled many of the features of the new monumentality, including an alliance with mural modernism, a concerted urban composition, and an emphasis on collaboration.

But the gap between two branches of functionalism—the architectural and the political—proved too wide to bridge. This failure has been extensively analyzed from the perspective of different views of the role that abstraction or modernism played as a universal language. But the historiographic focus on modernism's failure to become an official architectural language for UNESCO has obscured the missed connection between architectural modernism and buildings of other historical paradigms. Indeed, the move to a new monumentality was also a strategic one, to steal historicism's audience: to dull the avant-garde's polemical edge, and make modernism more accommodating to a public more interested in architecture's longevity than its newness. The proposal was also informed by earlier architectural theorizations of monumentality drawn from the historical styles, whether Classical, Egyptian or Gothic.[85] In that sense, the new monumentality resembles UNESCO's other work for Museums and Monuments. In fact, in 1943, Giedion had also contributed to the Allied Military Government's massive ongoing effort to make lists and maps of monuments not to bomb, directing the attention of "those who govern" to monuments both existing *and* new, and helping to jump-start the historicizing of modern architecture's own set of canonical "monuments."[86] And a few years later he would petition the organization to help in the preservation of Le Corbusier's 1924 Villa Savoye.[87] To be sure, as a "new monumentalist" Giedion implicitly condemned much of the architecture that was listed in the Allies' lists: public buildings built by governments since the late 1800s and well into the 1930s that were so many "empty shells," products of a "pseudo-monumentality."[88] But in passing, the new monumentality manifesto gave a definition of monuments that was consistent with the Allies' own: monuments were "human landmarks [which] form a link between the past and the future."[89] The new monumentality manifesto simply proposed to reverse directions: from looking backwards to looking forward, from inheritance to legacy, and from architecture's collective reception to its collective conception.

A useful snapshot of this missed connection can be gleaned by considering

Figure 0.7 Eugène Freyssinet, Halles du Boulingrin (Reims, France), 1927–1929. One of two structures Sigfried Giedion suggested adding to the Allies' lists of monuments for France. Photo: Chevojon.

how modernists and preservationists both celebrated the monumentalization of structure in this period. When he was asked to add to the list for Northern France in 1943, Giedion provided two names: the bridge of Plougastel and the Halles du Boulingrin in Reims[90] (figure 0.7). Both by the engineer Eugène Freyssinet, both were dramatic feats of reinforced concrete engineering, that Giedion thought opened new sculptural possibilities for architects. Structure also appeared in UNESCO's first publication about monuments, from 1951, which showed the rebuilding of the roof of the cathedral of St. Stephen's in Vienna, destroyed in 1945. What looked like an identical reconstruction, was in fact a wholly re-engineered modern structure, made by pouring a vast concrete floor on top of the gothic walls, and using this floor to erect and support a massive steel frame on top. Where there had once been a dense lattice of wood, a new space had been opened up: a modern steel shed built atop an ancient cathedral (figure 0.8). Photographed in the same visual style that Giedion used in his advocacy of the "spatial interpenetration" of modernism, St. Stephen's new roof was an advertisement for structure as much as for historicism. In an alternate scheme that a Viennese architect had proposed in 1945, the space under the roof was made into a bunker, whose protective function was then expressed emphatically in stylized parabolic concrete ribs (figure 0.9). There, structure, form, and image were each separately achieved. Whatever else their differences, new monumentalists and international monument advocates were aligned in that they hoped the structural behavior of architecture itself would deliver a kind of monumental aesthetic, regardless of style or meaning.

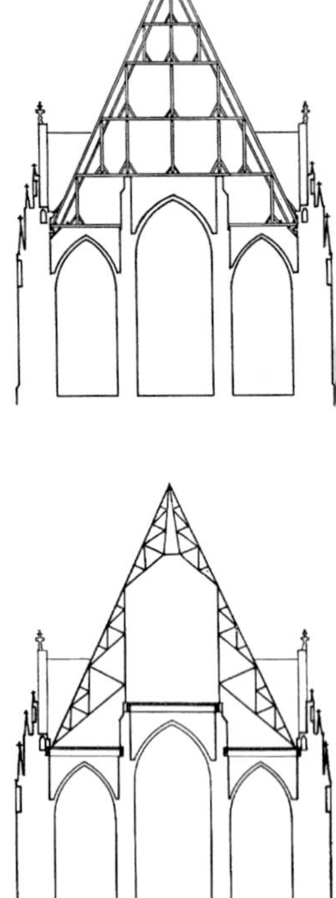

Figure 0.8 Reconstruction of the roof of St. Stephen's Cathedral in Vienna, as depicted in UNESCO's first manual in the Museums and Monuments series, *Sites and Monuments: Problems of Today* (Paris: UNESCO, 1951). Photo: BDA-Archiv.

Figure 0.9 Hoffman und Wagner, Project for the reconstruction of the roof of St. Stephen's Cathedral (Vienna, Austria), April 1945. BDA-Archiv, topographische Materialien, K 5A, St. Stephan, M 1945.

In a sense, the international bureaucrats who pushed for monument survival in this book were also forging a new monumentality. They, too, turned to architecture to supply a substance rather than form. But unlike the international avant-garde, they were willing to attach this substance to material remnants of former architectures, and to inherit their formal, material, or stylistic aspects. For UNESCO's internationalists, new materials such as concrete and steel could support not only the "growth of a new tradition" but the rebirth of old ones.[91] The second half of this book—consisting of a bridge and two chapters—is devoted to parsing the consequences of this attitude for monument conservation as a thriving global architectural practice in the postwar. Just as postwar international organization relied on de facto accomplishments to lead to ideological conviction (rather than the other way around), similarly these postwar projects of monument survival were orchestrated first, and then used as evidence that "culture" had a place in new world order.[92]

From Cultural Content to Cultural Technique

UNESCO picked up the thread of monument protection left behind by the League, and wove it along the same two parallel strands: the legal and the technical. The International Committee on Monuments (MonCom) was created in 1949, as a subdivision of Cultural Affairs (CUA).[93] Its earliest heritage missions were modest in scope and budget, but provided the content for a series of manuals titled Museums and Monuments. Meanwhile UNESCO's more general publication also featured monumental architecture. The *UNESCO Courier*, conceived as a "window open on the world" in the manner of *National Geographic*, featured many vistas of camera-friendly monumental sites.[94]

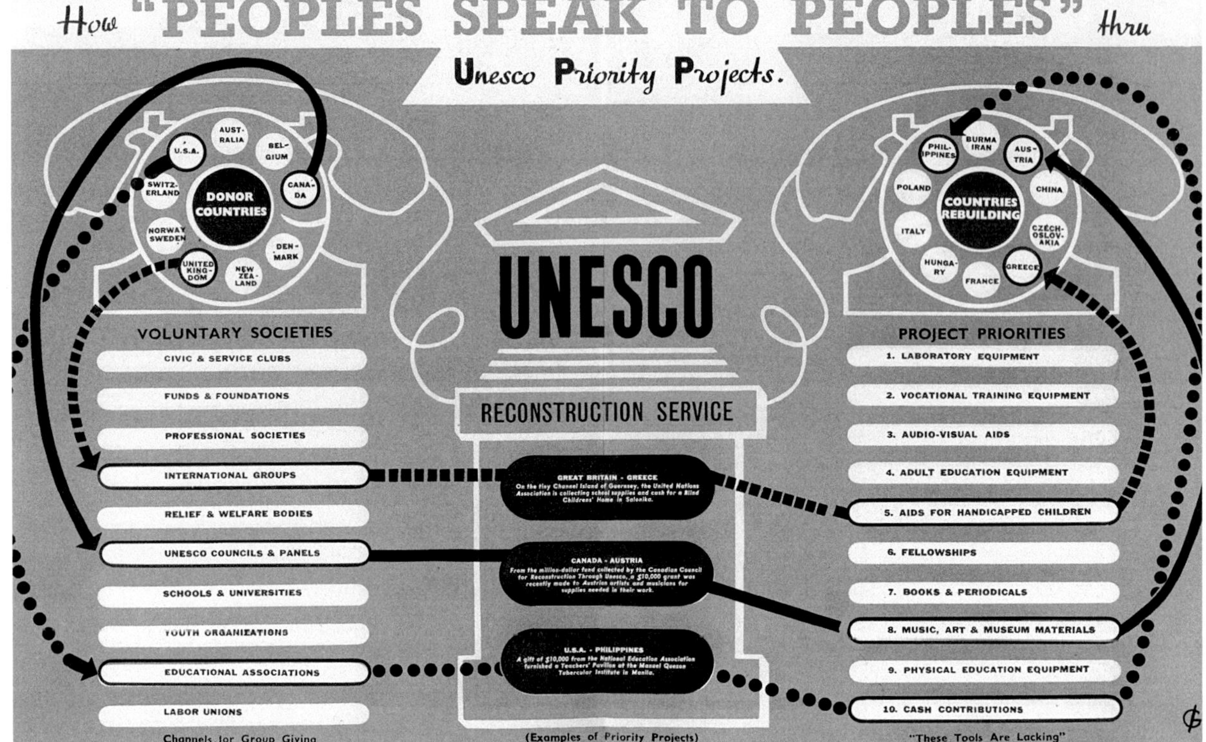

Figure 0.10 "How Peoples Speak to Peoples." UNESCO combined architecture and electrical imagery to depict the organization's special projects in 1948.

Similarly, the massive publishing endeavor that was *The History of Mankind* frequently punctuated its narrative arc with architectural examples, in part in order to build consensus between over a thousand working historians. The organization's letterhead, which was adopted as its logo in 1946, made the acronym UNESCO into a classical temple's colonnade, and seamlessly combined this appeal to monumental solidity with the imagery of electric communication (figure 0.10).

But monument conservation became a focus of UNESCO activities only after the organization made a concerted shift, in the mid-1950s, from cultural content to cultural techniques.[95] In the words of Director General Luther Evans, the organization was to go from "telling nations what to read" to "teaching them to read."[96] All UNESCO projects were subordinated to the requirements of Technical Aid—the kind of aid that could be disbursed as technological know-how and hands-on training. A new organization, the Technical Assistance Administration, became the driver for the political economy of development that presided over the UN's involvement with the decolonization of the Global South, beginning in 1945 and greatly accelerating after 1960.[97] When UNESCO's leadership attempted to determine how culture would get more "technical," the saving grace for monuments was that the formula for Technical Aid prized longevity:

A Technical Assistance Programme, as distinct from a programme of material aid, is a means of promoting economic development through the spread of technical knowledge. This process is not merely a matter of teaching particular techniques. An essential element is the training of local leaders capable of carrying on, and in turn training others to carry on, the work of development in their own country. Such educational activity must of its nature involve long-term projects.[98]

What mattered was the exploitation not of material objects but of human capital; thus, what the MonCom lacked in geographic coverage or economic leverage, it would make up for in social continuity: with appeals to tradition or to history, and to practices of monument preservation as a repository of human knowledge.

Technical continuity gave the MonCom access to better budgets; it also allowed its officials to reach back to unfinished prewar business. The two main international laws about cultural property signed in the 1950s were continuations of the two legal projects that had begun in the 1930s.[99] The 1954 Hague Convention for the Protection of Cultural Property in the Event of Armed Conflict, especially, was based on the prewar drafts, although discussions of "civilization" were replaced with considerations of "culture." The Hague preparations also became an opportunity to shore up UNESCO's standing as a technical authority. After all, World War II had been a massive experiment in monuments protection, from which one could now draw lessons and propose standard norms and procedures. Thus UNESCO's monuments experts found themselves planning for a new war in a cold war climate, adapting their know-how to the nuclear threat of the 1950s. An almost delirious aura of technicality emanates from the compendium they published as an appendix to the Hague Convention text, illustrating everything from the precise dimensioning of an underground bunker to the six steps through which one should protect a turbine through a "standard process of cocooning."[100] Many of these new technical norms were borrowed from industrial planning and have not aged well. Indeed, they demonstrate all too well that relying on technological standards for consensus means risking that the consensus will rapidly become obsolete.[101]

Such was the paradox of technicality: it was better for an international committee to continue to publish new standards, for the sake of "continuity," than not to publish anything at all. Regular updates of building and preservation norms began to substitute for regular meetings of cultural diplomats. Although the MonCom had initially hoped to become an international administration modeled on Germany's *Tagung*, it was never given the funds to grow into one.[102] Instead, two more conferences in the manner of the Athens Conference were held, in Paris in 1957 and Venice in 1964. To make a case for ramping up UNESCO's monuments work, the directors published a compendium of case studies in 1951 that showed how war-damaged monuments across a remarkably diverse number of countries had been rebuilt or preserved in record time.[103] But this slim volume also inadvertently underlined how the reconstruction of monuments had been a huge success story for monuments without being coordinated as an international architectural project.

Thus, postwar functionalism only compounded what I have called the politics of syncopation: the sense of a continued delay between the cultural and other branches of diplomacy. But many opportunities were opened up by this delay. Chapter 4 shows how the umbrella concept of "cultural property," which had been defined almost in passing during the Hague negotiations, acquired a whole new applicability in the rush of postcolonial museum-building after 1960.[104] Instead of legal instruments, it was the museum interior that became a delivery method for international values, disbursing spatial standardization and cultural normativity. Indeed, the top recommendation for modernizing a monument in the late 1950s was to transform its interior into a museum. Similarly, the massive project to salvage Abu Simbel, which is described in chapter 5, came out of an International Campaign for Monuments that was originally intended to be little more than a public relations initiative, but gave rise to wholly new economic instruments for funding cultural projects.

In architectural history, these monument and museum projects of the 1950s and 1960s are usually seen as marginal to the main lines of the modern movement: compromised by contact with local building cultures, diminished as interior architecture, or periodized as transitional to a more deliberate return of monumentality in postmodern architecture. This is in part because, although Giedion and others in modernist circles turned their attention to ancient monuments such as Egyptian pyramids and Roman temples during this period, they interpreted them abstractly, in terms of evolving "space-conceptions."[105] In fact, the international heritage missions of the postwar also offered a plethora of opportunities for designing distinctly modern monumental effects around historic structures, without committing to their particular architectural style. For example, the Italian architect Franco Minissi traveled to Egypt in the late 1950s as part of a mission to conserve and display an ancient ritual boat that was unearthed by archaeologists near the Giza pyramid.[106] The prismatic "museum" he designed for the boat was as much a jewel case as a viewing envelope (figure 0.11). Delicately suspending the visitor in mid-air between boat and pyramid, making cunning use of the kinship between their two shapes, Minissi opened up a new kind of monumental interiority, enlarging to an architectural scale a space of encasement that had only ever been, in UNESCO's literature, a pragmatic and uninhabitable buffer-zone.[107] We could even say that Minissi monumentalized the envelope-building strand of international cultural protection that had been building up since the 1930s—from the sandbags of the Spanish Civil War, to the *populit* of Ancona's arch, and the cocooning of American turbines.

Minissi's Giza boat-museum is but one of innumerable examples of UNESCO-sponsored projects where the link between artifacts as distant in

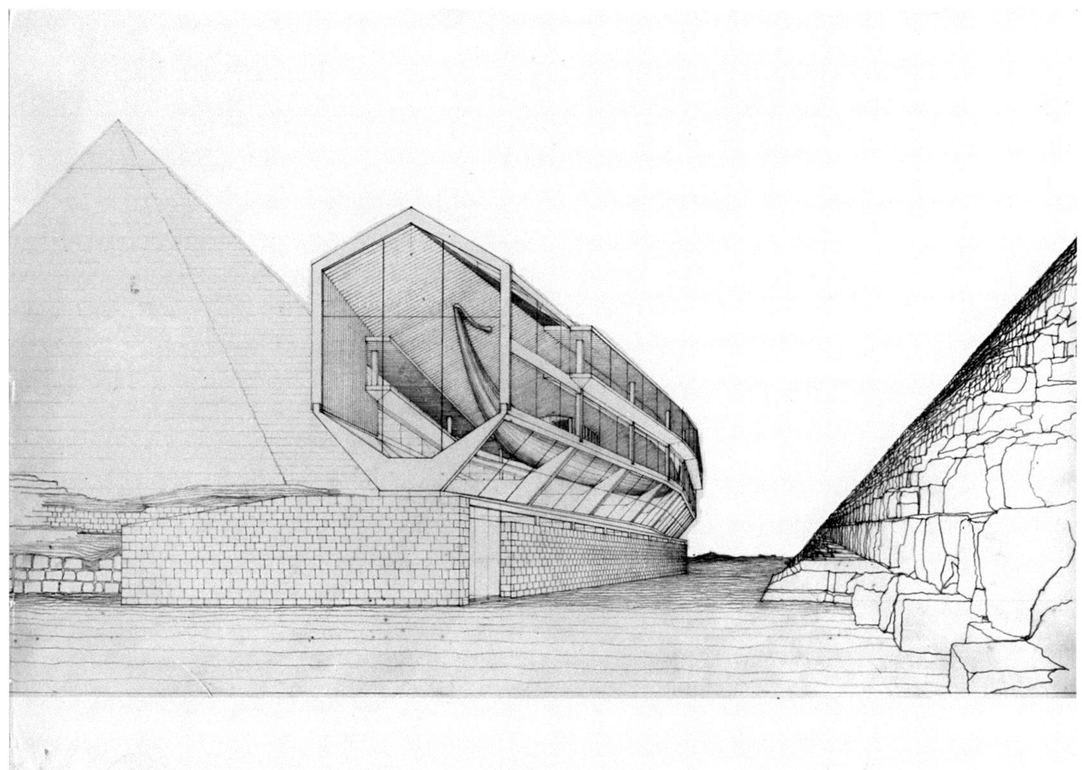

Figure 0.11 Franco Minissi, Perspective rendering of the Gizeh Boat Museum. Archivio Centrale dello Stato. Fondo Franco Minissi. Used with permission.

time as ancient Egypt and the international development decades was not just metaphysical or exegetic, but was also designed as an architectural project. The second half of this book is full of such case studies. They show how the soft power of culture drew legitimacy from an architectural aesthetics that was neither historicist nor modernist, and stealthily mobilized the budgets of cultural ministries and international organizations well into the 1970s.

Gorée, or Collective Memory

The phrase "world heritage" was coined in 1965 in Washington, DC, during a White House Conference that had been convened to assess America's interests in a shifting landscape of international cooperation.[108] At this conference, architectural historians joined archaeologists, technologists, and nature conservationists to propose a "world heritage trust" that would treat the "cultural diversity of the earth" as a resource to be conserved, akin to oil or gas. The use of "world" signaled the advent of environmental thought, where heritage is not made of punctual goods to be shared between nations but rather a territorial resource shared among among them. By the time the United States made a proposal for a World Heritage Convention to UNESCO in 1972, the phrase helped to resolved two projects that had been competing within the organization to become international law: one for protecting "culture," the other for protecting "nature." The shift to environment was prepared through the same processes of bureaucratic shuffling that had long characterized cultural internationalism. "Preparatory documents" announced a new universal value by warning of its immanent disappearance:

> [B]esides the traditional natural and man-made causes of decay, [calamities, cataclysms, fires, earthquakes, landslides, volcanic eruptions, floods, tides, vandalism, abandonment, and neglect] changing economic and social conditions, urbanization, industrialization and pollution threaten the existence of thousands of sites, monuments, buildings and natural areas throughout the world. Unless urgent measures are taken to recognize, protect, preserve, rehabilitate and present this heritage, it will be lost forever.[109]

Continuing a now-familiar pattern, destruction was used to re-classify some material threats as natural or traditional, so that others could be categorized (and culturalized) as newly urgent. As the "salvage campaigns" studied in chapter 5 show, the "environment" was always already cultural in the 1960s: accompanied by "man," and describing equally the thing to be protected and the substance threatening to overwhelm it.

The word that held together these natural, cultural, and environmental agendas in anticipation of 1972 was "site." It could denote a building, a park, an oilfield or, significantly, a city containing an entire social fabric. Among the UNESCO missions in the late 1960s, none helped to coalesce the microcosmic meaning of "site" more than Gorée, an island off the coast of Dakar, in Senegal. The international rehabilitation of the island of Gorée first began in 1965 in preparation for the Festival Mondial des Arts Nègres, organized by the Senegalese president-poet, and founder of the Négritude movement, Leopold Senghor.[110] UNESCO gave international aid, expertise, and legitimacy to this project, helping to dissimulate one continuing bilateral relationship (between France and its former colony) and to open a new one (with the United States.) Senghor wanted to turn the island into a place to which diasporic populations could "return," recreating for them an aesthetic experience of their ancestor's original enslavement and liberation. One building on the island in particular, the "House of Slaves," was conserved and rebuilt to heighten the logics of slavery embedded in its section: slaves to be sold had lived in crowded cells on the ground floor, while owners enjoyed a lavish life at the *piano nobile*, up a set of stairs arched in an oversized and patronizing embrace[111] (figure 0.12). This 1965 project continued a chain of reconstructions that had begun in the colonial period under French watch, but the Festival further leveraged spectacular, performative, and commemorative artforms to turn Gorée into an "island of memory." A nightly boat took visitors to the island to witness a "magical spectacle" of dances and songs. Other temporalities were removed to other sites: to the new market in Dakar, for example, where tourists shopped in a timeless present—the time of "craft."

Figure 0.12 The House of Slaves in Gorée, Senegal, photographed in the twenty-first century. © Jean Krausse. Used with permission.

The claim made by Senegalese cultural officials that they have "situated" a global memory of slavery precisely in Gorée island has given rise to a bitter controversy. The debate centers around the questionable authenticity of the "door of no return"—an opening at the back of the House of Slaves, that leads directly to the beach and from which slaves were supposedly loaded onto America-bound ships. In the 1990s historians went to great pains to show that this narrative was likely invented in the 1930s, transposed from a *different* slave-house on the nearby island of St. Louis, and then continually instantiated after the Festival ended, by a conservator and on-site narrator, Boubacar Joseph Ndiaye, that Senghor appointed to "re-memorialize" it.[112] Yet this debate over the authenticity of the door detracts from the more obvious architectural transformation that the house and island have undergone, whether one calls it a modernization or re-vernacularization: a stripping away of signature *colonial* elements, such as balustrades and façade ornaments, which appeared both on ground and upper floors (figure 0.13). All subsequent heritage missions in Gorée have in fact concentrated on policing the visibility of the colonial and precolonial past in the built environment.[113] But the protagonists of Négritude who launched this new phase in the island's history knew very well that collective memory was an artificial construct. Many of them had studied in midcentury Paris at the time when Maurice Halbwachs first proposed that the "substance" of history was the "collective memory," and willfully filling lacunae seemed the basis of all history-writing.[114]

The discourse of collective memory locates a monument's modernity in the act of interpretation. Ancient, historical, and traditional architectural objects stayed relevant in the twentieth century, according to this interpretation, because they acted as supports for a social imaginary that was uniquely

Figure 0.13 "Une habitation à Gorée (Maison d'Anne Colas)," 1887 engraving after a 1838 painting by Adolphe D'Hastrel of the building now known as the "House of Slaves" in Gorée (Senegal).

modern: diffuse, collective, and topographic.[115] Scholars of collective memory often turn to monuments to democratize historical discourse, to show that history was not made of great men or individual events, but also of "memories" of ordinary people. Yet memory discourse's return to the forefront of Western European historical discourse in the 1980s coincided with a moment when the word "monument" lost its specificity as an architectural, authored, thing. The advent of poststructuralist memory discourse in architecture tended to imply that all architectural and urban research should be socially grounded and location-based, a proposition that is particularly ripe for political recuperation. Even Pierre Nora, instigator of the massive and discipline-changing project *Lieux de Mémoire*, warned of the "problematic" convergence of patrimonial interests and history-writing in France.[116] One of the aims of this book, then, is to follow how objects have been re-memorialized not only through nationalism but also in willful transnational displacements.

Willful recuperations of memory are a powerful weapon as well. The proponents of Négritude would likely claim as their proud legacy the fact that an estranging display of slavery through "tribal" dances has become an obligatory experience for all global visitors to Senegal, including the first black President of the United States, who traveled to the "door of no return" in June 2013.

They might even reveal that theirs was a strategy of long-term syncopation, for a delayed culturalization of global politics, that imposed upon the "world court of public opinion" a debate about what, exactly, was memorialized in this gesture. But equally part of this legacy is the epistemological dance that every architectural historian in now compelled to enter into when facing these world heritage sites as objects of historical inquiry. Analytical skills must be honed to detect the peculiar alignment of political and architectural commitment that implicated design in this global rememorialization, and to see it as such.

This book offers four decades of historical material on which to hone this critical capacity. All the sites in this book are of this oscillating kind: they once forced designers to make a decision between building and destroying, between monument, document, instrument, and so on, and they demand that historians do the same with their narrative choices. They show us modernity being constructed through intense committee negotiations over a period of intense destruction. They uncover that bureaucratic paperwork and design innovations were equally necessary for monuments' shape, form, outline, longevity, material composition, spatial disposition—in short, their architecture—to be understood as modern. Monuments in this book are not stable objects, but building projects.

1 “Wardens of Civilization”

CONSERVATION AND DIPLOMACY AT THE 1931 ATHENS CONFERENCE

A commemorative photograph, dated October 25th, 1931, captures the event where monuments first entered into the agenda of an international organization (figure 1.1). Seven scholars, in dark suits, pose amiably on the steps of the Erechtheion, an ancient Greek temple built on the north side of the Athenian Acropolis in the fifth century BC. They are not dressed for digging, or tourism. They have come to Athens as cultural diplomats, delegated by the League of Nations to host the first international conference devoted to "the conservation of historic and artistic monuments."[1] The group sits off-center, sharply delineated against a vast backdrop of gray skies and stones. Towering behind them, four armless caryatids carry the temple's architrave atop their heads, bearing the seams of a recent archaeological re-constitution. Below, new marble has been added to hold up the assemblage, sharp-edged and smooth-faced pieces that stand in proud contrast to their weathered neighbors. This committee was not the first to pose for the camera on the Acropolis; a steady stream of congresses had convened in Athens since the turn of the twentieth century and been photographed among the Acropolitan monuments. But there is something unique in the way this photograph is grandly framed as both a portrait of a committee and a picture of a monument. Observe in contrast how two years later another group of internationalists, the architects of the Congrès internationaux d'architecture moderne (CIAM), assembled in the same spot, for a crowded snapshot where the monument barely appears. One of them is even aiming his camera lens at us (figure 1.2). While modern architects seem to blur out the past as they look toward a modernist future, the cultural diplomats exude a different attitude towards time, a different kind of synchronicity. Like new stones paired with old, they proudly embody the double nature of modern heritage: the idea that monuments are objects from the past, whose conservation in the present is also an event worthy of commemoration.

Figure 1.1 Delegates of the Arts and Letters Committee of the CIC pose on the Erechtheion of the Athenian Acropolis, on October 25, 1931. Jules Destrée is sitting in the center. © Musée Jules Destrée, Charleroi.

Figure 1.2 Delegates of the Congrès internationaux d'architecture moderne (CIAM) pose on the Acropolis in late August 1933. Courtesy of the Loeb Library. Harvard Graduate School of Design.

The event where this photograph was staged, the Athens Conference, has come to be seen as a landmark in the history of international heritage production and protection. Its seven-part conclusions were published in four languages in 1933, and have retroactively been named the first international

"Charter" of preservation.[2] This renaming has elevated the profile of the Conference, inviting historic architecture into the evidentiary cabinet of modern intellectual history, notably to illustrate the rise of "presentism" as a cultural attitude characteristic of the twentieth century.[3] But it has also set up a dichotomy between two architectural expressions of modernity, one modernist and one conservationist, further reinforcing the self-differentiation of these two opposing architectural camps.[4]

Yet as an event, the Athens Conference remains a mystery. Little has been written about how it unfolded, and the ambitions of its organizers. The relationship of its textual legacy with the political and diplomatic program of international organizations in the 1930s remains to be parsed. Even a cursory investigation shows that there is more to the ten October days—four in Athens, the rest on a boat tour of Greek sites—than these facile dichotomies. Why, for instance, did the League diplomats not pose in front of the infinitely more famous Parthenon? For much of the 1920s this building had been partly hidden behind a massive scaffold, during the extensive rebuilding program that the French-trained, Greek government-sponsored, and internationally sanctioned architect Nicolas Balanos had been managing at the site since 1895. In 1930, Balanos had completed the "repair" of one of the Parthenon's colonnades and re-inaugurated the building in an official ceremony.[5] But when the Athens Conference met, the second phase of his works was in full swing. In other words, the Parthenon that was visited by this group was a construction site. The Erechtheion, in contrast, had been an earlier project of Balanos, and was now completed. In fact, by the time the CIAM arrived in 1933, modern struts would reappear there too, one between each caryatid, to help them carry their load. So whether staged as ancient or modern, the Greek monument was in no way to be pictured, or understood, as under construction.

In this chapter, I hope to recover the institutional and intellectual scaffold that made the Athens Conference possible, and that, like Balanos's scaffolding on the Acropolis, has apparently dissolved into a historical vacuum. The architectural historian Can Bilsel has interpreted the Athens Conference in performative terms, as a yardstick event that not only "resacralized" the site of the Acropolis but also inaugurated an international regime he evocatively names "the bureaucracy of the authentic."[6] Building on this insight, I emphasize less the conclusive triumph of authenticity than the difficult birth of an international bureaucracy.

The legacy of the Athens Conference is mostly paperwork, but as Ben Kafka has suggested, paperwork must be taken seriously as a "medium of bureaucracy" that disciplines its practitioners in very specific ways.[7] The object of my inquiry is the relationship between monuments and documents that was established in Athens to fit monument conservation into the League of Nations as a bureaucracy. As Susan Pedersen and other historians have argued, despite its failure in high politics, the League pioneered the diplomatic rhythm and institutional blueprint that would continue to define international politics for the rest of the century, notably by creating lasting "technical" successes in specialized fields.[8] The Athens Conference, I argue, sought to make architectural conservation one such specialized sphere, setting a course for technical achievements despite possible legislative and political failures.

The chapter moves in three broad strokes. I begin by reading the conference's conclusions through the lens of intellectual cooperation as branch of the new diplomacy. I then reconstruct the disciplinary snapshot that was offered to conference attendees, by recounting the three contexts—the law, the laboratory, and the city—where monuments work was becoming increasingly and avowedly "technical." Finally, I revisit the last session of the Conference on the Acropolis, where new forms of international authority encountered existing channels of cultural diplomacy, including the competing ones of German archaeology and American philanthropy. More than revealing lingering frictions between the new diplomacy and the old, this encounter must be read as multiplying the means through which to blur the distinction—in architecture as in politics—between old and new.

Monuments at the League: Concrete Testimonials

By the time the Athens Conference was convened in 1931, monument conservation had already been an object of interest among the "reformist nebula" of architects, urban planners, and art historians who met periodically in international congresses and world fairs across Europe and the United States in the first third of the twentieth century.[9] But the Athens Conference was the first formal meeting of experts convened exclusively around monument conservation. Over a hundred participants from seventeen nations were invited, and from the beginning, the League's organizers were adamant that this was not to be yet another academic event or professional congress.[10] "Even when we concern ourselves with a specialized topic such as monument restoration," explained the Conference president Jules Destrée in his opening speech, "we must be mindful to elevate ourselves to a higher level, to a better understanding between peoples, a bringing together of nations, and towards anything that may one day establish solid foundations for peace."[11] Destrée had been one of the founding members of the CIC and, to elevate the professional meeting into a peace-building event, he asked participants to speak in a kind of disciplinary shorthand (*parler à demi-mots*) and leave time for broader discussion.[12] This was the trademark method of "intellectual cooperation," a kind of discourse where technical issues were brought up but not fully explored, and it explains the signature disjuncture that exists in the textual legacy of all CIC events: a gap between the agendas of conferences, the transcripts of discussions, and the volumes published in their aftermath.[13]

In the case of the Athens Conference, the agenda had been prepared by Destrée in Geneva and was driven by internationalist concerns (such as collective ownership of heritage, international legislation of monuments, and education reform).[14] But the discussions over the four days in Athens were structured to reinforce internal debates among preservationists, foremost among them the famous debate between "restoration" and "conservation" that had staged itself across the English Channel since the mid-1800s, pitting followers of Viollet-le-Duc in France against those of Ruskin and, later, William Morris in England.[15] These two aesthetic sensibilities approached the question of architecture's completion from opposite ends—one wanting to rebuild monuments to an ideal state, the other seeking to barely touch the material object, hoping at most to manage its inevitable ruination and decay. Despite the many subtleties that had come to moderate these two positions, "to conserve or to restore?" was made into the discipline's official question in Athens.[16] Speakers were "invited to explore two positions," renamed "architectural or archaeological" but clearly referring to the two long-established camps.[17] As a Swiss observer remarked, from the perspective of this longstanding controversy, the conference did not "pose new questions" but rather "reinforced existing convictions."[18]

However, when the conference's proceedings were edited for publication in a massive tome in 1933, this duality was both forefronted and overlain with a layer of diplomacy. Expositions of "doctrine" and "principle" were placed first (even though they had not been given such prominence in the event itself), and some of them were submitted after the fact, as if to even out the two positions.[19] In contrast, the language used to craft the conclusions was conciliatory. Conclusion I reframed ongoing discussions as a kind of diplomatic dynamic. "The conference," it read, "endorses the general tendency to abandon restorations *in toto* and to avoid the attendant dangers by initiating a system of regular and permanent maintenance calculated to ensure the preservation [in French: *conservation*] of the buildings."[20] This recommendation appears at first glance merely to instantiate the consensus that, in Paul Léon's words, "conservation ha[d] replaced restoration."[21] But its phrasing also signals the influence of diplomatic thinking. As an international agenda, to "initiate a system of regular and permanent maintenance" was to apply the temporal mindset of the new diplomacy to monumental objects. Just as the League would regularize international relations, so the Athens Conference would regularize monument maintenance and create appeasement. Similarly, Conclusion II asked conservators to act "in keeping with the trend of public opinion" and determine projects that would attract "the least possible opposition." Just as the new diplomacy was meant to supersede an ad-hoc system of state relations that gave rise to wars, the Athens Conference would interrupt the tendency for restoration projects to attract controversy and be trailed by seemingly endless debates.

What kind of document was this, then? The Athens Conclusions were never titled a charter as such and their preface announced that the intent was *not* "to offer a treatise of conservation."[22] Using the terms of international political theory, we could say that this document was supposed to have regulatory, not constitutive power.[23] Certainly the idea of a government-issued "charter of conservation" was already in vogue in 1931. As we will see later in this chapter, the head of the Italian delegation, Gustavo Giovannoni, had just finished authoring one such national charter, *La Carta del Restauro*, which was exactly what the League's conclusions were not: an architectural constitution for the Fascist regime, a manifesto full of formal prescriptions for the country's architects to follow. [24] Italian historians have pointed out that many of Athens's so-called technical recommendations closely resemble the principles of this charter. But if in Italy conservation was an architectural practice subject to government control, the League had no architects in its ranks. While the Athens Conclusions do offer a set of general principles, they are written in clauses that follow the term "recommend," and where the active verb is about accommodation, not design: *respect*, *maintain*, *empower*, *adopt*, *initiate*, *allow*, and the list goes on.

If the designation "charter" has stuck, then, it is partly because a charter is a kind of document that has historico-political power more generally. Another use of the word "charter" in the Athens discussions makes these stakes clear: Paul Léon, Giovannoni's counterpart as the head of the French delegation, refered to *the monument itself* as a charter. In his presentation he tied the development of modern restoration in France to the rise of history-writing. "The idea of monumental restorations," he wrote, "is linked to the birth of history. Monuments became historical: a testimony to the mores, ideas, and lives of the past. They are documents of the same order as a historical charter (*charte*) or a treaty (*traité*)."[25] Several French historians have singled out Léon's description of a documentary turn in conservation as equivalent to its modernity and argued that it is the broader lesson of the Athens gathering.[26] French government-sponsored preservation doctrine had advanced by a kind of bureaucratic writing; Léon even spoke of monuments as "great archives of stone."[27] This French conception was clearly influential on the CIC, whose subcommittee for Arts and Letters was headquartered in Paris. When a preparatory subcommittee met there in October 1932 to construct an agenda for the Committee on Historical Monuments (the one that never met), it accomplished one piece of business: to define a monument, by paraphrasing a 1913 French law, as "an edifice *the conservation of which* is of interest to the community, generally for reasons of history or art."[28] This definition presumed regular maintenance first, and then named the monument as its object.[29]

But if, in France, monuments were a kind of internal official historical document, in contrast, the international system owned no objects. How then would the archival capacity of monuments be activated? This problem provoked some of the most creative language in the Conclusions. For example, Conclusion VIIa leveraged a notion of guardianship: "The question of the conservation of the artistic and archaeological property of mankind," it read, "is one that interests the community of the States, which are wardens of civilization."[30] This clause became an important precedent in the development of international legal protections, surviving successive edits as the Athens Conclusions traveled up the League's channels to the General Assembly.[31] Here, diplomatic language and heritage discourse were hybridized, mixing two claims of belonging: first, that architecture belongs to "mankind" (a claim cultural agents had been making since the Enlightenment) and second, that civilization belongs to "the community of states" (a legitimizing tenet of the League of Nations, borrowed from British trust law.)[32] To disseminate this principle of a "trust," or "tutelage," then, all participating nations were asked to "publish an inventory" of their monuments. The League also resolved to dedicate a special section of its own publications to building up what it called an "international documentation" of monuments.[33]

The Conclusions also took a radical step further, implying that the monument would itself become a kind of mass medium, capable of constituting its own public through an act of witnessing. Buildings were "concrete testimonies of all ages of civilization," and it was the public reception of this testimony—"the respect and attachment of the people themselves"—that was the "best guarantee" that these objects might be conserved.[34] Therefore, the resolution passed by the Committee on Intellectual Cooperation in the wake of Athens asked that "the general public" be educated "with a view to associating the latter in the protection of the testimonies (*témoignages*) of any civilization."[35] Note the circular reasoning: monuments were powerful enough to catalyze public opinion, but the public then needed to be educated about how to understand them in a new way, as universal rather than national heritage. The public, then, must be taught the power of the monument in order to "associate" itself upon "witnessing" it.[36] The imperative to create new associations was the third problem to taking national monuments administration as a model: not only did the international system own no objects, and employ no architects; it also had no directly governable constituency. This was resolved by suggesting that children should be taught to "respect" monuments, and that the League could help provoke an educational reform. The apparently anodyne addition of children as vectors of monuments conservation is crucial. To begin with, it implies that the League was willing to wait a generation for its program of monument conservation to take effect.[37] Secondly, it offers a clue that the monument was a medium that had a creative, forward-looking potential—that rather than being a passive archive of past experiences, it was a kind of incubator of future value.

The Athens Conclusions' framing of the monument as a creative, generative object is important because it situates architecture among many other intellectual products that had been considered as possible targets of international regulation since the early 1920s, as the leaders of intellectual cooperation grappled with assigning themselves tangible tasks. It was not the first time that monuments had been brought up. At its very first meeting in 1922, the CIC had tried to set an international agenda in the field of archaeology, calling for new regulations for obtaining archaeological permits and for the sales of found artifacts. This agenda, published widely, began by asking all governments to draw up "a list of such archeological treasures that have yet to be brought to light."[38] The hubris of this request was not lost on Francesco Ruffini, the Italian legal scholar who had been asked to draft the proposed law. This would "require special powers of divination," he quipped; were archaeologists supposed to *predict* what was underground before starting to dig?[39] Instead, Ruffini drafted a law that simply asked states to list all of their *existing* archaeological finds, and used the word "monument" to describe those objects. This seemingly small renaming gesture was highly significant, because it allowed Ruffini to recruit monuments into his ongoing efforts, as part of a broad movement of legal internationalists, to reform intellectual property law. Indeed, in his landmark *Report on Scientific Property*, submitted to the League the following year, Ruffini redefined scientific "discovery" as a kind of creative activity, and brought under a single conceptual umbrella the invention of abstract concepts, the creation of artworks, and the discovery of archaeological artifacts.[40] The point was to argue that scientists should be compensated for their discoveries, as artists were with their creations.[41] If comparing science to art helped Ruffini depict scientists as creators, archaeology helped him depict—indeed, calculate—the future value that would be produced by basic science research.[42] So it is not that Ruffini was against prediction, but simply that he sought to use it to calculative ends. Scientists' ideas should be protected, he implied, because like future "monuments" they delivered increased value over time.

This early appearance of archaeological fragments shows the monument's historical depth being used, long before 1931, to try to force the League into innovative ways of concretizing its work, and especially to leverage *prediction* as a modern way of doing and thinking. Many of the CIC's members saw that a new kind of predictive temporality was at hand, but few agreed on the political consequences of this shift. For example (and it is the crucial one) the group's founding president, French philosopher Henri Bergson, took "time" as the crux of his philosophy but resisted any calculative operations, focusing instead on the internal processes of thought, such as "memory," that made past and present ever-evolve into one another. Bergson upended the assumption that time is a primary datum against which truth unfolds, and also questioned the Cartesian hierarchy between mind and matter. Thus he was a staunch anti-positivist and it is difficult to imagine him supporting the depiction of monuments at Athens as so many archival texts upon which to build official histories. Certainly he virulently attacked the French historical profession for its claim that history was a positive science.[43] Yet as Max Horkheimer already noted in the 1930s, despite this apparent anti-positivism Bergson's work on temporality was clearly, if dialectically, informed by the scientific "instrumentalizations" of time that were occurring all around him.[44] We can see his work as leader of intellectual cooperation at the League as one such instrumentalization. One of the best-known debates to take place within the CIC was the feud that Bergson instigated with Albert Einstein about the nature of relativity. The debate is remembered for having established a lasting opposition between "the philosopher's time and the scientist's time," and it also aptly describes Bergson's stance about what kind of activity would best serve the League's new cultural diplomacy.[45] There was a difference, Bergson insisted, between agreement achieved by technical commissions that dealt with "things" (such as "hygiene or the railroad") and the higher kind of agreement that could reached between "persons" (such as delegates on a League committee).[46] And so, paradoxically, while the CIC in its early years often conceived of itself in frankly Bergsonian terms, as an international "mind" leading an international "body," Bergson's intellectualism held little sway when questions turned to how to *force* this political body to act, or more specifically, how philosophical dialogue could direct techno-scientific cooperation.[47] To wit: both of Ruffini's attempts to advance international regulation (of research and digging) dead-ended in the mid 1920s, faced with an increasingly competitive international market for cultural goods.[48]

These early debates about different modes of prediction helped pave the way for the Athens Conference. On the one hand, they recast cultural objects as things with speculative properties rather than dead matter—something we have heard in the Athens Conclusions. On the other, the first decade of the CIC showed that such things needed to be extracted from the intellectual mixing chamber of Geneva in order to have that power activated. The Athens Conference was an opportunity to do just that. It fell to Jules Destrée, the Belgian art historian and former Culture Minister, whom we heard earlier convening the Athens Conference participants by asking them to move quickly from technical debate and to peaceful dialogue, to make this jump. Like Ruffini, Destrée was trained as a lawyer. And while Ruffini worked on redefining "discovery," Destrée focused on "witnessing" as a mental operation that unfolds around monuments—now defined as urban objects—activating their cognitive potential in spatio-temporal terms.

Monuments in the Law: Founts of Beauty

Among the specialists he had convened to Athens, Jules Destrée was keen to emphasize his own status as an architectural amateur. "For the passerby that I am," he declared in his opening speech, "what matters is that the monument remain as beautiful, as moving, as radiant as possible."[49] But behind this self-imaging as mere passerby Destrée dissimulated a longstanding engagement with cultural heritage law, which dated to his years as a young "radical-socialist" lawyer in turn-of-the-century Brussels.[50] He frequented a circle of writers and painters who led the workers' party, the Parti Ouvrier Belge (POB). Theirs was a lawyerly and aesthetic socialism: they advocated workers' rights and Symbolist poetry, and veered the Marxist critique of private property towards artistic themes. Destrée's mentor, the expropriations lawyer and gallery director Edmond Picard, preached "the socialization of art" in the journal he founded, *L'Art Moderne*.[51] "For whom do we own works of art?," he asked in one editorial, and answered that even the artist was only a temporary keeper of his own works. Because art was the product of a special category of labor that did not alienate its author, it was destined to become part of what he called "the condominium of humanity."[52] Picard and Destrée organized art-appreciation classes for industrial workers where they told of social liberation through aesthetic experience. In 1896 the young Destrée wrote his own pamphlet, *Art and Socialism*, which addressed how monument conservation would be transformed by this coming "socialization." Citing William Morris, he described monuments as collective property that the state has "the obligation to restore, maintain and transmit."[53] But if socialism would collectivize modes of production, modes of consumption—including, crucially, modes of aesthetic consumption—would, according to Destrée, remain individual. Monuments typified this kind of public property: owned together, enjoyed individually. Since aesthetic enjoyment was precisely a kind of consumption that does not deplete the object, "statues and buildings" were "inexhaustible founts of beauty" that could be indefinitely shared, and would continue to dispense "sublime sensations" for generations to come.[54] So it was as founts of beauty dispensing collective value that monuments were to impress the passerby of Destrée's 1931 speech.

When Destrée took on the task of organizing the Athens Conference, he began by commissioning a comparative survey of the legislation that governed various nations' monuments to ensure their longevity. His timing could not have been better: a wave of new laws had just been passed protecting monuments across European nations: the British Ancient Monuments Act of 1931, a Belgian Law on the Protection of Monuments in August 1931, a revision of the French Historic Monuments Law of 1930, and the preparation of an Italian Charter of Conservation in 1931. Presented together in Athens, these laws revealed a "surprising uniformity," as the Institute's legal advisor summarized.[55] States had given themselves emergency powers to intervene to protect monuments against their private owners, when those owners threatened to destroy or damage them.[56] Adding a layer of regulation onto existing private property laws, states had created new ways to control monuments, rather than claiming outright "ownership" of them.[57]

Destrée could barely wait for the end of the first Athens session to endorse this "new, as-yet ill-defined right." He eventually authored Conclusion II, where the Conference consecrated the "right of the collectivity in regard to private property."[58] To put this emerging juridical consensus to work, he asked the League lawyer to consider "the possibility of classifying certain objects as *common heritage of mankind*."[59] This strategy was the same one as states used on a national level: to establish a list of protected monuments, then "impose certain obligations" on their owners. But working between different nations was entirely different than working within them, and required a significant ideological leap.[60] In Destrée's prewar socialist writings, the condominium of humanity coincided with the nation-state. Now, in his text advocating monuments protection to the General Assembly of the League of Nations, he recommended "a restriction of the right to national property, insofar as it is a selfish right."[61] Between 1896 and 1930, Destrée went from defending artworks against the "selfishness" of bourgeois private property, to defending monuments against the "selfishness" of the nation-state. He addressed this shift in a 1931 editorial that called for "the modernization of sovereignty"—a reform of what he saw as an inherently bourgeois social formation, the nation-state. Just as the state was increasingly forcing private citizens to give up some of their so-called sovereignty for the sake of new collective public goods, so the international community could ask states to limit their national authority for the sake of protecting international goods.

Destrée's theory of monuments as triggering a socialist sentiment places him in a trajectory of internationalist thought about monuments that had coalesced around 1900, in a debate between Austrian art historian Alois Riegl and his German counterpart, Georg Dehio. Dehio, a proponent of the motto "conserve, do not restore," justified the need to maintain monuments because they provoked in the beholder a selfless piety. But as Riegl pointed out, Dehio's altruism ended at the national border. "We conserve a monument," Dehio wrote, "not because we find it beautiful, but because it represents a part of our national life." Riegl agreed that the cult of monuments was born from a quasi-religious feeling that overrode objective judgments of significance. But he also pointed out that for Dehio "the altruistic moment . . . immediately becomes selfish, as soon as it is put into relationship with another nation."[62] Instead of making national, historicist value judgments, Riegl based his proposal for a conservation law on the idea that monuments prompted in the modern mind a "socialistic" sentiment, a "feeling for humanity" that was international and universal. This debate recast nationality and internationality as subjective modes. In 1931 Destrée sided with Riegl, proposing that architecture triggers a transnational "socialistic" altruism. But the conditions for leveraging the emotive power of monuments had changed considerably since the turn of the century.

Indeed, if Destrée's prewar socialism was marked by the optimism of the Second International, by the 1930s his writings had taken on a post-catastrophic tone. "The world is traversing a worrisome crisis," he said in his opening Athens speech, picking up on themes he developed that same year in a collection of essays, *Doing Away with War*, where he warned of the current "disequilibrium of Europe," which was certain to provoke a "catastrophe so radical that no country, no man in no country, can reasonably hope to escape it."[63] Physically this catastrophe would manifest itself as a "generalized ruin." Here Destrée drew from his personal experience during World War I, when he had toured destroyed cities in Italy and Russia, found his own home demolished by bombing, and even published a provocative town-by-town guide of the destruction wrought by invading Germans upon the picturesque townscapes of Wallonia[64] (figure 1.3).

Figure 1.3 Jules Destrée poses in uniform among the ruins of Naumur, in 1915. Musée Jules Destrée, Charleroi.

The way to salvage Europe from becoming another landscape of ruins, for Destrée, was to federate the continent through exchanges of expertise and technical cooperation across political borders.[65] "Technique creates bonds between all parts of the world," Destrée wrote. A federal political structure would gradually graft itself onto transnational networks of energy, transport, trade. These kinds of material links, federalists believed, were to be solidified first before the political will for unification could be achieved. Destrée clearly imagined the monuments of Europe connected by one such transnational web, to be explored and exploited.[66] It was in this spirit that he called for the protection of monuments: not only to preserve their physicality, but to build an infrastructure—the closest thing to an electrical network—around these objects he considered a renewable cultural resource.[67]

But Destrée was ahead of his time in conceiving of monuments as a geographically dispersed aesthetic resource and few of the conservators assembled in Athens shared his federalizing impulse. Despite the rise of motorized touring in the first decades of the twentieth century, the geographic imaginary of Europe's tourist industry was national, or regional.[68] For Destrée electrification was a model of cultural diffusion; but most conservators had spent decades protecting townscapes against the proliferation of telephone infrastructure.[69] Even the Athens Conclusions included a specific recommendation to "suppress unsightly telegraph poles" in the vicinity of monuments.[70]

Furthermore, to unify monuments protection across Europe would have required integrating variegated national administrations, from France's highly centralized authority, to Italy's network of regional outposts, and Britain's largely local controls. One country that had successfully federalized its monuments policy was Germany, which had adopted since 1900 a method of conferences (*Tagung*) for coordinating monuments policy across its disparate states (*Länder*). There, German conservators led by the medievalist Paul Clemen met annually to report on important cases and recent developments in their jurisdictions.[71] This method closely resembles the diplomatic conference mechanism proposed in Athens and may well have served as inspiration for the League. But Germany sent not a single delegate to Athens. Officially the reason was that the economic crisis made travel too expensive, but responding to one of several invitations, Clemen also questioned the need to internationalize monuments administration at all. The questions raised in Athens, he argued, seemed "to be entirely national and to bear little international character."[72]

Germany was the clear loser of the Versailles treaty and already by 1931 its participation in League activity of any kind was limited and soured by general resentment. But the German state was not alone in effecting a nationalist retrenchment around its monuments. Many Athens presentations showed that conservation policies progressed hand in hand with nationalist ideologies. The Polish delegate Jarosław Wojciechowski credited national sentiment for continued monumental protection during long periods of foreign rule.[73] Francesco Pellati announced that in Italy the category "national monument" was obsolete, only to continue that all monuments were now gathered under the banner of *romanità*, an expansive category of Italian culture that represented "the civilization of the whole world."[74]

As historians have pointed out, the introduction of "civilization" as a moral standard in Geneva's internationalist circles at the turn of the twentieth century originated from an effort to find a common ground for adjudicating disputes among warring European states, but it also had the devastating effect of excluding the peoples of entire continents from the protection of international rights for decades.[75] Monuments were no different; as soon as they were designated as civilizational products, their fate was de facto removed from the hands of any population not included in the community of states. When Athens presentations mentioned architectural structures outside of Western Europe, all under colonial administration, the rhetoric of architectural and colonial tutelage seamlessly became one. Destrée himself was a Pan-Europeanist—which means that his progressivist hope for a dissolution of borders between "mother-countries" in the north presumably depended on pooling colonial resources into a mega-colony in the south.[76]

Faced with defensive nationalism, and prey to their own imperialist views, Destrée and the other legal advisors of the Athens Conference ultimately deferred to state governments as agents of internationalization when they designed an international protocol for monuments protection. An expert commission would sit in Geneva, they proposed, ready to advise any member state on any threatened monument. But not anyone could petition this body. States were given the power to block their citizens' access to this commission, and then conversely to select which of its recommendations to adopt. Similarly, the

Conference sought to establish an international "inventory of ancient monuments," which effectively anchored monuments to their homeland.[77] Destrée mapped artistic rarefaction onto national geography, specifying that "to be classified [as 'common heritage,'] works would have to be of a truly unique interest in the artistic patrimony of the country in which they are found."[78] In the pyramid of aesthetic distinction, international value would rest atop a decidedly nationalist base.[79] At best, as the Swiss observer ultimately remarked, the League offered a forum for "peaceful competition" between nations.[80]

However, Destrée's fundamental insight, that monuments could be treated internationally as an aesthetic resource, resonated with the arguments of other conference participants, and especially those who explored architecture's visual capacity to support and feed the international imagination. While Destrée conjured a world sustained by never-depleting founts of architectural beauty, this younger generation of architectural specialists had come to Athens with experiences in the laboratory sciences, which led them to a stark reevaluation of architecture's finite material life.

Monuments in the Laboratory: Disaggregated Bodies

A variety of scientific discourses came to inflect preservation theory and practice in the twentieth century, marking a significant shift in tone from the literary debates of the previous century. An experimental ethos transformed how questions driving the field could be probed. Spanish architect Modesto Lopez Otero expressed this condition with the quip that "what was a philosophical problem has become a technical one."[81] Over the course of three days, a plethora of case studies focused not on the why but the how of preservation.[82] Even as people hung on to the doctrinal opposition between restoration and conservation, it was in fact revealed to be a spectrum of possible action. As French delegate Paul Léon put it, a new "experimental era" in preservation had begun.[83]

A number of historical changes had made the choice between restoring and conserving simply impractical. To begin with, it became increasingly difficult to distinguish between the action of human and of nonhuman agents. Ruination had been conceived as the aesthetic mark of linear, continuous, slow, and unstoppable natural forces onto manmade objects, and conversely, human interventions were perceived and performed as a break in this historical continuum. But the temporal chain that had been assumed to motivate ruination was being increasingly confused. Many buildings needing restoration looked historic but were in fact modern.[84] Conversely, some historical buildings appeared "newer" than their modern descendants, causing architecture's very historicity to lose its visual cohesion. Secondly, most of the damage affecting buildings looked natural but was in fact manmade, manifesting the effects of industrial pollution. "Monuments are being threatened to an ever-increasing degree by atmospheric agents," read Conclusion V.[85] There had also been the destructions of war, which complicated the assumption that damage was limited to certain buildings. And there were the innumerable instances when a monument was damaged by previous waves of restorers, who had defaced monuments under the guise of saving them. "Sometimes," avowed one participant, "the worst enemies have been our predecessors."[86] While nineteenth-century architects imagined that monuments were either restored or not, twentieth-century monuments were more likely to be hybrids, equally damaged by neglect and zealotry. In this context, preservationists could no longer trust decay to signify the uniform passage of time.

Authenticity, time-passage, decay: all of these morally charged concepts were presented in Athens as quantifiable variables in a new branch of architectural science. And the analogy motivating this new science was with medicine. All participants spoke of life and death, health and old age, surgery and medicine, normality and abnormality. "The architect holds the life of the monuments in his hands, so to speak," declared Lopez Otero, who broke down conservation into a 3-step process: first, "understanding the building's pathology," second, "diagnosing and comparing symptoms of ruination," and last, devising a "course of treatment."[87] This medicalized language was not new, but conservators now used it to systematize preservation as a field, which progressed through applied research rather than abstract speculation, building on a set of clinical precedents. This clinical approach, in turn, inverted the taxonomic impulse that had long sustained preservationists, defying stylistic categories by emphasizing outliers and exceptions such as the Minoan palaces of Crete.[88]

Classifying monuments based on decay involved developing a new vocabulary of disaggregation, dissolution, and "denaturation."[89] The more monuments were presented as a pool of available matter, for humanity to experiment on, the more a materialist notion of heritage took hold. Unifying all of these different types of monumental damages was a new atmospheric type of destruction called weathering. Open-air archaeological sites were now grouped together with urban monuments, bringing together conservationists who dealt with modern cities and archaeologists were used to dealing with "little more than a chaotic amassing of enormous stones."[90] Paradoxically, their efforts to protect monumental matter from these atmospheric effects drove conservators to simulate and, eventually, accelerate the effects of time through "a kind of artificial ageing of the material," bringing the decaying matter into the laboratory to see how time-passage could be registered at a molecular scale.

This material approach to monuments did not void them of metaphysics; on the contrary, the empirical search for the causes of material disorder led to a heightened awareness of the possibility of discovering a new, exalted monumental substance. Belgian architect Jean Hendrickx, for instance, explained that the scientific method rendered obsolete any approach to monuments that only projected sentimentality *onto* them because it was better to extract affect *from* them, "allowing the material itself to secrete spirituality in its purest form."[91] This animistic expectation that monuments would ooze with restored spirituality turned the idealisms of the nineteenth century—both rationalist and romantic—on their heads. "Order" and "harmony" were no longer purely visual criteria that regulated architectural facades. Now, moral and aesthetic values were to be extracted from the building itself. Indeed, the new experimental apparatus also provided techniques for actively visualizing the processes of decay, since the naked eye alone would not suffice. Lopez Otero for example vaunted photogrammetry, because it could "graphically render the process of ruination," revealing the imperceptible change of buildings over time, through a "cinematic history of deformations."[92]

Still, most of the technical "solutions" proposed in Athens deferred to a classical understanding of monuments as surface-bound objects.[93] In fact, the Athens Conference was organized to follow up on a first conference on paintings and sculpture. Accordingly, in Athens, Jean-François Cellerier, the head of a newly established monument unit at the Conservatoire des Arts et Métiers in Paris, followed a practice common in painting restoration, with its emphasis on "varnishes," by gearing his research towards perfecting a substance to "coat" historic facades. Yet while painting conservation and monuments preservation shared many procedures, such as chemical analyses and microscopic examinations, the two fields had markedly different goals.[94] To place a painting in the laboratory was to reveal the secrets of the masters. But in architecture there was no hidden image to be detected behind decay—indeed, rather than an insight into genius, the observation of building surfaces only threatened to reveal a depersonalized logic of decay. As if to fill this scientific void with narrative over-compensation, many of the material experts found political ontologies inside building stones, using them to legitimize national narratives. Indeed, the new conservation science, with expensive laboratory experiments, lent itself to patriotic showcasing.[95]

If there was one clear voice for a more scientific internationalism at the Athens Conference of a more speculative—rather than applied—kind, it was that of Viennese art historian and scientist Alois Kieslinger, who explicitly presented his experiments as a neutralizing force and a liberation from the dogmas of previous years. Kieslinger was unique for suggesting that new methods for conservation required new modes of architectural perception. His presentation on "the Disaggregation of Building Stones" summarized the research he would publish the following year in a slim but groundbreaking volume, *Zerstörungen an Steinbauten* (Damage to Stone Buildings).[96] Trained as a geologist, Kieslinger argued that the right analogy for conservation was with petrography, the study of mineral substances. "In both domains," he wrote, "what is needed is a regular schedule of chemical, microscopic, photographic experiments." Only this regularization of experiments could identify the molecular causes of illnesses that might not be detectable to the naked eye. Thus Kieslinger vaunted the pedagogical value of photography to recognize the symptoms of the "maladies" afflicting buildings visually. Peeling marble, bending tombstones, eroded volutes, mangled sculptures, rusty rails,

Figure 1.4 Alois Kieslinger, illustrations of the "malady of the crust" (*Krustenkrankheit*) in *La conservation des monuments d'art et d'histoire* (Paris: Office International des Musées, 1933).

and oozing cornices—these are but a few of the varieties of decay that Kieslinger collected in his photographic catalog, armed with his trademark black and white checker-board measuring scale, calibrating the eye.[97] As a photographic literacy substituted for being able to look inside these built artifacts, Kieslinger hoped, architects would "learn to see geologically"[98] (figure 1.4). Even readers of the conference proceedings were invited to train their eyes into this mode of scientific seeing by the use of metric scales giving each material sample a measure.

Geological "vision" had the potential to revolutionize the epistemology of architectural preservation. To begin with, the effects of time on architectural matter were visible, but not necessarily legible as such. Secondly, Kieslinger discovered that time proceeded not along a single line, but rather according to cycles of humidity and dryness. It was the "rhythm of moisture" (*Feuchtigkeitsrhythmus*) that was the true motivator for architectural history. And most importantly, he showed that monuments were not passive recipients, but rather active participants in their own deterioration. The romantic conception of time as a tactile agent that layers its visible marks onto architectural surfaces was entirely undermined by Kieslinger's geological research.

Kieslinger collected these three insights in a detailed exposé of "crust-formation" [*Krustenkrankheit*, which the Conference translated as "malady of the crust"], a type of decay that appeared to afflict the outside surface of architectural works but really grew from deep within their material texture. Previous theories had held that the chemical byproducts of industrial production—salt, soot, sulfur—decayed architecture by depositing themselves on the surface.[99] Instead Kieslinger demonstrated that through complicity with rainwater, a variety of atmospheric agents penetrated to the center of the stone and then migrated crucial minerals from the interior to the exterior, leaving a void at the center. Even when monuments appeared to be solid bodies, they were disintegrating from within. And this malady did not discriminate between styles or forms. Even the strongest of monoliths tended towards disaggregation, and even the most prismatic objects would eventually succumb to a pathetic faciality. From the perspective of materials science, monuments' existence was simply unstable.

The Athens Conference did not yield new standards for conservation science, but Kieslinger's participation in the conference, alongside other experimentalists, gave scientific credence and empirical support for the project of diplomatic regularization, apparently showing the new diplomatic age would be punctuated by an experimental tempo.[100] Another branch of conservationists approached the problem of re-visualizing historical architecture at an urban scale, as part of the project for making entire cities visually coherent. In fact, many legal and scientific advances in monuments protection that I have been discussing so far had unfolded on an urban stage, and against the drama of Europe's rapid urbanization, to which the Athens Conference devoted an entire session.

2

Hier ruhet
Frau

4

Frisches Gestein
Übergangszone
Mehlige Schicht
Jnnenkruste
ehemalige Oberfläche
Außenkruste

5
10
15

3

0 1 2 3 4 5 6 7

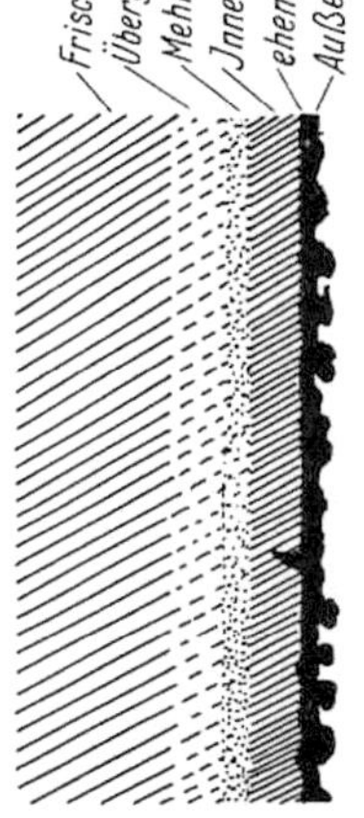

4

1

2

Monuments in the City: Destructive Objects

Many of the new laws that were discussed in Athens were first tested during the unprecedented growth of European cities since 1900, and especially after World War I, when city authorities began to develop and maintain "plans" for expansion. Over three tumultuous decades of harsh competition for urban land, preservationists had protected monuments against speculative and embellishment schemes, fought over adjacencies, and generally tried to argue that protection should extend beyond the buildings to their urban surroundings.[101] By 1930, social and physical planning, sealed together by reformist mentalities, had begun to erode private ownership for the sake of newly defined "common goods" such as parks, infrastructure, and public squares.[102] As the British delegate in Athens summarized, European cities had arrived at "the principle of expropriating for the cause of public utility."[103] Preservationists rode this wave of reform to achieve their own victories, by reconceptualizing their work as the provision of an urban amenity. The newest wave of monuments' legislation in 1930 and 1931 had simply elevated these urban controls from city to state.

The dangers of urban expansion were everywhere in evidence during the Athens Conference presentations, and were addressed in Conclusion III, "The Aesthetic Enhancement of Monuments" (Mise en valeur des monuments). Despite the lack of any reference to cities in this heading, the section was about the regulation of new construction around monuments, and argued for control over these surroundings by combining two discourses that had long been familiar to urban authorities. First, the notion that monuments should be "valorized" [through *mise en valeur*, translated into English as "enhancement"] appealed to socio-economic planners, because it implied that monuments provided planners with a calculable value.[104] Secondly, the term "physiognomy" implied that each city has an identity legible in its built form. According to an organicist analogy in usage since the early nineteenth century, engineers understood cities as bodies, with buildings for organs, streets for arteries, parks for lungs, etc. By extension, preservationists developed a habit of describing façade profiles and even street patterns as a city's "face."

Originally, these two discourses worked at cross-purposes. Enhancement was a euphemism for demolishing to "liberate" historic monuments from abutting structures, as applied in Haussmann's reform of Paris, and many other European cities. Physiognomy in contrast was usually invoked precisely by post-Haussmanian urban thinkers to protect "minor" urban architecture. By 1931 they were poised to become compatible tools in a constructive strategy for the design of the historic city, shaping urban demolition into a cohesive urban image. Two Athens attendees, Belgian architect Victor Horta and Italian preservationist Gustavo Giovannoni, were pioneers in this new synthesis.

Horta opened his speech by evoking the modern European city as a theater of eclecticism. "We still build in every style, we are not afraid to restore mon-

Figure 1.5 View of the demolished "Quartier des Putteries" from the Rue Montagne de la Cour in Bruxelles (Belgium), photographed in 1905. © KIK-IRPA, Brussels.

uments of every age, we shake up entire neighborhoods in order to enhance them, to embellish them, to adapt them to the uses of today—all of this happens too often without a method."[105] Any attentive listener could have easily identified in this unnamed chaotic city Horta's native Brussels, which a building boom had left marked by disorder, visual exuberance, and stalled embellishments, and where Horta himself had built many mansions as leader of the Art Nouveau movement.[106] The transformation of Brussels into a European "capital of commerce" had begun under Leopold II and was still underway in the early twentieth century. By 1931, Brussels was a city in patches: strings of showy private houses, interspersed with monumental nodes, around which vast swaths of demolished fabric awaited rebuilding[107] (figure 1.5). In the process, Brussels's monuments appeared to have become destructive objects, seemingly provoking the demolition of city fabric around them.

Horta proposed to use monuments to establish architectural continuity amidst "permanent change." City fabric would be regulated by visual guidelines derived from monuments, propagating outwards, in three concentric zones, allowing the neighborhood to become "the envelope to the building's soul." First, the monument was to be surrounded by an open zone (*zone libre*) of deambulation. To create "the most favorable view," Horta recommended

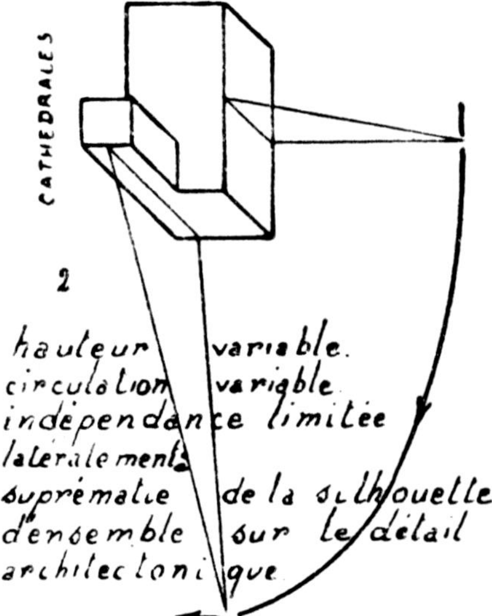

Figure 1.6 Victor Horta, diagram of the proper viewing angle for "vertical architecture," 1935. From Horta, "Etude objective sur les auteurs des Serres du Jardin botanique de Bruxelles," *Bulletin de la Classe des Beaux-Arts* 5, no. 17 (1935).

drawing a 45 degree angle from the top of the building to the ground, and opening this angle more or less, depending on whether the architecture was horizontal (classical, which would benefit from deep vistas) or vertical (Gothic, which would look better close up)[108] (figure 1.6). After this buffer zone of visual appreciation began "the neighborhood," composed of "utilitarian and decorative structures." Here not only geometry, but also a dimensional and material lexicon, would be inspired by the architectural characteristics of the monument. Like "a frame to a painting," the neighborhood was to be harmonized with the principal monument to "enhance [*mettre en valeur*] its practical and aesthetic value." Massing, light, volume, shadows, materials, proportions, and coloration—all took part in this visual subordination, so that the monument's effect might "ricochet" off the "urban ensemble." Finally, a third zone of architectural influence extended beyond this neighborhood along the public streets of the city.

Horta used these rules to justify demolitions as part of an expressionist agenda—preserving "the envelope of the building's soul." In a sense, he expanded the lessons that he had worked out as an Art Nouveau architect (about spatial interpenetration, plan fluidity, and aesthetic form as paths towards political liberation) to the scale of the city. In this modernist reconfiguration, the internal circulation patterns of historic buildings would extend into street geometry. No longer self-enclosed, the image of the monument oozed and propagated into the city, reaching concentrations in important buildings and dissipating again in more utilitarian structures. Preservation was not just a defensive stance but a reciprocal accommodation of building and city, a dynamic of creative destruction that channeled the "rapid change" of the city to optimal aesthetic effect.

When presented in an international conference, Horta's accommodationist language struck a geopolitical chord. Against "a lack of coherence and intellectual dispersal," he proposed to "neutralize the disaster." Horta's conservative architectural politics had already debuted on the international stage in 1927, when he presided over the jury for the competition for the League of Nations's new headquarters.[109] Similarly, in Athens Horta positioned himself as a middler of extremes, appealing to "reason," "agreement," and "understanding" and issuing a rallying cry that sounded as much like a political slogan as an architectural manifesto: "Let us agree on how to order architecture!" Ricocheting throughout the city, total design would make space for political neutrality. This was a very weak architectural politics to be sure, but a politics nevertheless: Horta implied that architectural cohesion would necessarily create an architectural public.

If private capital had brought destruction to Brussels, in Rome it was state power that had taken hold of the pick-axe. Since the late 1870s, the government had gutted entire swaths of the capital in the name of embellishment, and the Fascist regime had intensified the trend. As soon as Mussolini had come to power in 1922, he announced a plan to cut new avenues through Rome's old neighborhoods, demolish structures deemed secondary, and expose archaeological remains at the expense of medieval buildings. By 1930 the *Duce* had taken to being photographed at the sites of demolitions, pick-axe in hand. These demolitions were not without their own preservation agenda—the fascist state was committed to promoting monuments of art and architecture as part of its own image, both internally and abroad.[110] In contrast to Horta's more dynamic image, this one was to be photographic, staged, and dependent upon freezing a view of imperial grandeur along monumental axes.

It was also as part of this campaign to brand the fascist regime as preservationist that Mussolini dispatched over twenty architects to Athens, the largest national delegation by far.[111] The Italian government had been trying to steer the CIC's work towards visual culture, to make it a continuation of its own cultural politics at home, and had been the host for the 1930 conference on art conservation.[112] Giovannoni, the leader of the Italian group, was director of the Royal School of Architecture in Rome, and at the height of a multivalent career as a practitioner and theorist of preservation.[113] Giovannoni duly tabulated the number of delegates from each country in his conference notes, noted the dominance of Italians, and, in the two speeches he gave, offered "the phenomenon of Italian restoration" as a model for the rest of the world. He also brought with him the habit of addressing his theory to the *Duce*, whom he credited for no less than having "re-valorized the life-force of the nation."[114] Italian architectural culture was divided among several factions, each with a competing idea of how historic architecture could best serve fascism, with Mussolini himself as arbiter. Within this crowded field, Giovannoni advocated what he called a "scientific" theory of preservation—by which he meant a practical set of rules, set down in drawing, to help architects make decisions about

Figure 1.7 Benito Mussolini and members of the Commission for the Plan of Rome take a tour of ongoing embellishments around the coliseum in Rome (Italy), September 1933. © Istituto Luce.

monumental projects on a case-by-case basis, rather than through *a priori* polemics or urban plans imposed from above (figure 1.7). By 1931 he was actively working against the coming wave of demolitions that Mussolini had planned for Rome. Thus the vision he presented in Athens was entirely his own; couching it in patriotic language was a way for him to speak to the fascist regime as much as for it.[115]

The single theme that unified Giovannoni's various Athens speeches was continuity—as a political, urban, and architectural principle. Politically, Giovannoni argued that fascism continued the "reconstruction of the Italian nation" that had begun in the 1860s. Historically, he presented Italy's monumental heritage as a "continuum of development unique in the world for spanning over 30 centuries."[116] And spatially, Giovannoni offered a single principle to give material reality to this historical fact: an "extension of monumental value" not only to major monuments, but also to "secondary works" whose value was "typical," "collective," "relative," or "vernacular." Conservation now had to protect to entire zones of the city and their "monumental ambiance." The whole city, he argued, was a monument itself.

Like Horta, Giovannoni recommended an urban strategy that did not dissolve hierarchies (between high and low, old and new, large and small), but propagated them outward, through a system of urban renewal he called *diradamento* (which translates roughly as "pruning"). And like Horta, rather than forbidding demolition, Giovannoni incorporated it along smaller streets, giving shape and identity to distinct neighborhoods, "improving without radically transforming."[117] To provide visual continuity in the profile of buildings, Giovannoni asked architects to develop a neutralizing architectural language. New construction could be legibly more abstract than classical forms, but no modern interventions should come to undermine the clear visual perception of a historicist whole.[118] In plan, he sought to preserve a delicate ratio of solid and void through a system of "interconnecting piazzas" leading from one monument to the next, created by partial demolitions of buildings and street alignments. In his Athens speech, Giovannoni used euphemisms—"reintegration, recomposition, unencumberment," and "restoration of monumental unity"—which classified these demolitions as enhancements.[119] But despite his anti-radical rhetoric, Giovannoni's straightening-out of the city required extensive and opportunistic destruction. The stealth destructions of *diradamento* even reached inside buildings, especially large non-religious historical monuments that could be gutted to accommodate administrative functions, while surrounding historic urban fabric could become modern housing by having their interiors "regularized."

Giovannoni further codified his urban system as constructive, rather than destructive, by polemicizing against modernists' obsession with "structure," and counter-proposing the concept of "integrality"—another euphemism, this time implying a continuity not only between old and new but also between the moral fiber of the conservator and the material makeup of monuments. In fact, historians have noted that Giovannoni's theory offers many parallels with the ethos of international modernism he abhorred; his "integral architect" was comparable to the "total designers" of the Bauhaus and easily fit within a spectrum of rationalisms.[120] Similarly, Giovannoni's historical scholarship has been placed in a lineage of historians, such as Auguste Choisy, who systematized the study of historical precedents, and rationalized the teaching of architectural history under the influence of engineering culture.[121] But it was not only ideology or institutional politics that made Giovannoni a modernizer; the very tools of urban *diradamento* were invented to produce a thoroughgoing rationalization of space. His theories were shot through with the word "regolare." Inevitably in the new interiors he designed for historic building shells, he removed idiosyncrasies to produce regular shapes; and the new modest-size public squares (*piazzette*) he recommended peppering around the Italian built environment were ever-gridded and griddable. In fact, *diradamento* was only possible because the transition between monument, private, and public space was to be lined with a standard band of space that could be unfurled with varying lengths to patch the edges of half-demolished blocks. In this, Giovannoni was inspired by his analysis of the Renaissance reform of Italian cities, which

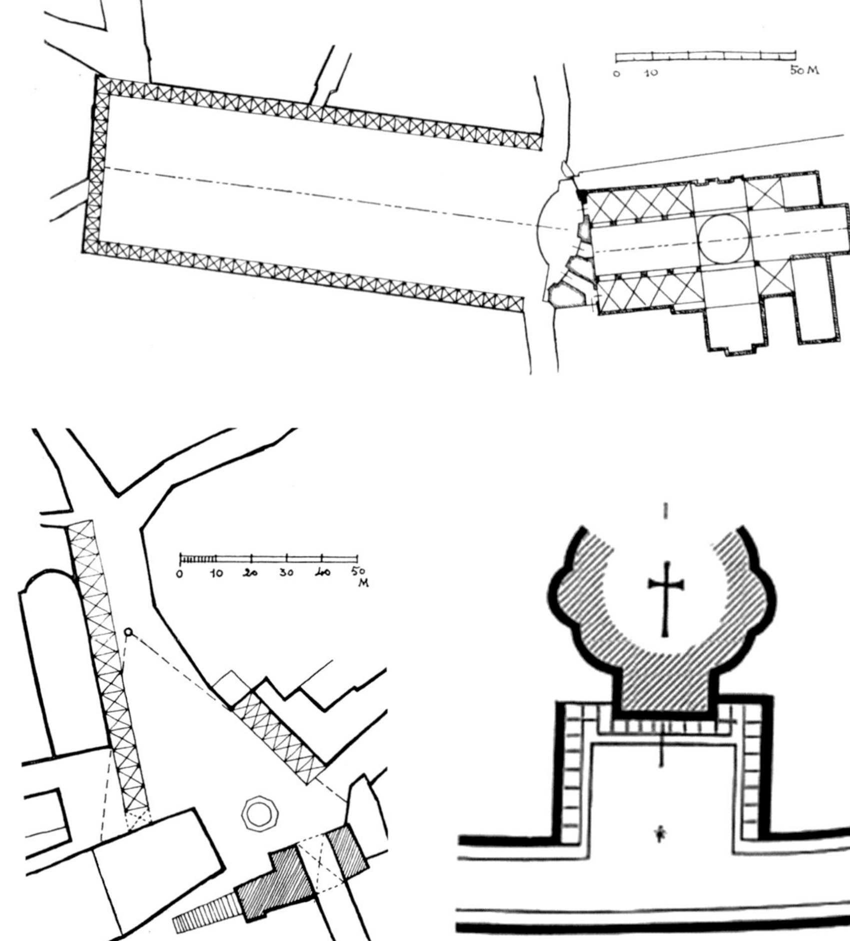

Figure 1.8 Gustavo Giovannoni, plans of Italian monuments and their surrounding piazzas, drawn to show groin-vaulted cloisters, 1930–1935: Top: Piazza Grande, Vigevano (15 C.); Bottom Left: Piazza in Fabriano (14 C.); Bottom Right: San Carlo Borromeo, Milan (19 C.).

he drew in plan vignettes, with a consistent graphic style where all new arched cloisters appeared as a band of repetitive, modular space, criss-crossed by groin vaults and punctuated by columns[122] (figure 1.8). Giovannoni's new pattern could absorb any defect, straighten out any irregularity.

Rather than speaking of space itself as a tool for reform, Giovannoni closed his Athens speech calling for the architectural empowerment of "the simple citizen." Anyone who showed empathy for the form of his city was entitled to make choices as to what should be restored, demolished, or reconstructed. In closing, Giovannoni advocated giving inhabitants legislative control over the environment in which they lived.[123] But this historically conscious lifestyle—what he called a "genteel civility"—would only be available to some. Indeed, Giovannoni praised a new system of urban expansion (originally developed by the architect Marcello Piacentini and eventually applied in the new plans for Rome, Venice, Bergamo, Bari, and Siena) that expelled *both* architectural novelty *and* working-class populations from innumerable Italian city centers to the outskirts. Aligning historic preservation with social segregation, Giovannoni prefigured a much later trend of preservation through gentrification.

Giovannoni's design philosophy of "integrality" was uniquely suited to the chameleonic nature of the fascist regime, and fit just as well with the League of Nations's discourse of neutrality. The design skills he advocated were the tools of an architectural diplomat, and the Italian urbanite was a model for an international citizen, who would also "avoid extremes."[124] Furthermore, his ambition to place architecture in a historical holding pattern was perfectly in keeping with the League's plans to regiment conservation in a diplomatic present.

Like Horta, who worried about urban museumification, Giovannoni promised to regulate not only the form but also the temporality of the city. Horta had warned about the "museum-city," and Giovannoni agreed, adding that "cities are not archives."[125] But both relied on institutions and paperwork in essential ways to keep the city alive. Notably, both pioneered graphic techniques such as annotated plans and axonometric drawings of guidelines that could be flexibly attached to building's edges, whatever the original context, to recommend spatial improvements and record monumental changes. These kinds of annotations were essential tools for transmitting design ideas from one conservator to the next in any administration, and can be seen as antecedents of the annotations that came to pervade the plethora of expert mission reports produced by UNESCO in the later half of the twentieth century.

Destrée's legal project, Kieslinger's scientific experiments, and Horta and Giovannoni's urban ameliorations—all of these processes were proposed at the Athens Conference as rising international standards. But the one realm in which monuments had already been conceived as international property, and where their physical resilience had been tested by intergovernmental collaboration, was the archaeological site. Unlike in the CIC's early debates, archaeology here was not conceived as a digging practice but a reconstructive one. And archaeology imposed itself as a discipline for diplomatic negotiation, by sheer force of the location of the meeting on the Acropolis. Indeed, the temples of the Acropolis became unavoidable "test-cases" for all the conclusions that had been tentatively arrived at in the preceding days.

Monuments in Archaeology: Quasi-diplomatic Things

The final session of the Athens Conference was held on the Acropolis and revolved around the Parthenon, literally and figuratively. Nicolas Balanos, the Greek architect charged with the Acropolitan monuments, gave a tour of the work he had completed over three decades (which included restoring the Erechtheion and the Propylea, and lifting the northern colonnade of the Parthenon) and then invited the Conference to comment on his proposed plan for the Parthenon's south colonnade[126] (figure 1.9). The Conclusions record that

Figure 1.9 Nicolas Balanos presenting at the Athens Conference, with the Parthenon in the background, 1931. © Musée Jules Destrée, Charleroi.

the Conference unanimously endorsed Balanos's plan to perform "no restoration" on the Parthenon "beyond anastylosis," defining this term as the "reinstatement of any original fragments that may be recovered" and the use of "recognizeable new materials" to support these fragments.[127] In ancient Greek, the word "anastylosis" refers to the erection of a monument; its modern return to mean *re*-erection appears to have been native to the Athenian archaeological scene and can be tied to Balanos's appointment at the Acropolis site in the wake of the earthquake of 1894.[128]

Essential to framing the debate about *anastylosis* as a new scientific norm was the older practice known in French as *relèvement* (literally, "lifting back up"), which allowed fragments dispersed around a site to be reconstituted. In 1905, for instance, when the French journal *Le Musée* published a petition against the *relèvement* of Parthenon column drums, it was by arguing that once fallen, monumental fragments belonged to the earth. Proponents of reconstruction, in contrast, argued against abandon to earthly forces—including those of the "vandals" and "barbarians" who had willfully damaged the structures over the centuries.[129] *Anastylosis*, then, was not just a scientific variant of *relèvement* but a rupture from the very possibility of "leaving" the work of vandals or nature.

But anastylosis, this apparently highly rational practice, was in fact fraught with difficulties. Contrary to the published deliberations, the transcript of the Acropolis conversation reveals that every aspect of Balanos's method was challenged. He admitted, for instance, that some the column drums that he had used on the Parthenon's south colonnade might have been moved from the south to north of the site in earlier years. The alibi of stones simply "falling" from monument to ground gave way to another, more complicated story where human activity displaced fragments repeatedly around a site. The deliberations also forefronted the constructive nature of the technique, by defining anastylosis as "the use of new pieces to hold up old pieces."[130] In fact, modern materials dominated the discussion. If newness was to be "recognizeable," what kind of continuity could be designed between the new pieces and the old?

Balanos indicated that he had originally intended to use marble to replace the Parthenon's missing drums, as he had done at the Erechtheion, but since "new marble would never match antique marble," at the Parthenon he had switched to constructing new pieces out of a combination of stone and cement, which was stained and waterproofed. This was a temporary solution, Balanos specified, to be replaced once a more suitable "new material" had been "discovered." Old and new drums were fastened with iron connectors, sometimes in the same slots where ancient architects had once used metal ties, sometimes in newly drilled holes.

Objections to Balanos's method abounded, especially from those experienced with iron and concrete—Kieslinger, Horta, Giovannoni, Slothouver, and Pontremoli. Some pointed out that new iron would corrode, expand, and cause the ancient marble to crack. Others rehearsed the hydrometric dangers of abutting stone against concrete. A variety of alternative solutions were discussed—lead, bronze, or stainless iron; a different concrete, another marble. As Giovannoni summarized, "science could usefully intervene" by requesting both that "a different metal be used" and that a new marble be chosen to "*facilitate* identification" between old and new, rather than *suppress* it. But Balanos was deaf to these objections, and continued to refer to his system as a kind of cladding that might be replaced.

History has proven Balanos tragically wrong, and his restoration caused exactly the kind of damage predicted. New iron corroded and cracked the stone in the Erechtheion's architrave. Balanos was also cavalier in handling old stone, cutting away at old fragments, making straight lines out of irregular edges to fit them against new portions, like puzzle-pieces.[131] But despite having essentially predicted this damage, the opportunity to codify anastylosis as an international norm was too attractive for the Athens Conference to pass up, and the Conference endorsed Balanos's proposed work.[132] Underscoring the idea that no real set of best practices emerged from Athens, the Parthenon remained a special case.

Throughout the discussions, the Acropolis was repeatedly excepted from the general rules the conference proposed. For example, although the Conference recommended that no one style should be "proscribed" over another in restoration, Georg Karo justified the demolition of an "overly romantic"

Frankish Tower that once stood near the Parthenon, but still called for the protection of Frankish, Venetian, and Turkish buildings in the rest of Greek territory.[133] Similarly, Victor Horta argued that the Greek weather, which made marble look "crystalline," rendered moot any absolute judgment about the authenticity of conservation materials: ancient Greek iron did "keep (*conserver*) indefinitely" but most modern iron was of bad quality; bronze was not recommended in very humid climates, but in Greece it was acceptable.[134] The Parthenon became an example at the same time as it became an exception.

This contradiction gets to the heart of the relationship between architectural matter and international politics proposed in Athens. Because of the weight that was placed on monuments as possible media of intellectual cooperation, the recovery and piecing back together of dispersed stones was expected by most of the attendees to function as an allegory for the new diplomacy, with its goal of repairing frayed international relations. But defined by archaeology, anastylosis was a technique that gave new valence to architectural history on the international stage, by turning an architectural object into *both* a monument *and* a document. If, as Lorraine Daston has argued, two regimes have competed historically to preside over the judgment of things—the idolatric and the evidentiary—the Parthenon was called upon to perform in both.[135] On the one hand, it was to be authentically itself, radiating its aura. On the other hand, it was to bear traces of the modern restorers, to index a scientific process. Anastylosis was a technique that assigned these two aesthetic tasks—enchantment and visualization—in a tectonic analogy to two kinds of stone. New stones could be read like texts; old stones could be experienced as artifacts. But the relation between past and present in diplomacy was not so simple.

To begin with, the Acropolis had long acted as an international tribunal for the adjudication of archaeological knowledge. Archaeological institutes, foreign schools and academies, which had proliferated in historically rich sites like Athens since the second half of the nineteenth century, had acted as cultural embassies for competing European empires. These cities were described by Athens attendees as centers of "international thinking" in charge of "the collective patrimony of civilized nations."[136] Balanos himself had been appointed by an international committee of archaeologists drawn mostly from these archaeological institutes.[137] And presiding over the Acropolis deliberations was Georg Karo, director of the German Archaeological Institute and the only German attendee to the entire Conference.[138] The Athens Conference, however, recast this history of colonial and semicolonial oversight as a kind of proto-international "hospitality."[139] So the new diplomacy was rooted in the old. Indeed, negotiations of the most secret, bilateral, traditional kind had been necessary to agree on Athens as a location, to reassure the British delegates that the Greek government would not ask the League to request the restitution of the Elgin marbles from the British Museum.[140] The new international authority was shaped through encounters and frictions with existing semiprivate modes of international cooperation.

Within this longer international history of the Parthenon, the League appeared on the scene of Athenian archaeology not as a definitive new authority, but rather as one among several new actors in a new network that took over the management of cultural resources in this period: in a shift from quasi-colonial German control to an era of American influence. The Athens deliberations, in fact, can be situated at a very specific juncture in this transition, just after Balanos had completed work on the northern side, and was about to start on the south. This pivot from north to south, it turns out, constitutes a shift between old and new regimes of international preservation, brought largely through the intervention of a group of American philantropists with close ties to the American School of Classical Studies in Athens (ASCSA). This was, after all, a "formative period" in US-Greek relations, when the aftermath of the War was forcing the two governments to "discover each other in the diplomatic sense," fueling a wave of Hellenism in American learned circles.[141]

The United States first became involved in the Parthenon's reconstruction in the mid-1920s, when *New York Times* editor and former college president John Huston Finley found out that funds for Balanos's work were about to dry up as Greece struggled to repay its American war loans. Finley resolved to gather a group of contributors to keep Balanos working. By the time the Athens Conference was convened in late 1931, the north colonnade was completed with American funds, and fundraising was about to start for the south. But a debate about the placement of old stones and the choice of new materials—similar to those that would be raised at the conference—had already taken place.[142] In this earlier phase of debate, ASCSA classicist Edmund Capps advocated for Balanos against a set of donors, which included no less than American skyscraper architect Cass Gilbert, who objected to the "large unsightly patches of concrete" that Balanos had produced. Capps had also consulted with his colleague, the archaeologist William Bell Dinsmoor, who produced an extensive critique of Balanos's work and proposed an alternative rearrangement.[143] But ultimately the project had moved forward, after the American group successfully requested that Balanos replace his cement with American concrete, now to be supplied by the contractor of the American School's latest building, the Gennadius library.[144]

The Finley group that worked with Balanos both before and after the Athens Conference was not an official diplomatic body, but its correspondence shows that it succeeded in provoking precisely what the League was aiming for: the "association" of an international public through a monument. Of course, this was hardly the public of schoolchildren that the League had imagined. Instead Finley and his donors wielded a combined financial, diplomatic, and cultural leverage that took a small, elite, and largely American coalition as a sample of world public opinion. This process is worth recounting in detail, because it established the pattern through which the international value of monuments could be deployed through documents, a pattern that would continue to be used throughout the century, increasingly taken up to make monuments international media (combining a text and icon) by official organizations.

Originally, Finley and his group were entirely convinced by the vision that the northern columns had simply "fallen" and were now lying "prone," "in fairly complete fragments upon the ground."[145] In his letters and in the *New York Times*, Finley propagated the story that the columns "lay pathetically where they fell in 1690" and remained "practically intact," needing only to be "lifted up into position and secured."[146] To take advantage of this lifting image, Finley devised a fund-raising strategy that assigned one column per donor and encouraged them to think that they might "go over there and have a hand in the job."[147] Since there were seven columns, Finley looked for seven donors and branded them "the Mythical Seven." This man-to-column pairing was even rendered graphically in a sketch by Tom McAndrew where each donor was shown arduously lifting his own column (figure 1.10).[148] Anthropomorphic identification was also encouraged by the debate about anastylosis where, Finley learned, it was customary to liken the column to the body and the architrave to the head. [149] Bolstered by this architectural embodiment, the group soon began referring to each other by Ancient names—with Cass Gilbert calling Finley a "reincarnation of Euripides," Finley reciprocating with "brother Centurion," McAndrew invoking the "Seven Wise Men of Greece," and a general tendency to recount the project in poetic prose as if it were an episode of Greek mythology.[150]

There is more to this rhetoric than the self-mythologizing of a few American philhellenes. These donors saw themselves as civilizational wardens, conflating personal patronage with universal heritage. What one donor called "the proprietary feeling" that he felt towards the monument after having contributed funds, was continuous with what another donor called the pride of having protected "the ancestral patrimony of every thinking man."[151] The concept of guardianship we have been following in this chapter was now a quality that passed from architecture to person. The donors felt that they now stood in "mute company on that far and famed hill" as if they were columns, and the columns now performed as "sentinels of beauty" as if they were humans, "guarding, as it were, the traditions of the greatest of the arts for all posterity."[152]

If this architectural embodiment felt immediate, it is in part because Balanos never drew the project before he completed it, proceeding empirically, stone by stone. The beautifully intricate drawings Balanos published in 1936, with red and black ink distinguishing old and new, were an after-the-fact compendium of "scattered documents" made over the course of the project[153] (color plate 1). In other words, Balanos drew the puzzle only *after* he had completed it. But the Finley project was far from unmediated; it was interposed by various modes of transmission and transcription.[154] This involved wire transfers, newspaper columns, sketches drawn in the margins of letters—a whole host of para-architectural documentation.

Architectural annotations became particularly crucial during the second phase of the Parthenon's rebuilding, after 1931, because the number of columns on the south side could not so easily be matched to a number of donors. Too many pieces of the façade were missing to reconstruct it entirely—some columns would have to remain "stubs."[155] So, to communicate both to the donors and to Balanos what the reconstruction would look like and how to apportion funds, Capps and Finley drew their own sketches[156] (figure 1.10). The difference between these two sketches provides a good guide to the difference between the temple as icon and evidence. Finley's sketch, drawn in New York, corresponds to the façade as seen from a distance. It shows varying column heights against a horizontal datum. Capps's sketch, drawn in Athens, identified individual drums, as they would be seen up close. The difference between the near- and far-views was far from rhetorical: it was also incorporated into the design of the facade. The American architect Stuart Thompson, who had been asked to specify the building materials, designed the columns to be made of a "warm yellow grey" color in order "to harmonize with the old work when seen from a distance," but appear "separate and distinct" from up close. This difference in color was then petrified, so to speak, in an instruction that the concrete be waterproofed "to prevent a change of color."[157]

Stretching between the near view and the far, the famed path up the Acropolis hill was thus transformed into a reverse pilgrimage road. From afar, one would see "a temple instead of a ruin,"[158] but from up close the temple would offer "no false illusions."[159] Rather than experiencing the aura of an icon at the end of a long voyage, the sequence began with an iconic effect and guided the visitor towards a sobering witnessing of evidence.

Between 1928 and 1933, this path was traveled by innumerable American and British visitors who wrote Finley to attest to the "inconceivable magnificence" of the result.[160] "The general effect of the restored columns is admirable," wrote one architect, while another judged it "quite revolutionary." The director of the Rockefeller Foundation wrote to say that the Parthenon "got me like few other things." Finley used excerpts of these testimonials to elicit further funds. "Until he has seen the new Parthenon," one person wrote, no one could "argue the case" for or against restoration. "One has but to see it to be convinced."[161] This loop of witnessing and testifying was finally closed when the temple became sketchable again, as attested by one traveler who certified that Winston Churchill and his wife "put in their time making sketches of the Parthenon."[162]

The Finley episode returns us to the themes of witnessing and guardianship around which this chapter—and the Athens Conference itself—began, with monuments as "testimonies of all ages of civilization." By 1931, the stones of this one exemplary monument had themselves been consciously witnessed by a string of modern visitors, an educated elite who could testify to the imageability of the architectural object. It was through this incorporation of architecture into an apparatus of opinion-setting and image-making—in short, mass-media—that the "public" that the League hoped to "attach" to the monument

in the three columns of the south

ne and 4 in one. This will I think

that the four columns cannot be co

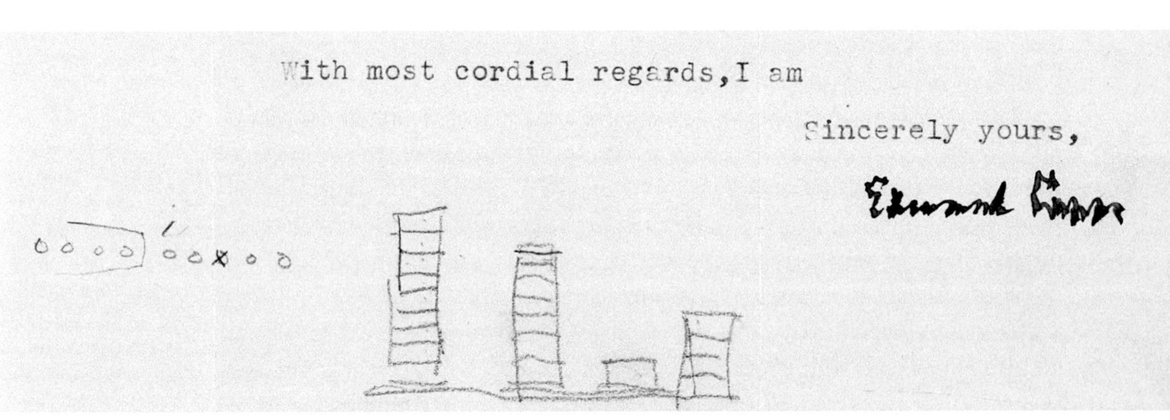
With most cordial regards, I am

Sincerely yours,

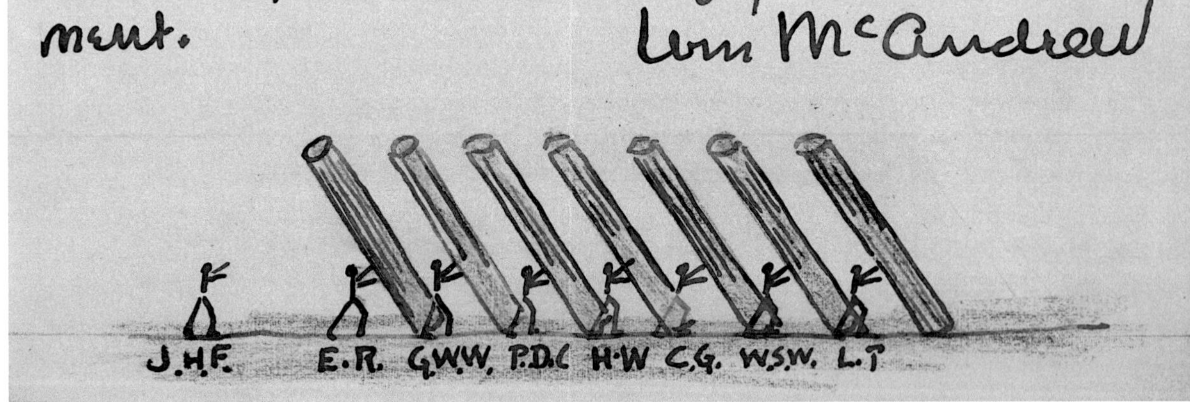
ment.

Wm McAndrew

was ultimately constituted. In judgments transmitted behind the scenes of an international conference and confirmed in its official pronouncements, cultural diplomats accepted an architectural object into the international imaginary.

The significance of this loop of witnessing for the League's cultural politics is two-fold. First, it situates the Athens Conference very specifically within a sequence of international "visits" to Balanos's work. Second, it helps extend the reach of the question—was the temple an icon or a document—to include the testimonials of other witnesses who were part of the League's official networks and *also* connected to the Finley group in more informal ways. Foremost among these, we find Gilbert Murray, a British classicist who had succeeded Bergson as president of the Committee on Intellectual Cooperation, and visited the Acropolis in April 1931. Although Murray was nowhere to be found during the Athens Conference, he had in fact written a letter to Finley weighing in on the debate about the southern colonnade, where he argued that the south side of the Parthenon should be reconstructed, despite the fact that there was "a case for having raised the N[orth] side and leaving the S[outh] side down." In arguing this, he spelled out what architecture's contribution would be to an international citizenry: "the imaginative assistance to be got" from restoring the south side, he argued, would "be worth a great deal."[163] This is less banal of a statement than might seem at first. Consider the alternative: that one side of the monument would be given "an image" and the other not. In effect, Murray argued that the south side should be transformed into an image (even if it was an image of a ruin) rather than have no image at all. If one side of the Parthenon had been redesigned to project an image of constructive completion, the other side could be designed to reflect destruction or incompletion.

Figure 1.10 Sketches of two Parthenon colonnades, drawn by members of the American donor committee who raised funds to re-erect them. Bottom: Tom McAndrew's sketch of the northern colonnade, each column being lifted by a member of the "Mythical Seven" in 1926; Top: South colonnade drawn by John Hudson Finley, 1933; Middle: South colonnade drawn by Edmund Capps showing the number of drums for each, 1933. John H. Finley Papers, Manuscripts and Archives Division. The New York Public Library. Astor, Lenox and Tilden Foundations. Middle sketch used with the permission of the American School of Classical Studies at Athens, Archives.

It should be noted that the idea that the Parthenon existed in two states (one as a complete object, the other partially demolished after the explosion of gunpowder that had toppled so many of its columns in 1687) was hardly new. Murray was involved in another debate over the reconstruction of the Parthenon's two images in his capacity as a board member of the British Museum in London, where the American architect John Russell Pope had been hired to design a new room to house the so-called Elgin Marbles.[164] Here too, a debate had flared about how to reconcile old and new—the new, modern room seeming to dwarf the ancient marbles in its majesty.[165] And here too, Murray wrote (during the same month) that he was willing to accept a combination of scientific accuracy with quasi-religious "enshrinement" since it was for the sake of bettering a previous, unsatisfactory arrangement.[166] This previous media, in this case, was the model: since 1845, the marbles had been located in a room with two models of the Parthenon in its two states. So, returning now to Murray's intervention with Finley: unlike these older media for reconstruction, at the Acropolis the new and the old both would be experienced on site. But rather than relying on anastylosis alone to convey a new strategy, Murray preferred to think bigger and project one image onto either side of the monument, as if each façade were a screen. Mediation, not embodiment, was the solution for bridging icon and evidence.

What kind of image was this, then? Finley offers an answer in a letter where he incorporated Murray's input. The difference between these two sides, he wrote, was that between two kinds of memories. "There will thus remain," he wrote, "on the one side a memory of the Parthenon as the world has known it for two hundred years and on the other the longer memory."[167] The two epochs of the monument's history were not only images but memories (implying that they had built-in audiences) and these two memories were not separate, discrete, or sequential; rather, they had overlapping durations, and were available simultaneously.

Using the Parthenon as a visual tool to design memories—Henri Bergson could probably not have asked for a better homage. Recall that Bergson's philosophy took memory as a motor of history. Bergson rejected any strict line separating objects and subjects and argued that human bodies and inert matter were philosophically indistinct, both ruled by "the undeniable fact of material succession." To explain this continuity, Bergson proposed to see the world as composed of images, and defined memory as a specific kind of image that jumps between past, present, and future. Indeed, memory was the concept through which Bergson redefined the role of the body in the act of cognition. "The task of the body," Bergson wrote, is "not to store up recollections" but rather "to select, in order to bring back to distinct consciousness, *the useful memory*, that which may complete and illuminate the present situation . . . with a view to ultimate action."[168] Thus, we can hear in Murray's and Finley's fund-raising machinations a Bergsonian argument for the importance of an international mission at the Acropolis. The Parthenon became an intellectual sorting tool, to "select the memory" that would be most "useful" in promoting international understanding—or any international agenda, for that matter.

To conclude, I want to return to the commemorative Erechtheion photograph that opened this chapter, and reread the relationship between monuments and the innumerable documents—from meeting agendas to lecture notes, from diplomatic agreements to fund-raising letters—that began to be produced behind the internationalist scene surrounding it. In a Bergsonian framework, the photograph illustrates how the League's monumental politics placed emphasis on the intellectual's physical presence and visibility. The delegates in the photograph are acting as the "mind" of the international body politic, by selecting "memories" from the history of the world, building them into monuments in order for these monuments to lead international citizens into action. The politics of this memory-making is conservative, in the sense that it relied on objects to present an image of history as moved by continuities rather than radical breaks. But this is not to say that the Parthenon was made to project an image of continuity. Anastylosis is, after all, a modernist technique, which partakes in an aesthetics of collage and discontinuity. Rather,

Figure 1.11 Photograph of the Acropolis in 1931–1932, showing the Parthenon with scaffolding at left, and Erechtheion on the right. Photographer: Hermann Wagner (?) German Archaeological Institute D-DAI-Ath 75/525.

and more complicatedly, the monument was designed to exist in a historical continuum that could absorb temporal differences, order them in a hierarchy, and make strategic use of the proliferation of images. In the holding pattern of the new diplomacy, monuments could enable certain continuities while disabling others.

From the perspective of techno-scientific cooperation, then, so many of the new preservation techniques that had been discussed and authorized at the Athens Conference remain entirely invisible in this photograph. Behind the diplomats, hidden deep inside the reconstructed architrave above the caryatids' heads, Balanos's new iron has probably already begun to corrode the ancient marble, forever affecting its material makeup. It is only by consulting a photograph taken from another angle, *between* the Parthenon and the Erectheion, that we can see the elaborate technical setup of the site itself, that was required for the picture to appear as it did (figures 1.1 and 1.11). This lateral view reveals that the cultural diplomats who posed in our photograph were not only *guarding* the Erechtheion on which they sat, but also *looking at* the Parthenon, and waiting for Balanos's repairs to be completed and take on their full effect. This lateral view also helps us to imagine the audience, the hundred or so conference attendees who likely watched the photograph being taken and who, like us, witnessed a building making its international reappearance, and the making of an international politics of visibility.

It is arguably this political visibility we seek, today, every time we photograph ourselves at a World Heritage site. The Athens Conference resacralized the Acropolis, and marked the beginning of an international politics of place. But incredible effort went into transforming this one site, the Acropolis, into a place where World History could be experienced. In order for thousands of other sites around the globe to enter into the new internationalist collection of world memories, something would have to give. A single committee could not visit every building; visitation would have to be delegated. It would take another eight years, and the outbreak of the most destructive conflict in human history, for the privilege granted to this single site to be extended to innumerable others.

2 “Battles Designed to Preserve”

THE ALLIES’ LISTS OF MONUMENTS IN WORLD WAR II

Today we are fighting in a country which has contributed a great deal to our cultural inheritance, a country rich in monuments which by their creation and now in their old age illustrate the growth of this civilization which is ours. We are bound to respect those monuments so far as war allows.

If we have to choose between destroying a famous building and sacrificing our own men, then our men's lives count infinitely more and the buildings must go. But the choice is not always so clear-cut as that.

Dwight D. Eisenhower[1]

In late December 1943, Dwight D. Eisenhower, Supreme Commander of the Allied Expeditionary Forces, issued a letter to all commanders that ordered them to "respect the monuments" they were about to encounter in their path up the Italian peninsula, "so far as war" would "allow." This *Letter on Historical Monuments* echoed the arguments that heritage advocates had been making on the international scene since the early 1930s. Like the conservators we heard speak at the Athens Conference in the last chapter, Eisenhower argued monuments were a transnational inheritance. And like many League diplomats, he called for monuments to be protected in war because wars should be fought in the name of "civilization," rather than against it. But Eisenhower's frank admission that cultural protection was possible only because "the choice" between physical destruction and human sacrifice was "not always clear-cut" signaled a blurring of prewar ethical and legal codes in the face of new destructive technologies. The conflict that had broken out in 1939 had grown into a full-blown aerial war. As entire city centers had been bombed by the German Luftwaffe and the British Royal Air Force, the principles of military "discrimination" and "proportionality," codified in the early 1900s to protect civilians, had been thrown entirely into question.[2] By the end of 1942, Allied and Axis leaders had entered a dynamic—a "military-political game of poker"—which forced them continually to justify their choice of what constituted a legitimate military target.[3] Issuing his *Letter* in this context, Eisenhower was careful not to compare destroyed monuments to *civilian* casualties, speaking only of soldiers' lives. But he did appeal to a distinction of a cultural kind. The "choice" between famous buildings and men's lives, he implied, was possible only if another choice had already been preliminarily made: between buildings that were famous and those that were not.

In this chapter (and continuing in the next) I trace how the international project of monument survival was taken up by Allied planners, commanders, and consultants during the years 1942–1945, and how they created a new model for transnational monuments protection by leveraging the sheer magnitude of destructive circumstance. Whereas, in the League years, monuments advocates tried to tie architectural maintenance to the regularity of diplomacy, here it was the monuments' qualities as exceptional objects that made them lynchpins of action. Thus, I examine how architectural distinction became entangled with military discrimination in the European war.

The subject of my study is the group that was behind Eisenhower's letter: the American Commission for the Protection and Salvage of Monuments in War Areas, or Roberts Commission. Named after Supreme Court justice Owen Roberts, who held the ceremonial title of chairman, the Commission was officially constituted as an American government agency in Washington, DC, in August 1943. But it relied on two existing channels of military-academic cooperation opened almost a year earlier. As early as December 1942, a group of art historians, archaeologists, and curators from various American universities and cultural institutions volunteered to help military authorities "preserve and protect Europe's monuments" and were, somewhat to their own surprise, recruited to the task.[4] In February 1943, the American Defense-Harvard Group (ADHG) began providing information on monuments to the Army, eventually recruiting sixty-one scholars to help. In April, the American Council of Learned Societies (ACLS) established a similar committee in New York, eventually bringing another hundred scholars into the fold. By the time Eisenhower issued his letter, these two groups had already come to include a veritable who's who of American art history, mobilized to the cause of salvaging Europe's monuments. The letter was intended to move the project from the home front to the battlefield, by granting official status to the Monuments, Fine Arts and Archives (MFAA) branch of the Army. Drawn from the ranks of art history, the fine arts, architecture, and the museum world, these "monuments men" would come to number about two hundred, accompanying advancing Allied armies, first in their European campaign, then in the Pacific.

Officially, the mandate of the Roberts Commission was "the protection and salvage of monuments in war areas"[5] (figure 2.1). But it would be more accurate to say that it was devoted to creating and maintaining a complex apparatus from which a choice of monuments could be made. This apparatus consisted primarily of lists and maps of art and architectural objects, annotated with a system of stars to indicate the relative importance of monuments, prefaced with introductions and sometimes appended with rules for selection. Within its first year, the Committee produced one fifty-page list of monuments for every country likely to be involved in war—with notable exceptions, as we will see; by the end of the war, over 25 *Civil Affairs Handbooks and Atlas Supplements* had been produced (figure 2.2).

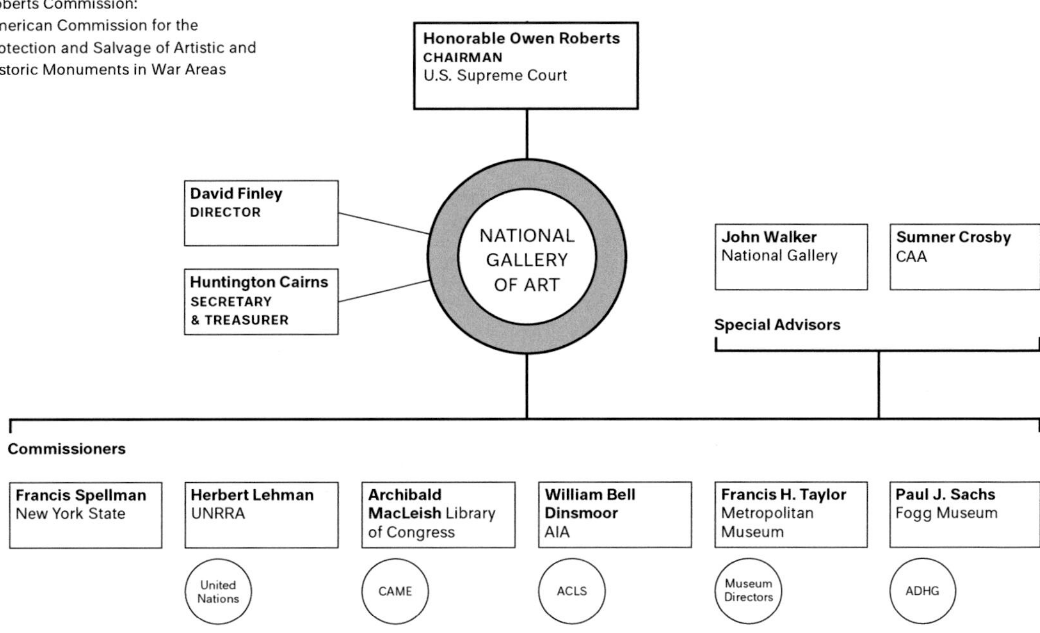

Figure 2.1 Lucia Allais, Organizational chart of the Roberts Commission, based on data from Roberts Commission, *Final Report* (1946). © Lucia Allais.

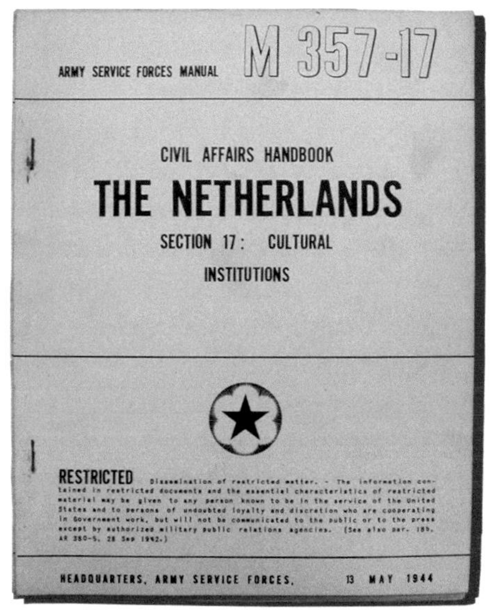

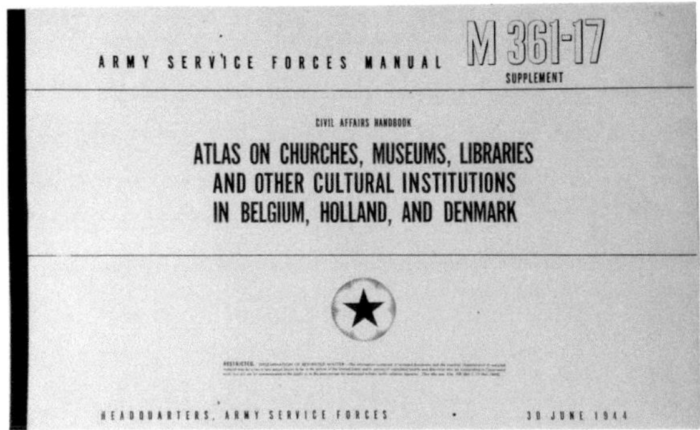

Figure 2.2 *Civil Affairs Handbook* covers. a. The Netherlands: Section 17, Cultural Institutions (13 May 1944); b. Section 17b, *Atlas on Churches, Museums, Libraries and Other Cultural Institutions in Belgium, the Netherlands and Denmark* (30 June 1944), NARA.

My aim in examining this Allied apparatus of protection is not to verify its efficacy. A before-and-after comparison of all the monuments listed and preserved would be far beyond the scope of this chapter, and greatly complicated by the fact that these lists were designed to expand and contract at will.[6] Instead, I ask how the Roberts Commission contributed to normalizing international monuments protection in the twentieth century, by providing a bridge between the tentative prewar work of the League of Nations and UNESCO's more aggressive postwar efforts. To address this issue of historical continuity, I consider the Allied monuments' policy as part of the phenomenon of total war, defined broadly as the "calculated, systematic conflation of the military and civilian dimensions of industrial warfare."[7] If any long-term legitimacy for monuments protection emerged from this rather exceptional episode, it was surely a product of such a conflation, a "militarization" that occurred not only on a pragmatic level, as historians and military commanders had to become unlikely collaborators, but also through an affinity between the political ideals that structured the social order of the United States, and its development of instruments and goals for violence and destruction.[8]

Existing histories of the Roberts Commission have tended to concentrate on the weakness of its authority, correctly pointing out that its protective mandate never once trumped the strategic needs of military authorities. The oral histories and memoirs produced by the Monuments Men Foundation evocatively reveal how the MFAA troops struggled to perform their protective duties, often working against the very military machinery that employed them.[9] Yet even understaffed, outnumbered, and outranked, as a growing number of regional and national case studies has shown, MFAA officers achieved surprising efficacy.[10] Their histories point us not to the unlikely nature of their efforts, however heroic, but rather to the structural possibilities for their success.

Any overall assessment of the Allies' treatment of monuments, however, has been hampered by thorny problems of historical interpretation. Many have ultimately classified the work of monument protection as a species of propaganda, concluding that "the physical effects of war on historic monuments was of more interest to propagandists exploiting the symbolism of this aspect of the Second World War than those with the power to damage those buildings."[11] In this chapter, I throw this distinction between power and symbolism into doubt, by showing that the line between monuments as material objects (subject to "damage") and their communicative potential (as "symbols") was crossed, negotiated, and reconceptualized throughout the war and with great dexterity by the Roberts Commission and its various military interlocutors. Such an oscillation between protecting a monument's concrete form and its transmissible content was constitutive of monuments protection, not an impediment to it. In particular, I argue it was precisely monuments' availability as nodes in a vast web of cultural communication—a ready-made propaganda network—that made their protection and salvage compatible with Allied strategy.

Ubiquitous, widely dispersed, filled with the power to influence minds, monuments were first an inevitable backdrop, and soon became irresistible

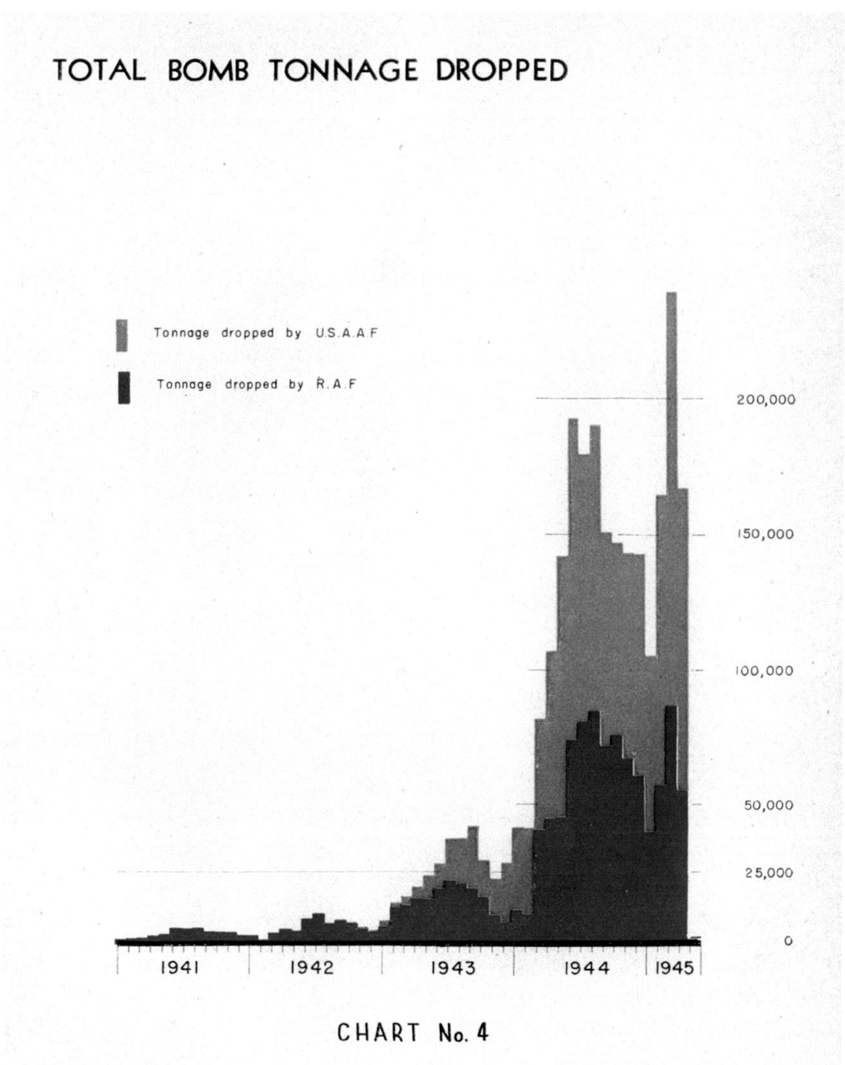

Figure 2.3 Total Bomb Tonnage Dropped by the Allies over the course of the European war. RAF bombs in black, and USAAF bombs in gray. Chart No. 4 in USSBS, *Overall Report (European War)*, September 30, 1945.

instruments, in a technologically driven and ideologically charged Allied endgame. Eisenhower's 1943 *Letter on Monuments* came at a specific juncture in the war, just before the Allies were about to embark on a dramatic crescendo of violence and destruction. The years 1944–1945 are when World War II became the most deadly and destructive conflict in history, leaving behind at least 60 million casualties and a rubble-strewn landscape of unprecedented scale.[12] The Allied contribution to this destruction is vividly illustrated by the sharp upturn in the curve of bomb tonnage delivered by American and British airplanes over the course of the war (figure 2.3). This curve also helps to show that the conditions in which the policy of monuments protection was designed (1943) were fundamentally different than those of its ultimate application (1944–1945) and from the way architecture had been implicated in psychological warfare in the first few years of fighting (1939–1942).

I have therefore divided the story of the Roberts Commission into two. In this chapter I focus on the first phase, when the protection policy was developed and accepted. I begin with the prophecies of total war that shaped military imaginations before the war, and the reception of cultural destruction until the end of 1942. I then address how various components of the Allied policy broke this pattern, through a reading of Eisenhower's two letters. Lastly, I reach back to examine the listing enterprise itself in greater detail as it developed over the first half of 1943. Listing was a fluid medium, which drew its legitimacy from heterogeneous sources: by borrowing institutional power from university administration, editorial standards from the tourist publishing industry, and collaborative models from academic research. I want to show that the choice to protect both anchored itself in the moral *habitus* of the American educated classes and took advantage of an exceptional concentration of scholarly power, much of it made up of émigrés, in the field of art history. In chapter 3 I move into the war's later years, transitioning from knowledge technologies to bombing technologies, from lists to maps, and from militarization to regionalization.

Bombers and Baedekers

For much of the 1920s and 1930s, the totality of war was identified with the adoption of aerial bombing as a new technology.[13] European nations tested out their air forces during the civil and colonial wars of the 1920s and 1930s, and airpower theorists used these experiments to predict that future wars would increasingly rely on air power as a "decisive" weapon—meaning that the spatial reach of the airplane would radically shorten the war.[14] Since nations would be conceptualized as uninterrupted battlegrounds, bombers were justified in targeting civilians as well as soldiers. In 1927, the Italian General Giulio Douhet famously predicted that the discrimination between soldier and civilian would no longer hold because "everyone takes part" in wars—and under this label he listed, in addition to "the soldier carrying his gun," a number of productive civilians: "the woman loading shells in a factory, the farmer growing wheat, the scientist experimenting in his laboratory."[15] Aerial bombs aimed at civilians would provoke "panic," "disorder," and, eventually, such "moral disgust" that war would end through the "revolt" of the population:

> A complete breakdown of social structure cannot but take place in a country subjected to this kind of merciless pounding from the air. The time would soon come when, to put an end to horror and suffering, the people themselves, driven by the instinct of self-preservation, would rise up and demand an end to the war.[16]

Douhetianism (as this theory was already called) thus relied on new weaponry and on the discursive structure of politics in a mass-society. Bombing would be decisive only if it triggered political action by sending a message to the masses, and then only if their response traveled back up the chain of political command.[17]

The first two years of the war can be understood as a testing out, and ramping up, of this Douhetian logic. As soon as the conflict broke out in September 1939, British and German air forces began aiming their bombs at civilian targets, and negotiating between their actual destruction and the threat of their potential destruction, each side claiming to approach that elusive "breakdown" of the other's social structure.[18] Cities emerged from this retaliatory logic newly objectified: as bargaining chips, and as units of civilian psychology.[19] By the end of 1942, a lengthening list of qualifiers had been appended to the gerund "bombing"—*area bombing, carpet bombing, indiscriminate bombing, mass bombing, morale bombing, saturation bombing, terror bombing*—all euphemisms for the "merciless pounding from the air" theorized by Douhet.[20] But if Douhet was proven right about the escalation in bombing, the decisive effect he predicted did not follow suit. Instead, the blurry psychological variable he had described as "the instinct of self-preservation" became progressively codified, in a discourse on morale that could turn even the most psychological losses into material ones, and vice-versa.[21] Already by mid-1942 certain raids had begun to show the flaws in the logic that tied entire cities' behavior to their level of destruction. In 1941 Hitler had threatened to "terror bomb" the center of Rotterdam, obtained the surrender of the Netherlands from the threat alone, and then ordered the bombing of that city anyways.[22] On the Allied side, Sir Arthur "Bomber" Harris was especially proud of the February 1942 attacks on Milan not for the "amount of material damage" but rather for the "utter disorganization" they created, although they did not provoke Italy's surrender.[23]

As a military variable, morale could be measured architecturally. A destroyed home equaled a "dehoused" worker, which equaled a weakened war machine. But the assumption that civilians would be demoralized in proportion to the extent of "home destruction" was tragically mistaken. As the *United States Strategic Bombing Survey* would chillingly summarize in 1945, civilian architecture as a target offered only "diminishing returns with increasing bomb tonnage"[24] (figure 2.4). It was not only the quantification of home destruction that came to complicate the architectural equation of morale bombing. Monumental architecture also soon made its appearance in Allied and Axis balance sheets. In April 1942, the Luftwaffe began bombing five historic British towns in attacks that soon came to be known as "Baedeker Raids" because these towns appeared to have been picked for their historical significance out of the popular German *Baedeker Guidebook for Tourists*.[25] The raids provoked a sharp intensification of bombing, and of propaganda. The British air forces retaliated by targeting the historic cities of Lübeck and Rostock, becoming, as Thomas Mann put it, "the apprentice who surpasses the master."[26] Together, these raids complicated the assumption that architectural damage to a city meant psychological weakening of its population in two ways. First, they showed that

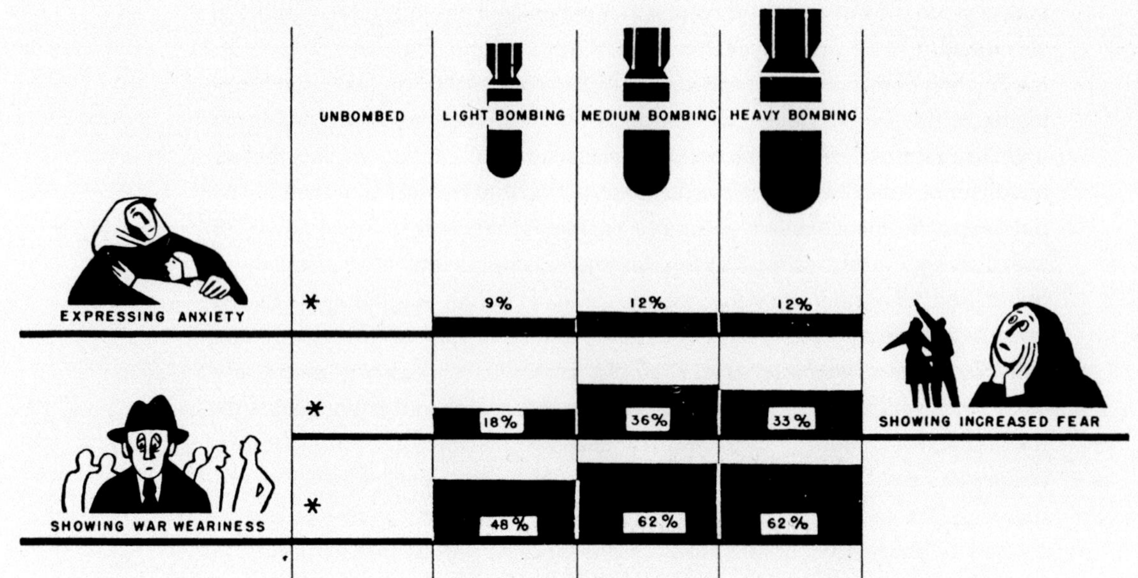

Figure 2.4 Excerpt from "Variation in Morale Factors and Intensity of Bombing," USSBS Morale Division, *Effects of Strategic Bombing on German Morale*, vol.1 (May 1947).

civilian sentiment could be concentrated in monumental architecture, rather that dispersed in neighborhoods. Secondly, they showed that this concentration of civilian outrage could, apparently, be triggered with some measure of precision. In a war where architectural destruction hitherto signified a willingness to act "indiscriminately," the Baedeker Raids introduced architectural monuments in a form that had been preliminarily itemized, chosen from a list, and with great discrimination.

The phrase Baedeker Raid implies a sinister marriage of bombing and tourism, and is usually treated as an especially atrocious instantiation of the arbitrariness of war, an example of bad taste piled upon moral decay. Indeed, in a rather crude mapping of military grade upon architectural importance, the German officer who first mentioned Baedeker invented more "stars" for monuments than actually existed in the guides themselves, threatening to "bomb every building in Britain marked with three stars" whereas Baedeker allowed only two, and called them "asterisks."[27] But in fact, the Baedeker name merely captured the systematic nature of this new kind of iconoclasm. After all, the phrase replaced an older linguistic pattern where each newly bombed city's martyrdom was individually memorialized by having its name turned into a verb—"to Lübeck," "to coventrate," *koventrieren*.[28]

Thus, the distinction bestowed upon these five British cities as Baedeker targets has to be seen against the backdrop of the increasing uniformity of Europe's cultural geography, a phenomenon that was a product of the massification of tourism and of modernity more generally, not of the war. The Baedeker company owed its success and name-recognition to having invented a new format to replace the "adjectival raptures" of previous guides, offering a faster-paced, more telegraphic style of commentary, which it delivered along specifically prescribed and timed routes, made possible by the technologies of travel-capitalism, and systematized through a ranking system. Judgments of taste were applied through asterisks not only to monumental sites, but also to hotels and shops. The entire tourist experience was now built around traveling to collect and consume architectural distinctions.[29] And since the early twentieth century, the increasing parcelization of European tourists' tastes into ever-finer regional points of interest (a phenomenon that created the need for continual revision and production of the Guides, fueling their standardization) was entirely compatible with the expectation that the modern tourist consume "the whole culture" he was visiting.[30] To refer to Baedeker in wartime, then, was to refer to the systematic adaptation of aesthetic judgment to the demands of mass society. Baedeker helped render the cultural topography of Europe's monuments compatible with the increasing sameness of its industrial geography[31] (figure 2.5).

Six months after the last of the Baedeker bombs hit Canterbury, the idea began circulating in Washington to use Baedeker guides to *avoid* monuments, rather than targeting them. The trigger for this mobilization was two-fold:

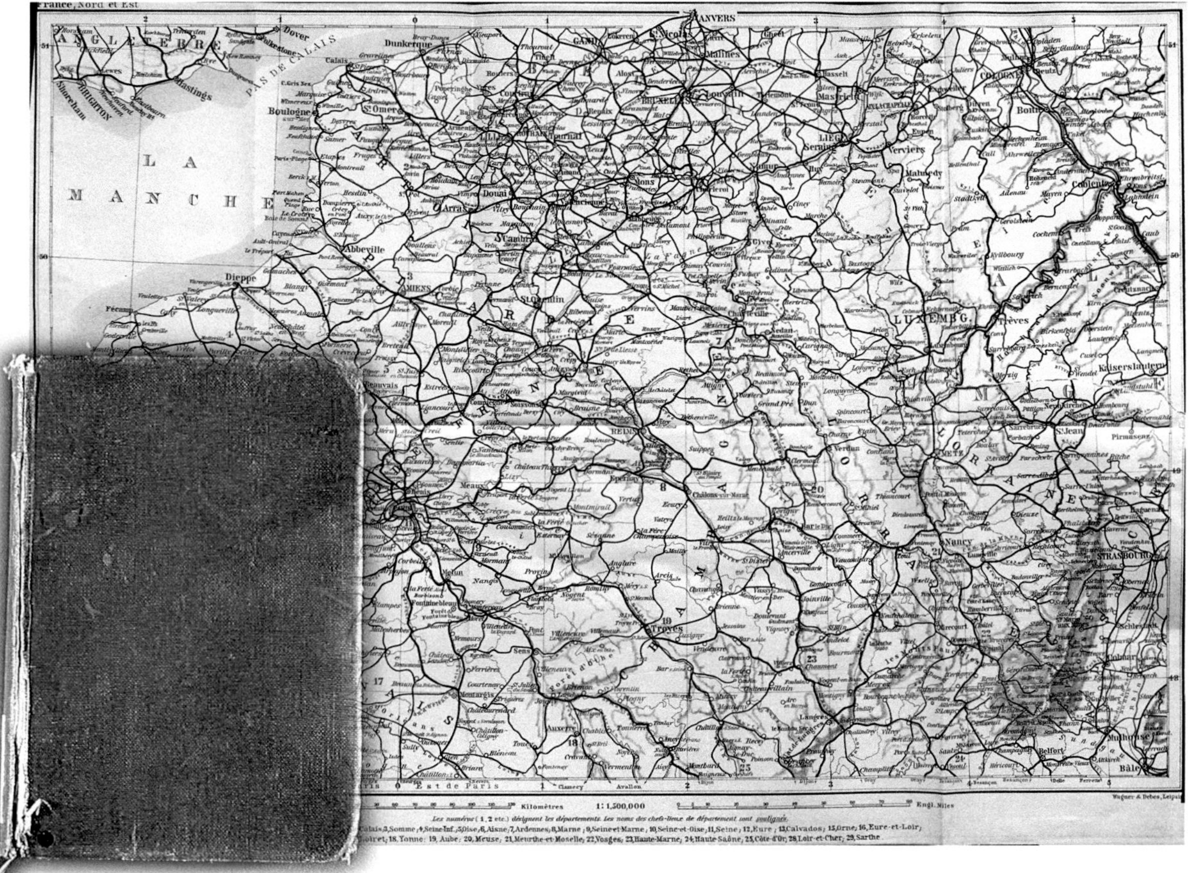

Figure 2.5 Karl Baedeker, *Handbook for Travellers, from Belgium and the English Channel to the Loire: Excluding Paris and Its Environs*; (1909). With map unfolded.

reports from the Eastern Front that German armies were systematically destroying Poland's libraries and monuments; and rumors at home that a new postwar planning bureau, the Office for Postwar Rehabilitation, was to be created. Two separate petitions, addressed to President Roosevelt in November and December 1942, made this proposal. The first was authored and cosigned by several cultural politicians in Washington, DC, and suggested that American air forces "avoid damaging" certain monuments in Europe and offered to "prepare information," including "maps of targets," based on a library of material containing "Baedeker and other guides to foreign countries."[32] The second originated from Harvard University and suggested that army officers be issued lists "which in the case of Europe might well be Baedeker's two stars and one star monuments," along with "very simple instructions as to what to avoid and what to do, for safeguarding these."[33] This phrasing, "might well be," encapsulates the stealth conversion of civilian knowledge into military intelligence that ensued. In contrast to Axis bombast, the Allied militarization of Baedeker would be more silent yet profound, relying on Baedeker for its systematic cultural hierarchy, spread large and wide over Europe. Throughout the rest of the war, at every level of the Roberts Commission, from the art historian who was told "your list will look like a Baedeker, but an edited Baedeker" to the MFAA officer who sent "an urgent request for Baedekers" from the German frontline, Baedeker became and remained the group's most valued primary source and standardizing framework.[34]

Anyone following the Baedeker arc in the propaganda storyline of war would have undoubtedly understood these two petitions—I propose to call them Baedeker Memos—as inverting the logic of the Baedeker Raids, transforming Europe's monuments from targets to non-targets. But in terms of the totality of war, they only further closed the gap between civilian knowledge and military instrument. As W. G. Constable, the British curator of paintings at the Boston Museum of Fine Arts, and one of the authors of the Harvard Baedeker Memo, would put it a decade later, what made Baedeker useful to the tourist was his "impersonality," which he likened to "that of a compiler for a railway timetable or a telephone directory."[35] Far from being at odds, the infrastructure of mass communications, including rail and telephone, were of a piece with the systematization of aesthetic appreciation.

Constable also called Baedeker's impersonality "merely a mask," however, and conceded that even serialized, Baedeker's judgments delivered a totality, a *Weltanschauung.* Constable and his colleagues also had a worldview of their own when they suggested using Baedeker to preserve monuments: not only a disembodied list of buildings, but a whole cultural infrastructure—the underlying shape of monumental urbanity. Constable had devoted some thinking and writing to this shape. In a lecture titled "Art, Its Place in a Changing World" that he developed in the 1930s, published in 1938, and delivered as late as November 1942, he asked his audience to "imagine a utopia"—by performing a mental act of erasure: think of a city, imagine its civic core, then erase the urban fabric:

All of you who cherish a Utopia—then imagine Washington in terms of its cathedral, national gallery, library of congress—all would be preserved [while the] rest, except as monuments, disappeared.[36]

In this urban template for a utopia, created by emptying a familiar city of its buildings, anything that was leftover could be called a monument.

A month later, as the US began to plan for the postwar, and Constable and his colleagues were prompted to mobilize, he stopped delivering this lecture. But he tacitly transferred this mental urban erasure onto the war in a December 1942 memorandum, this time addressed to the army.[37] Here, Constable scoffed at the suggestion that had been made (by those in the competing ACLS committee) that "plans of places containing important monuments and collections, with the position of those marked on the plans, be supplied to the armed forces of the United Nations, with a request that they should try to avoid damaging such monuments, etc." Constable called this idea of deliberate avoidance "little short of fantastic." But he made the remarkable suggestion that by slightly changing the temporal viewpoint, "after a place is occupied, steps might be taken to protect monuments, etc, from careless use, looting, (or even from deliberate destruction suggested by military necessity)."[38] Constable stopped short of suggesting destruction as a method to achieve the utopian urban template he had imagined, but endorsed its feasibility in an army-occupied place.

The Baedeker Memos were part of a broader shift in Allied targeting practice and theory. This shift is best captured by another use of the Baedeker name in this period: a target list published in January 1943 by Britain's Ministry of Economic Warfare (MEW), titled *The Bomber's Baedeker* and subtitled *Guide to the Economic Importance of German Towns and Cities*[39] (figure 2.6). The MEW had taken on the task of "investigating the possibility of the [bombing] effort being directed in a more selective manner" and notably at industrially significant urban targets, rather than just civilian ones, which it ranked using fourteen criteria.[40] This work was initially only a marginal aspect of British policy, as Harris continued to focus on destroying housing fabric. But the MEW began to acquire new valence when the American Air Forces entered into the European war with a stated preference for precision bombing.[41]

Rather than attempting to destroy large swaths of urban fabric, US bombs would be aimed at crippling nodal points in the German war machine.[42] Precision was not only a technological criterion for designing weapons. It also implied an entirely different way to imagine the geography of the enemy's territory: Germany became a set of points rather than a continuous and inhabited horizontal field. In the words of one popularization, the goal was "bombing

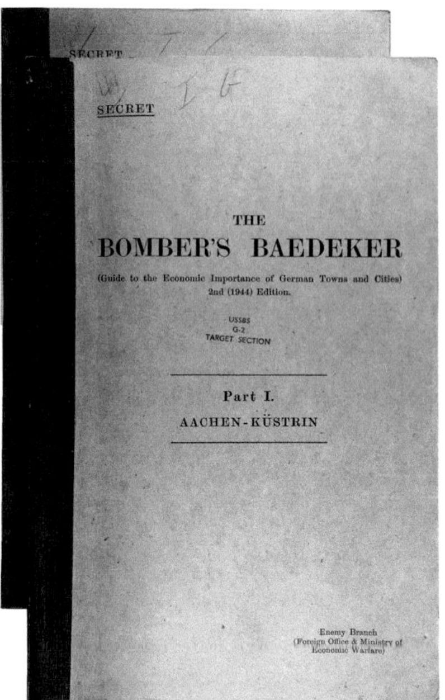

Figure 2.6 Ministry of Economic Warfare (UK), *The Bomber's Baedeker: Guide to the Economic Importance of German Towns and Cities*, Part I (1944). Cover.

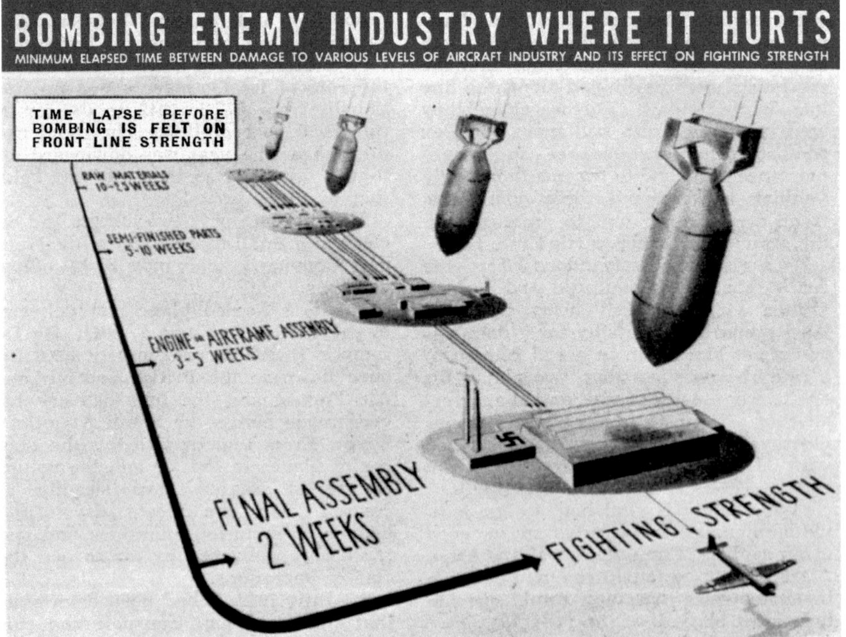

Figure 2.7 Precision bombing explained as "Bombing Enemy Industry Where It Hurts." *Flying Magazine* (January 10, 1944), 55.

enemy industry where it hurts" (figure 2.7). America's emphasis on precision intensified the widespread civilian contribution to the war, producing a new breed of civilian experts who could, in Peter Galison's words, provide "a methodical theoretical reconstruction of the interconnections that held together the German economy and war machine and that asked how it could be blown apart."[43] Scientists, engineers, and economists became "operations analysts," producing target systems that listed industrial assets as nodes in this military-industrial web. British target lists produced by the MEW such as *The Bomber's Baedeker*, then, were somewhere between these dispersed American lists and the Baedekers themselves: they still referred to whole cities as targets, but gave reasons to aim at one or the other by ranking them according to industrial capacity.

By early 1943, the Baedeker name stood in for the networkability of Europe, and the increasing pointillization of Allied military engagement with this network, whether of its industrial sites or its monumental sites. From the Baedeker Raids of early 1942, to the twinned appearance of Baedeker Memos and *Bomber's Baedeker* at the turn of 1943, the Allies' aerial strategy shifted away from Douhetianism, with its staccato rhythm of bombed city centers, towards a broader spatio-temporal coverage that included cities and its civilians, but was anchored in the infrastructural ubiquity and interconnectedness of its networks, whether that of its factories and railyards, or that of its monuments. When Roosevelt and Churchill met at Casablanca in January 1943 to agree to a joint Allied strategy, this networkability of Europe became the explicit basis for a militarization of American expertise about monuments.

Two Letters

Perhaps the best way to understand the Casablanca Conference as a basis for the Allied monuments policy is to say that it provided answers to some of the more daunting logistical questions about how the British and the Americans would combine their very different strategies, while also elevating destruction to an even greater level of abstraction, by calling for "the destruction of the philosophies in [Axis] countries which are based on conquest and the subjugation of other people."[44] This use of philosophical language to concretize the still-distant prospect of victory had crucial consequences for shaping the American monuments protection program, and serves as my guide for reading Eisenhower's two *Letters on Monuments*.

The most important aspect of Allied strategy agreed on at Casablanca was the endgame of "unconditional surrender": the idea that no Nazi or Fascist leader could negotiate to remain in power after capitulation, and that the whole of enemy territory would have to be handed over to Allied occupying forces. Like "decisive," "unconditional" was a euphemism for the massive socio-technical investment that America was willing to make in the war. Techno-

Figure 2.8 A course in Civil Affairs at the School of Military Government in Charlottesville, VA. Photograph John Collier. Library of Congress.

logically, this investment meant that the US was willing to combine their own bombing technologies with those of the British. A "round the clock" bombing system would allow American precision-bombing raids during the day to be followed with British area bombing by night. If these two apparently divergent attitudes to violence against civilians could be combined, it was because America's strategy of precision was not driven only by ethical concerns but rather, as Sean Malloy has argued, by "the lure of precision" that exerted itself at multiple levels on American liberal society.[45] Thus American and British bombs could equally contribute to having a single effect, "to utilize the resources of two great nations with the decisiveness of single authority."[46]

On the human side, unconditional surrender required the militarization of yet another sector of American society to staff the American Military Government (AMG)—that vast machinery for occupying conquered territories. A School of Military Government was established in Charlottesville, VA, to teach "soldiers to become governors" and prepare them for the work of occupation.[47] The goal was to ensure that "by the time the war is won, [the US] have not inadvertently undermined some of the aims for which it is being fought"[48] (figure 2.8). Civil Affairs Officers were to keep temporary watch over civil society in Italy, Germany, Japan (and wherever else a collaborative government had come to power, such as France). They were armed with "guides" of all kinds, called *Civil Affair Handbooks*, authored by civilian experts. The series began, in volume 1, with a broad picture of "the country and people, government, public finance" and continued with specialized volumes such as "agriculture" and "police." Lists and maps of monuments concluded the sequence, as volume 17, named "Cultural Institutions" and its "Atlas Supplements" providing maps.

Monuments would be preserved, then, as part of the infrastructural backbone for rebuilding after surrender. To military government officers, the logic of monument preservation was explained as follows: people living in any conquered territory would be more likely to accept an occupying force that had shown sensitivity to cultural landmarks in its advance, and continued to do so during the temporary governance. "Those in military government could obtain greater cooperation on the part of local populations" if they salvaged their monuments.[49] This calculation weighed the military means of achieving victory against the political instruments for future occupation.

Given the extensive military machinery that was needed to make this promise possible, it was not the first paragraph of Eisenhower's first Letters on Monuments, which I quoted at the opening of this chapter, but rather the less bombastic and more pragmatic *last* paragraph, that enunciated the Allied protection policy:

> It is a responsibility of higher commanders to determine through A.M.G. Officers the locations of historical monuments . . . This information, passed to lower echelons through normal channels, places responsibility on all Commanders of complying with the spirit of this letter.[50]

As outlined in this paragraph, the Allied protection system had three components: "information" on monuments (provided through Civil Affairs Handbooks), "channels" of transmission (ensured by Military Government Officers) and another, third term, which was behavioral, here tersely conveyed by the words "responsibility," "compliance" and "spirit".

This human ingredient, and the role it would play in making monuments the seeds of a new brand of psychological warfare, was more fully explicated in a second version of the Letter on Monuments, that Eisenhower issued in advance of D-Day on May 26, 1944. The very fact that there is a second letter also reflects the third aspect of Allied strategy agreed upon at Casablanca: the timeline of European invasion, which depended on two dates: one for landing in Italy and another, a year later, for landing in France. This timeline made Italy into a testing ground and explains why Eisenhower's second letter reflected a certain learning curve, itemizing the protection policy in four points. Point 1 reiterated the "responsibility to protect and respect" monuments as "symbols" but also expanded it to "the whole Continent of Europe" and recast the war as a battle of preservation. "Shortly," the letter began, "we will be fighting battles *designed to preserve our civilization.*" The title of the letter was also changed to include the word "preservation." Then, rather than connecting European and American "civilizations" through past history and shared growth, this connection was actualized through war. Monuments were described self-referentially as "symbols of that which US armies are fighting to preserve."[51] An internal cohesion of war and preservation ensued.

But Eisenhower quickly qualified this mapping of strategy onto architectural policy with a disclaimer about military necessity. This time, rather than abstractly describing this principle as in the first letter, Eisenhower used the example of the Abbey of Montecassino, which had been flattened by Allied bombs during the winter of 1943, after a bitter and protracted battle prompted in part by its nature as a "revered object." Eisenhower justified the destruction by saying that the enemy had used the Allies' "emotional attachment" to the monument "as a shield."[52] Allied bombs had been aimed at this shield, not the monument itself. Thus—and this was the third point—the protection policy was to be judiciously lubricated by human qualities of "restraint and discipline":

> But there are many circumstances in which damage and destruction are not necessary and cannot be justified. In such cases, through the exercise of restraint and discipline, commanders will preserve centers and objects of historical and cultural significance.[53]

This language of personal responsibility was undoubtedly authored by Eisenhower himself.[54] The adaptability of American soldiers and citizens was one of his signature concerns, as a leader of the Italian campaign and later as US president in the heydays of the war of ideas against the Soviet Union.[55]

Indeed, Eisenhower's war memoir, *Crusade in Europe,* is coursed through with lessons about how individual human qualities can be turned into military assets. "The individual now works differently," he wrote; and conversely "personal characteristics" were "more important than ever in warfare," because individual behavior was propagated through the vast and complex assemblage that was the modern army.[56] What Eisenhower valued was a soldier's "ability to continue changing his methods, almost even his mental processes" in reaction to new technologies. In this context, it is easy to see that monuments were tools in developing this flexibility.

Eisenhower's two letters on monuments changed the narrative arc of cultural destruction in the European war, not only because they contained orders from on high, but also because they supplied to the army a new link between human psychology and monuments. This new link was, precisely, the nature of monuments as communicative links. Eisenhower moved away from the monument's meanings. To protect meant to refuse to engage with the monument's symbolic content—as an iconoclast or a worshipper might—and instead to place it in a human system that could pass along information about culture, and its role in a war. Immense pressure was therefore placed on the format of the information so it would suit the massive American war-making apparatus.

Information about monuments was prepared for use by American military intelligence quickly, in the crucial months between February and December 1943.[57] In that span of time, a project that started "as a strange and slightly ridiculous undertaking" by its own protagonists' admission, became one of the most broadly applicable cultural initiatives in the Allied strategy.[58] The next section of this chapter follows how art-historical knowledge was transformed into military information, by recalling the disciplinary structures that made such militarization possible, and the cascade of crises that it provoked in the military/civilian chain of command.

Everyone's Monuments

Stacks of typescript and mimeographed lists of monuments had already arrived in the battlefields of North Africa in spring 1943, long before Eisenhower ascended to the head of the Supreme Headquarters Allied Expeditionary Force (SHAEF), and a mere four months after the Baedeker Memos had first circulated in Washington. The Harvard Committee had gotten to work first. Paul Sachs, associate director of Harvard's Fogg Art Museum and a close collaborator of Constable, contacted the founder of the American Defense-Harvard Group, the Harvard philosopher Ralph Barton Perry. Perry then created a Monuments Subcommittee to host them, and they recruited anthropologist Hugh O'Neal Hencken of Harvard's Peabody Museum as secretary, and the Byzantinist art historian Wilhelm Koehler as chief list-maker (figure 2.9). They made contact with the School of Military Government at UVA in February. The School, in turn, sent its first "request for material on monuments" in late March. After an intense back-and-forth during which they negotiated with the War Department and a growing list of collaborators at home, the first set of long "Harvard Lists" was issued in May 1943.[59]

"It was desired by the War Department that this work should be done quietly, unofficially and promptly," wrote Sachs in retrospect.[60] This swift militarization was due to the increasing systematization of art history as a self-assured academic discipline, not only at Harvard but in many American universities, in the interwar period. Staging itself as a robust, pragmatic, and systematic field of research, art history attracted a disparate mix of scholars with widely divergent methods—from philologists to curators to archaeologists and artists. A remarkable institutional momentum in the 1920s and 1930s produced a proliferation of museums and art history departments, along with a whole constellation of associated collections, archives, and libraries, across the country.[61] Indeed, this institutional growth seemed to obscure any scholarly achievement, to the point that Colin Eisler described American art history between the two wars as being "all medium, no message."[62] What he meant was that art historians seemed more interested in institution-building than in producing novel interpretations of artifacts. What matters for our purposes, however, is that

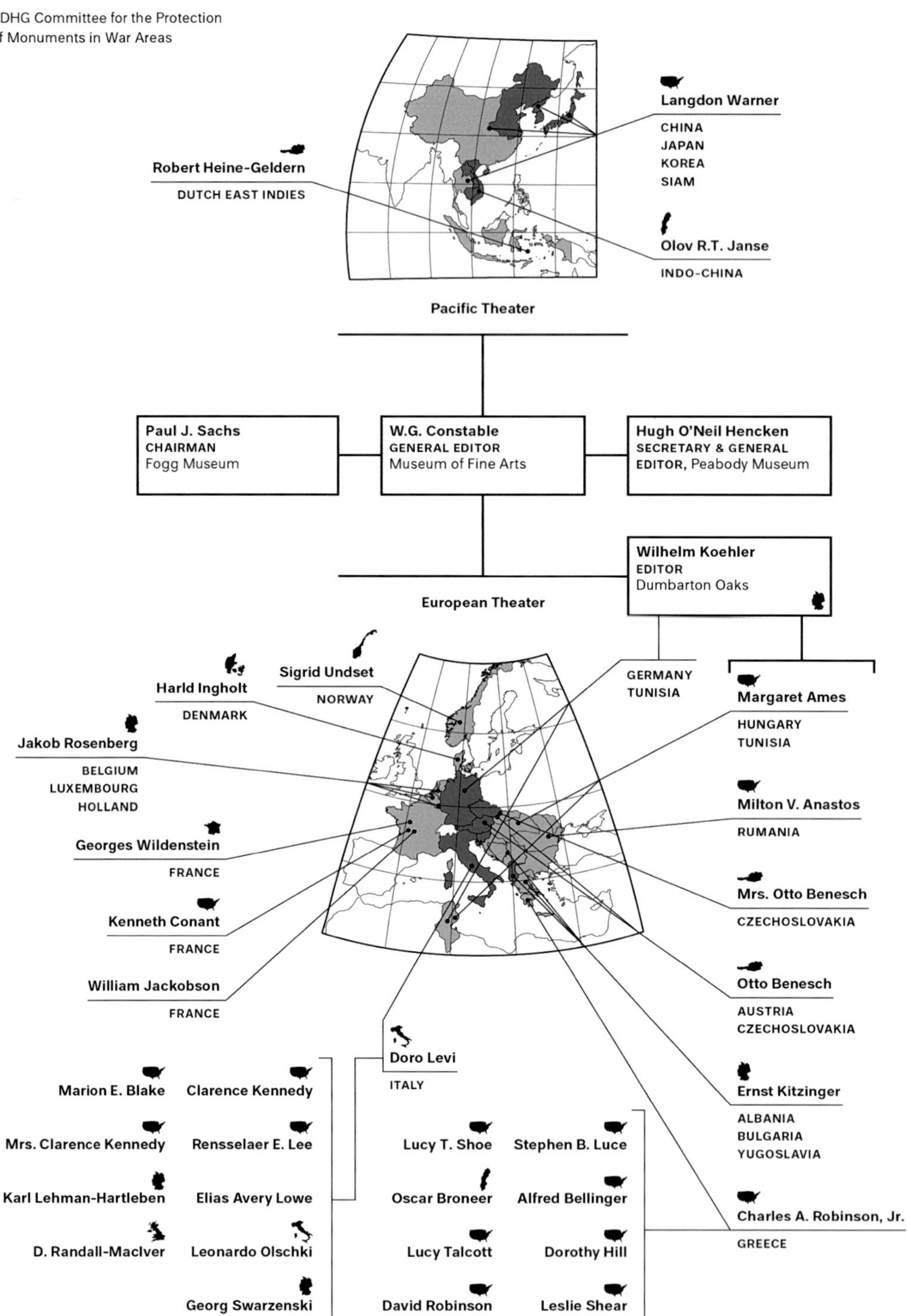

Figure 2.9 Lucia Allais, Organizational chart of the American Defense-Harvard Group's Monuments Committee, based on data from Roberts Commission, *Final Report* (1946). © Lucia Allais.

the practice of making lists was one of the privileged disciplinary traditions that allowed these institution-builders to conceive of themselves as taking part in one of the central conceits of art history as a humanist pastime since the Renaissance.[63]

The redirection of the "medium" of art history towards monument protection in spring and summer 1943 can be apprehended through a composite sketch of those who did the listing through a three-part division of labor. Museum curators such as Paul Sachs and W. G. Constable, heirs to the "gentlemanly and ethically oriented art history" of the turn of the century, became list editors. Wilhelm Koehler, Erwin Panofsky, and other émigrés who were "masters of the empirical method" were recruited in large numbers to make lists. And archaeologists like William Bell Dinsmoor and Sumner Crosby, who had turned the discipline towards "scientific aims," came to oversee the lists' implementation in the field of war.[64] Before the war, these different types of art historians had already worked together to make art history a legitimate branch of the humanities, rather than a subjective and self-indulgent pastime. "Art history is no longer a mere embroidering on the other humanities . . . but a humanistic discipline of independent value, nay, of paramount value, by reasons of its power to coordinate and integrate the other humanistic pursuits."[65] This bold claim to autonomy was authored in 1928 by the Princeton medievalist Charles Rufus Morey, who later became the vice-chair of the ACLS's monuments committee. In 1937, Morey helped to organize the Trask Lectures on the theme "What Is the Meaning of the Humanities," where many of the arguments that would be made for the importance of monuments in war were rehearsed as arguments about the significance of the humanities in American liberal arts education.[66] Here, too, art history was presented as a kind of humanistic "shield" against the creep of technology and science in university education.

One of the speakers in the series was none other than Ralph Barton Perry, director of the Harvard Group, who was one of the most prominent voices in the nationwide debate that animated 1930s university circles about how to "defend" the humanities against the threat of laboratory-based scientific research.[67] A self-described philosopher of "militant liberalism," Perry was imbued by the pragmatism of his mentor William James and a critic of vocational reform in education.[68] Invited by Morey to speak about philosophy, Perry defined the humanities as "any activity conducive to freedom" and presented the "enlightened choice" faced by a student in humanistic study as training for the freedom inherent to living in a liberal society.

> The extent to which a man is free, that is, exercises enlightened choice, depends in the first place upon the extent to which he is aware of the possibilities. Insofar as a man is ignorant of what there is to choose, alternatives are eliminated not by rejection but by accident. Freedom is proportional to the range of options.[69]

This philosophy, wherein freedom was conceived in "proportional" terms, also functioned as Perry's description of American liberal arts education, and also of the humanist's contribution to war.

The war only intensified Perry's advocacy for the humanities. He created the ADHG in 1941 to "mobilize the Harvard community" in a double counter-propaganda effort: to "counteract the appeal of totalitarianism" and show universities could be useful to the war "over and above the technical research conducted in its laboratories."[70] By 1942, Perry became the institutional sponsor who first got the monuments protection project off the ground, by advising Sachs to pursue the Army's educational channels in Charlottesville's School of Military Government for the protection project. Indeed, the Army had explicitly decided to make use of universities, instead of army posts, for its Civil Affairs training, because it gave access to better faculty.[71] This meant that existing links between universities (such as between Harvard and the University of Virginia) would continue to have influence in the planning stage of the war. This was the case with monuments policy. Only after the idea of making lists of monuments was endorsed as *curricular* did it rise up the ranks, eventually reaching the Director of Military Government in Washington, DC, who appointed an army contact in Charlottesville, Colonel Shoemaker. The Harvard directors agreed to keep this connection efficiently "unofficial" while they worked out the formatting of lists.[72]

This nimble use of the Army's educational network differentiates Perry's Harvard Group from Dinsmoor's ACLS committee, which mobilized at the same time but initially failed to get any traction despite its many Washington connections.[73] British art historians were also skeptical of this academic volunteerism. When Constable tried to enlist his former colleagues from London's museums, Kenneth Clark and Eric MacLagan, they replied that they "doubted" that there was "anything art historians could do" in these times of war.[74] (In fact, Anglo-American cooperation was already at work in protecting, or at least surveying, Britain's monuments. The National Building Records had been incorporated in 1942 and was conducting surveys of "Cathedrals, Cathedral Cities, and country towns" in "vulnerable areas" with funds from the Rockefeller Foundation.[75])

For Perry, the line between "militant" liberalism in a university and "military" freedom at war was easily crossed. Ballistic overtones pervade his philosophical writings. During World War I, he had published *The Free Man and the Soldier*; and in his massive 1926 tome, *A General Theory of Value*, objects acquired their value by becoming "targets" of human interest and then being "defended" or "preserved."[76] By 1937 he described college as a place where students "endeavor to preserve their humanism" to counter "the pulverizing effect of specialized research and administrative decentralization."[77] And within the humanities, the arts and literature were especially resilient because they possessed "an uncommonly stubborn quality," presenting "life concretely." It was this same concreteness that Perry helped attribute to monuments during the war, with projectiles and pulverization no longer institutional metaphors but now ongoing material processes.

Perry's philosophy helps to flesh out one of the ideological valences of the Roberts Commission, then, and in particular the idea of presenting cultural protection to the Army as a "choice." The very first proposal Perry arranged to send to Shoemaker contains an argument that Eisenhower later used in his Monuments Letter—namely, that cultural destruction was a question of "choice":

If destruction of a fine building, for instance, is essential to the execution of a military operation, the building must be sacrificed. But there is often a choice open, and those in authority should bear this in mind.[78]

Under Perry's influence, this offer of "information on monuments" was motivated at least in part by a liberal philosophical agenda of always allowing choice.

But a slippage already occurred, around the word "choice," in this early document. In Perry's philosophy, choice was always between several options. For example, he thought liberal arts education should help the student reconcile the "humanitarian distribution of goods" and "their 'humanistic' or cultural quality," in order to become "a chooser of the best."[79] In this sense, interchangeability was key to choice. Yet in this early document sent to Shoemaker, monuments were to be protected precisely because they were not interchangeable. "Monuments are for the most part unique and irreplaceable," the memorandum said. "Cultural monuments, once gone, are gone forever."[80] This passage was likely contributed by George L. Stout, the conservator of the Fogg museum, for whom the choice between destruction and preservation was fundamentally different than the choice among monuments. But by allowing these two contradictions to stand, Perry inaugurated a method of cultural protection that conflated the decision of *whether* to preserve with the choice of *what* to preserve.

Motivated by this pragmatist view of choice, Perry and Shoemaker convinced the Army to take monuments information into account for what they called "practical" purposes first, and to concern themselves with their designated "cultural" value later. In March 1943, as the listing project was just getting underway, Shoemaker argued to the head analyst at the Office of Strategic Services (OSS) that information on monuments was valuable for its training value, apart from its more "fundamental purpose":

Quite apart from the fundamental purpose for which [this material] is being prepared, there is another and very urgent need for it in connection with the training of military administrators.[81]

A week later, he conveyed this argument to Perry himself:

> Quite apart from its more fundamental purpose, this project has important values in establishing confidence in the Army in the minds of intellectual leaders in occupied areas and in changing some of the popular misconceptions in the US in respect to the character and the interests of the Army.[82]

With every passing week, and as the lists were already being compiled by a growing number of art historians at Harvard, Princeton, and Brown Universities, the "fundamental" purpose of monuments protection remained unspoken even as it was reasserted that its more pragmatic and "confidence-building" uses were becoming more urgent.[83] This matters because a tentative enunciation of the purpose of protection might have brought back the themes of the Baedeker Raids: the unique symbolic content of monuments, and the fact that "once gone they are gone forever." By using the word "fundamental" these themes of survival were implied, but the word (and the reality of) "destruction" were kept entirely at bay.

In mid-June, Shoemaker finally offered a definition of the "basic purpose" of the Committee's work:

> The basic purpose of this work is the protection of those media through which culture is carried from one generation to the next. We also have a more immediate and practical interest in it, however.[84]

In a neat bifurcation, it was only after their "practical interest" had been locked in place that monuments lists' longterm aim was described. Additionally, this purpose was now defined not as a content at all, but as transmission, a historical "carrying" of culture. Monuments protection was defined by a double mediation: first, monuments were media through which culture passed; then, their value was passed on through the protection program. Aside from the possibility of a building being preserved by the policy, the secondary value (which was here placed first) was that this preserved monument would transmit the "good character and interests of the Army" by its survival alone. Protection was essentially a highly efficient form of propaganda that required no message, just medium.

This expansion of the scope of cultural protection from monuments to "those media through which culture is passed on" was a turning point in the making of the lists of monuments. Originally, the Harvard editors had asked list-makers to include only "churches, shrines and pilgrimage sites."[85] After June 15th they composed a revised set of instructions for their list makers, giving them a new taxonomy of what they still called "monuments" but now distinguished between churches, monuments (defined narrowly as commemorative structures), art museums, and six other categories of buildings:

a. Churches and other religious buildings.
b. Secular buildings, including private houses.
c. Sites of archaeological, historical, or religious importance.
d. Shrines, places of pilgrimage, and other places of special local importance.
e. Works of art (movable or otherwise) such as statues, monuments, fountains.
f. Art collections, both public and private (including arms and armour collection).
g. Archaeological collections, both public and private.
h. Scientific collections, both public and private.
i. Libraries and archives.[86]

Thus, "the monument" emerged as the overarching protective category during the war not through a nominal definition, but through a demonstrative list. Furthermore, this new expanded meaning (the monument as an empty vessel) emerged while the older one (the monument as an intentional memorial) was still in use.

The addition of libraries and archives in the expanded list is particularly significant as it returns us to a theme—the relationship between monuments and documents—that we heard so many committees discuss in the first chapter. Prewar internationalists had paired built and written historical records only very abstractly, largely to invent new legal arguments that monuments should be treated as a kind of intellectual property. But American cultural leaders were used to relating books to buildings in much more informal ways, and did so repeatedly and productively during the Harvard Group's early negotiations with the Army about monuments. Libraries were frequently cited as examples of monuments to be protected. Persons from the library and archive world in Washington, DC, including the Librarian of Congress and the Archivist of the United States, were involved in the listing project almost from the start. In contrast, the National Park Service, which was technically the corresponding organization for European monuments administration, was never consulted, despite the fact that the Service had commissioned a memorandum in 1940 explaining how monuments protection worked in Europe.[87] Furthermore, arguments about books and buildings equally containing a history of civilization were seen not as erudite but as especially resonant with nonspecialist audiences. The opening sentence of Morey's draft for a "Lecture on Monuments" to be delivered to all the troops read, "The history of civilization and liberty is written in the artistic and historic monuments of Europe."[88] Similarly, the Rockefeller Foundation explained its financial support of the Roberts Commission by arguing that architectural structures ("The acropolis in Athens, the monasteries of the Balkans countries, the churches in Rome, the paintings in Florence, the vast architecture and artistic wealth of Italy") were "as much part of the present as the poetry of Shakespeare."[89] This use of poetry to concretize architectural buildings in the "present" is striking, and shows what an important (indeed monumental) role was given to the literary canon in American liberal education, with its great books and core humanities programs.[90]

Despite the apparently casual manner in which books and buildings were linked in the Commission's public rhetoric, a more serious epistemological reframing of the relationship between monuments and documents lurked not far beneath. Both Perry and Morey had been exposed to a whole new way of thinking about the "monument" as a disciplinary object in 1937 by the art historian (and eventual list-maker) Erwin Panofsky. Panofsky was the fourth speaker Morey had invited in the Trask Lectures. In his lecture, "The History of Art as a Humanistic Pursuit," he proposed to recenter all humanistic scholarship around "monuments" and make this word an all-encompassing descriptor for historical records.[91] If all human records could be understood either as "primary material (a *monument*)" or "secondary material (a *document*)," Panofsky argued, then one could generalize that the Humanities were the realm where "everyone's 'monuments' are everyone else's 'documents' and vice-versa."[92] In fact, it was the delicate balance between experiencing a primary source firsthand and studying it for meaning that constituted the true mark of a humanist. Whereas the scientist could directly address the natural phenomena he worked on, the humanist needed first to engage in a synthetic act, to "mentally re-enact the actions and to re-create the creations" that were his object of study.[93] Hence, every historical record was in some sense a monument.

By depicting the monument as an object to be "recreated" in the present, Panofsky added an experiential component to prewar internationalist theories of the monument as a kind of testimonial that needs to be presented, as if in court. This concretization was a significant departure from the definition of a "monument" that was operative in Europe's National monuments administrations. As the aforementioned 1940 National Park Service memorandum cogently put it, "The question for what reasons are monuments classified in Europe, cannot be answered by enumerating specifically a number of criteria." Instead, the best one could do was to define a monument as "an object of conservation" and to trust that this practice would be "seasoned by the experience of more than a hundred of years."[94] The Panofskian definition freed the monument from this institutional weight, giving free reign instead to an oscillation between in-person experience and information from books. This was exactly how a Civil Affairs officer would experience monuments on the ground: in person, and with list in hand. A hidden practicality, wholly unforeseen by Panofsky, lay behind his definition. It was this practicality that Colonel Shoemaker activated when he called monuments "cultural media" and authorized the mass-production of lists in June 1943.

Starred Things

The first drafts of lists were sent to Colonel Shoemaker in Washington in March 1943. He promptly returned them to Paul Sachs with a complaint that they contained "too many discussions of an art-historical nature." Shoemaker had asked the art historians to include in their lists a brief description of the "significance of the item to the local population," so that military commanders would be able to "exercise judgment in respect to the importance of action."[95] But the historians had gone too far and *argued* for "the artistic merit of the material listed" after listing them. "Please refrain from instructing the army in art history," Shoemaker complained, and the lists' editors dutifully passed on this admonition. In a new set of instructions, they warned list-makers not to "talk down to the Army," and assured them, "the Army will accept your judgment as to what items should be given priority."[96] But if the Army accepted the judgments of art historians, it also robbed them of the language through which they usually arrived at them. The judgment that would be unconditionally accepted, instead, was a kind of ranked popularity.

The disjunction between art historians' erudite tendencies and the Army's need for practical information had the potential to derail the entire listing endeavor in 1943. But Paul Sachs and W. G. Constable were lifelong collection-builders, and well versed in the art of making relative judgments. Sachs, especially, acted as a kind of institutional gasket between the different parts of the protection project in its early phase. Sachs's contribution was anchored in the practices he had pioneered in the famous "museum course" he taught at Harvard to several generations of curators and historians, many of whom would become "monuments men" (figure 2.10). Also important to his wartime work were his extensive European connections, and his having helped launch other institutional venues for art history at Harvard: the Fogg conservation laboratory, and the Dumbarton Oaks Research Library in Washington, DC. In all of these ventures and his teachings, Sachs was driven by the need to build up collections and professionalize America's curatorial class.[97] As such he worked constantly to redirect aesthetic judgement from the work of art to the collection. "Every distinguished collection," he wrote in the 1930s, "is a work of art in itself, revealing qualities of proportion and harmony which spring from a controlling idea. A true collection manifests a sense of design."[98]

Similarly, as a recurrent guest in Sachs's class, Constable gave a lecture on "Ethics for Museum Men" where students heard that the best purchase for an art museum, especially a regional one, was not necessarily the "best" work but rather "best fit" for its collection.[99] "Indiscriminate buying" was a weakness of American museums and to blame for many second-rate collections, Constable cautioned. "Avoid the gap-filling policy," he advised.[100] During the war, he enunciated similar principles to the list-makers, encouraging them to think that "the best was the enemy of the good," especially as they asked for more more time to complete their lists.[101]

Figure 2.10 Paul J. Sachs (seated) teaching in the Naumburg Room at the Fogg Museum. Photograph by George S. Woodruff, 1944. Harvard Art Museums /Harvard Art Museums Archives, Fogg History Photographs, ARCH.0000.265 Photo: Imaging Department © President and Fellows of Harvard College.

It was Sachs's and Constable's experience in spreading aesthetic value across objects in lists and collections that kept the protection project on track despite what they saw as their colleagues' baffling "incapacity to grasp what was required." In response to Col. Shoemaker's complaints about lists being too erudite, in early April 1943, Sachs and Constable introduced a new structure for the lists: they would restrict all art historical discussions—such as a summary of the major periods of art history and different kinds of monuments for each country—to the lists's introduction.[102] Secondly, together with the other Harvard Group editors, Koehler and Hencken, they created a system of asterisks that became the primary tool for designing the lists.

Once the asterisk system was invented, a working hierarchy was established under Koehler's and Hencken's direction, where senior scholars (usually émigrés) coordinated the work of several (usually junior) contributors for a single country's list, and the list then returned to the editors, who would combine them. The stars quickly became the visual index that editors used to discern the quality of the lists they received. For example, Princeton classical archaeologist Doro Levi, who was in charge of the Italian list, described a discrepancy in contributors' "generosity of stars" and said that, in a "final revision to bring in uniformity," he had "cut or reduced for the balance of the whole."[103] List composers began to speak the language of composition and design, noting the "sparseness" of some lists and the "evenness" of others; expressing a desire for "variation," or a need for "uniformity."

After this re-formatting, a visual and linguistic rhetoric of fame quickly came to permeate the Harvard Lists as a substitute for art-historical discourse. For example, after gallerist Georges Wildenstein wrote an unsatisfactory French list, Koehler revised it by appending each listed item with a single fact to justify its "fame"—age, meaning, architectural features, form, beauty, style, popularity with tourists, usage by authorities, and even presence in the literature. A condensed excerpt from the list for Northern France looked like this:[104]

Bernières (Loiret)	**Church with beautiful spire*, famous**
Blois (Loire & Cher)	Chateau*** remarkable for first-rate historic interest and architectural form
[. . .]	
Carnac (Finistère)	Menhirs*** alignments*** etc. most famous of their kind
[. . .]	
Champdeniers (D.S.)	Church*, parts about 1000 years old
Chantilly (Oise)	Chateau* and stables* famous and much visited
[. . .]	
Chartres (Eure & L.)	Cathedral***, unquestionably one of the finest of all medieval buildings
[. . .]	
Chaumont (Hte.M.)	Chateau* used by Pershing and GHQ of AEF
Chauvigny (Vienne)	Chateau** and church* ensemble, very picturesque
[. . .]	
Domremy (Vosges)	Birthplace of Jeanne d'Arc*** French heroine; important for that reason only
Josselin (Morb.)	Chateau**, famous and rightly so; church
Le Dorat (The V.)	Church*, bold and interesting design
Le Mans (Sarthe)	Cathedral** very noble building, apse one of finest in Gothic style
Le Raincy (Seine)	Parish Church**, one of the most interesting of the modern French churches
Loches (I. etL.)	Chateau*, well-known medieval building; church of St. Ours*, curious 4-spired Romanesque building, unique in form
Morienval (Oise)	Church***, widely known example of primitive Gothic, cited in all books on the subject

Instead of an ekphrastic recreation of each object, it was the list itself that could be directly experienced as a starred, almost bejeweled, recreation of Europe's monumental collections. This format became specific enough that later guides for list-making would feature a "sample page" to work from.[105]

Thus formatted and introduced, the French List of Monuments performed a cultural function that Pierre Bourdieu has described as paradigmatic of art: the proliferation of distinction. "Works of art," wrote Bourdieu, while "distinctive in general, enable the production of distinctions ad infinitum by playing on divisions and subdivisions into genres, periods, styles, authors, etc."[106] Here, the production of distinction was propagated through geography.

Constable was well versed in the art of distributing distinction geographically. In his lecture on museum ethics, for instance, he encouraged his students to conceptualize geographically the proportion of artworks to the population density of various nations, by thinking about the distance people had to travel to see "fine work."[107] Similarly, during war, he conceptualized a double act of distribution. First, he imagined that he was "designing" the lists of monuments for a hypothetical soldier with no training in art history, "Captain John Smith, of Kalamazoo, in real life a bond salesman."[108] Second, Constable added to the list's introduction a blanket statement conferring distinction to the entirety of the French people:

> Consciousness of their national artistic supremacy, of the value of their art treasures and monuments . . . is one of the distinctive characteristics of the French people.

Having worked out this distribution of art-historical value across the social fabric, Constable sent this French list to contributors to use as a template for the whole of Europe. From the introductions that resulted, the people of Western Europe emerged as a homogeneous mass, animated by a generic attachment to their monuments:

> To the Norwegians every kind of monument of the past . . . is precious and valuable.

> In short, the Belgian nation as a whole is highly conscious of the great significance of its artistic heritage.

> The Dutch people hold their monuments and the art of their past in high esteem.

> The Hungarians are extremely proud of their nation, and all classes of people are deeply interested in its history and culture.

> Italy is a nation of art lovers who are intensely proud of their history and of the monuments in which it is given visible evidence, and all classes of the Italian people hold these things in the very highest esteem.

> The Austrian has a great respect for tradition, and is very retentive of habits and practices sanctified by custom.[109]

Read as a composite work, these introductions confirm Panofsky's famous 1953 description of the émigré American art historian as a surveyor of transatlantic panoramas.[110]

It is not that Constable and his art historian colleagues consciously thought of the war in a sinister sense as an opportunity to reduce Europe to a collection of monuments. But reflexes they had developed in order to collect objects and especially to give the impression of geographic evenness within the confined space of the gallery, were here re-territorialized. The result was a wholly simplified regional architectural history, based on monuments being famous with surrounding people, who might visit these buildings, as one does a museum.

If the tools and methods invented for teaching art history to an American liberal educated class living in a mass-society were so easily transferrable to the war effort, it is also because the quantification of the geography of art had penetrated art history to the core of its discursive network, transforming the scholarly grain of the field into subfields. In practice, most art historians worked on a small geographic "area" anchored around a "monument." The Dumbarton Oaks Library is a case in point. The library had opened in 1941 under the leadership of Wilhelm Koehler, who had himself had emigrated to Harvard in 1935 and brought with him the methods of the new *Kunstwissenschaft*. Determined to undermine the hierarchies between major and minor arts, regions, periods, and schools, he had established a "principle of collaborative research" whereby each graduate fellow was assigned a geographic area, contributing to building a comprehensive Research Archive of "all available information about any monument important for the development of Christian art."[111] When the Army requested that the Harvard group expand the geographic scope of the countries covered by their lists in Spring 1943, Koehler and Sachs arranged to keep Dumbarton Oaks open for the summer and make it "a home center for the protection project."[112] Fellows were given stipends to stay for the summer, and produce the Army's lists for Germany, Bulgaria, Hungary, Albania, Rumania, Yugoslavia, and Tunisia.[113]

Thus "militarization" owed a particular debt to the regional parceling of the study of art and architecture in the United States. This debt became especially clear when templates worked out in Western Europe were applied elsewhere. For example, Constable worried at one point about Mittleuropa seeming comparatively sparse, writing to Koehler to ask, "Don't we need more starred things in Yugoslavia, Bulgaria, and Rumania?"[114] A similar issue arose with introductions where the art historians felt they could not appeal to the empathy of the American readership, as they had when speaking of the French as "a nation of art lovers." In North Africa it was the "notorious religious fanaticism" of Muslim inhabitants that was cited as reason for protecting religious shrines, complemented with economic arguments that echoed the colonial "trust of civilization" themes that we heard in League of Nations discussions.[115] Similarly, the whole Japanese people was described as having "almost fanatical reverence for even the most humble shrine," apparently to make up for in ardor what the country lacked in number, since the introduction opened with the dubious statement that Japan was characterized by a paucity in cultural monuments "compared to a small European country."[116] Comparative regional coverage, not individual analysis, drove the protective project.

This comparative mentality led Wilhelm Koehler to have a crisis of conscience that constitutes the only explicit moment of internal critique in Harvard's listing endeavor. Koehler was the person largely responsible for having "evolved a form" of list that the Army deemed "satisfactory for all countries,"[117] and because he was stationed in Washington, he had an unusually close connection to the project. He met with Col. Shoemaker several times, sometimes handing over lists in person; he heard firsthand of the ambitions of the competing ACLS committee, and of plans to merge the two.[118] Having taken on the writing of the German list by himself, he began to have misgivings in June of 1943, when the Roberts Commission proposed a press release that would have described its mission as protecting monuments "for their own sake." Koehler wrote to Perry in Cambridge, reminding him of the practical conceit that had motivated the listing: that monuments were to be taken not as ends in themselves (as in art history) but as means to an end (as in propaganda). A reply came from Henken, that he thought they "should think of as many reasons as possible for protecting these things."[119] But this too fell flat. Koehler thought the monuments of Germany were under a threat not for "many reasons," but for the very particular reason that they were under Nazi control. He opened the first draft of his introduction to the German list with a "Parthenian shot at Hitler," and continued with a detailed description of the country's monuments service, the *Denkmalpflege*, whose decades of "impartial work" the Nazi regime was threatening to undo.[120] Also in deference to the *Denkmalpflege*, Koehler searched far and wide that summer for a copy of Paul Clemen's book about the protection of monuments during the First World War to give personally to Shoemaker.[121] In a sense, Koehler sought to act as the lone personal connection between two enemy monuments programs. But he struggled to overcome the same obstacle as others before him: the fact that in Germany a monument, *Denkmal*, was defined in a circular manner, as an object of listing and therefore of protection, whereas the American system defined monuments through a demonstrative list.[122]

By mid-June 1943, the time for such informality had passed. Given the quickening pace of events in the European theater, the Harvard Lists began to seem impracticably long, and the unofficial personal ties that had oiled the university's connection to the army had become unsustainable. Constable rewrote Koehler's introduction, removing references to the Nazi regime, leaving only a reduced version of his description of the Commission's mandate and including Germany in it.[123] That summer, the project's logistical heart also moved from Washington to New York where, under the new supervision of William Bell Dinsmoor, the ACLS committee produced shorter and anonymized lists that became Civil Affairs Handbooks.[124] Dinsmoor was the same classical archaeologist whom we heard in chapter 1 weighing in on the Parthenon reconstruction in the 1920s. After this expatriate experience in Athens, he had returned to teach at Columbia University, and had been trying to get a monuments committee sponsored by the ACLS since January. He finally succeeded in establishing a formal channel for monuments work, getting all contacts with the Army re-routed to the chief of Civil Affairs in Washington, DC, General John H. Hilldring, and securing financial backing from the Rockefeller Foundation to begin constructing its own card file in the basement of the Frick collection in New York.[125] In principle, this workshop functioned in the same way as Dumbarton Oaks but with more resources, a full-time staff, and a capacity to update information about the state of destruction of Europe's monuments, and the names of their various administrators, in real-time (figure 2.11).

In actuality, the ACLS's card file was itself an infrastructure, from which information could be retrieved at will. It assigned each monument a card, and cards could also represent an object, place, or person. Dinsmoor even hoped to use this apparatus to make new lists. But the more expedient way to proceed was to shrink the Harvard lists from 50 to 25 pages by including only its 2- and 3-starred elements[126] (figure 2.12). Some list-makers took this news in stride and began strategically planning for the shrinking of their lists by "adding stars here and there."[127] Koehler, in contrast, argued that Germany was a special case. Having initially refused to take part in the "starring" scheme at all, he had allowed asterisks to be added to his list only after an extensive back-and-forth.[128] When, in November, he realized his German list had been reduced to only these "starred things," and realizing that the Italian list had in contrast been expanded seemingly at will, he wrote Col. Shoemaker to protest.[129] He had always objected to "such a radically abbreviated list in the case of Germany," and asked if the list could be retracted:

> After having finished I am more convinced than ever that any list reduced to such an extent is completely arbitrary, subjective, and therefore open to thoroughly justified criticism, and that in this two-fold process of elimination certain monuments of the first importance have had to be dropped.[130]

Koehler was the only person who had personally been involved in every phase of making and editing a list. He had witnessed the conversion of a hierarchy between starred and not-starred into a hierarchy between listed and unlisted and therefore potentially into saved and destroyed. He felt himself to be the victim of a uniquely American kind of militarization: a process that organizes civilian activity to prepare for war, while "concealing its purposes and obscuring its consequences."[131] The monuments protection work, he implied, was granting legitimacy to a project of destruction by even publishing a list at all.[132]

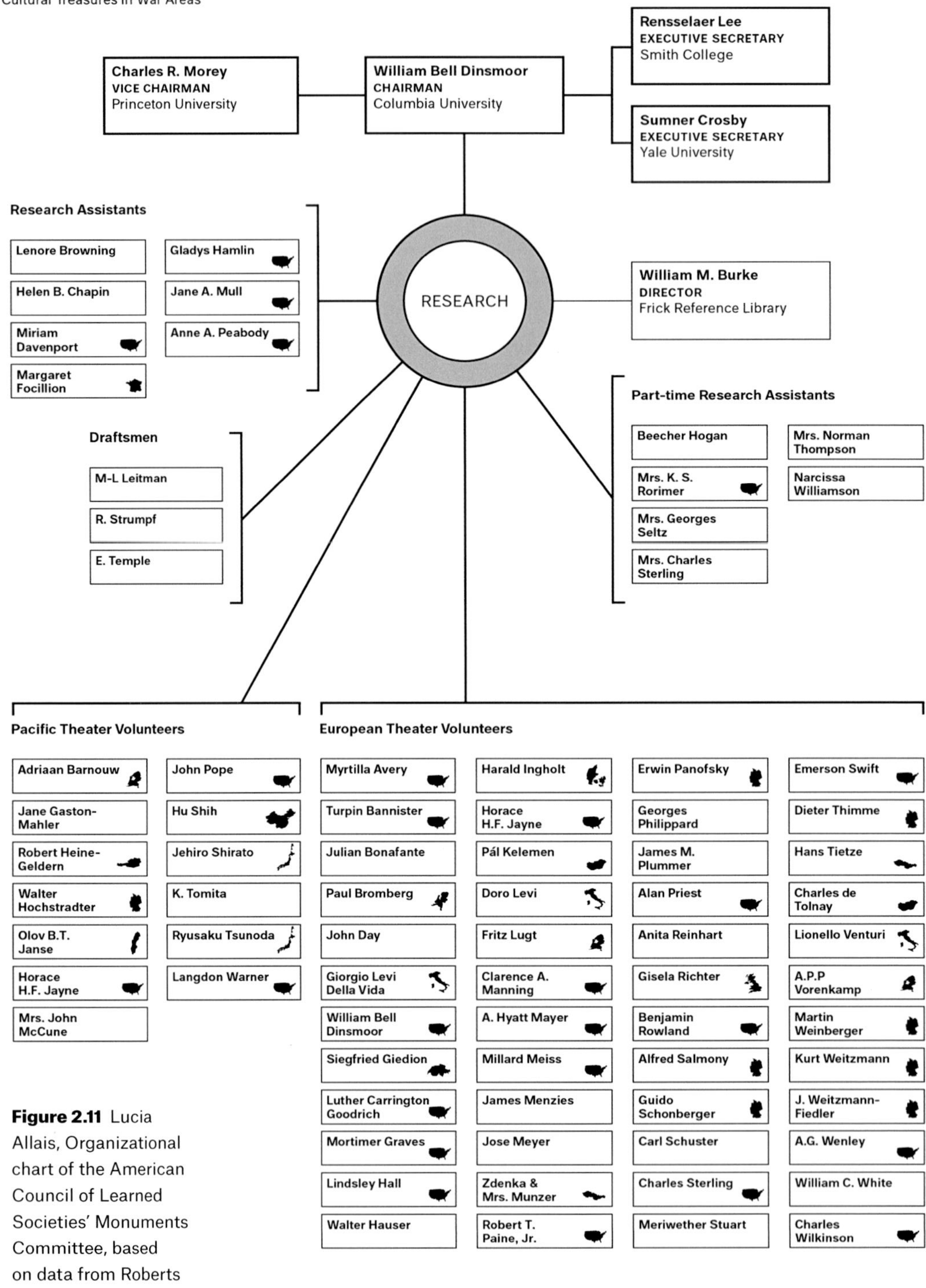

Figure 2.11 Lucia Allais, Organizational chart of the American Council of Learned Societies' Monuments Committee, based on data from Roberts Commission, *Final Report* (1946). © Lucia Allais.

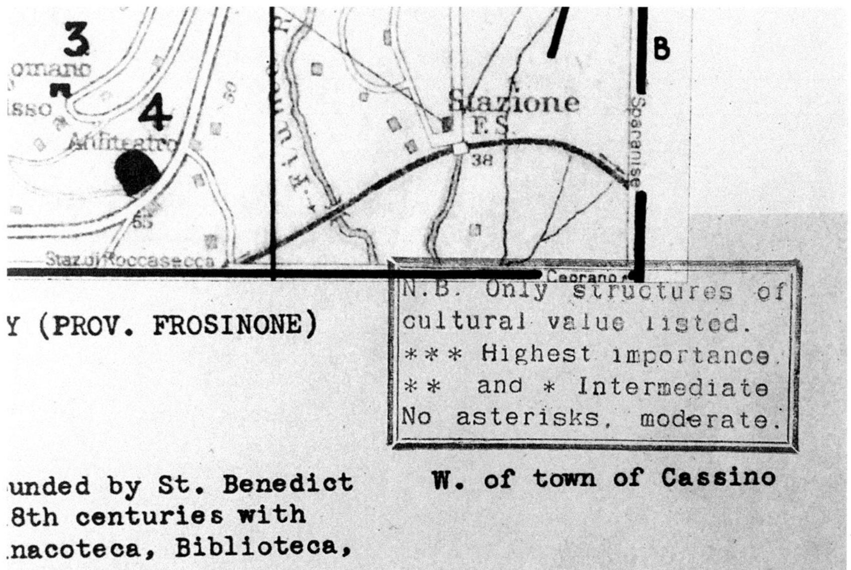

Figure 2.12 Detail of the legend explaining the use of asterisks in a *Civil Affairs Handbook*, Section 17: Cultural Institutions. (1944). NARA.

In fact, being named in a list or on an index card was not the only way an architectural monument could be militarized. Consider an anecdote told by Margaret Ames, a junior fellow at Dumbarton Oaks and the author of the list for Tunisia. "In Tunisia," she is reported as saying, long after the war had ended, "a number of buildings were carefully protected from bombing, because somehow they were thought to be shrines. They were, in fact, tobacco and newspaper kiosks."[133] This story projects us a year forward, and places us on the North African coast, among a blanket of destruction that had been wrought by several competing armies—first the German, then the Allied bombing campaigns, and eventually varying occupying troops. Picturing protected kiosks among this devastation helps to parse several limitations of the list as a protective tool. First, soldiers on the ground had taken liberties in choosing which monuments to protect, showing that the "freedom to act," as Eisenhower called it, was felt all the way down the chain of command. Second, the introduction Ames had authored (where she described fanatic religious devotion of Muslims) had unintended consequences. The soldiers had gotten from the lists the need to find shrines, along with an idea that monuments exist everywhere, and in a network. As for the specific confusion—a lowly newsstand kiosk taken for a revered object—it reveals that scholarly distinctions were no match for architectural stylizations in hard materials[134] (figure 2.13). Whoever was in charge on the ground had relied on visual cues to decide the kiosks were monuments because of their Orientalizing forms. What they had protected were not shrines but colonial infrastructure, built by the French colonial government since the early twentieth century to furnish Tunisian cities with modern amenities and give its civilizing mission a gentler, more regional appeal.[135]

Figure 2.13 Postcard showing a view of the Avenue de France in Bizerte (Tunisia) with a newspaper kiosk built by the French colonial government.

Shrinking as Strategy

At the end of this story of the tumultuous events of spring 1943, it may seem to the reader that the Harvard scholars merely reconstructed from scratch a format of information that was readily available in Baedeker and elsewhere. But the scholars' intense work in the early months granted lists of monuments a legitimacy that a Baedeker did not have. To begin with, they produced what Lisa Gitleman has called "typescript books": publications that flatten hierarchies between author and reader, and circulate to the uninitiated some specialized information usually cloaked in secrecy[136] (color plate 2). Furthemore, the language of social distinction that was blanketed across these documents conveyed in the mind of the reader that protection required no other reason except the availability of information. Observe in contrast the hand-wringing later expressed by British officers debating which "approach" to adopt in convincing their troops to protect monuments.

> It seems likely that the aesthetic or art history approach would mean little or nothing . . . and . . . the "common heritage of civilization" line would mean very little more. . . . it is possible that the aspect of antiquity, i.e. the appeal of sheer age and long continued use will go down. . . . The social significance of buildings might get across . . .[137]

This internal debate constitutes an almost parodic rehearsal of Alois Riegl's catalog of monumental values, and stands in stark contrast to the American method, which made all monuments subject to protection, de facto.

Furthermore, the strategy for shrinking and expansion of the list that was established in these early months was consistently followed for the rest of the war. As several more types of lists were issued, a proportional logic was used. The fate of the material prepared in the United States continued to vary according to the timing and geography of the war. There were places the American historians were asked to exclude: Italian colonies (since the British would occupy them), areas of Russian interest (Finland, Baltic States, and Poland), and Burma, Malaysia, and Philippines (where the British claimed to have more specialized knowledge).[138] In most European places, the lists were appended with maps. In Northern Europe, including in the Netherlands, Belgium, and Germany, additional Zone Handbooks were issued for use in the field.[139] In Italy, in addition to these handbooks, the data was transposed onto aerial photographs by and for pilots of the Mediterranean Allied Air Force, as we will see in chapter 3. In France, one list containing only 25 monuments for the country was eventually made. Every time, the same two questions were rehearsed: first, whether to make a ranked list or rather a basic list "not weakened by discrimination," and second, which of the "lesser monuments among which the choice was not so portent" to include.[140] These manifold variations were perceived as strengthening monuments protection, because they enabled the kind of decision-making that Eisenhower had entrusted to the "new individual" at war (figure 2.14).

One of the most dramatic demonstrations of how new choices in the field came to sustain the protection program occurred in October and November 1943, between Naples and Tunisia, just as information about monuments was about to pass from street maps to aerial photographs. I will return to this moment in the next chapter—for now it suffices to note that the British archaeologist Paul Baillie Reynolds was given three hours to submit a list of 45 monumental cities that, "in the opinion" of the MFAA, and on a "sliding scale of importance," had "asterisk value."[141] Baillie Reynolds made a ranked list, with help from two other MFAA officers, and attached corresponding maps. Within a month, this list was rejected as too regionalized and insufficiently prioritized. New instructions were issued, where the asterisk metaphor disappeared and a blunter thought experiment was proposed: "If the whole of Italy had to be destroyed except one city," he was asked, "which city would you choose? If two cities were allowed to remain, which would they be? Etc."[142] This phrasing is remarkable because it not only performed the same mental erasure Constable had imagined for a single city, now at the the scale of the entire country, but asked him to repeat this radical act to produce a hierarchy, proliferating distinction *ad infinitum*, to use Bourdieu's language.[143] And for every additional allowance, the new lucky surviving city had the burden of representing the same geographic "whole," Italy.

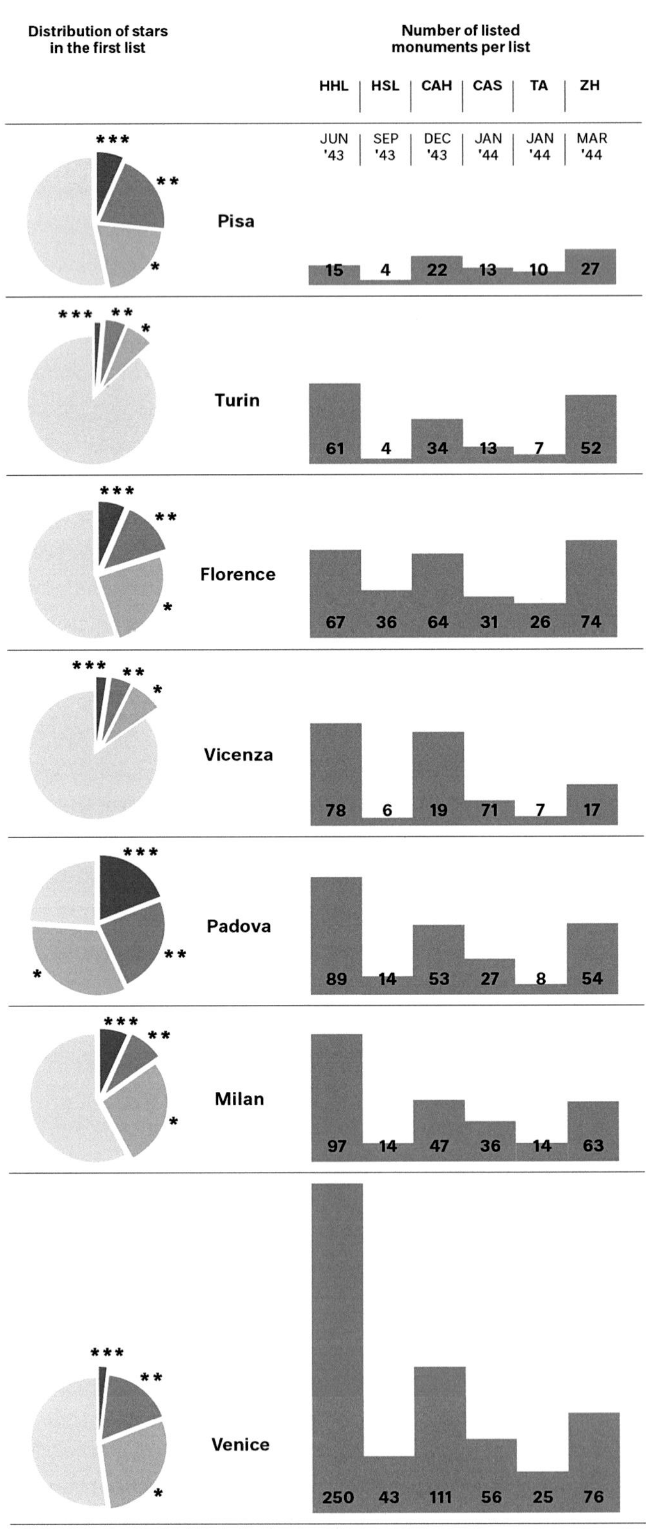

Figure 2.14 Shrinking and expansion of the Allied lists and maps of monuments for seven Italian towns, between May 1943 and March 1944. © Lucia Allais.

If every listed object had to represent a geographic whole, conversely every category of monument had to be present in every list. Consider one alternative shrinking method that was proposed on the eve of the invasion of France during D-Day. In order to create shorter, "wallet-sized" lists for use by disembarking soldiers, Civil Affairs planners suggested issuing "churchless" lists. The idea was that churches would be protected de facto: by military order (whereas other palaces, for instance, might be "billeted" temporarily for administrative use) and by predisposition of the soldiers.[144] And since churches were so numerous, the resulting lists would have been about 40% shorter.[145] Yet to publish a churchless list—and to remove an entire category of building—would violate the principle that a country's entire pyramid of aesthetic distinction had be represented in its list. In fact, churches continued to play a crucial demonstrative role in MFAA publications long after the word "monument" had been replaced by the more overarching "cultural institutions." Manuals issued in fall 1944 were titled *Atlas on Churches, Museums, Libraries and Other Cultural Institutions*. Much later, as the Tunisian episode shows, the MFAA troops on the ground became real-time human discrimination machines. Their presence in the theater of war was sometimes interpreted to mean that they could take any list and add stars on the spot, and other times to mean that they could expand the list at will.[146] Initially justified by expediency, mundane features of the lists became means of flexibility.

All of these acts of discrimination, distinction, separation, hierarchization, created a structured flexibility that would become essential in choosing targets and weapons, and more generally in making strategy—as the next chapter describes. By early 1945, Eisenhower's office could issue a blanket reminder to all Allied troops that "the locations of monuments are known to us and published from time to time."[147]

The legitimacy of the list of monuments came at the cost of a displacement of questions about ethics onto the methods of aesthetics, however. As we have seen, in order to get the policy authorized, scholars had to supress any discussion of the possibility of human violence, and they experienced the dilemmas, debates, and anxieties that might have arisen around destructive scenarios as disciplinary ones instead. Furthermore, each scholar faced the struggles of transforming an academic pursuit into military work individually, in a kind of relay-race, each borrowing variously from the sciences, and under increasing pressure from an army organization that took such claims of scientific objectivity seriously. It is under these conditions of epistemic violence that information on monuments was passed, in June 1943, to what was then the most powerful destruction machine in modern history.

Conclusion: Elective Affinities

As I have already suggested, Panofsky's evocative depiction of a monument as a humanist "recreation" can be expanded from the narrow philological sense he intended it, to decsribe more broadly the American art historians'

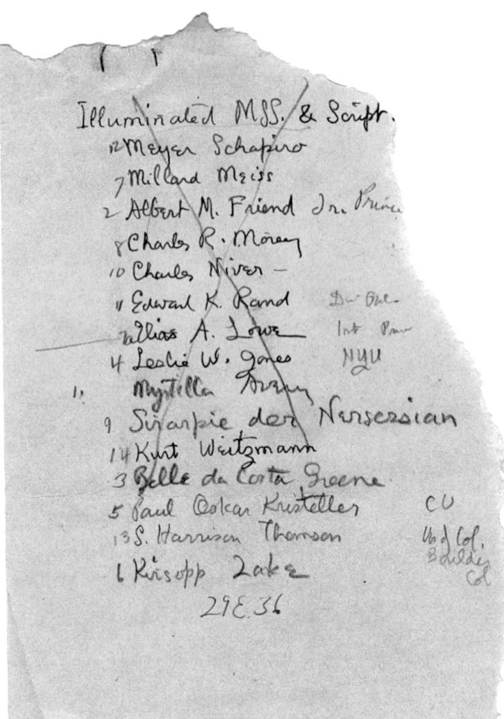

Illuminated MSS. & Script.
12 Meyer Schapiro
7 Millard Meiss
2 Albert M. Friend Jr. Prince
8 Charles R. Morey
10 Charles Niver —
11 Edward K. Rand
Elias A. Lowe
4 Leslie W. Jones NYU
1, Myrtilla Avery
9 Sirarpie der Nersessian
14 Kurt Weitzmann
3 Belle da Costa Greene
5 Paul Oskar Kristeller CU
13 S. Harrison Thomson U of Col. Boulder Col
6 Kirsopp Lake

Figure 2.15 William Bell Dinsmoor, list of scholars to consult on the location of illuminated manuscripts in Europe, 1944. Papers of William Bell Dinsmoor. Used with permission of the American School of Classical Studies at Athens, Archives.

contribution to the war. Of course, humanistic reenactment was for Panofsky not fanciful reconstruction; it was bound by rules policing the scholar's work. In particular, Panofsky excluded from the act of interpretation any insights a person might derive from experiencing art as aging patrimony—the aesthetics of patina, the possibility of "accidental" additions to the work, the conditions under which he saw it, etc.[148] As "a private person" the art historian could consider these factors, but as "a professional man" he set them aside, by "bracketing" them off. Yet when war struck, Panofsky proved to be an apt wielder of the list as a tool that blurred these two modes. He contributed to listing not only monuments but also people, notably adding to the so-called "White, Grey and Black Lists" of scholars who may have collaborated with various Axis looting schemes[149] (figure 2.15). One of the most evocative lists he made was titled, simply, "List of Libraries Where I have Studied."[150]

More broadly, then, we might ask how the art historians of the Roberts Commission navigated the sudden "unbracketing" of their art-historical practice from world events. One answer is found in the critiques directed at the Commission immediately at war's end, which attacked its methods as too efficient, too rationalized. In 1946, the German émigré architectural historian Paul Frankl published a pointed attack of his colleagues who had produced lists of monuments, for doing too little, too late. Monuments protection had been a kind of "value-blind-flying," he wrote.[151] By this he meant that art historians had busied themselves with the superficial affairs of monument survival, only after they had closed their eyes to deep-seated causes of the war in earlier years:

> Can these art scholars who agonized about their beloved artifacts, really be exonerated of guilt? What did they really do to prevent the catastrophe? At the last minute, they made maps. But they should have organized themselves decades earlier: first, to protest a prevailing lack of culture and blindness to values, and then supplementing this critique with a positive plan for world government. In their own field, they are highly educated; they discriminate between values as keenly as the artists they study, and far more objectively. But should they not also educate themselves in the problems of world politics and world morality?[152]

Frankl was not alone in implying that American art historians had been ideologically indifferent to Europe's descent into war. From the other end of the political spectrum, in 1945 Metropolitan Museum director Francis Taylor accused "teutonic" art history of having facilitated the rise of Nazism in Germany, and warned that this same art history, guided by "method" over "values" and driven by "iconological thinking," was now threatening to infiltrate and undermine American cultural institutions.[153] Although Taylor had been an active member of the Commission, and even claimed credit for its successes very publicly, by the end he lamented that "something intangible had been lost" even in monuments' survival.[154]

The response of the Roberts Commission's members to these accusations is telling. George Stout reacted in private by objecting that Taylor and other "art politicians" were taking credit for monument survivals that they "knew to be caused purely by accident."[155] What mattered to Stout was not the result of the salvage effort, but the "process of its planning" and the lessons that could be learned. Looking ahead, he called for more militarization: to make protection more systematic by "building it into the fabric of military organizations" and then "maintaining it during peacetime."[156] From the other end of the spectrum, Ralph Barton Perry also cared more about process than result. But for Perry it was this element of accident—the possibility of destruction—that coated monuments in an ideology of freedom, making them communicate the message that the Allies were fundamentally "free" to act.[157]

What Frankl and Taylor missed was that the American protection policy had been the product of a choice not between "method" and "values," but rather a choice between methods. The scholars making lists, and later the MFAA troops on the ground, continually struggled to identify a system of aesthetic distinction by which monumental objects could instantiate the values of one political system (liberalism, or choice) and not the other (totalitarianism, or the lack of choice). At every turn, they had struggled with *how* to be value-blind: how to disentangle real decision from mere choice. The connection between daily acts of choice and personal freedom broadly construed is one of the fundamental themes of post-Enlightenment political thought; as Walter

Benjamin put it a decade earlier, "choice is natural and may even be elemental; decision is transcendent."[158] In that sense, the American lists of monuments were bearers of a liberal politics, reflective of a broader Allied mission, drawn from American political ideals, and which eventually became the dominant internationalism in the West after 1945.

If there is one aspect of this method that the scholars of the Roberts Commission could not control, however, it is that they dealt with each monument one by one, as individual objects, separated from the built environment and only later re-anchored to a place through little more than regional art-geography. My next chapter unfurls the consequences of this epistemic anchoring, which subjected monuments to blindness of a more technological kind. This phase begins in early June 1943, as soon as the Roberts Commission was asked not only to make lists of monuments but also to locate them on a map.

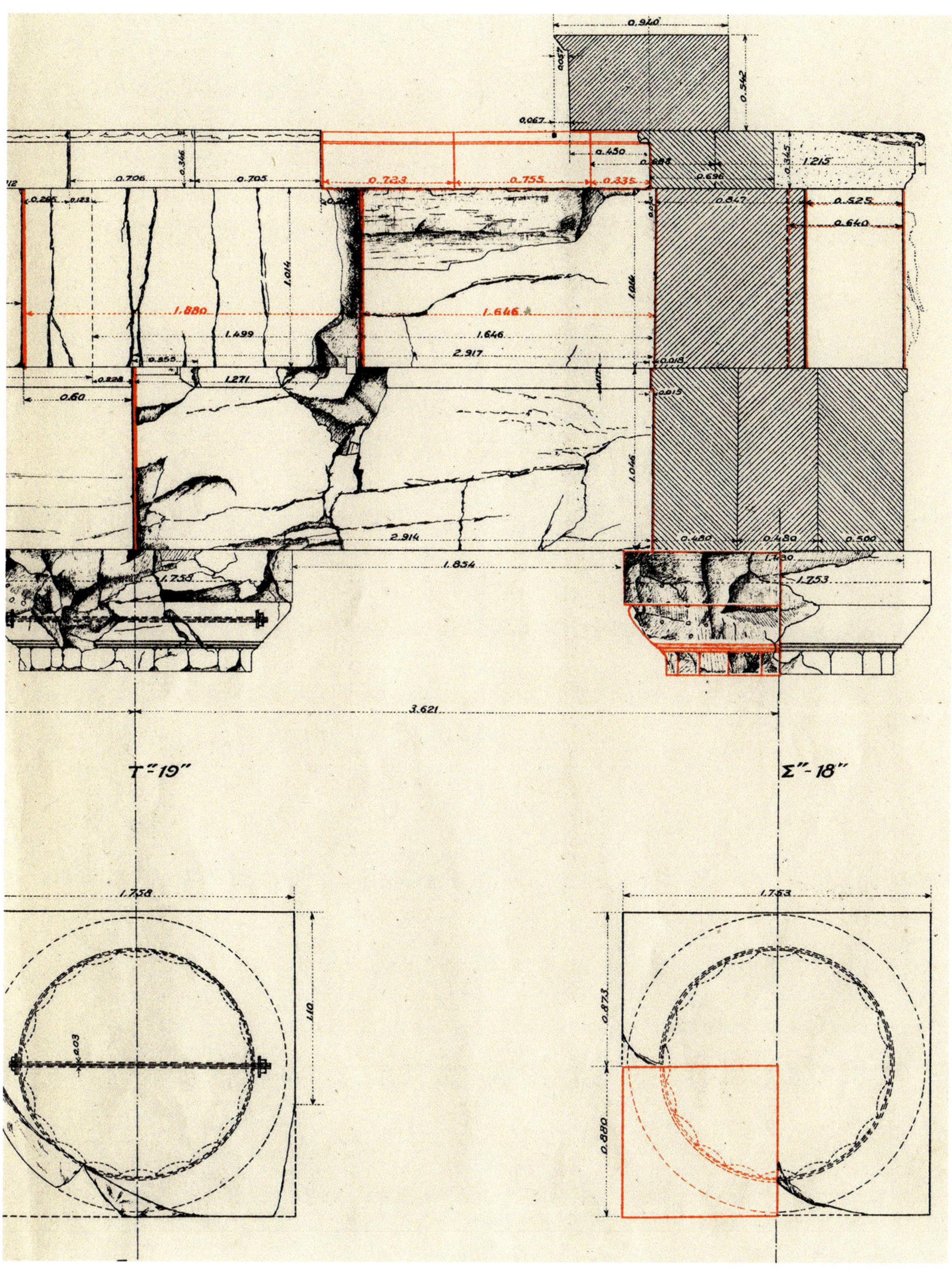

Plate 1 Nicolas Balanos, detail from entablature and capital (interior elevation) of the northern colonnade of the Parthenon, from *Relèvement de l'Acropole* (Paris: 1936).

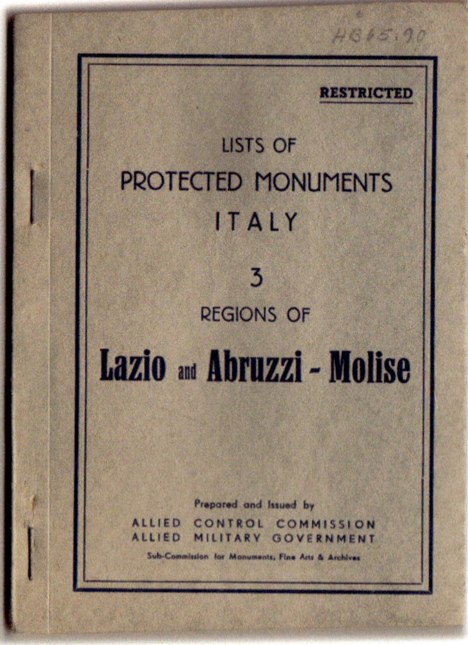

Plate 2 Covers of the Zone Handbooks for Italy issued by the Allied Military Government to Civil Affairs Officers in 1944. NARA.

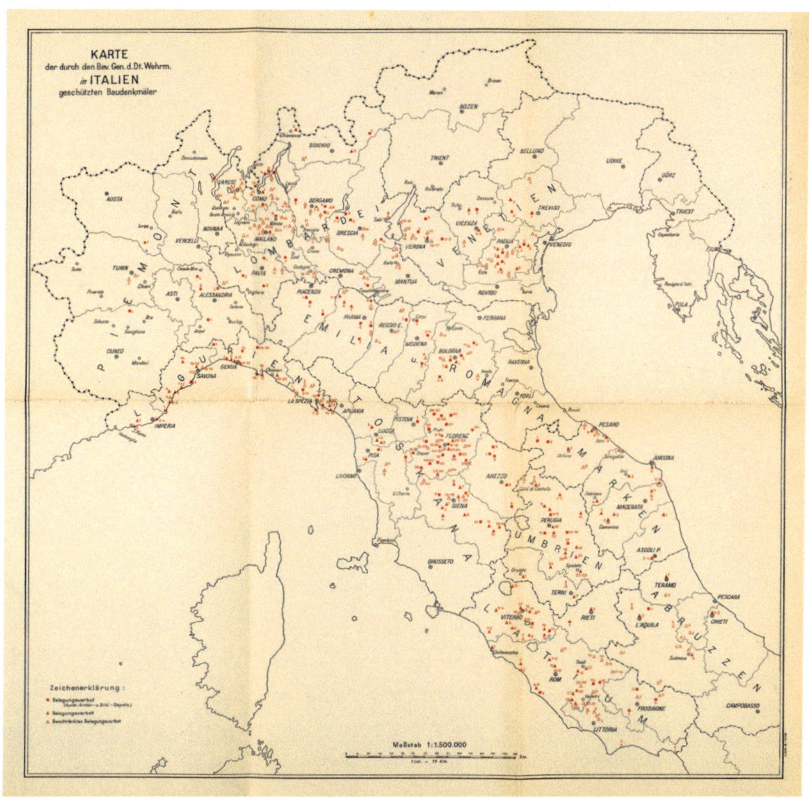

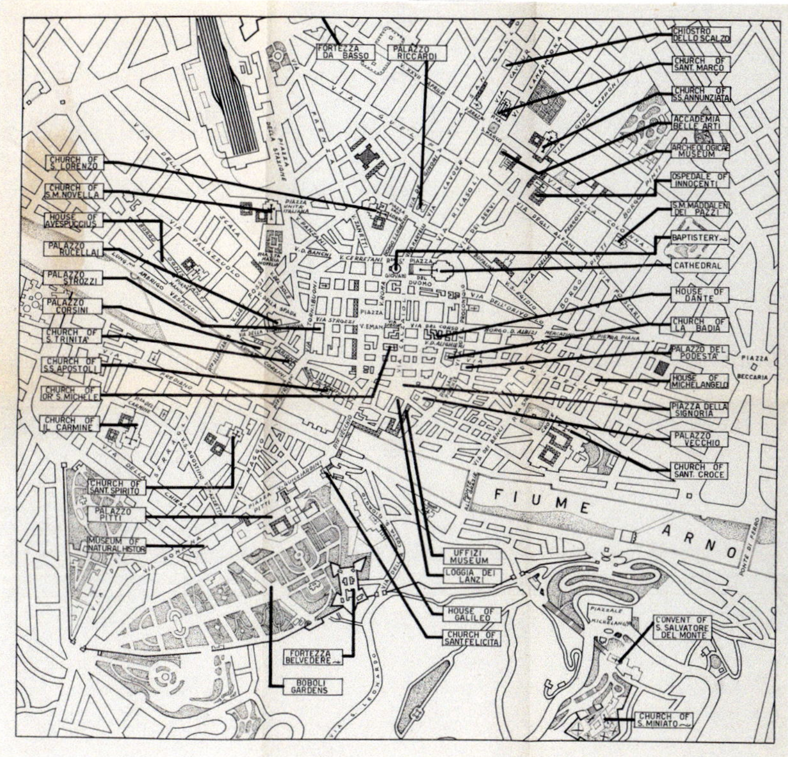

Plate 3 a. Map of monumental sites in Northern Italy made by the German Kunstschutz, 1944. *Verzeichnis Und Karte der Durch Den Bevollmächtigten General Der Deutschen Wehrmacht In Italien Geschutzten Baudenkmäler*. Frederick Hartt Papers, National Gallery of Art, Washington, DC, Gallery Archives. Used with permission. b. Map of monuments in Florence from: Allied Military Government, *Soldier's Guide to Florence* (1944). Theodore DeWald Papers (C0420), Manuscripts Division, Department of Rare Books and Special Collections, Princeton University Library.

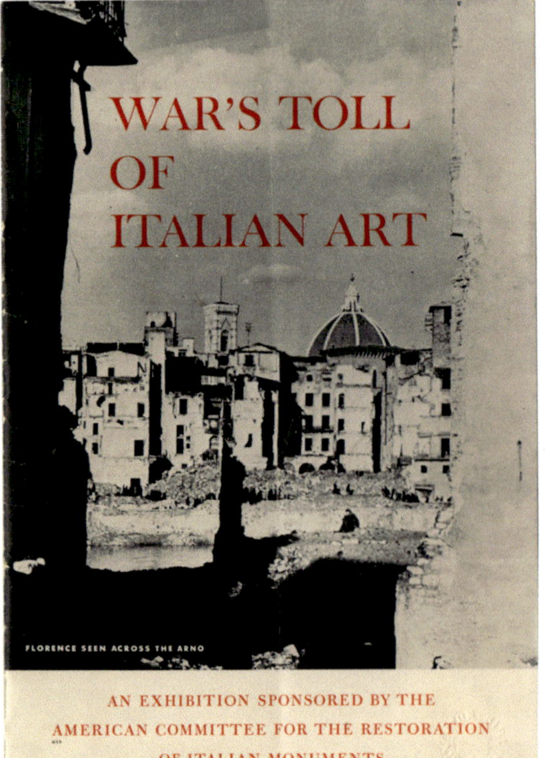

Plate 4 Wartime pamphlets about Italian monuments: a. *Profanazione* (1942) Italian propaganda pamphlet. Frederick Hartt Papers, National Gallery of Art, Washington, DC, Gallery Archives. b. American Military Government, *Soldier's Guide to Rome* (1944) Ernest Theodore DeWald Papers (C0420), Manuscripts Division, Department of Rare Books and Special Collections, Princeton University Library. c. American Committee for the Restoration of Italian Monuments (ACRIM), *War's Toll of Italian Art* Exhibition Catalog (1946).

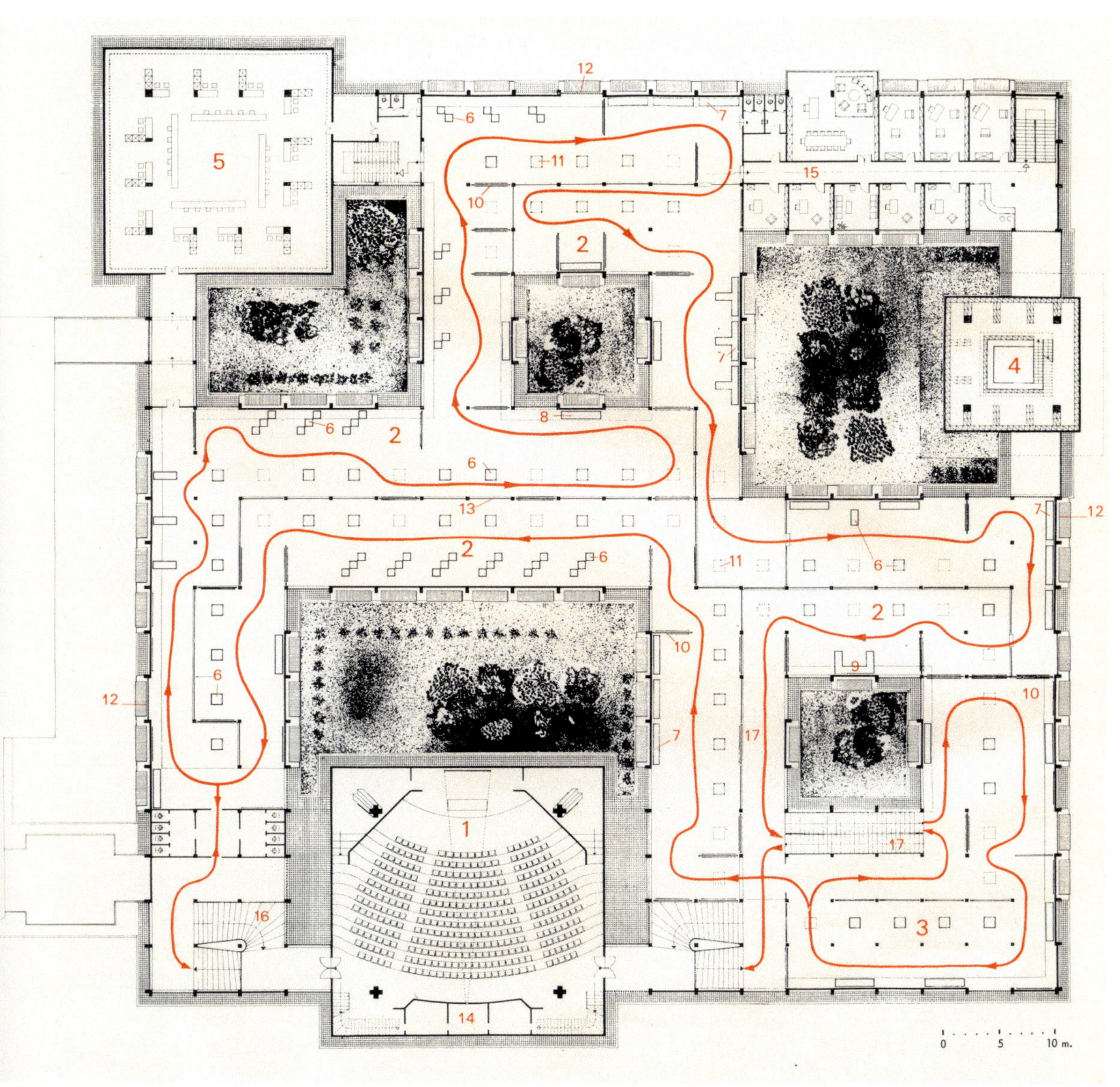

Plate 5 Franco Minissi, plan of the proposed addition to the National Museum in Accra, Ghana (1964). Archivio dello Stato.

Plate 6 Photographs of Franco Minissi's unfinished addition to the National Museum in Accra, Ghana (2017). Photos © Kweku Obeng.

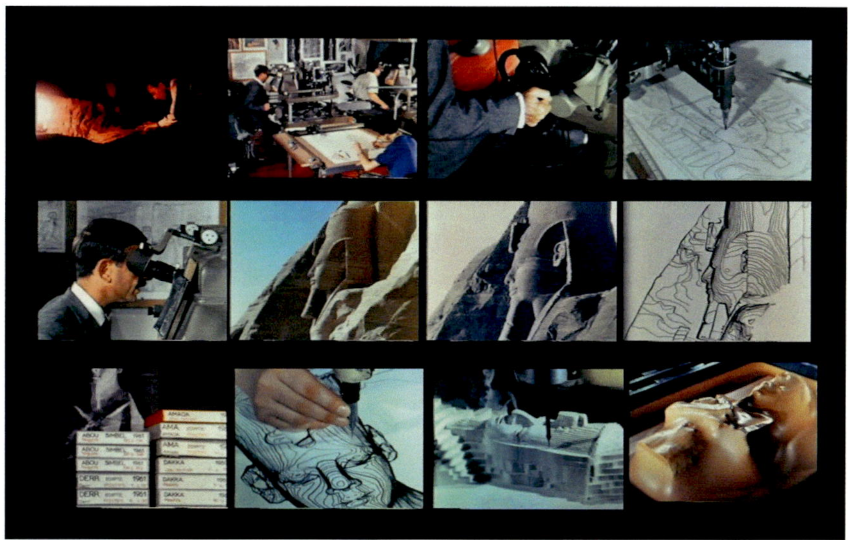

Plate 7 a. Stills from Robert Génot, dir. *Nubie 64* (1968), showing photogrammetric recording of the temples. Institut National Géographique. Used with permission. b. The temple-fronts were covered in sand to protect them from falling rocks from the mountain above. Photograph © Georg Gerster. Used with permission.

Plate 8 Material from the Campaigns for Florence and Venice: a. Postcard of a Florence street during the flood of November 1966. b. Photograph of the fortifications of the island of Sant'Andrea in Venice, 1954. Published under concession number 4/2017 del Ministero dei beni e delle attivita culturali e del turismo-Soprintendenza Archeologie, Belle Arti e Paesaggio per il Commune di Venezia e Laguna. Used with permission.

3 Unwitting City Planning

MAPS OF MONUMENTS AND THE AMERICAN BOMBING OF EUROPE, 1943–1945

The first Allied bombs fell on Rome in late morning of July 19, 1943.[1] That afternoon, commanders on both sides of the war rushed to assess the strategic consequences of the raid. American reconnaissance missions flew over the bombed sites to survey the damage.[2] Mussolini, who had been meeting with Hitler in Northern Italy, returned to Rome to face an anxious Grand Fascist Council. Pope Pius XII ventured out of the Vatican for the first time since the beginning of the war, and was greeted in the bombed neighborhood San Lorenzo by a hysterical crowd, which flocked around him as he stood in a Christ-like pose, arms outstretched. But one of the most consequential turning points in the war's cultural front occurred much more quietly in Washington, DC, where the German émigré architectural historian Richard Krautheimer was working as an intelligence officer for the Office of Strategic Services (OSS). Krautheimer had just learned that US bombing crews had been "briefed by means of maps and photographs on which primary monuments to be avoided were marked."[3] Finding this report "encouraging," he composed a letter to colleagues he knew to be engaged in the preparation of Lists of Protected Monuments for the Allies, to suggest that they immediately begin making maps. Such maps "would have the advantage of presenting in concise and graphic form the more important data, which the air forces could constantly relate to their projected targets." Krautheimer was careful to speak of *con*cision, not *pre*cision, and cautioned that these would not be target maps; that they would be "informative" and not "advisory." Still, the letter changed the course of the American monuments protection project that we have been following since chapter 2, because it opened the door to an entire line of argument that had been advocated by one faction of the Roberts Commission but hitherto suppressed: namely, that monuments might be avoided during bombing, rather than being salvaged on the ground afterwards.[4]

All of those who had voiced this hope had associated mapping with precision. In November 1942, for instance, art historians gathered in Princeton imagined "maps showing the precise location of historic sites in the hope that, where possible, they might be spared bombing."[5] When details of the Rome

Figure 3.1 The thirteenth-century church of San Lorenzo Fuori le Mura in Rome (Italy) after it was damaged in an Allied raid on July 19, 1943. NARA.

raid were released, they appeared to confirm this association of monument survival with the signature visual rhetorics of precision. "Precision Bombing Problem Was What to Hit and Also What Not to Hit," announced a headline in the Air Force magazine *Impact*. The point was illustrated with aerial photographs where four sites in Rome had been labeled "must on no account be damaged."[6] And yet, as the article acknowledged and the art historians already knew well, among the destroyed railyards and housing blocks of San Lorenzo lay the half-destroyed basilica of San Lorenzo Fuori le Mura, which had now lost its thirteenth-century frescoes—the same frescoes that had earned it two stars in the Allies' Lists of Monuments—obliterated by what was labeled "a few stray bombs" (figure 3.1). So the raid on Rome, which inaugurated the Allies' monuments-avoidance aerial war, also laid bare the struggle that lay ahead. The monument, that unit of protection, was well within the margin of error of Allied destruction.[7]

This chapter follows the American monuments protection project as it moved into the European theater after June 1943, newly emboldened by the request for maps, but increasingly encountering the fiction of the non-target, that elusive object "not to hit." As maps of monuments became the preferred platform for the Roberts Commission's work, the dilemma of combining aesthetic distinction with military discrimination, which was the subject of the last chapter, turned into a struggle to reconcile visual concision with technological precision. As I will show, as the war progressed visual criteria were increasingly used to make a choice of monuments. Yet maps only deepened the problems of associating monuments protection with the liberal ideology of choice, because "choice" was now mediated through the optical and statistical technologies for destruction. Protective action was split into two realms. From above, art historians became reliant on machines of aerial warfare and their blindnesses, while on the ground, Monuments, Fine Arts and Archives (MFAA) troops borrowed fieldwork tactics from archaeology. In both realms, the problem of constantly updating information on monuments so that it resembled target intelligence, and later the shape of destruction, overtook the broader mission of planning the survival of monuments as cultural infrastructure.

Focusing on maps of monuments and their formatting helps us dismantle the main conceptual difficulty that has faced historians investigating the fate of monuments in World War II—the question of whether avoidance of damage to historic monuments was intentional or not.[8] The vocabulary that has been hitherto employed matter-of-factly to evaluate the monuments policy—words such as *intention*, *effect*, *target*, and *avoidance*—was itself completely transformed by the war. Indeed, theorists and historians of technology have drawn the terms for a new, machine-inflected philosophical understanding of human volition from the history of precision-bombing technologies and their cybernetic transformation of the mind and body. Building on this literature, I argue monuments contributed to this new predictive ethic of action, reaction, and uncertainty even when they were excluded from the bombsights of what Peter Galison has called "the ontology of the enemy."[9] It was their nature as triggers of cultural choice on the blurred edges of targeted vision that rendered monuments useful and compatible with technologies of destruction. They allowed art historians, and ultimately soldiers, to resort to art historical judgment as one way among others to deal with the ethical uncertainty of war.

Blacked-Out Spots

One of the recipients of Krautheimer's report on Rome was the archaeologist William Bell Dinsmoor, who was, as we have heard in the last chapter, heading the American list-making project at the Frick collection in New York. Dinsmoor wasted no time converting this enterprise into a map-making workshop (figure 3.2). He also repeatedly tried to involve the Army's own map-making agencies in the process.[10] But traveling to Washington to obtain what he called "aerial maps," he was disappointed to be told that he would only be given "ordinary ground maps" and that his committee was also welcome to use maps from tourist guides. Dinsmoor rationalized this, but he continued to encourage a language of precision among his colleagues.[11] In December 1943, a proposed press release talked about the maps showing "important

Figure I

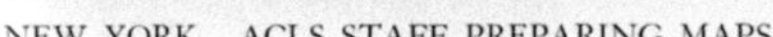

Figure 3.2 William Bell Dinsmoor (left) poses with Jane Mull (pencil in hand), Bill Burke, and Miriam Davenport at the Frick Collection in New York while making a map of monuments, 1944. Photograph from Office of War Information. NARA.

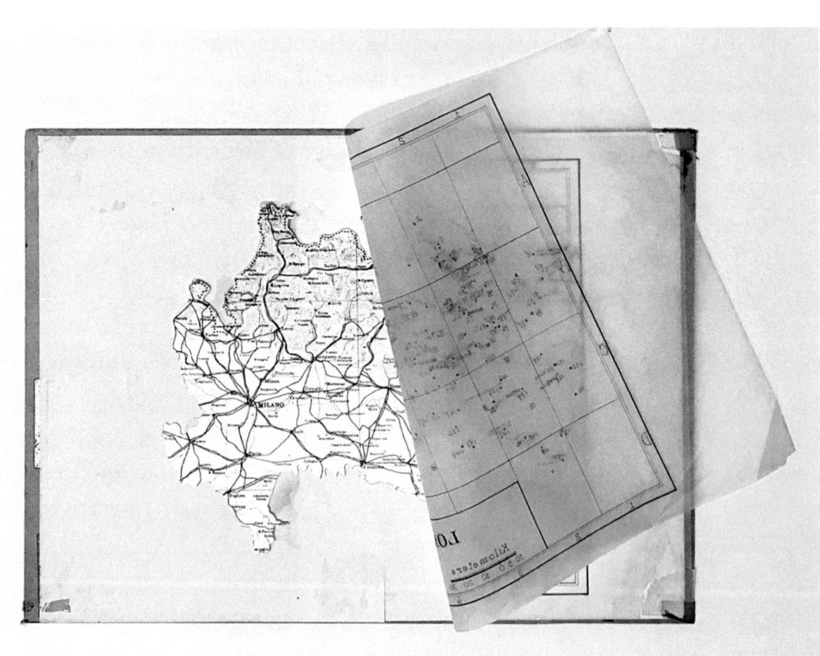

Figure 3.3 Assembly of the base for a Frick map of Lombardy. NARA.

cultural spots . . . blacked out," so that they would "show airmen exactly what to stay away from."[12] This blacking out was the result of a laborious procedure of montage. First, base maps drawn from different kinds of tourist guides were copied (cut out if they were of a whole region), then overlain with a vellum sheet that included a standardized grid, a title, and other graphic infrastructure (figure 3.3). Monuments were then marked onto another superimposed vellum layer, their plans filled in with black ink, each shape affixed with a number, and keyed to typewritten list. The entire assemblage was then Photostatted, and the several layers of vellum produced an effect where "the town map [was] in gray and the important buildings in black."[13] Maps were bound alphabetically in Civil Affairs *Atlas Supplements*, country by country. Two atlases—for France and Italy—were ready by the turn of the year 1944. In February, the whole project was moved to the west of England, where more atlases were made, and soon after again to London, where various representatives of Allied governments in exile helped construct and refine the lists and atlases for their own countries.[14] From that point on, the Atlas maps acquired the dual purpose that they would retain throughout the war. For the Air Forces, they became reference documents, acting as a kind of "long list" from which a number of other protective documents were made. For the MFAA officers, they were guides for navigating the conflict, recording damage, and coordinating "first aid" after battle.[15]

The switch from lists to maps to coordinate monuments protection provoked two fundamental changes in the Roberts Commission's work. First, "the town" became the primary numeric threshold for monument choice.[16] A map of any town would be included in the Atlas Supplements only if there were at least 5 monuments to show. Just as had happened when the starring mechanism was introduced, art historians began judiciously planning for this fact by adding monuments "here and there" so that certain towns earned themselves a map. Secondly, map-making encouraged the committee to think in spatial terms, and to suggest expanding protection from a monumental point to an entire urban zone. This happened over time. The Frick map of Rome, one of the earliest ones made, showed a spattering of black spots so concentrated that one could read the plan in a gestalt oscillation of positive and negative urban space, including in the highly recognizable baroque shape of St. Peters (figure 3.4). No attempt was made to name this as a singular monumental "area," however. But the nearby archaeological sites of the ancient Roman Forum were hatched, by hand, to represent a larger zone. Within a half year, these two graphic nomenclatures had been combined, so that entire urban areas around monuments would be hatched in an apparent spatialization of their architectural value. In the Frick map for Frankfurt that was produced in late March 1944, for example, this "hatched region" was also called out as a three-starred entry, "characteristic medieval streets and houses from 14th–18th Centuries," to be considered as a historic whole[17] (figure 3.5).

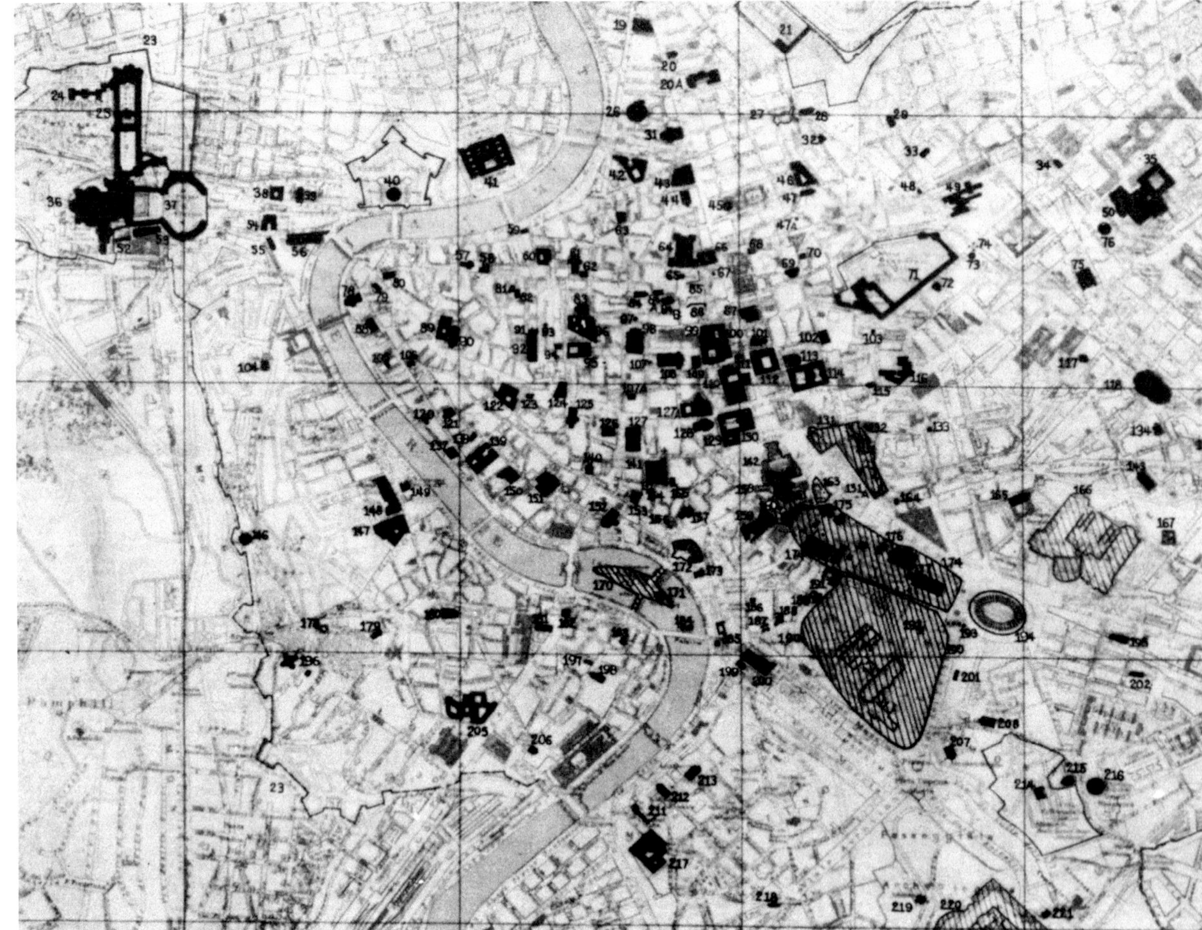

Figure 3.4 Detail of a map of Rome, with monuments (blacked out) and archaeological sites (hatched) prepared for the *Civil Affairs Handbook, Italy.* Section 17. Supplement on Cultural Institutions. *Supplementary Atlas on Churches, Museums, Libraries, and Other Cultural Institutions in Italy.* (Headquarters, Army Service Forces, 4 January 1944). NARA.

Despite this spatial bleeding of blacked-out spots into hatched-over areas, however, the Roberts Commission's maps of monuments were never taken as a particularly powerful argument against the kind of area bombing aimed at city centers. Already at this early date, in late 1943, when British and American Air Forces had yet to coordinate their two very different air targeting strategies, the words "planning" and "briefing" were used expediently to convey the *indirect* way graphic information on monuments would affect bombing practice. After the first batch of maps was sent off to Europe, Roberts Commission officer David Finley inquired about their use and received confirmation that "the maps [were] used in its planning of aerial operations," immediately followed by a disclaimer: "your attention is called to the fact that the RAF also participates in aerial operations."[18] Later that same month, General Hilldring frankly conceded that "the RAF bombing made it difficult for them to utilize the information," but that "the theater commanders were trying to influence the British."[19]

One of the first persons the Americans approached to make this influence felt was the British evolutionary scientist Solly Zuckerman, who was advising British Bomber Command. Zuckerman was trying to perfect a formula for combining statistical methods and material surveys in evaluating the efficacy and accuracy of British bombs, and he traveled periodically to the battlefield to study "fresh damage," as he called it.[20] During one such trip he was approached by MFAA officers, Frick lists in hand. Although he was sympathetic and, as we will see, eventually became an important conduit for British-American cooperation, he was fundamentally skeptical of the maps' usefulness. As he explained to the art historians, avoiding individual monuments within a city was simply impossible, whereas avoiding entire cities might be.[21] Given his calculative power in studying damage morphology and recommending design changes to weaponry, Zuckerman's judgment is significant: in a British military organization devoted to area bombing, he was the closest to an expert on precision.[22]

Given these early experiences, Dinsmoor was likely not deluded about maps becoming a deterrent against area bombing. His attachment to the map arguably lay elsewhere. As an archaeologist he was able to think of the relation of monument to map metonymically, as a part-to-whole relationship. Information on monuments was to be presented on a map, by this logic, because it was the best way to convey the message that the monument was a fragment of a whole city. This was different from pure lists, which had been composed with

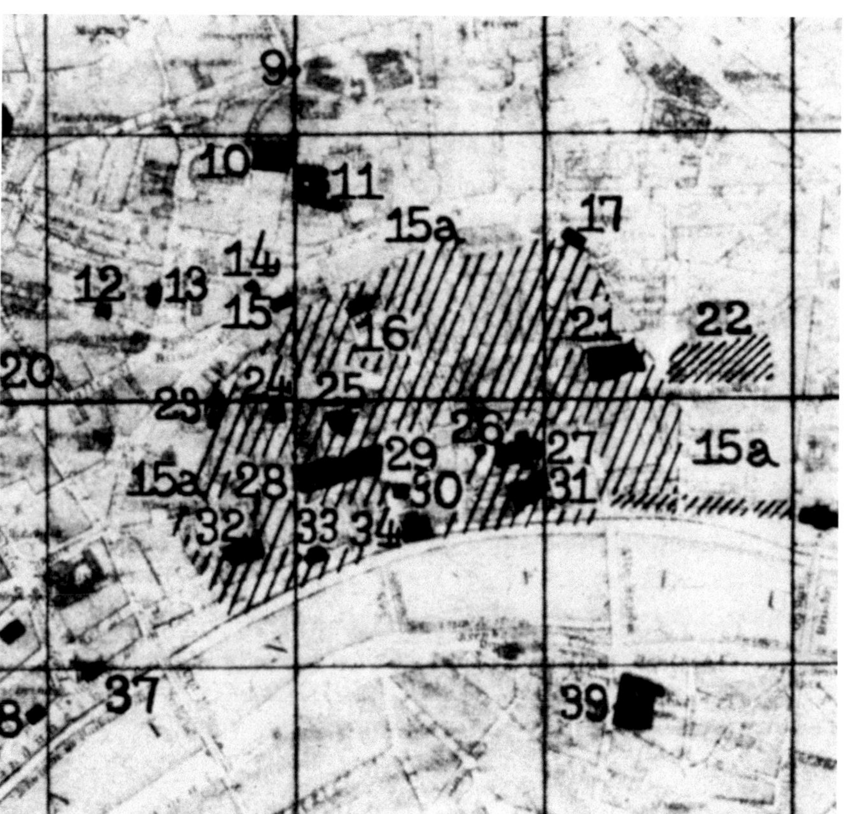

Figure 3.5 Detail of the map for Frankfurt, with entire "historic city center" hatched in. *Civil Affairs Handbook, Germany*. Supplement 17. *Atlas on churches, museums, libraries and other cultural institutions in Germany*. Army Service Forces Manual M356-1 (March 1944). NARA.

an open-ended idea of wholeness, only loosely tied to any geographic reality. Now, issues such as scarcity, evenness, and proportionality would be visualized on one page, within limited bounds. In that sense, the Frick maps visualized the navigable web of monumental infrastructure—the "reasonable utopia" that Constable had imagined, but dared not invoke, in his Baedeker memo in 1942.[23] Dinsmoor also revealed that he thought of monuments in urban terms when he took it upon himself to rearrange the Army's introductory Lecture on Cultural Monuments around a virtual tour of the city of Dijon. His lecture began with an overview of the policy but proposed to conscript the examples to one city. Dinsmoor then stopped at every monument to both explicate each category of monument and give another example of the type somewhere else in France: thus the value of Dijon's Notre Dame was "just about as great" as the eponymous one in Paris; and the royal palace, now converted into a museum, was of "equal importance" to the Chateau de Chenonceau, etc.[24] In this metonymic manner, the monument's value derived from the town, and the town's from the nation.

Dinsmoor's archaeological viewpoint also meant he was uniquely positioned to appreciate the value of a fragment of a destroyed building, and of a preserved building in a destroyed city. He was not alone. On the British side, it was archaeologist Leonard Woolley, who had spent two decades "digging up the past" in Ur, who became the highest-ranking member of the MFAA.[25] These archaeologists brought vastly different managing styles to their task, but they had all been trained to imagine a fully built city from a field of ruins, no matter how little of it was left. These disciplinary reflexes provided the concluding link in a chain of specialization we began to trace in the last chapter: lists were made by art historians, manuals were edited by curators, and now, destruction would be surveyed by archaeologists. Once he arrived in Europe almost a year later, Dinsmoor's first task was to try to eliminate what he called the "cultural lag": the two weeks between the end of the fighting and the arrival of MFAA troops, when a lot of "avoidable damage" was done by troops who couldn't tell "characteristic fragments of important buildings" apart from more generic demolition material.[26] "Many of us," Dinsmoor had already pleaded in October 1943, "have devoted entire lives to the reconstruction of monuments from broken fragments."[27] Important monuments could be rescued not only as wholes but also in their inevitable states as heaps of broken fragments, he explained frankly, since fragments were all that archaeologists dealt with anyways.

This archaeological scalability had its limits, however. In fall 1944, Dinsmoor traveled to Europe and was faced with a blunt visualization of the way his actions potentially determined not only what to preserve but also what to destroy. As he recounted at a symposium convened upon his return at the Metropolitan Museum of Art, Dinsmoor had witnessed first-hand the state of Europe's cities and began to worry, that the cities were beginning to "resemble" the maps:

> I very much fear that, unwittingly, we have been engaged in a city planning program and that some of the towns, in which the most severe fighting has occurred, now very closely resemble our maps, with only the marked protected monuments now standing.[28]

We should not diminish the importance of this turn of phrase, "unwittingly engaged in city planning," or its evident reference to modern urbanism with its history of destructive embellishments. (Dinsmoor was familiar with contemporary developments in urban design and, judging from the introduction to his seminal work, *The Architecture of Ancient Greece*, willing to accept modern architecture as long as it was informed by history, "choosing the good and refusing the bad."[29]) In fact, Dinsmoor never spoke the reference to urban planning aloud; in the final script of his Met talk he crossed it out and left only the second phrase, about the resemblance of town to map. Still, Dinsmoor's fear is revealing as he claimed unintentional success, despite the incredible energy he had devoted to making maps and ensuring they were used in planning military operations.

What, then, are we to make of this ambivalent concession? To what extent, and in what way, can the Frick maps of monuments be said to have contributed to creating a field of ruins? First, we should note that Dinsmoor's assessment was colored by a statistical approach to destruction that began to take hold in Europe on both sides of the war since the escalation of bombing in early 1944. "I began to acquire this impression," Dinsmoor confessed, while hearing of "an announcement of the French Ministry of Information," that "out of the 17,000 monuments historiques of France, 8,000 of the 17,000 have been injured."[30] The *Service des Monuments Historiques* had begun publishing damage reports that dryly listed every French monument and its state of demolition on a scale from one to four.[31] This nomenclature was similar to the one Albert Speer's ministry used in Germany for rubble-clearing and construction—and indeed would be used in reconstruction authorities across Western Europe after 1945. Just as a building's individual destruction was expressed fractionally, so damage to monuments was expressed in proportional terms relative to the national patrimony ("only 2% of French monuments" were damaged) and accompanied by comforting speculation about reconstruction.[32] Later Woolley would even warn against listing the buildings that were destroyed by name. Such lists might well make it appear, he warned, "as one familiar name follows another, that little has survived from the orgy of destruction." Instead of an additive list, he recommended taking a statistical area view.[33]

This statistical-geographic turn in the perception of monuments' destruction confirms a trend in the history of the Roberts Commission with which we are familiar: that the formatting of information about monuments mirrored evolving destructive strategies. We are therefore better informed by analyzing this format than concentrating on the state of any individual building, or the question of the intention that lies behind its survival. The historical agency of monuments maps, then, has to be seen in terms of the processes and instruments that were used to convey the information they contained. Briefing, transferring, seeing, recognizing—all were used to convey the location of monuments during the act of destruction. Such an analysis means examining the conditions under which any "advisory" information became useful in bombing, and specifically as it passed through the techno-human apparatus of precision bombing.

Bloodshot Eyes

Closing the gap between intention and result was a problem that plagued all aerial raids. "Briefing" was one among many steps in a chain that broke down destructive action to make precision prevail against significant technical constraints. Take the Rome raid with which we began this chapter. Before the raid, four "target folders" containing aerial photographs of monumental sites were distributed to flight crews.[34] The lead pilot recalled the intense process of visual memorization that ensued:

> That evening and the next morning, my time was spent poring over the intricate details of approach, IP, etc, until the last potential unforeseen item was covered. The maps and photos were branded into my bloodshot eyes. The target area—its relation to outstanding landmarks was fixed in my mind. Never in all my missions, had I worked so hard in briefing and poring over maps as I did for this mission. So much depended upon the success.... I had memorized the map and photos so well that if I were to visit Rome, I would be a well qualified tourist guide.[35]

There is something chilling in the way that first-hand aesthetic experience (and the tourist reference to certify it) entered the cockpit. Like the art historians before him, the bomber used the disposition of monuments to memorize an urban totality. Once in the air, he was rewarded with a recognition of this monumental blueprint: "The layout and the target area was the same as I had learned it from the maps and photos." Then, after the bombs were dropped and "nothing had been hit but the target," he felt the satisfaction of knowing that "my study and planning had paid off."

But the link between recognition and destruction was not in fact as immediate as this account implies. Memorization was but one link in a chain of transmission of information, that was threaded continuously, from the bomber's eye and mind, via his commander, his sighting machine, the bomb itself, and even its victims below. At one end of this chain, the Allies had communicated their intentions to bomb by dropping leaflets in the city, on two separate days ahead of the raid.[36] At the other extreme of this chain was the intimate relationship between the two or three humans in the plane (bomber, pilot, and sometimes gunner) who collaborated on coursing of the plane, locating the target, and releasing bombs. In order to "see" the target the bomber had to do

Figure 3.6 Bombardier demonstrates sighting a target through his Norden Bombsight, November 1944. Photograph: AP Wirephoto from Army Air Forces (JH61045AAF).

it with his entire body, holding the crosshairs of the bombsight over a target. By the time the Norden bombsight—that vaunted precision instrument—became standard on American airplanes, the bomber was asked to hold this cross-hair long enough that an "automatic bombing computer" could derive enough information about the movement of the plane to calculate sighting angle, and eventually, wait for the plane to "lurch" as the computer released the bombs[37] (figure 3.6). Furthermore, the bomber made *two* passes over the same target: the first time to lock the sight in place, and the second time to correct for a smaller deviation and launch the actual bomb. This waiting, too, required intense training. One step in the instructions for the bombsight was devoted entirely to asking the bomber to resist his instinct to "overcontrol," instead "accepting the small remaining errors."[38] Under certain conditions bombers in a formation were to wait until they saw not the target but the bombs of the leader of the raid. This practice extended the flow of trust from the eyesight and reflexes of one pilot into the airplane of the next. In other words, the same human qualities that we heard Eisenhower invoke in chapter 2 when he asked soldiers to "respect" monuments, were activated here at infinitesimal doses across wires and pupils.

The breaking down of the gestures of warfare into steps is characteristic of modern decentralized armies' attempts to "lower the decision-making threshold by granting local responsibility" to commanders.[39] Of course, helping to smooth over possible misconnections between these two extreme ends of the communication chain—pounds of paper dropped onto city-dwellers from the sky and precision-bombing equipment manned by the minute gestures of the flying crew—was the Air Force leadership. They also imparted know-how for calibrating destructive judgment to the built environment. The Rome Raid was led by General James Doolittle, who had been one of the first, in the 1930s, to conduct demonstration flights "by instrument alone."[40] As he explained in a rousing speech to the crews beforehand, to bomb Rome without "going down in history as ruthless barbardic hordes" would present a "challenge to precision."[41] This was not only because of its monuments. The architectural features of Rome were entirely bound up with its perceived symbolic nature as the capital city of Italy, its religious heart, the party seat of Fascism, and the site of Vatican City, as well as the "common knowledge," in Eisenhower's own words, "that the Germans were taking advantage of our restraint to use Rome as a principal link in their communications network."[42] When the bombing restriction on Rome was lifted, restraint was spread out to all: Doolittle handpicked his pilots and allowed Catholic ones to recuse themselves. Broader targeting choices were also made: to steer clear from the administrative center of the city, although the Germans had set up a Headquarters there. Doolittle's speech to crews, where he appeared geared up in his flying suit and announced he would himself be flying along, added a final cognitive touch: "Listening to him," recalled one navigator, "I somehow *knew* that we would find the target, hit it, and get back."[43]

The briefing formula that Doolittle used to make the Rome raids stand out in the pilots' minds was one he first developed in December 1942 for the raid on Tokyo. This raid was radically different than Rome: retaliatory against the attacks on Pearl Harbor, it was shrouded in secrecy, and designed to have one-time "significant psychological impact," as opposed to any strategic effect.[44] But it offers a useful comparison as Doolittle's brief to pilots contains monuments as part of the same raw ingredients that would continue to make up the Allies's destructive recipe for the war as a whole. First, the two destructive morphologies: demolition bombs were to be dropped "where they will do the most damage," and incendiary bombs were to be dropped "in an area that looks like it will burn." Then, three instructions of avoidance: first, certain building materials ("avoid hitting stone, concrete, and steel targets because you can't do enough damage to them"); second, civilians ("nothing to be gained by attacking residential areas")—and finally, monumental architecture ("Leave the imperial palace alone").[45] The monument was therefore already an architectural ingredient even in a raid such as Tokyo designed essentially to signify destruction. In Rome too, monuments had to fit in the crowded cognitive field of the bombing crew. But in a neat reversal of Tokyo, Doolittle mentioned no firebombs, and no material distinctions between targets. Instead, one forbidden monumental site became four. Considering the history of Rome, four was not many. But the multiplication shows that what mattered in avoidance was the relative distance of these sites to one another. In Rome, this distance clearly showed a calibration of avoidance to the scale of mechanical, weapons-dependent precision. Indeed, these four sites were well farther apart than the 1,000 feet that was assumed to be the margin of error for a precision raid at that point in the war.

The Rome raid was deemed a "decisive" success, and provoked Mussolini's almost immediate fall and Italy's eventual surrender in September. Among the many consequences of this turn of events is that Italy became the feeding tube for the European theater, and the aerial photography of monuments that had been tested out in Rome was applied systematically to all of Italy.

Beginning in December 1943, a special set of aerial images of monuments was commissioned by the Mediterranean Allied Air Forces. Tellingly, this initiative came not from the American Doolittle, who had been steeped in the ideology of precision and trained in its instruments, but from a British officer, General Arthur Tedder, who is known for having later invented a version of carpet bombing (or "Tedder carpet") that adapted area bombing to tactical needs.[46] Tedder had been appointed Eisenhower's deputy in the wake of Casablanca, and eventually became "the aviation lobe of Eisenhower's brain."[47] He was closely advised by Solly Zuckerman, the British expert whom we have heard express skepticism at the Frick Maps' usefulness as he was approached by MFAA troops in Naples. It was through Zuckerman and Tedder that the the American precision mentality and area-thinking of the British Ministry of Economic Warfare (MEW) entered into a confrontation, and eventually compromise. Through a three-month negotiation about format, the British practice of ranking cities gradually adjusted to American planning for ranking monuments, and vice-versa.

MFAA troops had arrived with unbound Frick maps in North Africa and Sicily as early as September 1943; once bound atlases began to arrive, they had already had an effect on British and American enlisted soldiers.[48] "The maps have been arriving regularly and made a great impression," wrote Ernest DeWald, who had been asked to give a lecture on monuments to every new batch of incoming troops.[49] It was here that the episode I recounted in the last chapter occurred—where three art historians were given three hours to produce a ranked list of cities to Zuckerman. A month later Zuckerman reported Tedder's dissatisfaction, and his new instruction said what was needed was a list of cities that should survive "if the whole of Italy were to be destroyed."[50] This second list was eventually produced in November. By then, news of the Frick maps had also traveled to London. In December British political leaders wrote to Tedder to ask whether he wanted British command to make their *own* maps, or whether "the American ones would do."[51] Tedder eventually resolved to go straight to aerial photography. He sent Allied planes on a series of reconnaissance sorties over 79 cities in northern and central Italy. Each city's photograph was then annotated with outlines showing monuments, accompanied with a typescript and numbered list naming them. Gone were the asterisks—only a numbered list of individual buildings remained. By December 12, 1943, Tedder was able to reply to London that "aerial photographs" of cultural sites were being used in bombing.[52] In February, these maps were bound in a "bombing book" called *The Ancient monuments of Italy*, informally known as the "Tedder Atlas." In a continuation of the Rome technique, Tedder asked that these "be readily available to bombing crews at all times" so they could be memorized.[53]

This Tedder Atlas constitutes the closest that monuments protection ever came to being integrated into bombing culture for a theater as a whole. In a vindication of the conceit of practicality that motivated list-making in the first place, the RAF came to accept a policy of monument protection through pressure both from below and from above: in meetings with lowly MFAA officers, through the de facto presence of lists and maps in the theater of war, and in reaction to their evident usefulness to calm the growing political anxiety in London over the invasion of Italy.[54]

The Fiction of the Non-target

The scholars of the Roberts Commission made much of the fact that these annotated aerial photographs offered "a picture of the area as the pilot and bombardier actually observe it."[55] It is true that photographic depth changed the visual dimension of monuments protection. Whereas Frick maps graphically flattened the image of the city, the Tedder maps in contrast captured a specific moment in time. Consider the Tedder map for Venice (figure 3.7). It was taken as clouds were clearing over the city, and annotations hover above these clouds. Thick white lines are drawn in a consistent lineweight around the urban shapes of buildings, some making boundaries around them; others filling them in. Together, this whiting out, outlining, and numbering, pull the eye forcefully out of the center of the city, expanding the characteristic shape of it river bend, as if to figure the act of seeing itself.

Yet these aerial photos were not target maps. While a Tedder aerial map would have been studied by the bomber, it would not have been taken in the air. Documents that *were* included in a "target folder" for any raid were of a different kind. To begin with, each pilot was given an aerial reconnaissance photograph, where targets of varying urban shapes were outlined in white, most of them shapeless masses labeled with circled numbers, with no particular attention to the resulting composition.[56] In addition to this aerial image, a target folder contained a map that was topographic, with urban built-up areas in purple, water features in white, and infrastructural elements in black (figure 3.8). For example, a target map used for the raid on Florence on March 26, 1944, showed four urban targets, drawn as black shapes, and labeled by letter. But the most important graphic feature of this map was the set of concentric circles—a

Figure 3.7 Aerial photograph of Venice with 25 monuments outlined and numbered, from Mediterranean Allied Air Forces, "The Ancient Monuments of Italy," also known as the "Tedder Atlas" (March 10, 1944). NARA.

VENICE.
GSGS 4164
SHEET 51. REF. 7051
4004
NA82Q

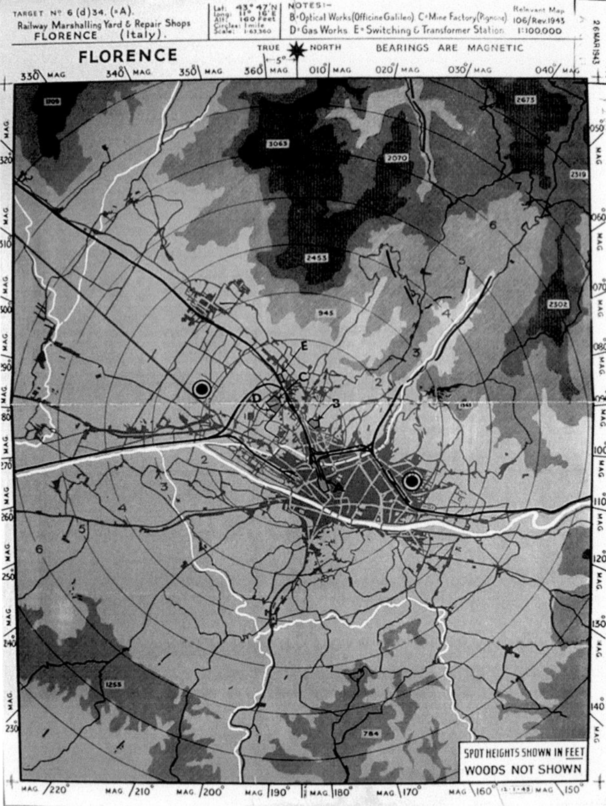

Figure 3.8 Target map included in an Allied target folder for a raid on the marshalling yards in Florence, dated 26 March 1943. NARA.

bull's eye offset every mile from these targets. The only other elements on the map to speak this concentric language were two airfields, drawn as encircled black dots.The aerial photograph *pictured* vision; the target map *structured* it.

Nor did the Tedder Maps restrict bombing on their own. Unlike in Tokyo and Rome, where pilots were briefed in person, here a set of rules for selection, written by the Commander of the Mediterranean Air Forces, Lauris Norstad, were appended *in writing* to the Tedder Atlas. These rules are worth parsing because they systematized the combination of bombardier vision and destructive know-how previously conveyed by a live brief.[57]

The original choice of which cities to photograph for the Tedder Atlas was based on a list made by Norris, which ranked cities by number and also divided them into three categories.[58] At the top of this list were Rome, Florence, Siena, and Venice, which each represented "a complex and indivisible mass of important monuments essential to the Italian tribute to European Civilization." Then came two more categories: "quintessential creations of world famed importance," and cities "essential to the main body of Italian Art as a whole."[59] The distinction between "quintessential" and "essential" amounted to the same pyramid of art-historical distinction that had motivated listing since late 1942, as we saw in chapter 2. But once these 79 cities were photographed to be included in the Tedder Atlas, a new set of bombing priorities was applied and the list was reshuffled into three new categories, named A, B, and C. Cities whose very urban fabric was indivisibly monumental were now called "not to be bombed":

Category A:
ROME, FLORENCE, VENICE, TORCELLO.
These towns are in no circumstances to be bombed without authority from this headquarters.

In contrast, "quintessential and essential" sites were described by way of their proximity to military objectives:

Category B:
RAVENNA, ASSISI, SAN GIMINIANO, PAVIA, URBINE [*sic*], MONTEPULCIANO, PARMA, AOSTA, TIVOLI, UDINE, GUBBIE [*sic*], VOLTERRA, SPOLETO, BORGO, SAN SPOLONE, ASCOLI, PICENO, COMO, PESARO, AQUILLA [*sic*], and the Dalmatian coast towns of SPALATO and RAGUSA.

The bombing of those towns which have at present no particular military importance should be avoided if possible. If however it is for operational reasons considered essential that objectives in any of them should be bombed, there should be no hesitation in doing so, and full responsibility will be accepted by this HQ.

Category C:
PISTOIA, MODENA, BRESCIA, CREMONA, ZARA, SIENA, PISA, PADUA, VERONA, BOLOGNA, AREZZO, ORVIETO, FERRARA, VICENZA, PRATO, VITERBO, CORTONA, PIACENZA, LUCCA, RIMINI, FRASCATI, BRACCIANO, PERUGIA, ANCONA.

There are important military objectives in or near these towns which are to be bombed, and any consequential damage is accepted. [60]

Inside every class, the order of priority stayed the same as Norris had given it. But every monumental class was now defined by the possibilities for declassing.

A number of "if... then" scenarios gave the conditions for demoting a city from one class to the next. For Rome and other A cities, time functioned as a shield: restrictions could be lifted if bombing "intentions" were forwarded "28 hours prior." In contrast, while flying over cities of the B and C categories, bombers could make judgments *in the air*. Then, weather conditions would matter. Cities were not to be bombed if they were "obscured by clouds by day or night," and the formation leader was to decide whether to wait for cloud clearance. Going further down toward reduced visibility, at night these towns were to be first illuminated by dropping flares "with reasonable certainty." In a revealing addendum, in the case of bad visibility, the pilots were specifically forbidden from dropping "'in the target area' when the actual target cannot be located." And since it was the pilot who now made these decisions in the air, one final qualifier was added to all the others—that in the final instance the value of a monument was lesser than the value of a crewman's life, and that, if a choice had to be made between them, the Army would take responsibility for a monument's destruction.[61]

These rules mark the return of Tokyo-like criteria for architectural guesswork and partial visibility, which had been suspended over the skies of Rome. They show the creep of the reality of area destruction onto the point-based idea of precision. Norris, the art historian, had created a pyramid of art historical value, with unique objects at the top and more typical creations below. But Norstad, the airman, translated this pyramid into the statistical area-thinking of destruction. Indeed, the bull's eye that had trained the pilot's eyes during target practice, and directed his vision during bombing, also signified his ability to operate within an area rather than on a point. The success of precision bombing was measured according what was later called "circular error probable" (CEP): the diameter within which it was likely that at least 50% of dropped bombs would fall. As historians of weaponry have pointed out, the fact that error came to be understood in circular terms shows that area-like destruction became a "certain, unmistakable reality" even at the height of precision-bombing ideology.[62] For a weapon designer, the circle was a way not only to highlight a point at the center, but also to relax the criteria for accuracy, and to probabilize it.

As briefings became systematic, monuments undoubtedly came to figure among the growing number of architectural approximations that contributed to bombing know-how, although it is difficult to find evidence of this in written archives. One factor complicating the idea of an absolute exception for monuments is that this technological apparatus always involved choices not only between area and precision, or between civilian and monumental architecture, but also between "primary" and "secondary" target—an alternative site where bombers were instructed to drop their bombs (rather than bring them back) if the primary one was not visible. And if this second target was also not visible bombers were still advised to drop their bombs on something else rather than bring them home. This "something else" was undoubtedly chosen using rudimentary architectural approximation from the air, as to a building's size, shape, materiality, typology, etc. In this context, a bomber having been previously briefed about how to avoid damaging monuments might well decide not to drop bombs on objects recognizeable as such—a church, or a castle.[63] Indeed, one hint that monuments were integrated into the destructive habitus of American bombers is that restrictions against bombing civilians and against bombing monuments were increasingly paired in the months following the making of the Tedder maps. By January 12, 1945, Eisenhower's office circulated a note that "the civilian population, cities and historical and cultural monuments should be spared from bombardment or attack by our land, sea and air forces," subject to military necessity.[64] Cultural protection never became a pure architectural exception. It resulted more from the accumulated choices to preserve rather than from any single choice to destroy, all mediated by the same technological apparatus.

What the Tedder Atlas reveals, in other words, is the fiction of the "non-target." There was no such thing as avoiding something precisely; there were only targets to be destroyed and their tendency to spread out into circular areas and catch unfortunate nearby monumental sites in this expansion. (The United States Strategic Bombing Survey [USSBS] chillingly summarized that more than 84% of all American bombs aimed at oil targets had fallen outside their target area.) In this context, the transformation of the bull's eye, from an icon of accuracy into an allowance for error, seems to make some monument survival more likely than not. The scale of the Frick and Tedder maps, with their one- to two-thousand-foot grids, seems fortuitously well-calibrated to the likely margin of error of an American bomb. The Tedder Map of Verona, for instance, captures an image of the falling of some high explosive bombs on a rail yard outside of town (figure 3.9). The scattered density of these bombs resembles the density of monuments in the center of town on that same map. This illustrates clearly why art historians may have been given the opportunity to select between 5 and 10 monuments in any given European city center: because the space between those monuments resembled in value the CEP of a precision bomb dropped over that city's center. In other words, it was possible to spray a city center with high explosive bombs and hit only areas between monuments. But the likelihood of this happening *intentionally* was, as we have seen from the preceding analysis, extremely remote.

The point of spending this time in the skies with Allied destroyers and those who issued their orders, designed their strategy, and led their missions, has been to show how the values of technological precision were incorporated into the problem of monumental distinction in the air. By analyzing the instruments used to convey and implement the policy we can see that the project of monument avoidance exploited the same property of the American military command structure that historians have shown characterized the adoption of precision, and later nuclear, targeting: the fact that influence flowed both ways, top down but also back up the hierarchy, through the innumerable steps delegating the design of weapons, battles, and information. Just as the "accumulated momentum of previous technical decisions" came to normalize nuclear targeting, just as the "lure of precision" exerted itself on the Air Force via its manifold training and research departments, and just as an "embrace of urbicide and domicide crept onto the map" of nuclear bombers, so the accumulated requests for consideration of monuments, and the presentation of their survival as both optional and practical at every level of decision-making, helped to make restrictions against monuments in Europe as more or less acceptable across all ranks.[65]

How, then, was this combined Allied strategic instrument, and the different kinds of architectural information it assumed, used to shape the destruction of Europe? To begin with, the effects of American bombings soon came

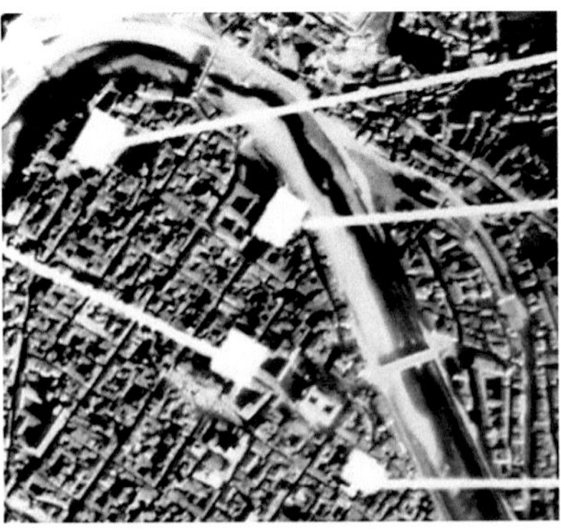

7
1
12
3
6
5
10
13
9
11
2
4
8
N
VERONA
G.S.G.S.4164
Sh.49/6554

to resemble those of British raids. As British experts such as Solly Zuckerman continued to refine area bombing's capacities, gradually a kind of "precision" was imparted onto British pilots and their weapons, and a type of "blindness" came to be accepted in American bombers and their bombsights.[66] Second, if proponents of area bombing and precision bombing appealed to different histories to define the city as target, then monuments arguably helped to anchor both. As Joseph Konvitz has argued, area bombing targeted the idea of the city from the Renaissance, as "a community founded on social relations," and aimed at disintegrating those relations. Precision bombing recalled the Enlightenment notion of "the city as an economic entity," necessarily networked between important nodes.[67] The association of European monuments with a deep cultural history unified these urban legacies, and created leeway for implementing a policy in different theaters through one "combined" offensive.

Figure 3.9 "Tedder Map" of Verona, with two details showing a spattering of bombs falling just outside of town, and the monuments in the city center. NARA.

The solution Tedder and Zuckerman devised to create "one integrated target group" for both air forces, so that they could together bomb Europe in advance of D-Day, was called "the Transportation Plan."[68] The plan was to concentrate both night- and day- bombings on "German communications," literally slowing the German war machine by making difficult the circulation of essential materials that fed it, from troops, to fuel, to repair parts. The cleverness of the plan was that the word "communication" both encompassed "German transport networks, rail, roads and canals," which tended to go across the city centers the British were already bombing, and also contained point targets away from urban centers, such as oil and fuel supplies, radio control points, and missile development sites, where the Americans were conducting most of their raids.

This plan had crucial consequences for monuments work: first, rather than thinking in terms of territorial sovereignty, the bombers would decide targets by taking what Eisenhower called "geographical cues" from how the Germans themselves were using Europe's transportation network.[69] Bombing strategy was therefore further unmoored from spatial assumptions about the effects of urban bombing on provoking "surrender," making a way for *other* factors of morale, such as monuments, to be increasingly emphasized. Yet, Tedder and Zuckerman continued to focus on cities as targets because they contained larger-sized nodes in transportation that were more easily damaged with fewer and less precise hits.[70] Tedder and Eisenhower hoped to shape destruction to provoke certain movements in the German armies—to "canalize surviving traffic to make it more vulnerable to subsequent attack."[71] On the one hand, Europe was deterritorialized, becoming a pure network dotted with urban sites, and a canvas against which a coherent path was to be drawn through destruction. On the other hand, the Transportation Plan implied different monuments policy for each theater, depending on which government needed to be toppled and/or liberated along this path.

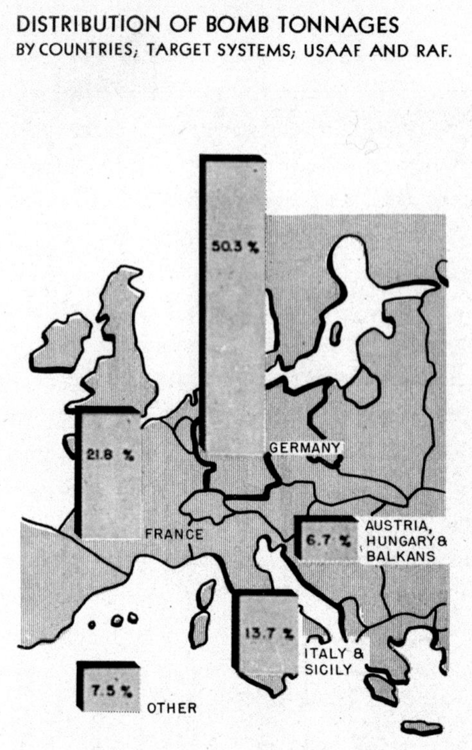

Figure 3.10 Excerpt from Chart No. 4, Total Allied Bomb Tonnage, European Theater of Operations in United States Strategic Bombing Survey, *Overall Report (European War)*, September 30, 1945.

In the remainder of this chapter, then, I examine how the monuments protection system was implemented in Europe in 1944 and 1945, by taking a comparative cut of three countries where the Allies dropped most of their bombs: Italy, France, and Germany, during the well-known historical arc of the European war after D-Day[72] (figure 3.10). Far from being comprehensive, my aim is to sketch out the range of destructive morphologies that became available to the Allies in their combined offensive, and to ask how these shaped the monuments policy and transformed the expectations that had been set in its design. I also want to tease out how the MFAA's techniques for monuments salvage and reconstruction left behind specific legacies that were picked up by international organizations in the postwar.

Italy: Relatively Minute Fragments

Italy was the place where Tedder's Transportation Plan and the MFAA's policy of protection intersected most felicitously, for two reasons: first, because Italy's cultural geography coincided largely with its industrial web (Rome for instance was both the center of all rail traffic and the artistic and cultural capital of the country), and secondly, because the fighting in Italy was designated as "subsidiary to and in support of" the later landing in Normandy. Italy was the place where the Allies would stall the conflict and keep the Germans occupied.[73] It was thus in Italy that the obsolescence of the old concept of Military

Government became fully apparent. American Military Government officers were originally charged with "securing their own lines of communications," but found that those lines also pulled up an entire socio-economic web, which confronted them with "daily problems of extreme moment to thousands of human beings." Thus AMG eventually established "an entire program of economic and social reconstruction" and while the avowed guiding principle was "indirect rule," in practice the AMG inherited the imbalances of the Fascist state and often compensated for them with extensive financial and administrative support to mayors, to builders, and eventually, to monuments administrations.[74] Italy's monuments service had first been regionalized in the teens, and its procedures had been further standardized by the Fascist state. But regional imbalances remained, placing uneven pressure on MFAA officers in different places.[75] The political conceit of Allied monuments protection—that monuments are a kind of cultural infrastructure, which can be found anywhere and be actively protected to earn local goodwill—was both legitimated and put to the test.

The Tedder maps had ranked Italy's cities for their monumental importance, but the difference between "quintessential" and "essential" sites of Italian art and architecture was really one of degree. The Allies in Italy were conscious that they were, in the famous words of one general, "fighting war in a Goddam art museum."[76] Furthermore, Allied bombers in Italy had always been encouraged not to over-bomb. This was not only because of its monuments. The Italian built environment was built mostly out of masonry, which created voluminous rubble that would slow down Allied advance.[77] As early as November 1942 British MEW researchers had produced a report on *Italian Domestic Architecture*, where they noted that this architecture was "considerably less vulnerable" to fire-bombing "than its counterpart in Germany" because "the thickness and mass of the walls" made it "relatively resistant to High Explosive damage" (figure 3.11). However, whole Italian towns could be heavily incapacitated with little bombing, because of poor "workmanship," and the "extensive use of vaulting and stone facings," meant that even lesser bombs would take advantage of "ease of collapse."[78]

The turning point, where this material knowledge of the Italian built environment was combined with a policy for monuments protection, was the battle of Montecassino. As we have seen in the last chapter, the Allies hesitated over destroying the Montecassino Abbey for two months, and this stalled their advance up Italy.[79] But by the time the order came to destroy the abbey at the top of the hill, the bombing of the *town* of Cassino below had created a massive roadblock. One of the damage reports put the point bluntly:

> There comes a point, however, in the destruction of any stone town when additional damage merely makes the fortifications stronger by piling rubble about them. . . . Any such utter destruction as was visited upon Cassino cannot fail to produce a complete road block, giving an advantage to the defender and inevitably delaying the offensive.[80]

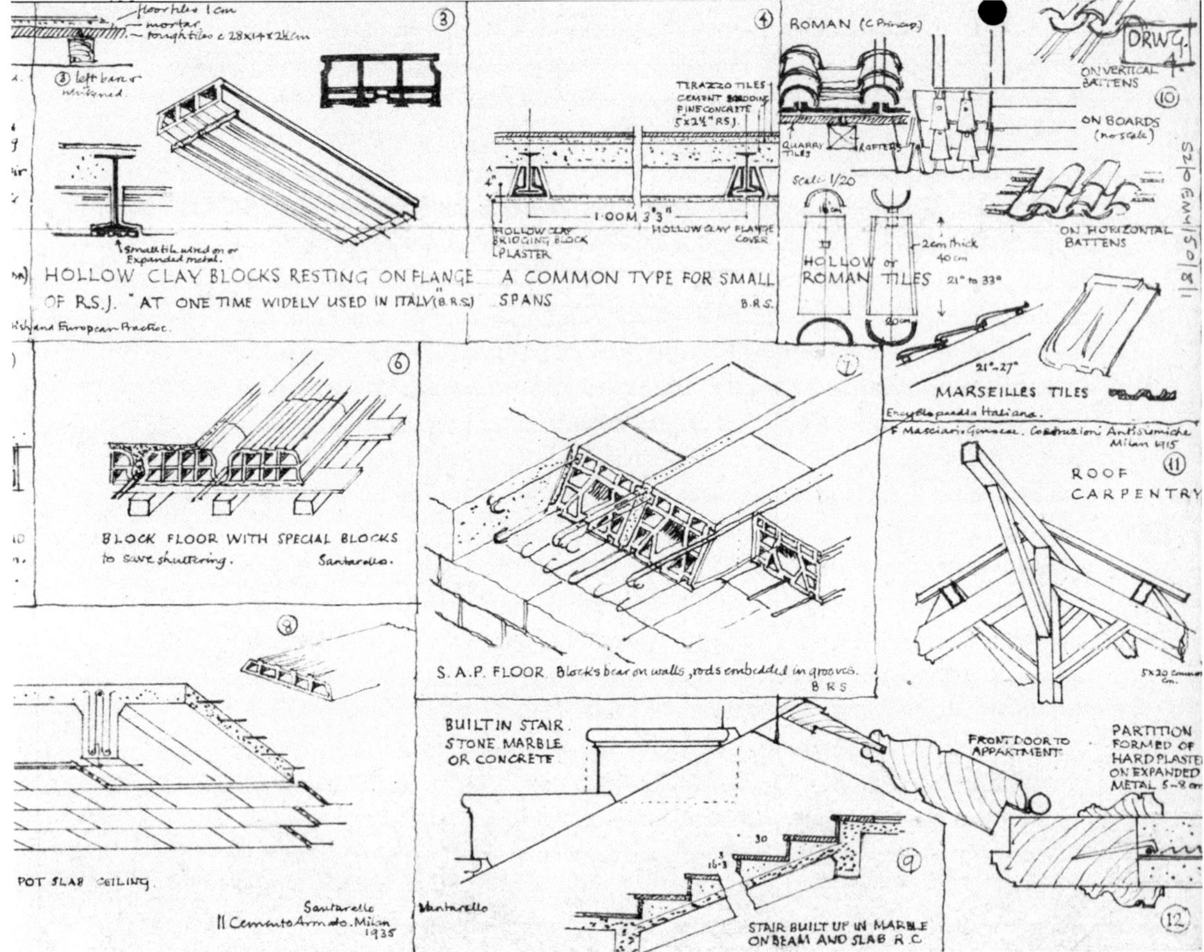

Figure 3.11 Construction details of Italian domestic architecture, from (British) Ministry of Home Security, Research and Experiments Department, "Note on Italian Domestic Construction and its Vulnerability to I.B. and H.E. Bombs." SZ.OEMU.50.8.2. Zuckerman Archive, University of East Anglia.

Hesitating around a monument had meant over-bombing its surroundings. After Cassino, then, destruction would be planned to create an easy path forward and around monuments. The bulldozer gave the Allies a clear advantage, allowing them to surprise the retreating Germans with the speed of their advance.[81] On the one hand, this allowed Monuments officers in Italy never to be too far behind the most recent destruction. On the other hand, the discrepancy in scale between the Italian road system and this American-made construction technology meant that it was usually urgent to swoop in to rescue "characteristics fragments" from listed monuments away from the bulldozer's path before they were cleared away with ordinary rubble.

Accounts of Monuments officers in Italy in the early days of the Italian campaign tell of exhausting days spent methodically visiting each listed monument, and making a decision as to its fate. These one-man judgment machines were armed with two documents that further reinforced the apparent "all-overness" of Italy's architectural distinction and destruction. The Frick maps showed where monuments were located; a pamphlet on *First Aid Protec-*

tion gave instructions on what to do with them. This pamphlet echoed Eisenhower's rhetoric, by describing monuments salvage as one way "to preserve our civilization from destruction," but applied it literally to the salvage of even the smallest broken pieces of art and architecture.[82] The focus was on authenticity. "Restoration often can be made from relatively minute fragments," the manual said; and "if the moving and piling of debris" was necessary, it was "essential . . . to keep related portions of the structure together."[83] The principles of archaeology were now applicable across the urban environment.

Thus in the field, maps of monuments became lists again. MFAA officers produced three kinds of written documents: a diary, a bi-weekly report, and a cumulative inventory of the monuments in their charge. Even entire villages were treated as monumental environments. Dean Keller reported that in one Italian town, he had simply "tried to put a little in order."

One comes to a palace, doors blown, and a piano leaning out the window—tapestries, books, pictures askew, statues in pieces on the ankle-deep carpet, no windows, raining, no one around, try to put a little in order.[84]

Similarly, Frederick Hartt's report on the Emilia region noted that "no list can convey the ruin of the little villages and townships of Southern Romagna," which had few monuments "of intrinsic importance, but together they formed a picturesque and vital part of the essential Italy."[85] This regional understanding of destruction in the early part of the Allied advance was reinforced by the work of the German *Kunstschutz* organization, who also constructed a three-tiered list of Italy's monumental sites, and made maps that showed entire regions spattered with minuscule red dots[86] (color plate 3).

It was through these material practices for sorting and recording the rubble that the communicative, morale-building potential of monuments returned to the Italian campaign. Aside from their own lists and paper (and sometimes a typewriter), MFAA troops were issued Historical Monuments signs to be posted "in and about important historical monuments"[87] (figure 3.12). The goal was to make visible the process of repair. Putting up signs, posting guards, directing bulldozers: these acts all showed a return of the imperative to think of monuments as cultural signifiers and morale boosters.

It was also through mass-media that visual records of the state of monuments passed smoothly from one side of the war to the other. The Fascist state had been accumulating and publishing monuments information, as we saw in the introduction of this book. As late as 1943 the Istituto Luce put out a pamphlet titled *Profanazione* that juxtaposed images of destroyed objects with propaganda about British and American iconoclastic intentions. By July 1944, similar visual material was published in a pamphlet, by the Allied and Italian authorities. Stripped of rhetoric, these images of damaged buildings were meant to demonstrate simply that the condition of Italy's monuments was being monitored.[88] As Tedder's Transportation Plan canalized troop move-

Kunstdenkmal!
Betreten für militärische Zwecke verboten!
Der deutsche Kommandant
Monumento artistico!
E' proibito l'uso per scopi militari! 
Il Comandante Tedesco

Name of building
2
THIS RUINED BUILDING IS OF HISTORICAL, EDUCATIONAL OR ARTISTIC IMPORTANCE
Demolition or carrying away of materials will not be done without consulting A.M.G. Monuments Officer, under SAE Instrs. Section R-1110, (Notice type 2).
LUCIAN K. TRUSCOTT Jr.
Lieutenant General, U. S. Army
Commanding Fifth Army

ments, and conflict in Italy ground to an increasing slow pace, Allied troops also spent more time in historic sites and the MFAA produced several touring guides—*A Soldier's Venice*, *A Companion to the Visit of Pompeii*, *A Soldier's Guide to Florence*; *What to See in Florence*. Once Siena was captured, they even curated an exhibition of *Masterpieces of Sienese Art*[89] (color plates 3 and 4). At war's end, it was suggested that the Frick material be reused to make multilingual tourist guides.[90]

Figure 3.12 Signs posted on Italian monuments, 1943–1945. a. Sign in German and Italian posted on the outside wall of the Cathedral of Pisa, as found by the MFAA. Photographer unknown. Ernest Theodore DeWald Papers (C0420), Manuscripts Division, Department of Rare Books and Special Collections, Princeton University Library. b. Sign posted by the MFAA at the Archbishop's Palace in Ancona. BRS Photographic Archive, Ward-Perkins Collection, wpwar-0406.

Tourism, the MFAA argued, built up the morale of Allied troops and also the good will of the Italian population. Pompeii is a case in point. Bombed several times by both sides, it was visited as early as October 1943 by MFAA Officer Paul Gardner, who arranged to reopen it to visitors. By the winter of 1944, as fighting in Cassino stalled the conflict, a propaganda reel showed a steady stream of Allied soldiers boarding a train to Pompeii.[91] Over the next two years, the site's conservator Amedeo Maiuri noted, "no less than half a million visitors in uniform came through the excavations, a whole colorful panoply of the United Nations, for a few hours of afternoon drunkenness but all things considered not without mutual benefit."[92] The benefit was both financial and in-kind: MFAA Officer Theodor Sizer insisted that Maiuri charge for entry, and use the funds to pay the salaries of restorers, who immediately got to work sorting through the damage, using "Carthusian patience to find, recompose and re-stitch the mangled flute of a column of the crushed crumbs of painted plaster."[93] As for the soldiers, their thousands of marching feet helped to clear the site's path of any remaining rubble. They were guided with brochures that showed images of Pompeii "before and after" the eruption of the Vesuvius, but made no mention of the current conflagration all around them. Pompeii acquired more popularity as a site in this short period of time, when a stroll in *any* bombed city in the north felt, in the words of one Italian journalist, like "a stroll through Pompeii."[94]

Once the archaeological phase of the monuments protection project came to an end, however, and as Allied protection turned to reconstruction, the expertise of the MFAA officers in the fine arts began to lose out against the more heavy-duty tools of those performing architectural, engineering, or urban planning tasks. In his report from Florence on September 24, 1944, Ernest DeWald noted in the same breath that Florentine bridges had been destroyed, and that rubble-clearing was being channeled towards creating a new urban piazza anchored by four newly discovered medieval towers:

> It is a sad sight to see Florence with its bridges gone and with all the demolition around both ends of the Ponte Vecchio. However, the clearing up is being done by the Army, supervised as to objects in the debris by our officers. In the area between the Mercato Nuovo area and the bridges four medieval towers came to light which have been completely hidden by the houses built around them. Every effort is being made to preserve these and have them stand clear in the new piazza which will probably be created in that area.[95]

Clearly no longer "unwitting," city-planning decisions were supported by the opportunity to unearth a deeper past, in a continuation of Italian planning practices established in the 1930s.[96] Indeed, we could say that like so many other emergency workers in this period, MFAA officers became "planning-minded."[97] They participated in the transitioning of damage assessment into reconstruction, by helping to re-monumentalize the Italian built environment. Acting as managers of the monumental layer of the city's architecture, they allocated resources to monuments, and produced administrative records for them (figure 3.13).

Monuments officers soon became bureaucrats. Reporting a month later from Florence, DeWald described his work solving problems of administration and paperwork:

> I have to decide what is to be repaired, how far the repairs are to go, comb out everything unnecessary from the estimates, hire archives, ferry them to safety through the AMG engineers and finance officers, intervene in a thousand petty cases, not to mention having to pass on requisition of any monumental buildings on our lists for the accommodation of troops.

Italian cities that had been temporarily understood as a lumpy field of ruins soon began to take shape as landscapes of architectural projects. Between the lines of MFAA reports that describe a surplus of monumental value and an infinity of urgent first aid, we can begin to discern that the efficacy of the Allies' contribution was measured by looking at a few important structures:

> I am repairing 21 churches in Pisa, but the huge job was the new roof on the Campo Santo, which was put on directly by the fifth army engineers. All over Pisa the destruction is terrible. Some parts of the town are earth already and grass is growing on them. Along the smashed lungarni which are so beautiful the stucco has fallen in sheets . . . from many places to disclose unknown Dugento structures underneath with fine Gothic arches and walls. You can quote this report the next time anyone tries to tell you that Italy hasn't suffered much. At any rate the continued physical existence of most of these damaged monuments is due entirely to us.[98]

The initial description of Pisa as a vast field of more or less finely made architectural fragments quickly gave way to the Camposanto, a privileged job site: it received first-aid from engineers, expert opinion from Rome, and his own attention.[99]

The American scholars of the Roberts Commission continued to contribute to this re-concentration of Italy's cultural value in famous buildings at the end of the war. Many in the Harvard Group, including Paul Sachs, Constable, Finley, and George Stout, reorganized themselves as the American Committee for the Restoration of Italian Monuments (ACRIM). This work began in 1946 and returned the scholars to the curatorial activities of the earliest "list-

Figure 3.13 MFAA officers inspect the San Francesco convent in Ancona (Italy) while archaeological excavations are underway below. BRS Photographic Archive, Ward-Perkins Collection, wpwar-0537.

ing" days in 1943, with liberal "choice" now a method for postwar financial aid. The same procedure for elimination that had been used for listing monuments to protect them was repurposed for choosing monuments to rebuild. This was the final loop in an ever folding thread of distinction we have been following in these two chapters, stitching the values of the American educated classes into the Italian environment. The process began with an exhibition of photographs of Allied-damaged monuments, "War's Toll of Italian Art," which traveled to museums in major American cities, enlisting donations[100] (color plate 4). Then, a list of "priorities" was created in collaboration with the Italian monuments authorities, to put candidate buildings into three "classes":

Class 1. Monuments of absolutely first artistic importance, seriously damaged but not involving prohibitive sums.
Class 2. Monuments of great artistic importance, so badly damaged that enormous sums will be necessary for their repair or restoration.
Class 3. Monuments of considerable importance and medium expense, but not of the absolute supremacy or urgency of class 1.[101]

Eventually, sites such as Montecassino requiring more "reconstruction" than "preservation" were excluded, and a regional exclusion was made for sites where the Military Government had already spent large sums.[102] The use of the word "monument" was questioned as it implied more construction of buildings than preservation of art.[103] Yet the final list of candidates reinstated the definition of a "monument," as an object of spatially concentrated value. Even in Pompeii, ACRIM eventually voted to fund "the restoration of a single house, to be selected by Maiuri."[104]

While the Americans were focused on reconstructing objects, among Italian preservationists the reconstruction was experienced as a moment when the problem of rebuilding the urban environment became "continuous with that of restoring an individual piece."[105] The Allied protection program helped inaugurate a split between two parallel lines of heritage maintenance and publicity in Italy: one aimed at an international public, the other at local memory-making.

For example, in Rimini, the ACRIM helped direct the reconstruction of the Tempio Malatestiano, a late-Gothic church onto which Leon Battista Alberti had added a new exterior shell around 1450. Over the course of centuries, the building had become a congealed assemblage of masonry old and new, Gothic and not. When Allied bombs caused the façade to be dislodged and one side to sag, the restoration divided the structure into two again. The Gothic interior was consolidated, while the Albertian exterior was meticulously disassembled and re-built following advanced archaeological standards. In fact, this process occurred so quickly that inhabitants, stoked by local leaders, became convinced that American armies were in fact dismantling the temple to bring it overseas. Only after it was agreed that elevation drawings would be produced, showing every stone numbered, was the Allied-backed project able to proceed.[106] The only addition to Alberti's façade was a dedication plaque indicating that the American businessman Samuel Kress had provided the funds for the reconstruction.[107] And while the exterior stood as the work of a singular Renaissance author, the Gothic interior was rebranded as paradigmatic of an earlier regional building idiom.

This project thus helps to situate the war in the narrative arc of the book. Like the Parthenon in chapter 1, the Tempio Malatestiano was reconstructed to convey two separate states of completion at once. But in Rimini two architectural paradigms that had originally been materially intermixed, were now taken apart, a gap made between the two. Furthermore, whereas the Parthenon

Figure 3.14 Disassembly and rebuilding of the Tempio Malatestiano in Rimini: a. Photograph of the façade midway through the disassembly. b. Elevation drawing of the front façade with each stone numbered. ©ACS. Used with permission.

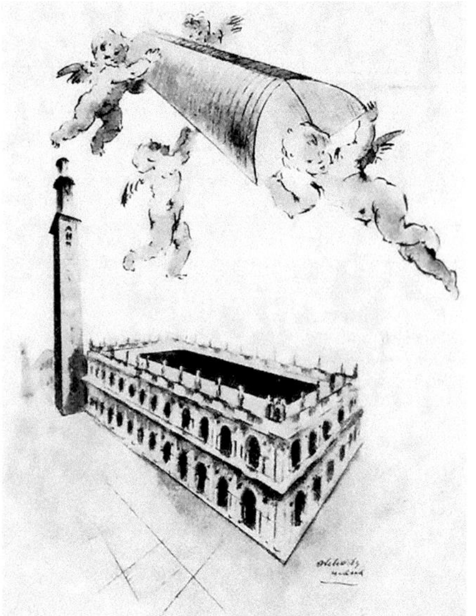

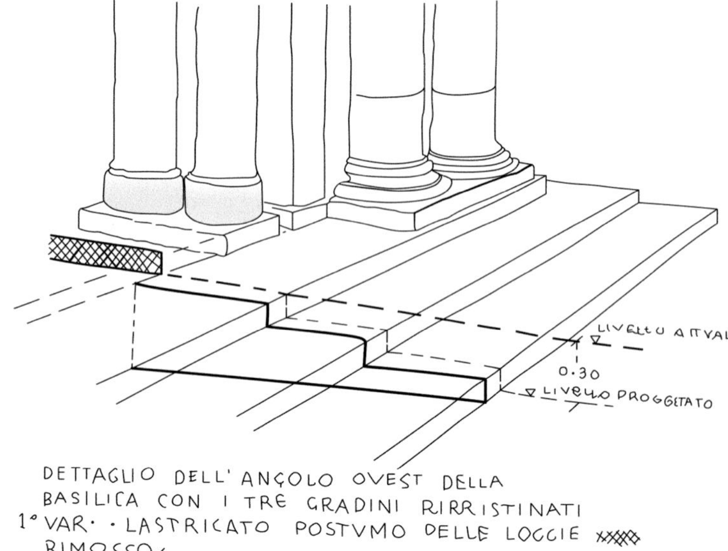

Figure 3.15 Reconstruction of the roof and steps of Andrea Palladio's Basilica in Vicenza (Italy), in 1946–1947. a. Vignette of angels delivering a new roof. b. M. Vucetich, Detail of the "Study for the design of the Piazza dei Signori in Vicenza with the reconstruction of the three steps of the Basilica Palladiana." Archivio Communale di Vicenza.

reconstruction was drawn after the fact, the Malatestiano drawings acted as a kind of advance contract. This was one of the earliest uses of an architectural drawing as basis for transnational agreement, and the drawings were widely republished by UNESCO in the postwar period, as Italy became a favorite training ground for monuments experts looking to learn precisely these kinds of techno-scientific methods[108] (figure 3.14).

The use of these increasingly precise architectural drawing tools for heritage reconstruction in Italy in no way prevented grander metaphysical narratives from being locally attached to particular monuments' survival. For example, the ACRIM voted to send funds to the "Basilica Palladiana" in Vicenza, a sixteenth-century palace at the center of town, which had been damaged by Allied bombing. A competition to rebuild the nearby piazza was launched in 1947, and this urban work became an opportunity to implement a never-completed part of the building's design: the entire piazza was lowered so that three steps could be added to correct the façade's proportions—based on a drawing that Andrea Palladio, the architect, had published in his treatise *Quatro Libri*.[109] The result, as Damiana Lucia Paterno has noted, was "more Palladio than even Palladio," and helped establish him as a regional architect.[110] But if the reconstruction of the piazza was achieved with carefully dimensioned section drawings, popular representations of the reconstruction focused on the rebuilding of the roof, as a story of angel-assisted salvation (figure 3.15).

France: More Likely to Be Destroyed than Not

By the time the Allies landed in Normandy on D-Day, June 6, 1944, the MFAA program had been tested out in Italy and it was possible to replicate many of its features in France. Tedder's office sent a first "request for material" for

France in May, in two tiers: lists of towns for "framing a strategic bombing programme," and lists of buildings "for use in tactical bombing operations."[111] MFAA reports from France resemble those of Italy: they describe the work of "putting order" in damaged cityscapes, making contact with local officials, giving financial and logistical support for rubble-clearing. After D-Day, the most urgent task became making monuments off limits to "billeting" troops. After all, historic monuments, likely to be empty and "owned by nobody," seemed like a ready-made solution for housing the thousands who were marching across the country.[112]

But France differs fundamentally from Italy because Tedder and Eisenhower decided that under exceptional circumstances a strategic air force would have to be used to tactical ends. Given the enormous amount of risk and uncertainty facing Allied troops disembarking in Normandy, a heavyweight force would act as a "decisive" factor in allowing the Allies to reach the German border.[113] This meant that destruction would be literally over-designed. Operation Overlord carved a frightful band of destruction through the North of France, from the Normandy beaches to the border with Germany; by 1945, conventional wisdom about the fate of monuments in this swath was that the "damage had been inversely proportional to the speed of advance."[114] This too was a proportional understanding of destruction. In terms of monuments protection, speed meant that there was little time to adjust the Frick format to evolving needs. Instead, France became the subject of the most abbreviated list of monuments that was produced in the entire war.

In July 1944, a 100-page Frick list of French monuments became a one-page list of 25 buildings. This list originated not from military but civilian channels: a new commission, the Vaucher Commission, which had been created to coordinate between the Roberts Commission, its British equivalent the MacMillan Committee, and representatives of the Free French government. Members of this group gathered on July 10, 1944, in London, to compose a letter to Tedder and Eisenhower that pointed out the contradiction between the existence of Frick Atlases and the "carpet bombing" that was being used in Overlord:

> Despite the distribution of maps and lists of cultural monuments in France to the Air Forces, the employment of the technique of "carpet bombing" has resulted in the destruction of a considerable number of cultural monuments. The Vaucher Commission and the MacMillan Committee were disturbed by the extent of the devastation in Normandy and the prospect of further obliteration of entire areas in France by Allied bombing. The Vaucher Commission passed a resolution ... to be forwarded to appropriate governmental quarters, expressing the hope that (1) some alternative to "carpet bombing" might be devised ...

But, they continued, *should carpet bombing be necessary*, a new list could be made that would restrict the French monuments to be spared to a "special" few:

> ... or (2) if modification of that technique were not feasible, then a few areas containing monuments of outstanding importance be selected for special consideration.[115]

The most remarkable part of this letter is the rapid switch from a demand for total restraint to a request for "consideration." An earlier version of this document made the calculation even clearer, in a probabilistic reversal of destruction and survival:

> the Commission would suggest that the problem of preservation be approached anew with a frank recognition of the fact that every monument located in a theater of military operations is more likely to be destroyed than not.[116]

There is perhaps no other document that encapsulates with such raw bureaucratic rationality the shift in attitude towards monument protection that is the subject of this book: from *interdicting* destruction, to *predicting* it.

The Vaucher Commission was so convinced of the real possibility that France would be reduced to a blank slate adorned with 25 cathedrals that they were ready with a list of "the 25 most important monuments in *all of France.*" On August 26, 1945, they sent this list and an accompanying Frick map to Tedder, via William Bell Dinsmoor[117] (figure 3.16). On the one hand, it was not very unusual for architectural historians to reduce France to its monumental sites. Histories of French medieval architecture customarily represented the whole country as a blank slate punctuated by cathedrals.[118] On the other hand, we might imagine that Dinsmoor had this particular annotated Frick map in mind when he reported, two months later in his lecture at the Metropolitan museum, that many French monuments had "miraculously survived" and that he feared he had been engaged in "city planning."

The Vaucher resolution elicited no response from Allied leaders but provided a new visual and geographic threshold against which the French bombings were perceived by Allied monuments officers. In fact, this regional scale of monumental proportion (one object per city, and twenty-five cities per nation) was compatible with the specific compromise on the principle of proportionality that Tedder had brokered with the British political leadership in the design of Operation Overlord. Civilian leaders in London had spent two months trying (and failing) to convince Tedder to promise to limit his bombings by calculating this threshold in human casualties: asking him to agree to a certain number of civilian deaths per city.[119] But the D-Day raids needed to seem unplanned, Tedder argued, and raids on French cities in advance of D-Day needed to resemble the most banal of Allied raids. Any additional restraint would have given away the planned path of the Allied invasion. The city of Caen, for example, would be a crucial stopping point for advancing Allied troops, but it could not be spared in the days preceding D-Day lest the Axis suspect it was being spared to facilitate Allied occupation and/or passage.

SECRET

aug 226

(49)

— Cathedrale de CHARTRES × p. 109 6B ; × p. 122 3F

— Cathedrale de ROUEN × p. 115 7CF

— Cathedrale d'AMIENS × p. 112 3F

— Cathedrale de REIMS × p. 95 4D

— Cathedrale de BEAUVAIS × p. 105 3D ; p. 125 7A.

— Cathedrale de LAON × p. 105 6C

— Cathedrale de STRASBOURG × p. 84 4C

— Cathedrale de BOURGES × p. 117 4D

— PARIS: Notre-Dame × p. 105

La Sainte-Chapelle

Le Louvre

? Eglise de VEZELAY × p. 95 3I-86 (5C-89A)

? Eglise de SAINT-BENOIT-SUR-LOIRE × p. 117 4B-22 (5C-78A)

×— Eglise et cloitre de MOISSAC × p. 103 6E

— Chateau de VERSAILLES × p. 105 3F ; × p. 123 7/8 A/B

— Chateau de FONTAINEBLEAU × p. 105 4H ; × p. 121 3F

— Chateau de BLOIS × p. 117 2C

? Chateau de CHAMBORD × p. 117 3C-31 (4C-88A)

? Chateau d'AZAY-LE-RIDEAU × p. 109 4F-48 (9D-86A)

? Chateau de CHENONCEAUX × p. 109 4F-46 (4D-87A)

— Chateau des Papes a AVIGNON × p. 129 1D-F

— Theatre d'ORANGE × p. 129 1C-B

— Maison Carree a NIMES × p. 106 6E-D

? MONT-SAINT-MICHEL × p. 115 2E/F-69 (2/3 B-43A)

— Cite de CARCASSONNE × p. 132 4B-A.

SECRET
BY AUTHORITY OF THE
CHIEF of the ARMY AIR FORCES
SWT 24 Aug '44

SECRET

COPY/w

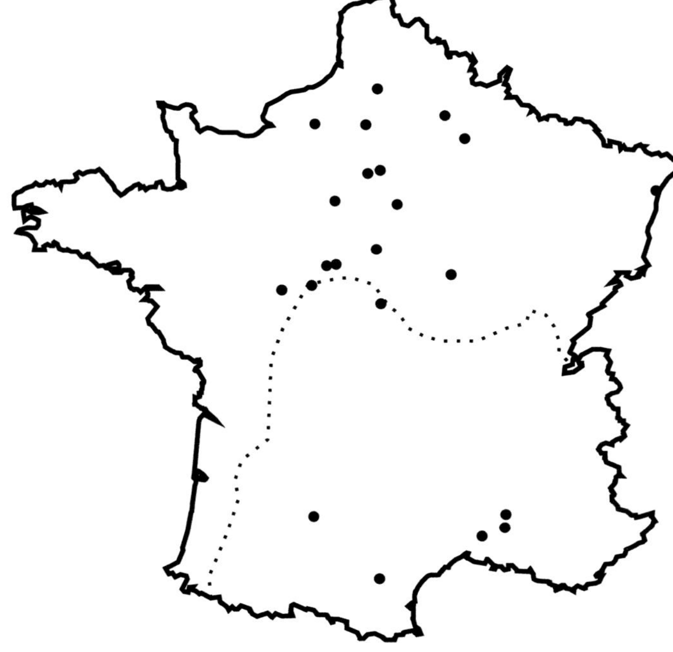

Figure 3.16
a. Vaucher Commission, List of 25 French monuments to be avoided, dated and annotated by William Bell Dinsmoor. NARA RG 231. b. Map locating these sites in France. © Lucia Allais.

After some hesitation about whether Caen should be placed on a list of cities to bomb on Days "D-1 to D-4," its first bombing came on July 6 and led to two weeks of continuous day and night bombings by Allies trying unsuccessfully to create a physical roadblock to German advance. The city's Palais des Ducs and its church of St. Etienne were severely damaged. The Cathedral of St. Pierre survived.[120] One bombed city, one surviving cathedral.

By August 1944, it had become possible for a commander to pass along a request to the Supreme Headquarters Allied Expeditionary Force (SHAEF) for monuments protection that took the form of a short list of French cathedrals. This order read as follows:

Request the following Cathedrals be spared as far as possible from bombing and artillery fire:
ROUEN
AMIENS
RHEIMS
BEAUVAIS
LAON
STRASBOURG[121]

Despite these connections between the planned destruction of French cities and the projected survival of a handful of cathedrals, the MFAA officers tour encountered no narratives of cultural martyrdom to undo.[122] Instead, the American Military Government (AMG) emphasized French self-government and a speedy hand-over into French authorities.[123]

France was now twice-occupied, and the Vichy government had taken the first armistice as an opportunity to reorganize the administrative structure of the French architectural profession, including its Service des Monuments Historiques.[124] Indeed, a new 1941 urban planning law presciently implemented a 1-km circular radius of protection around each monument, a distance obviously informed by aerial bombing technologies. Because of this reorganization, everywhere in France MFAA officers encountered a robust monuments administration, highly organized, if understaffed. When reconstruction was launched, the Service favored a functionalist segmentation of urban tasks. The reconstruction of the city of Saint-Lô, for instance, was divided into three: the half-demolished Cathedral was rebuilt by the French preservation architect Yves-Marie Froidevaux, as we saw in the introduction; a new hospital was built by a Franco-American modernist, Paul Nelson; and the urban reform of the town was overseen by the chief urbanist of the town.[125] There was little opportunity to perceive, receive, interpret, or indeed design, the city as a project, even though this is in fact how it is perceived today—the "capital of the ruins."

The Italian campaign may well have set an expectation, among the Roberts Commission, that all theaters of war would be covered with aerial photography. But in fact the Tedder Atlases were the exception. If the war had unfolded

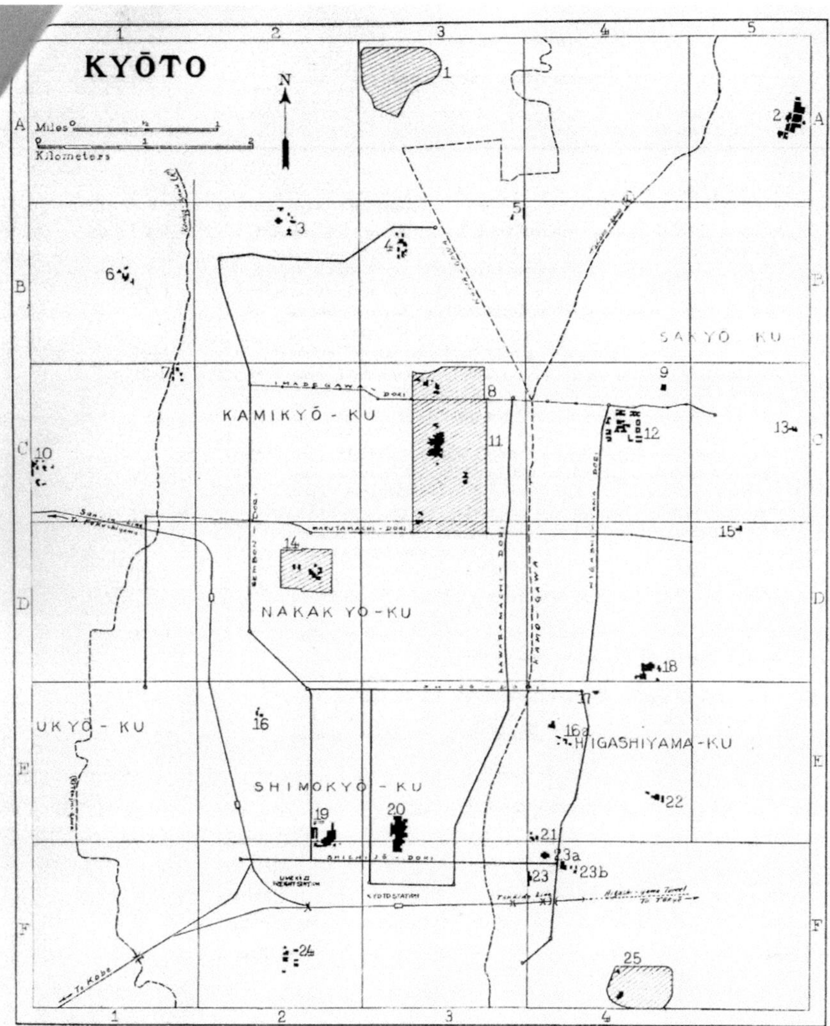

Figure 3.17 Frick Map of Kyoto (Japan), with underlayer base map removed and only city walls and monuments remaining. Army Service Forces Manual M 354–17. *Civil Affairs Handbook, Japan.* Section 17A: Cultural Institutions (May 1945), 9.

differently, proceeding first through France, for instance, these kinds of aerial maps would likely not have been made at all. Moreover, now that a single map had been made for all of France, the precedent was set for an entire country to be understood as a monumental collection graspable at a glance. This radical reduction is the legacy of the protection project in France, and it is most significant for the case of Japan. Historians studying the way the Americans mapped Japan in advance of its nuclear bombing have detected a "cartographic fade to black" on the surface of the maps, arguing that cartography functioned as a sinister premonition for the nuclear annihilation that was to come.[126] A similar premonitory effect can be seen in the Frick maps of monuments for Japan, but as a "fade to white." The first Frick atlas of Japan had used tourist maps as bases, as with all other countries. But when these were deemed too illegible, in a second edition the maps were redrawn as spare white outlines dotted by a handful of black marks (figure 3.17).

Germany: A Stony Desert

To say that Germany is a special case in the European bombing war is perhaps less useful than to say it was the exception around which all strategy had been designed. The Transportation Plan specifically allowed for the continued and continual strategic bombing of German cities by *both* the US and the British air forces. The listing of monuments for Germany was also always different—it was shorter than Italy's and more difficult to fit within the broader scheme of "distinction."[127] The fear was that over-articulating German people's attachment to monuments might provoke their destruction rather than prevent it. In June 1944 the German list's introduction was revised twice. First, all references to the sentiments of the German people were removed and replaced with a legal-economic argument about protecting "the richness of Germany in all kinds of cultural material" as "matter of international concern."[128] Secondly, Germany was made into a place for *the study of art*, and the likely site of looted art from around Europe.[129] Furthermore, the list for Germany was developed while some of the most destructive fire-bombing techniques in the history of the European war were still being developed, in an attempt to replicate a firebombing that had been achieved in Hamburg in June 1943.

The raid on Hamburg holds a similar place in the history of the German bombing war as the raid on Rome for Italy: a turning point. If the Rome raid suggested that there was such a thing as a city of non-targets, contemporane-

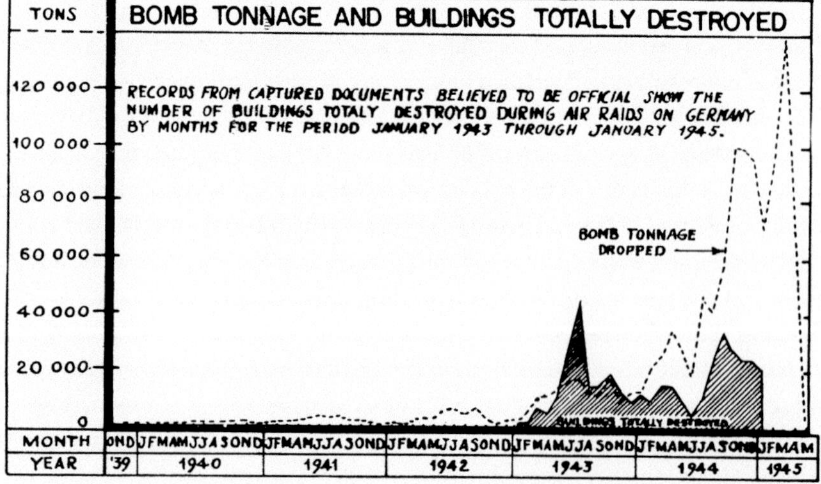

Figure 3.18 "Buildings totally destroyed" showing a peak in 1943 representing the raid on Hamburg. United States Strategic Bombing Survey, *Physical Damage Division Report, European Theater of Operations* (1945).

ous preparations for Hamburg show a continuing desire to achieve "the total destruction of a city."[130] The raid itself has become a landmark of the atrocities of war for featuring "the first man-made firestorm in history." An uncontrollable column of fire raced through the city at hurricane-speed, leaving 12 square miles of death by burning, asphyxiation, and a massacre so vast that it registers as a spike in the timeline of destruction *for the war as a whole* (figure 3.18). In fact, this raid appeared to confirm the predictions of British strategists who had banked on "incendiarism." Already in 1942 a report on flammability titled *German Domestic Architecture* classified German cities into four types, with detailed drawings and tabulated data about how they were built: materials, construction techniques, average dimensions, and location of stairwells and courtyards.[131] The report remained silent on the city's monumental architecture, despite the pervasive *visual* presence of monuments in its illustrations. There, each city was depicted with a birds-eye photograph of the urban center, showing housing fabric built *around* monumental sites: cathedrals, plazas, city centers, bridges, city halls, etc. (figure 3.19). Taken out of context these could easily have been mistaken for an album of an aerial tour of Germany's cathedrals and their picturesque surroundings.

This visual prevalence of monuments in an apparently functionalist document about urban zoning for morale bombing should not surprise us. The first person who had suggested that the RAF should analyze German cities in concentric "zones" of vulnerability, the British geographer Robert E. Dickinson, was a keen scholar of the role played by monuments in the history of German cities. In 1942 Dickinson published the first in a series of articles on "The Development and Distribution of the Medieval German Town," where he argued that Germany cities began to acquire an "urban character" around the year 1200, when "the lands between the Loire and the Rhine had become studded with urban nuclei gathered around church and castle."[132] This co-dependence of urban fabric and monumental anchors would have been aptly illustrated by a Frick map, with its graphic nomenclature of "hatching" the former and "blacking out" the latter. But the deep history and cultural metonymy that bound the monuments of Germany to their cities, was entirely suppressed in these fire-bombing architectural analyses.

After Hamburg was bombed, however, the association between its monuments and their surrounding urban life returned *en force*. Many stone-built monuments remained partially standing among the charred city fabric. German newsreels focused on these standing towers, and churches especially, to associate German martyrdom with piety rather than raise questions of political ideology.[133] Most survivors' accounts included monument recognition in the prelude to the shock of encountering mass-death. Hans Erick Nossack's poignant memoir recounts how he and other evacuees reentered the city a month after the firestorm. Recognizing their town's familiar monumental profile, "Everyone began to count the towers of the city":

Fig.2. FRANKFURT-am-Main

Hessen-Nassau

Material		a) R.E.8. Studies in German Domestic Architecture
Tile	(1) Thickness	12 mm. (½" +)
	(2) Length	36 mm. (14¼")
	(3) Overlap	20% 2 layers of tiles 80% 3 layers of tiles
Battens (laths)	(4) Sizes	3 cms. x 5 cms. (1¼" x 2") 4 cms. x 6 cms. (1½" x 2¼") 5 cms. x 8 cms. (2" x 3¼")
	(5) Spacing. centre to centre	15 cms. (for doppeldach) (5⅞")
Spars (Rafters)	(6) Sizes	8 cms. x 12 cms. (3¼" x 4¾") 8 cms. x 15 cms. (3¼" x 5¾") 10 cms. x 14 cms. (4" x 5½") 12 cms. x 16 cms. (4¾" x 6¼")
	(7) Spacing centre to centre	80 - 90 cms. (31½" x 35½")

Figure 3.19 Graphic and photographic information drawn from (British) Ministry of Home Security, Research and Experiments Department, "German Domestic Architecture" (1943) a. Aerial view of Frankfurt-am-Main (Germany). b. Detail of a comparative table of different material specifications. SZ.OEMU.50.8.2. Zuckerman Archive, University of East Anglia.

Oh, and with what affectionate nicknames they were summoned, one by one! And where was the most beautiful of them all, the tower of Saint Catherine's Church? And why had the town hall turned into a pagoda?–But at that point we had already crossed the river and were driving into the cemetery.[134]

Monuments became understood in this way as funereal markers for the city life that once surrounded them. Solly Zuckerman himself confirmed this understanding of the monuments of Cologne as memorializing dead civilians. "To this day, I incorrectly visualize that great church as standing in some vast square"[135] (figure 3.20).

This same sequence, of monumental recognition followed by urban shock, was experienced more or less in real-time by MFAA troops in Germany. They entered German city centers that had undergone several cycles of bombing. Walker Hancock waited two weeks on the other side of the Franco-German border, as the city of Aachen was repeatedly pounded from the air: "For two weeks we had watched Aachen burning below the horizon—an unsteady glow in the sky at night, by day a constant column of smoke. Now it was time to go in."[136] Radically short-staffed and arriving late, in cities emptied of civilian populations, the MFAA had little to work with but their powers of persuasion. By the time he entered Germany in October 1945, James Rorimer reported that "the destruction of monuments" was simply too great and that both first aid and documentation of damage were declared "secondary considerations."[137] Another officer reported that:

The line between avoidable and unavoidable damage was impossible to draw since each case could ultimately be judged only by one man, the commander on the spot. Consequently, beyond what could be accomplished by advice and persuasion, MFAA on its own authority could do little in the way of active protection.[138]

In a sense, the amount of bomb tonnage dropped on Germany up-ended one of the basic assumptions that had been made when designing the scope of the Civil Affairs division: namely, that the Allies would enter into enemy territory under "unscorched conditions."[139] Faced with this overwhelming destruction each MFAA officer became "less a guardian than an insurance adjustor assessing the loss, looking for what was salvageable, and attempting to forestall unwarranted claims."[140]

The switch from unscorched to scorched placed renewed pressure on paperwork. Sometimes documents became a kind of monument—targeted or protected for their cultural value. Consider the cultural factors that went into the third and final firestorm of the German campaign, the bombing of Dresden. The city remained frankly "unbombed," in part because of its cultural richness, but was chosen as a target in part because it allowed the British and Americans to coordinate (and compete) with the Soviet armies arriving from

Figure 47

SIGNAL CORPS PHOTO

FRANKFURT, GERMANY. DESTRUCTION IN AREA OF THE CATHEDRAL.

Figure 40

AIR CORPS PHOTO

COLOGNE, GERMANY. CENTRAL PART OF THE SEVERELY DAMAGED CITY.

the East.[141] As Richard Overy has pointed out, the alibi for the bombing became that Dresden was acting as an "administrative and control center," and its bombing would slow the German war machine by literally creating problems of paperwork:

> The administrative problems involved in receiving the refugees and redistributing them are likely to be immense. The strain on the administration and upon the communications must be considerably increased by the need for handling military reinforcements on their way to the Eastern Front. A series of heavy attacks by day and night upon these administrative and control centers is likely to create considerable delays in the deployment of troops and may well result in establishing a state of chaos.[142]

Figure 3.20
a. Aerial photograph of the center of Frankfurt (Germany), Photograph: Signal Corps. b. Aerial photograph of the center of Cologne (Germany). Photograph: Air Corps. From Roberts Commission, *Final Report* (1946).

Thus Dresden was bombed with full knowledge that the city would be full of over 500,000 refugees, and under the pretext that those deaths would register as a massive administrative problem. This is all the more poignant in light of the fact that in its earliest days the Roberts Commission had already warned that, in the context of mass-death and mass-displacement, bureaucratic records whose physical presence was usually unremarkable would take on the monumental function of remembrance, especially for refugees of exactly the kind that had fled to Dresden. "Not only property rights but human rights" were at stake in the destruction of administrative records, argued argued Solomon Buck, the Archivist of the United States.[143] In the Dresden bombing this administrative erasure was not only sought, but used to justify the mass murder of the refugees themselves. The logic of the monument as a container of documents was pushed to its most sinister conclusion.[144]

We might expect this turn of events to have provoked widespread protest among the MFAA officers. Certainly between the lines of their final report we can read a critique, that, in the guarded words of one, "more courage" should have been used in approaching the air forces.[145] But the bodies and the attention of all MFAA troops were diverted away from Germany's city centers at the same time as some of the most brutal destruction of civilians, of their housing, and also of their monuments was occurring. As soon as MFAA officers entered German soil in fall 1944, they encountered the hundreds of Nazi repositories of art—"castles, monasteries, cathedrals, private residences, farm houses and barns, office building basements, various mines and air-raid shelters"[146]—containing thousands of movable cultural objects, from confiscated Jewish collections, to artworks requisitioned for Hitler's and Göring's personal collections, to furniture evacuated from state museums. Rather than progressing right behind advancing armies, MFAA troops were dispersed, sent far and wide to search for these hidden caches. The recovery and inventorying of these movable works were "full of melodrama" and took over the entire MFAA division, as "all other operations were curtailed."[147] Even the MFAA realized that "the scattered and often isolated character of repositories" in Germany was keeping them from dealing with "the extremely severe destruction, especially in the northern part of the Rhine Province."[148]

This turn of events exposed the flaw in the Allied vision of Europe's monuments as cultural infrastructure. Hitler's army had used the same feature of Europe's geography that the Allies had identified as the basis for its cultural protection—its widespread, networked "communicability"—but used it to redraw the cultural map of Europe. The scale of the diversion was commensurate with that of Hitler's looting and dispersal plan. Art repositories were found as far as Czechoslovakia; the stained glass of a French cathedral had been buried near the Eastern Front. Furthermore, this separation of "movable" and "immovable" monuments undermined the logic of containment that held together the expansive Allied definition of "the monument." This was more than a geographic dislocation. The Allies' principles of spatial discrimination and avoidance were suddenly replaced by a different kind of target-thinking. Suddenly, art was something to seek. Photographs of art historians in uniforms finding

Figure 3.21 Ernest DeWald holding the Crown of the Holy Roman Empire, recovered in the salt mine of Alt-Aussée (Austria). Princeton University Archives. Ernest Theodore DeWald Papers (C0420), Manuscripts Division, Department of Rare Books and Special Collections, Princeton University Library. Photograph: Princeton University Library.

Figure 3.22 Ernest DeWald (second from right) and two other MFAA officers (P. K. Baillie Reynolds, right, and J. Paul Gardner, left) and a civilian in the Cloister of Santa Chiara in Naples (Italy). Ernest Theodore DeWald Papers (C0420), Manuscripts Division, Department of Rare Books and Special Collections, Princeton University Library. Photograph: Princeton University Library.

Impressionist masterpieces and imperial regalia in underground salt-mines offered an image of redemptive beauty amidst chaos (figure 3.21). In contrast, the image of the same monuments officer "putting order" in a stony ruin offered at best an ambiguous image of victory (figure 3.22).

Furthermore, the same paperwork could be used to inventory, locate, and restitute looted art as the MFAA had been using all along: lists, maps, index cards, reports.[149] The Nazi regime had established and rigorously maintained its own paperwork about art, which itself became a prized "t-force target": to be gathered for a dossier on "The Plunder of Art Treasures" and used to bring the charge of conspiracy against the Nazi regime in the Nuremberg trials.[150] While this aspect of the trials was ultimately minor, the ideological discourse that was spun around art in its possible affiliation with other war-crimes helped to legitimate the widespread effort of "cultural re-orientation" that the Allied Military government put in place after the war.

At war's end, the return of art objects and the rebuilding of monuments became paired tools in the hands of American planners. Many Roberts Commission officers stayed behind to perform various "cultural" aspects of the reconstruction.[151] For the art politicians of the Roberts Commission, the discovery of Axis looting offered irresistible ideological leverage in painting an image of the Allies restoring democractic "choice" to German political life.[152] This narrative benefitted unwittingly from the Nazi regime's own planning. During the reconstruction, when large-scale cultural buildings bombed by the Allies were chosen for reconstruction—the Residenz in Munich, for example—their rebuilding was all the more seamless because they could be refurbished with the artworks, furniture, and other "movable" objects that had been safely stored away by the Nazi regime. This was a case of Hague-Convention standardization *avant la lettre*, a wholly unconscious and unplanned transnational cultural cooperation across enemy lines.

Conclusion: In the Minds of Men

By analyzing the Allied maps of monuments through their geographic and technological scalability, this chapter has shown that they evolved over the course of the war to accommodate new forms of contingency and new realities of inaccuracy. I concluded with a comparative view of how this instrument contributed to shaping destruction in three different theaters, regionalizing the military use of monuments and giving rise, in each theater, to new technical ways to standardize protection that had prolonged postwar afterlives. In Italy, amidst patchy and patterned destruction, the whole country became a cultural network of interrelated sites.[153] In France, a list of minimum irreplaceable monuments reflected the overdesigned caliber of destruction. In Germany, the perception of all surviving buildings as funerary "monuments" fit the calculated nature of the Allied attack, which was itself hidden behind a redemptive narrative of salvaging art. I have only scratched the surface of how the policy, whose origins I described in the last chapter, was implemented. But I sought to show what form protection took during the entire the time between the Commission's formation and its dissolution. The point has been to emphasize the effect that continuity had on protection.

Temporal, not geographic coverage, was the essence of monuments protection during the war. An entire region could always be dropped from the plan: no map for Poland was ever made, for instance, in deference to Soviet interests.[154] But it was possible to claim a continuous thread of protection. This innovation constitutes the Roberts Commission's foremost legacy in postwar international heritage theory and practice. Established in a moment of opportunity, and maintained against all odds through the militarization of European monuments into morale-communication devices, then again instantiated through the strategic emphasis on both sides of the conflict on Europe's networkability, the legacy of the Roberts Commission lies foremost in this tenacious attachment of at least *some* kind of real-time bureaucratic management of monuments throughout the war. This continuous control was threaded through destructive techniques first, and then protective ones—made possible by the same paperwork. Listing and mapping themselves constituted protection.

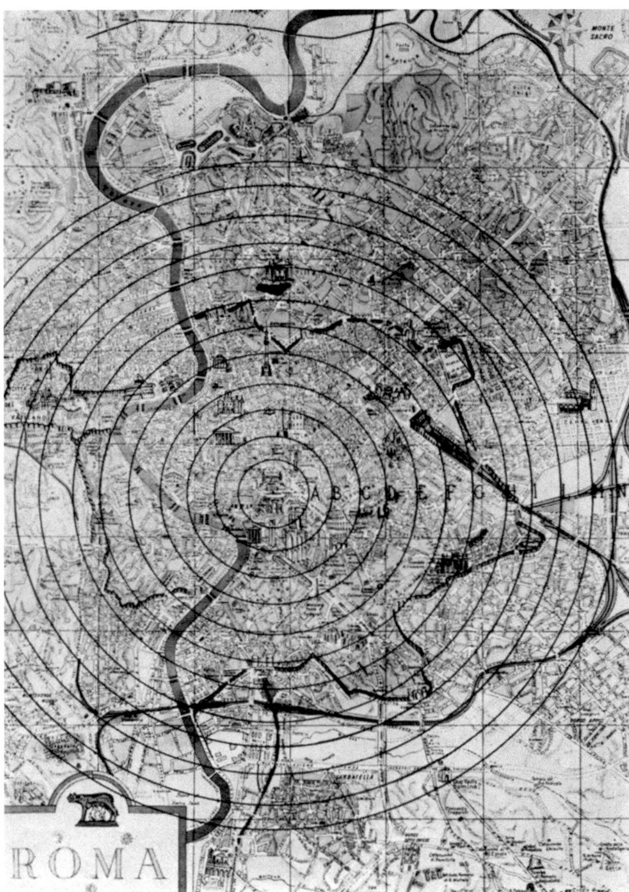

Figure 3.23 Map of Italy with nuclear target superimposed. *Bollettino dell'Istituto Centrale del Restauro,* 22–23 (1955). Unknown author.

When monuments protection became a major project of the United Nations' cultural agency, UNESCO, as the second half of this book will chronicle, monuments were made to convey a pacifist message—in the words of the Roberts Commission alumnus Archibald MacLeish, they were to help prevent "wars in the minds of men."[155] But UNESCO republished many of the protective inventions that had been achieved during the war through destructive plans and technologies. In fact, when MFAA alumni were asked to comment on UNESCO's proposed draft for a Hague Convention for the Protection of Cultural Property during Armed Conflict in 1954, all expressed skepticism that any preliminary legal pact between countries could ever be achieved. Instead, they pointed overwhelmingly to the various "practical" fortuities that made survival possible.[156] And in Europe, the return of monuments into the hands of national administrations did not mean a return to pre-war thinking. In its review of the Hague Convention, for example, the Italian preservation community produced one map that showed a circular target, superimposed on a map of Rome, with its monuments blacked out[157] (figure 3.23). The bulls-eye's dimensions were much larger than those of World War II—it had been recalibrated to the range of an atomic bomb. But the point remained: protective action would be envisioned through destructive eyes.

BRIDGE

Let's Visit UNESCO House

For the first fifteen years of UNESCO's existence, architectural monuments were far from the organization's top priority. This might seem surprising, given how closely the agency is identified with its World Heritage work today, and how frequently we are reminded of its origins in the cataclysm of World War II. But cooperation in the early years of postwar international organization was a concept in flux. Although each United Nations specialized agency was assigned its own function, UNESCO's contribution to the world system—the triad of "Science, Culture and Education"—was vague and controversial from the start.[1] The organization's motto spoke of achieving "peace in the minds of men" but it was unclear how this psychological territory could be accessed. The vagueness of this terrain was reflected in the graphic style of its earliest communications, where the head of an international citizen, looking as empty as the "o" in the organization's acronym, was repeatedly configured and conjugated through media old and new (from paint, to radio, to a globe) (figure B.1).

Heritage work as we understand it today rose to the top of UNESCO's agenda against significant obstacles, "without the benefit of designation as a major project," and under the leadership of a Director-General, the American Luther Evans, who was a reluctant culturalist.[2] As a former Librarian of Congress, Evans preferred to think of himself as an information manager than as a patron of the arts. If monuments conservation became a prominent and permanent channel for international cultural action under his tenure, it was because he oversaw a broader "technical" turn in the organization at large. So it was not until the early 1960s, when the budgets and mentality of Technical Assistance had fully permeated UNESCO, and cultural experts were systematically attached to all UN development projects, that monuments came to be seen as worthy emblems of world government—as internationalist ends in themselves.

Still, during this 15-year hiatus, we find a prospective mode of monument survival emerging from the organization's work. The monument was a suitable test-unit for probing how architecture might shape the meaning of culture

Figure B.1 Cover art of Julian Huxley's *UNESCO: Its Purpose, Its Philosophy* (Washington, DC: Public Affairs Press, 1947).

in world politics, especially since architecture seemed a suitably cooperative practice. Furthermore, unlike their prewar predecessors, UNESCO's monuments officials were empowered to send expert missions *on site*, and deliver its opinions *about a site*. Thus they sent their first heritage missions to places where diplomacy was needed: to the earthquake-stricken Peruvian town of Cuzco in 1949 (where American interests were intensifying); to the Yugoslav church of St. Sofia Ochrida in 1951 (where it was hoped that Eastern and Western blocks would cooperate); and throughout the early 1950s to the Middle East, where nation-building was unfolding at rapid pace.[3] These missions were sent not to consolidate the world-famous status of a building, as the Athens Conference had done at the Parthenon, but to jump-start new development opportunities. In that sense, these missions prepared the ground for later instances when conservation projects were fully integrated into transnational economic schemes. Paradoxically, then, in this period UNESCO fueled the increasing segmentation of monuments along national or regional lines—a technique that had worked well for the American Military Government in World War II. The older, prewar idea, where the League tried to institute international protocols for maintaining monuments one by one, was replaced with regular surveys of the whole cultural heritage of each nation. Tasked with reviewing entire state administrations, country by country, UNESCO experts helped forge a meta-bureaucracy.

One architectural effect of this turn of events can be seen in the organization's increasingly infrastructural view of architectural monuments. When a team of international architects and archaeologists traveled to the Middle East to advise national governments on the modernization of historic cities, for instance, the single most common recommendation they made was not that monuments should be preserved one by one, but that a narrative sequence should be designed to link them all together, often through the addition of a highway, that paradigmatic element of infrastructural development. They redesigned the Lebanese coastal town of Tripoli into a sequence of monuments, approachable by highway that bent in plan around the city and pierced a tunnel under its monumental core (figure B.2). Similarly, in the archaeological town of Baalbek, internationalists worked with Director of Antiquities Maurice Chéhab to modify a plan that had been drawn by the Swiss architect Ernst Egli, to connect the monuments via axial perspectives and roundabouts[4] (figure B.3). Instead of this Haussmanian, hub-and-spoke scheme, the UNESCO project proposed to gently curve the roadways, bending them to bypass important monuments in a series of lateral historic views.

Figure B.2 Material produced by the UNESCO mission, Paul Collard, Maurice Chéhab, and Armando Dillon, to Lebanon in 1953–1954: Section through monumental profile of Tripoli, and aerial view of the city center. IFPO.

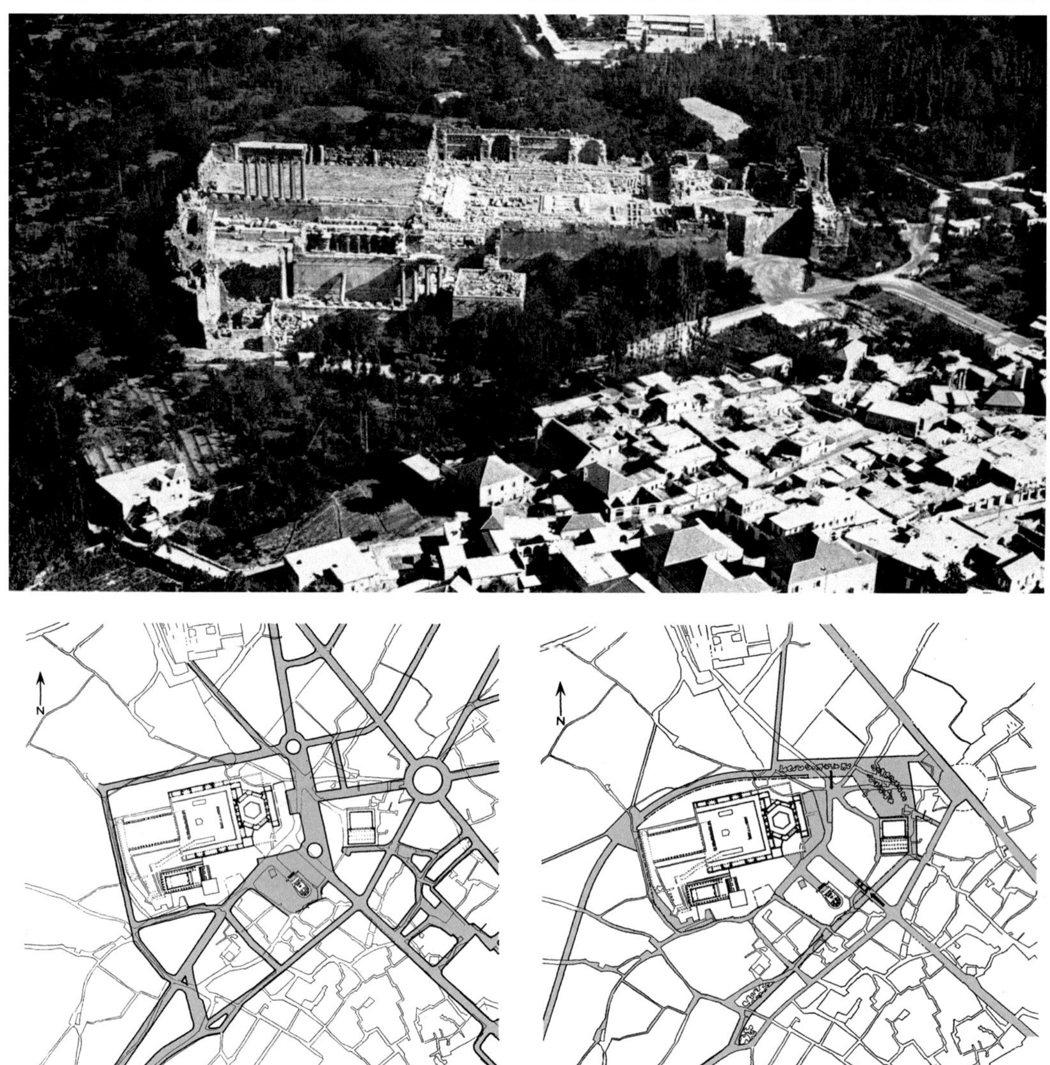

Figure B.3 Material produced by the UNESCO mission, Paul Collard, Maurice Chéhab, and Armando Dillon, to Baalbek (Lebanon) in 1953–1954: Aerial view of the fort (IFPO) and two drawings of an existing plan proposed by Ernst Egli (left) and by the UNESCO Mission (right). Diagrams modified by the author.

Insofar as these earliest heritage missions tethered monumental effects to infrastructural forms, they resonated with the design of UNESCO's headquarter complex in Paris in surprising and meaningful ways. UNESCO House, as it is known, was designed between 1952 and 1958 in a complicated and contentious process that came to involve two sites, three schemes, and no fewer than nine architects, including some of the most illustrious personalities of the modern movement.[5] This was not just another international building. As the UN's cultural arm, UNESCO was expected to be the keeper of collective values in cultural production at large, and to foster a global distribution of creative power in history and at present. In fact, the blur of collective authorship that was involved in the headquarter's *conception* helped to imagine its collective *reception* once it was inaugurated. A plethora of commemorative material showed off the irresistible iconographic potential of the curved

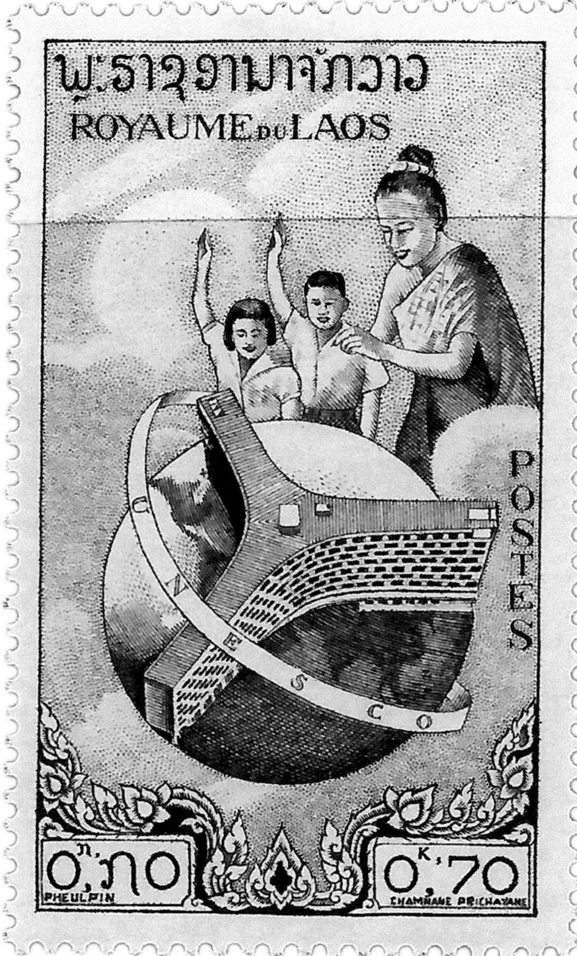

Figure B.4 Commemorative stamp issued by the Kingdom of Laos on November 3, 1958, for the opening of UNESCO House. Designed by Chamnane Prisayane and engraved by Pheulpin.

Y-shaped secretariat building: as an iconic star-shaped building, as a global network node, and as a world in itself (figure B.4). But UNESCO House was also always already anchored in Paris. Despite many frictions between the architectural team and the organization's leaders, one point of consensus was that UNESCO would help create a space for modern architecture in the heart of Paris.[6] Already in the late 1940s, the booklet *Let's Visit UNESCO House* collaged a graphic of Eiffel Tower and an aerial of the Place de l'Étoile into its tour of the temporary secretariat.[7] As soon as the schematic design was completed, a photograph of the model was collaged into an aerial photograph of the site (figure B.5).

Like a dam or a highway the UNESCO building was a large piece of architectural technology that brought to its clients and inhabitants a narrative of human progress. Photographs of the secretariat's construction highlighted the infrastructural connotations of its brutalist construction. And like the new highways of Tripoli and Baalbeck, the UNESCO House was designed from the start to bend around the monumental pattern of Paris. Urban diagrams

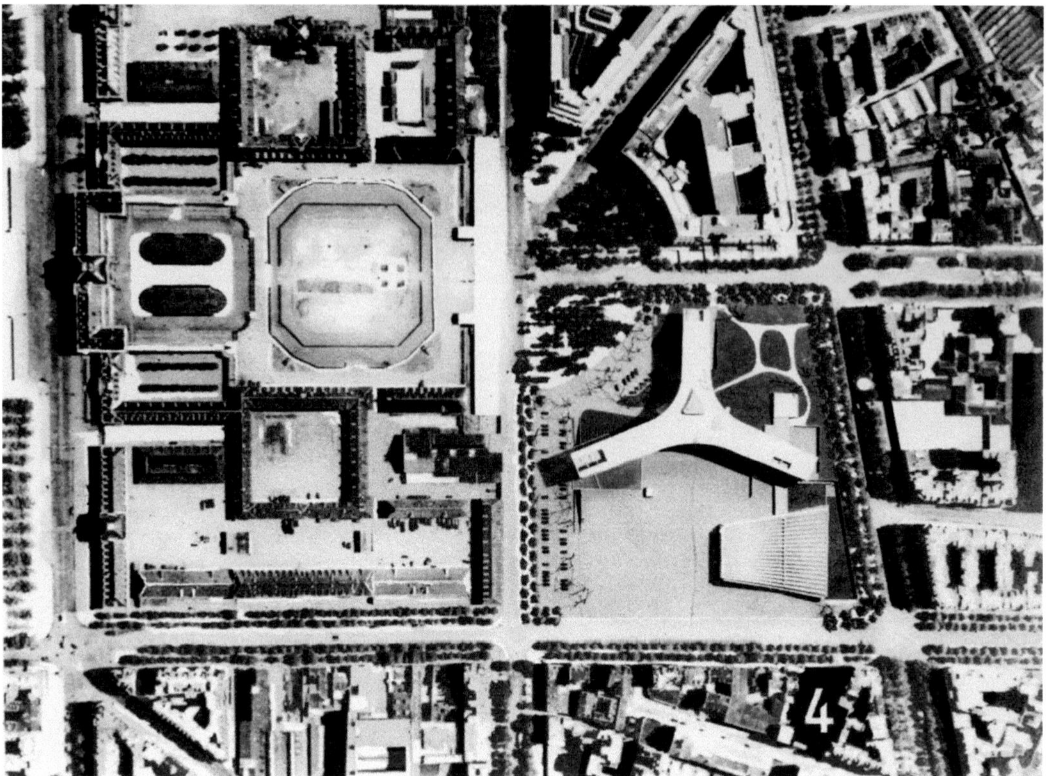

Figure B.5 Collage of the final schematic design for UNESCO House in Paris, on an aerial photograph of the site. From *UNESCO, Avant Projet, Place Fontenoy, Paris, 2 avril 1953* by Marcel Breuer, Bernard Zehrfuss, Pier Luigi Nervi (Paris: UNESCO, 1953).

included in the schematic sets showed the city as an outline traversed by the Seine and punctuated by a few monuments (figure B.6). These plans had originally been sketched out by Le Corbusier, and belong in a lineage of Corbusian work that begins in the 1920s, with the *Plan Voisin,* which blanked out Paris's city center, and reduced its historic fabric to a series of "vignettes."[8] Le Corbusier and his collaborators adopted a similar attitude to monumental Paris in the UNESCO design. But unlike his earlier urban polemics, where the city center was replaced with modernist housing and offices, here a single building helped to curate a modern city's monumental sights, with much less demolition.

It may seem anathema to compare UNESCO's work for heritage preservation on the one hand, and the design of its modern international secretariat on the other. But we should not let the apparent opposition between modernism and historicism fool us. To begin with, UNESCO House was itself conceived as a future monument. Even Evans tried his hand at a monumental rhetoric when he inaugurated the headquarters in a future-anterior mood in 1958, calling it "a structure which those who come after us may regard as a notable testimony to the genius of our age," and predicting that its "beauty" would "soon be recognized by all."[9] The building was a "testimonial" in the same sense that international lawyers had ascribed to intellectual property in the 1920s: an incubator of future value.

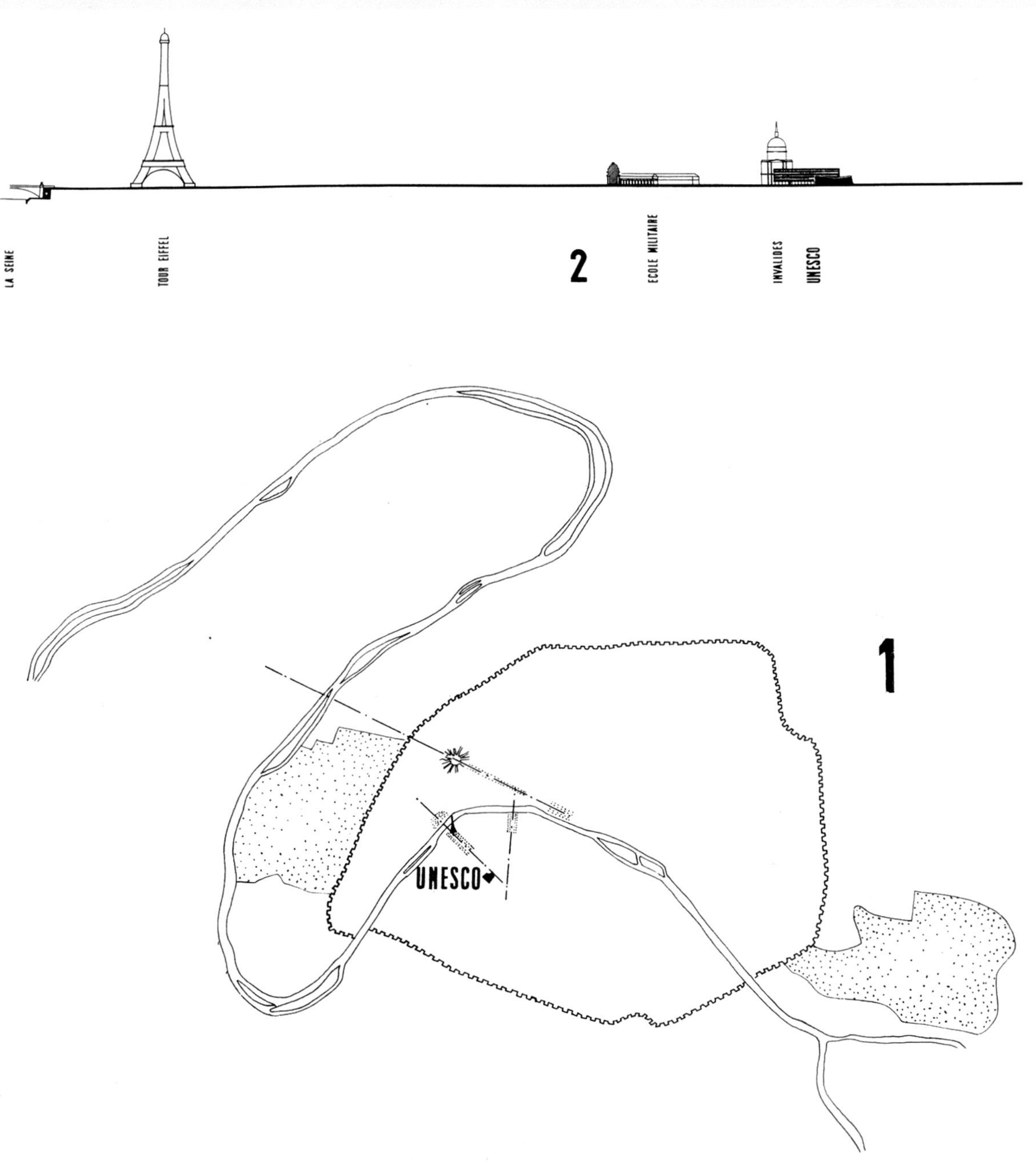

Figure B.6 Diagram of the city of Paris as an empty site traversed by the Seine and a series of monuments, from *UNESCO, Avant Projet, Place Fontenoy, Paris, 2 avril 1953* by Marcel Breuer, Bernard Zehrfuss, Pier Luigi Nervi (Paris: UNESCO, 1953).

Figure B.7 Marcel Breuer, Pier-Luigi Nervi, and Bernard Zehrfuss, UNESCO House (Paris). Unknown photographer. Marcel Breuer Papers 1920–1986, Archives of American Art, Smithsonian Institution.

Furthermore, UNESCO's heritage missions were not historicist but developmentalist—they sought to transform the past into a series of nodes, around which to weave a narrative. The UNESCO House site plan similarly curated and preserved a sequence of historical sights. Jacques-Ange Gabriel's École Militaire on the Place de Fontenoy was described as "preserved and protected" by the design. The roof garden of the Secretariat framed views of the Eiffel Tower and the dome of the Invalides, becoming one of the best places from which to photograph monumental Paris[10] (figure B.7). The Assembly Hall was even treated as a separate piece of architecture, a "hidden treasure" to be discovered along this infrastructural spine. Despite its unmistakably modernist *factura*, its "Egyptianizing" trapezoidal geometry also made it seem a building designed in a former age.[11]

Thus UNESCO House's architecture confirmed many of the emergent spatial characteristics of monuments we have seen in this book so far: the monument's status as an element in a touring circuit; its connection to infrastructural planning, and thus to destructive modernizations; and the elusive power of architecture as a collective art form against which theories of ownership and control of cultural goods could be tested. Yet unlike a highway or a dam, the UNESCO House was not only an instrument of urban planning but also an internationalist training ground. The main audience and constituency for this alignment between the narrative of development and architectural historicity was the bureaucrat making "rules for the world." After spending its first decade setting up "UNESCO Palaces" wherever the General Assembly traveled to hold its annual Conference (in Mexico City, Beirut, and Florence), the organization founded itself a House that brought home the lessons of monumental urban planning. This homing of UNESCO in Paris in 1958 can be seen as a starting point for the prodigious wave of re-functionalization of monuments that it would disseminate in the following decades. This wave is the subject of my next two chapters.

4 "Stones Also Die"

UNESCO AND THE DECOLONIZATION OF MUSEUMS, 1960–1975

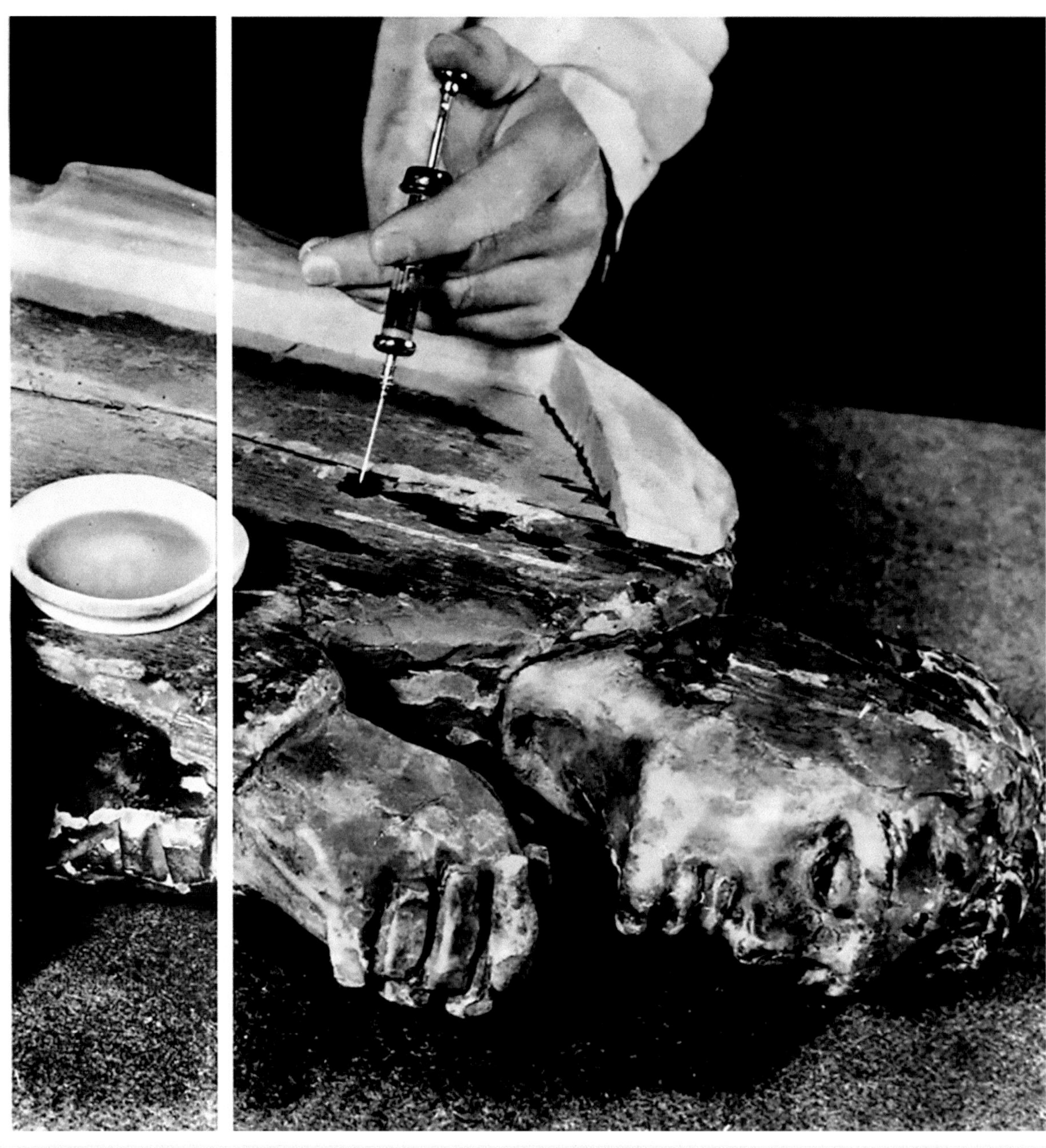

“Stones also die,” warned the Belgian museum conservator René Sneyers, in a 1965 special issue of the *UNESCO Courier* titled “Monuments in Peril.”[1] Edited by members of the organization’s Museums and Monuments Commission (MonCom), the journal showcased new directions in their initiatives for art and architecture. After two decades recovering from the experience of World War II, scenarios of emergency protection from war had waned, and the organization had turned its attention to more systemic risks. The dominant metaphor was with human life. Stones also died, and against this tendency of art and architecture to decay, conservators turned to “the new science of conservation” to set up patterns of long-term maintenance and ongoing palliative care. One two-page spread showed a wooden statue lying on a test-bed, receiving “an injection for immortality” from a lab-coated hand (figure 4.1).

Figure 4.1 “An Injection for Immortality” from “The New Science of Art Conservation,” *UNESCO Courier* 18 (January 1965), 9. © Solvay.

But this apparently benign medical metaphor was in fact borrowed from a highly polemical film, *Les statues meurent aussi* (“Statues also die”). Released by the Belgian filmmakers Chris Marker and Alain Resnais in 1953, it had almost immediately been banned by the French government for imputing the “death” of statues not to material decay but to colonialism. The haunting voice-over that opened the film indicted no less than the entire European culture industry as a “botany of death:”

> When men die, they enter into history.
> When statues die, they enter into art.
> This botany of death is what we call culture.[2]

The montage that ensued began among Gothic stone statues left to decay in the wild, and ended looking out from inside a museum showcase, alongside an African mask, under scrutiny from faces both white and black. The point was to show that European and African art objects “died” differently. Whereas European monuments were allowed to age, as the rest of the footage in the film showed, in Africa art objects were stolen and circulated, their makers brutally policed and dominated, all in full complicity with the human violence of

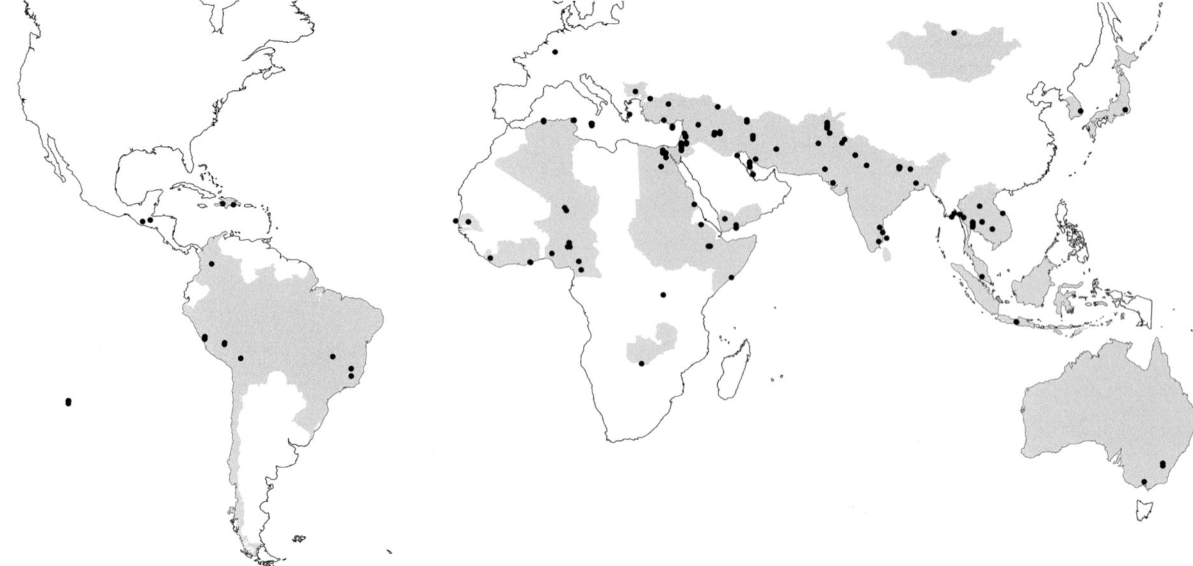

Figure 4.2 Lucia Allais, Map of every site visited by a mission delegated by UNESCO's monuments commission (MonCom) between 1960 and 1975. Data: UNESCO. © Lucia Allais.

colonial rule. So for Resnais and Marker, museum objects did not just "die." It was the institution of culture that killed them.

Twelve years later, the *Courier* tacitly redirected this critique. The French and Belgian colonies where Resnais and Marker had captured their footage were now independent nation-states. Indeed, seventeen new African nations joined UNESCO in 1960 alone. Many of these nations had leveraged some precolonial imaginary in their push for independence, promising that nationhood would also bring about a cultural renaissance. By 1965, the original membership of the organization had more than doubled. This southward shift in priorities would eventually lead to the election of Amadou M'Bow, the organization's first African Secretary-General, in 1975. Already in 1962, a *Courier* article had reopened the debate and questioned the idea that African museum pieces were still "meaningless relics," as Marker and Resnais had lamented.[3] Operating a subtle and strategic conflation, UNESCO's MonCom officials leveraged this anticolonial language to transform a "botany of death" into a science of cultural rebirth.

Between 1960 and 1975, UNESCO's heritage experts completed over a hundred fifty missions to states formerly controlled by colonial powers (figure 4.2). Wielding their influence as teachers of norms, they visited innumerable museums, monuments, and laboratories, and returned a plethora of recommendations for how to modernize them, or build new ones.[4] Funded through the United Nations' evolving Programs of Technical Assistance, and often coordinated through UN field offices, these missions were meant to trigger transfers of technology, funds, and expertise. But by far their more significant effect, I will argue, was the transfer of museums and monuments that empires had left behind into the hands of new states.

As Frederick Cooper and others have shown, during decolonization statehood itself was presented as a kind of inheritance, a legacy to be passed on from colony to nation.[5] The discourse of development that ushered new nations into the international system encouraged postcolonial leaders to think of independence as an administrative transition, not a political revolution.[6] In this context, the concept of cultural property offered unexpected advantages. Since the Hague Convention, the phrase had come to encompass a wide variety of material legacies spanning multiple scales, from objects, to buildings, and even "architectural ensembles."[7] The phrase implied historical depth, but also offered a vector for future capitalization. "Often," one official wrote, "a state that is poor in the economic sense is rich in cultural values."[8] But the logic of cultural property also dictated that such riches should remain at home. So, rather than being encouraged to trade their cultural objects, leaders of new nation-states hoping to join the international order were told that they could borrow, and borrow against, their own cultural heritage, which was not really owned by them at all, instead being effectively on loan to the state from its own people.[9]

My subject in this chapter is the architectural apparatus that was invented to leverage this slippage between heritage and inheritance, and render the nation-state knowable to its citizens as though in a museum. Every one of UNESCO's member-states was to be coursed through with a network of museums, whether free-standing or attached to (and inserted in) existing monuments. To construct these spaces, experts deployed the same repertoire of gestures through which the nation been comprehended in public museums since the Enlightenment: the design of itineraries; and the collection, disposition, and display of objects. They also drew on the many display architectures of the "exhibitionary complex," that formidable spatial apparatus that had developed in world fairs and exhibitions in the capital cities of the West, delivering the increasingly popular experience of being in a "world" designed only for visual consumption.[10] But UNESCO also augmented this repertoire with techniques that promised control over materiality itself. It is this material turn that we can hear in the shift from "statues also die" to "stones also die." The new emphasis on materiality, I will argue, gave a scientific sheen to the continuing assumption that tradition stands apart from (and prior to) modernity, and that a physical line should be drawn between them. Indeed, the new "science" also offered a panoply of new techniques for this line to be continually watched, monitored, even aesthetically contemplated. The primary design problem addressed in this chapter is therefore the boundary: the wall, the floor, the case, the vitrine, the window, the screen, and even "the open air"—anything that acted either as environmental enclosure or visual framing device, or both.

Historians of architectural heritage have argued that UNESCO's "object-focus" in this period came at the expense of other more "immaterial" or "spatial" dimensions of heritage.[11] But by performing an analysis of the spatial construct that *did* result from this object-fixation, I will reveal "space" not as an empty and frictionless plenum, but rather a space full of variation, materiality, activity, inflected by the Tropical Modernism that defines architecture as a dynamic rather than as a form. As in other chapters, then, destruction matters in my analysis because it was a way to replace certain patterns of building and making (and recording) with others.

The chapter is organized in a scalar progression from micro to macro. I begin with the conservation scientists who developed a playbook of chemical knowledge and administered the human capital in cultural institutions and their laboratories. I continue at the scale of the object, looking at the curators who designed object displays both in museum interiors and in the open-air. I conclude with the architects who invented principles of spatial continuity that were applicable to buildings of all kinds, from one-room huts, to modern museums, and sprawling monumental complexes. Conservation's imagined field of applicability was vast. While "the Tropics" were often invoked in UNESCO literature to legitimate this geographic breadth, it was the fiction of climate that drove its southward shift. For this reason, I have restricted my investigation to case studies in sub-Saharan Africa and, to a lesser extent, Southeast Asia, and I begin by navigating this field alongside one of its most ubiquitous denizens—the insect pest.

The Sample

Insects appeared in UNESCO's conservation literature in a 1968 manual titled *The Conservation of Cultural Property*, where no less than twenty-one species of "insect pests" were drawn, named, and categorized (figure 4.3). The creatures had also been trailed by a photographer as they burrowed through cultural property of all kinds: buildings, furniture, paint, books, wood, and even specimens of their own genus. This manual was the eleventh in UNESCO's Museums and Monuments series, and the first to present conservation as a normative practice, applicable wherever "individuals consider some object or artifact as being valuable."[12] But the subtitle promised *Special Reference to Tropical Conditions* and the map of the world locating the case studies in the book had the Northern Hemisphere cropped off. Dotted with sites in nations from Latin America, the Middle East and South-East Asia that had become independent in the 1940s and 1950s, and leaving blank all of Africa, where a second wave of independences was in full swing, the map implied a timeline of decolonization.

That colonies of pests appeared in UNESCO's literature at the same time as decolonization should come as no surprise; scholars of science and technology have long told us of the intertwined history of these two kinds of colonies.[13] In fact, pests serve as a useful guide for navigating how science figured in UNESCO's promise of cultural emancipation. To begin with, the insects

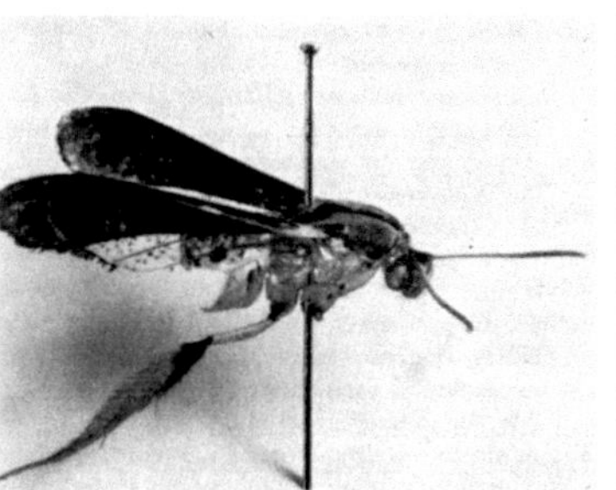

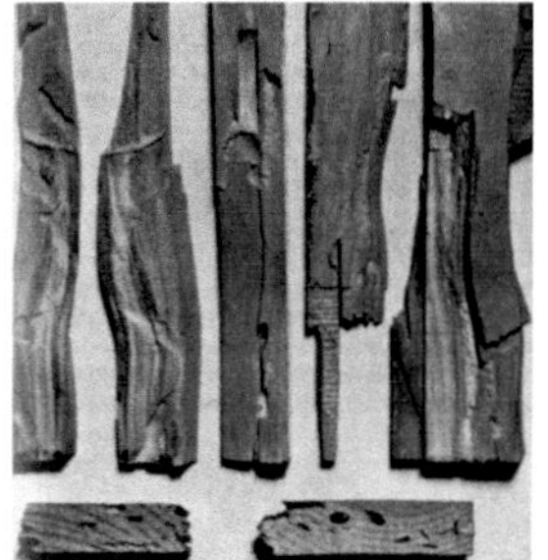

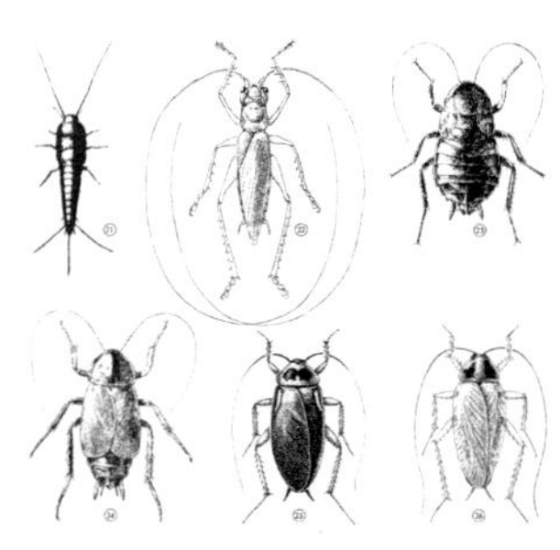

Figure 4.3 Insect pests illustrated in UNESCO's *The Conservation of Cultural Property, with Special Reference to Tropical Conditions*. Museums and Monuments 11 (Paris: UNESCO, 1968).

of the *Manual* evoke a deep history of coproduction of science and empire.[14] Colonial museums had been built for and by governors from the late 1890s to about 1940, to represent the colony as a more or less chaotic natural world to be encountered and dominated. Thus, even when they were also "art" museums, colonial museums functioned mostly as "scientific" collecting points for local curiosities of all kinds, including animal species, agricultural samples, human artifacts, and skulls.[15] By featuring mounted insects, UNESCO absorbed a legacy of colonial science that had collected them in the first place.

Second, the insects in the 1968 manual also appealed to a more recent branch of entomological science: a discourse about the "insect enemies of books" that had emerged in the early twentieth century among the rapidly professionalizing circles of European and American librarians and documentalists. For them, pests were not agents of nature but of culture. Manuals for bibliophiles described "burrowers" along with *human* threats to books, such as children, print sellers, inheritors, and, the worst human offender of all, "the borrower," who, ironically, depreciated the value of books by clumsily overusing them.[16] Similarly, the 1968 UNESCO Manual located pests in a branching tree of "causes of decay" of cultural objects, exactly at the intersection of human and environmental factors: the meeting point of "humidity" and "neglect."[17]

Insects carried this dual institutional pedigree (as object of colonial science and subject of metropolitan control) when they became an international "problem" in the postwar. Identified by the World Health Organization as vectors of malaria and targets of DDT, they were subjected to numerous United Nations initatives.[18] UNESCO took on the role of highlighting the presumed cultural aspects of malarial disease, such as its association with vernacular architecture. For example, one 1956 article titled "The Killer Insects of the World" showed a photograph of huts perched above a pond. These were "beautiful but . . .", the article warned, they acted as a nexus of insects and disease. Here, UNESCO recommended a combined remedy of science and architecture: first, to fumigate the hut, and eventually, to build modern housing.[19] The preferred solution recommended by the UN for such housing was the long and low horizontal section of Tropical Modernism that "caught as much breeze" as possible.[20] And so it would be for museums: UNESCO's 1968 *Conservation* manual recommended keeping insects out of museums and monuments by combining fumigation with "the design of buildings and furniture." Echoing the recommendations of the discourse on "tropical architecture" in modernism, where the insect was a proxy for Western discomfort in non-Western climes, and wielding similar data about the effect of climate on building construction, the manual recommended a conservation architecture that would be reactive to "climate and micro-climate."[21]

But there was also a major difference between housing people and protecting things. Whereas in tropical housing air was supposed to flow freely between inside and outside, in the museum the primary architectural task was enclosure, indeed, containment. The immense epistemic charge that was placed on museums as sites of protective interiority was illustrated in the manual's most famous diagram (figure 4.4a). Originally published by the director of the conservation laboratory at the British Museum, Harold Plenderleith, in his career-crowning *Conservation of Antiquities and Works of Art*, it showed three graphs tracking the "synchronous variations in humidity and temperature" of an object placed, first, in the open air, then inside a museum gallery, and finally inside a museum case.[22] The progressive flattening of these graphs illustrated the benefits of encasement, and implied a nesting of scales. The deeper-in the object, the flatter the curve.

But the search for chemical stability was elusive. Even when protected in a case, cultural matter always threatened to come alive again. As Paul Coremans, the editor of UNESCO's 1968 *Conservation* manual (and Plenderleith's counterpart at the Royal Laboratory in Brussels, Belgium), put it:

> When we glance casually at a museum object in its showcase, we tend to think that the object is inert and that the matter composing it is no longer subject to change. Nothing could be more untrue. . . . it is very much "alive".[23]

In other words, there would never be a flat curve. Rather, the three graphs exemplified the triumph of a bio-chemical view of art, which allowed the materials operative at microscale to be conceived as continuous as that of the macroscale. "Conservation [wa]s necessary," he wrote, "because matter is in constant evolution."[24] Conservators were needed to monitor this evolution.

This self-fashioning of the museum conservator as a manager of material variation was constitutive of conservation as an international field of expertise in the 1950s. Plenderleith and Coremans were protagonists in the midcentury shift from "passive" to "active" art conservation, where organic conservation materials (such as egg whites and wax) gave way to synthetic ones (such as epoxy glue).[25] In fact, the second manual to be published in the Museums and Monuments series was devoted to one of the most contentious episodes in the

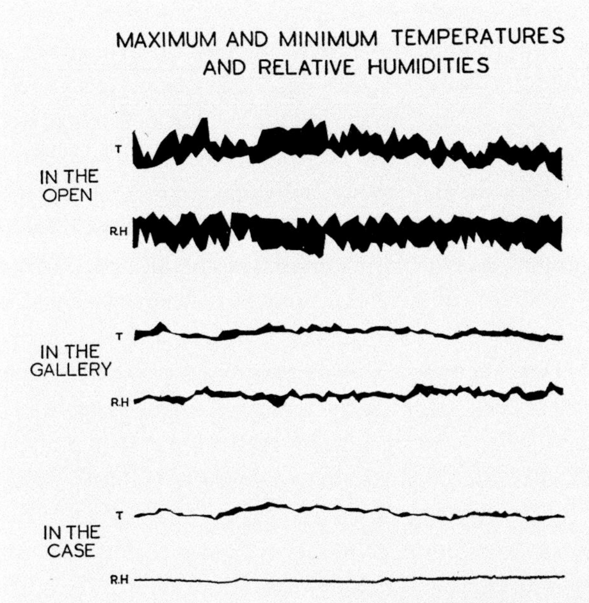

Figure 4.4 a. Variations in temperature and relative humidity in a London gallery over four months, published in H. J. Plenderleith, *The Conservation of Antiquities and Works of Art* (London: Oxford University Press, 1956). b. Maintenance work at the temple of Borobudur. *UNESCO Courier* (1968). Photo: Tor Gjesdal.

history of art conservation: the controversy over the so-called Exhibition of Cleaned Pictures at London's National Gallery of Art in 1946–1947.[26] The debate had pitted British, French, Belgian, and Italian conservators against one another, and ultimately thrown into question a century's worth of amateur conservation, with its attendant Romantic assumptions about what one side called *patina* and the other called dirt. Just as during World War II, when the polemics on *whether* to save monuments were eclipsed by debates over *how* to do it, here too old battle-lines between pro- and anti-cleaning gave way to a spectrum of positions about the *means* for cleaning, rather than its rationale.

In that volume, Coremans offered an early and explicit defense of science in the museum. The chemist and physicist were often viewed with suspicion, he readily admitted, because in their hands the museum object "ceased to be a work of art" and instead was "treated as a collection of particles with chemical and physical properties, which the uninitiated c[ould] never understand."[27] But Coremans assured readers that he and his colleagues were also artisans, whose hand was "guided by intelligence, sensitivity and a complete respect for the object."[28] Here then the role of insects in the UNESCO manuals becomes clear: they were avatars for the conservators. An inscrutable and difficult-to-remove species, with secret insights into the inner workings of art, they watched over objects others left behind—conservators were the sentinels of art.[29]

Thinking of conservators as in-house sentinels in a perilous environment helps us understand how museums and monuments fit in UNESCO's contribution to development economics, in two ways. First, conservation science offered not one value (not one "curve") but stabilization as a narrative: a controllable process, over time, to which economic growth could be tethered.[30] The constant "evolution" and potential devolution of the material's substrate was the kernel of cultural value that could be exploited for the national economic good. Second, if these charts carried forth a naturalist epistemology, where the distinction between inside and outside was one of degrees, cultural work on the contrary consisted in delimiting a specific scale in which the object could continue to exist distinctly, as such. It was only as an object that cultural matter was valued on the international market, even if it never left its case or was never traded abroad. Indeed, it was not by selling or even exchanging their objects that nations would exploit art as cultural capital; it was by serializing conservation. UNESCO's economic proposal for museum development, then, was to ask northern nations to invest in "training fellowships" that turned citizens of new southern states into conservators and laboratory technicians. This new cultural labor force, by monitoring art's material substrate, would do the work of international capitalization.

Labor is of course a crucial component in any economic development scheme. But here, the production of culture depended on an isomorphism between the artisan as a subject and the artifact as an object, both of which could be cultured in a laboratory. Listen for instance to a summary report about Paul Coremans's visit to the temples of Borobudur in 1962:

> Coremans took samples of the stone making up the monument. The stones were analyzed in Brussels and identified as a form of andesite, their composition being the key to their degradation by bacterial and cryptogrammic action. An Indonesian was given a fellowship to study laboratory techniques in Brussels.[31]

Traveling to the field, the conservator had returned with two samples: a piece of stone to test, and a citizen to train (figure 4.4b). This was described as an exchange—a stone is taken, a fellowship is given back. In this process, the postcolonial subject was treated as a sample of his environment, carrier of a quintessential substance from which the new state could be grown.

This process of exchange echoes Bruno Latour's theorization of "science in action," and his depiction of the modern laboratory as a space constitutive of the nation-state, characterized by mobility and scalability. In the example studied by Latour, Louis Pasteur gradually made his laboratory more mobile in the nineteenth century by bringing together laboratory and farm, scientist and veterinarian, microscale of the microbe and macroscale of agriculture.[32] What was produced was a new substance—a vaccine—that both carried and conquered disease. Similarly, throughout the 1960s UNESCO began to use museum laboratories and their various classes of inhabitants to construct nation-states as cultural "fields." As with Pasteur, the goal was to create something akin to a vaccine: "a very small nucleus of technicians that should acquire basic knowledge of ancient materials, of their degradation and conservation and who can . . . assist in the field."[33] This process happened in several steps.

A number of national conservation laboratories had been established in Europe in the midcentury, including under Coremans in Belgium and Plenderleith in Britain. In 1958 UNESCO set out to expand this European constellation into a global network by establishing its own center in Rome, the International Center for the Conservation and Restoration of Cultural Property (ICCROM). Rome was chosen because it already had the Istituto Centrale del Restauro (ICR) whose director, Cesare Brandi, had developed an extensive network of conservators who practiced a hybrid of science and artisanal craft. Rome was also chosen because Italy offered a better financial package than its competitors, and a supply of local teachers.[34] Rome was also, crucially, closer to former colonies. Over the next decades many British and Francophone practitioners came through Rome to train or be trained before going south, all of them going to former colonies but using UNESCO to purge themselves of any colonial associations.[35]

ICCROM's teaching philosophy was, on its face, materialist: it presented conservation as that branch of chemistry that is concerned with "the behavior of materials."[36] The syllabus that Plenderleith and Coremans devised for all ICCROM trainees was structured around raw materials (woods, textiles, paper, skins, stone, metal, bone). Each section began with lectures on the "foundational knowledge of the chemistry" for one material, continued with a taxonomy of artworks fashioned out of it, and concluded with the techniques for conserving them.[37] This was then complemented with applied laboratory lessons.

But when ICCROM set out to globalize this conservation network beginning in the 1960s, this materialism was tweaked to fit the conditions of the post-colony. In 1960 Coremans had opened an article with the authoritative statement that "Man is the worst enemy of works of art." Five years later, he wrote: "the climate is the prime cause of the deterioration of cultural property."[38] In the tropics, the diagnosis of an object's state of conservation came with an evacuation of human agency, decay now being attributed to climate. The further afield ICCROM experts conducted their work, the more human agency was evacuated from their theory of material decay.

Meanwhile, European conservators at home increasingly devoted their "pure research" to finding deep ties between various stylistic traditions and their soil of origin, in part by studying the material samples they brought home from UNESCO missions. For example, in the 1965 *Courier* Plenderleith presented a tropical material called "laterite" as "the next frontier of laboratory research in material science." Laterite, he explained, was a building material quarried in ready-to-use brick form. Having already been "baked" by the earth, so to speak, it made an optimal and workable artistic medium, but lateritic art and architecture were also inherently vulnerable to erosion—their very existence being somehow already destructive.[39] Recent scholarship has shown that the category of "laterite," invented by nineteenth-century natural historians, describes such a wide variety of materials that it points more to the desire to unify the tropics conceptually than to their morphological coherence.[40] The verb "laterization" was even coined to denote a specific kind of decay, which was then hypothetically blamed for the "decline of the civilization of Mesopotamia."[41] In other words, the great unifying material of the tropics was described in great scientific detail as having been designed to defeat conservation.

This definition of tropical materials, as self-decaying, was echoed in the treatment of postcolonial citizens as a material substrate from which new nations could be grown or built. The prevailing ethos trainees were taught at ICCROM was "integrity," a word that was applied not only to the matter from which cultural objects had been crafted but to the trainee too.[42] As we will see in the next chapter, the discourse of integrity became increasingly prominent in UNESCO's work as more large-scale engineering became necessary for monument salvage projects in the 1970s and 1980s. Already at the scale of the individual, the student who came to Rome (or Brussels) from former colonies was evaluated for his "integrity." Invariably, teachers were disappointed: students were described as being subject to inscrutable chemical imbalances, struggling to "acclimate" to life in the city and having difficulty "absorbing the substance of the teaching."[43] In response, UNESCO moved its laboratories closer to the field, opening a series of Regional Training Centers: in New Dehli, India; in Jos, Nigeria; and eventually in Churubusco, Mexico. The Pasteurian logic of transplanting laboratory life was followed again, now grafting trainees closer to their countries of origin. In these regional centers, administrators were encouraged "to develop a distinctive bias in the arts and crafts."[44] This might seem at first glance to mean that they would have the same "artisanal" know-how that Coremans and Plendeleith reserved for themselves. But in fact to be an artisan in a regional center meant producing objects for sale to visitors.

Figure 4.5 Lucia Allais, Provenance of students who received a fellowship to the training center in Jos (Nigeria) between 1963 and 1974. Data from UNESCO, *Report on the Regional Training Centre for the Preservation of Cultural and Natural Heritage at Jos, Nigeria* (JIU/REP/74/8). © Lucia Allais.

That conservation science helped erase colonial meanings, while salvaging colonial-era administrative setups, is most vividly illustrated by visiting the "Training Center for Museum Technicians" that UNESCO opened in 1963 in Jos, on the Central plateau of Nigeria. As a regional center, it hosted students from neighboring African nations on internationally awarded six-week scholarships. Jos's own vibrant museum scene would serve as incubator and testing grounds[45] (figure 4.5). There was a museum, a zoo, a pottery workshop, and a collection of structures built with modified tribal techniques—huts with doors; a restaurant shaped as a palace. Jos had already hosted several meetings of the Museum Association of Middle Africa / Museum Association of Tropical Africa (AMAT-MATA).[46] Under UNESCO, students from over 30 African nations traveled to Jos in 15 years to train in laboratory conservation. Just as with ICCROM, UN inspectors periodically reported that the students were

Figure 4.6 Students training outside of their living quarters at the Jos Center for the Training of African Museum Technicians. Technicians, circa 1964. Photographer unknown.

unable to "think technically" and had "trouble with abstraction." But closer scrutiny of their reports shows it was the debased materialism of the ICCROM syllabus that was ill-suited to the field. For example, practice in wood treatment proved difficult because there simply weren't any deteriorated wood objects around.[47] Furthermore, the course did not teach the history of British mining in Nigeria, which would have explained that the Jos Museum had been opened as "mineralogical museum," filled first with specimens from Nigeria's mines, and only secondly with the archaeological artifacts found inside these mines (figure 4.6).

Thus conservation trainees were prevented from confronting the colonial origins of the institutional lineage on which UNESCO depended heavily. But they encountered this lineage in daily interaction with the museum staff. A student working in Jos would have encountered three overlapping generations of colonial and postcolonial actors (figure 4.7). First, there was Sylvia Leith-Ross, who helped run the pottery studio for women at the museum. She had first come to Nigeria as the wife of a colonial British governor, and subsequently spent a career educating, or training, colonized women to make objects. In a continuation, she returned to Jos to help teach indigenous pottery, often expressing nostalgia not only for lost skill but also loss of colonial paperwork—since it would have been impolitic for her to be nostalgic for colonialism itself.[48] Second, there was the built legacy of Bernard Fagg, a progressive anthropologist who had been a member of AMAT-MATA. It was Fagg who been the first to find and study the now-famous Nok scuptures that have been identified as the oldest surviving art objects on the African continent. It was Fagg who lobbied the colonial administrations for funds to expand the existing Jos Museum to conserve them, and who had personally designed and directed the construction of much of the site's neo-vernacular architecture between 1950 and 1963.[49] Fagg returned to England in 1963, and was replaced by Ekpo Eyo, who would eventually become the first Nigerian-born head of Nigeria's antiquities department and who forms the third link in this human chain. Eyo knew first-hand that Jos's museum growth in the late colonial years was owed largely to the willingness of actors like Leith-Ross and Fagg to take a hands-on approach and build their practices into the local social fabric. But he gently critiqued the theories of material degeneration that fueled this intertwinement of making and curating. Instead Eyo adopted a social view of art. "Material decay," he wrote, "is not the greatest danger to the preservation of works of art and craft. Such danger comes from the disintegration of the old social struc-

Figure 4.7 Three generations of cultural property keepers at the Jos Museum. a. Sylvia Leith-Ross in the pottery workshop. Photographer unknown. b. Bernard Fagg with Chief Obalara. Photographed by W. B. Fagg (400. WBF.1953.05.11), 1953 © RAI. c. Ekpo Eyo (1964). Photographer unknown.

ture which was based on indigenous religion and a sustenance economy."[50] Eyo's mentor had been Fagg's brother William Fagg, who was also an Africanist. Fagg hypothesized that continuity in carving traditions originated in insects' continual eating away at wood objects. But Eyo dissented; "continuity," he wrote, "originates in families of carvers who train the younger generations as they come along." It is all the more remarkable, then, that despite this knowing critique Eyo recommended not abolishing museums in Nigeria but rather *proliferating them*, because they were the only way to "encourage and protect" a disappearing class of artisans.[51]

Colonial amateur, museum pioneer, and first-generation cultural leader—all agreed, that the Jos museum should survive after independence. This is because, as the rest of the chapter shows, the legitimacy of the museological structure—the power of "encasement"—was never explained by science alone, but also included a power of aesthetic framing.

The Case

To justify its interest in art objects, UNESCO's Cultural Affairs Division adopted the developmentalist line that to collect objects was to preserve a way of life. Museums were to "build up representative collections," by this logic, "before the old patterns of living, worship, etc. break down or disappear."[52] The idea of remediating the disappearance of traditions by collecting objects was not new. ICCROM and the MonCom built on a lineage of colonial object-hunting missions that began in the late nineteenth century and continued well past World War I.[53] The 1932 Mission Dakar-Djibouti was an especially important precedent. Sent by the French state in 1932 to sweep across its African colonies and collect objects for its new Musée Ethnologique (later Musée de l'Homme), it followed in the wake of Christian "missions" but adopted a documentarian, scientific ethos.[54] The objects brought back by these missions were engulfed into the primitivist artistic and literary fervor that was consuming Paris.[55] In a phenomenon James Clifford calls "ethnographic surrealism," the science of exhibition that was spun around this mission (named "museology" after the specifically French "ethnology") borrowed techniques from art museums and attached them to anthropological categories such as the gift, the fetish, and the totem. The effect, as he argues, was a ritualization of museum-going itself.[56] By the time UNESCO came onto the scene, this ethnographic aesthetics had become constitutive of the international culture industry that Resnais and Marker had critiqued, African objects and all.

Among the many continuities between prewar Parisian ethnology and UNESCO's postwar work, two are relevant here, aside from the reliance on the "mission" as a method: the epistemological conceit of the "object-as-witness" (where objects were collected, valued, and displayed because they can "testify" to the contexts of their making); and the person of George-Henri Rivière.[57]

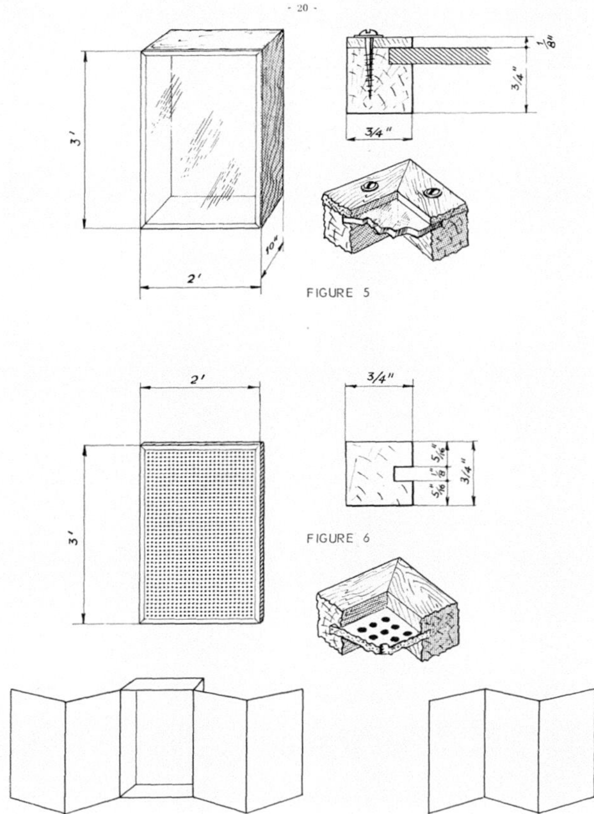

Figure 4.8 Diagrammatic instructions for building a museum showcase. From United Nations Report no. ESD-17-A, *Museum Techniques in Fundamental Education*, Educational Studies and Documents 17 (Paris: UNESCO, 1957).

Rivière had been one of the founding curators of the Musée de l'Homme, and became Associate Director of the International Council of Museums (ICOM) in the 1950s, and a dominant voice in UNESCO's museum work.[58] ICOM was an especially powerful institution in that it relied on an international network of museum personalities which was semi-independent from that of governments. It prepared a monthy journal, *Museum*, that was published by UNESCO and continued the tradition of transnational publication from the prewar *Mouseion*.

Rivière was especially invested in the atmospherics of exhibition design and his main instrument was the museum showcase, or *vitrine*. During his tenure at ICOM, the museum vitrine turned into a global norm. Showcases, in every possible shape and size, accessible from every direction, were detailed for different occasions and budgets (figure 4.8). High-end versions included light and air-conditioning, low-tech ones simply kept out dust and insects.[59] Vitrines were hardly new; but in internationalist hands encasement became a technique of nation-building. In fact, an implicit visual sequence can be detected in the pages of *Museum*: from altar-like symmetrical arrangements of objects, to matrix-like disposition; from ad-hoc displays on crowded shelves and stools, to fixed objects isolated or grouped by type; from informal labeling

Figure 4.9 Bakuba Room at the Museum of Art and Folklore in Luluabourg, Congo. From *Museum* 13, no. 2 (1960). Photographer unknown.

to maps and graphics orienting viewers in a universe of vitrines (figure 4.9). Although many of these reforms had occurred in the late empire, a casual reader would be forgiven for thinking that the decolonization of African museums had given rise to a continent-wide encasement.

None of these new display techniques changed the main epistemological conceits of colonial museography: the organization of collections by tribal provenance, rather than any identification by author or date. These categories were essential to the "institutional segregation" characteristic of late-imperial indirect rule.[60] In the post-colony, this provenance was still recorded in paperwork, displayed on labels, and increasingly also maintained via live performances of the persons from villages from whence the objects would be collected, sometimes now hired as guards for the museums. A photograph of the Kampala Museum in Uganda, for instance, showed these performers wearing uniforms and playing music on a platform, lifted and encased, as it were, as tidily as the vitrine objects behind them.[61] The architecture of vitrines therefore reinforced the nesting of scales found in the three-part "micro/macroclimate" graph of conservation science: the postcolonial subject confined to a modernist interior, the tribal object contained in a modernist vitrine, and the postcolonial museum out in the ethnographic field.

The Open Air

ICCROM's materialist frame functioned not only for objects in their cases but also subjects and their social milieu. Like Ekpo Eyo, many post-independence leaders hoped involvement with internationalists would offer a chance to remediate the risk of "deculturation" that came from inheriting a recently developed colonial museum.[62] The most successful by far was the Senegalese president and poet Leopold Senghor, who in 1966 orchestrated the Festival Mondial des Arts Nègres (FESMAN) in Dakar, to coalesce a *new* African literary and artistic movement. Senghor repurposed the museological apparatus of colonialism, with much support from UNESCO and the French government. Indeed, in a massive appropriation of the collecting techniques and aesthetic conceits of the Mission Dakar-Djibouti, Senghor mobilized UNESCO's experts in over a dozen missions to support his project.[63] Conversly, the Festival planted the seed for innumerable other UNESCO missions in Africa in the subsequent decade.[64] The centerpiece of this project, architecturally, was the "Dynamic Museum" (Musée Dynamique) in Dakar (figure 4.10). From the outside, it recalled a classical temple, with blank walls and a colonnade all around, but on the inside the building borrowed its name and section from the eponymous "Dynamic Museum" of Neuchâtel, Switzerland, which had been founded by Swiss museum director Jean Gabus. Like Rivière, Gabus was one of ICOM's most active members and throughout the 1950s he used the organization to popularize a design method he called "dynamic museography." What he meant by "dynamic" architecturally was flexibility in plan and fluidity in section.[65] Like Rivière's vitrine-building details, the wall section for this building was reproduced innumerable times in UNESCO's publications. Like Rivière, Gabus thought spatial disposition was the "basic datum"of an exhibition, but he made much of the nature of ethno*graphic* work as a kind of writing. All objects were witnesses in the sense that they were made to look like evidence, or traces, of daily life as a kind of mark-making.[66]

Thus Gabus's dynamic architecturalization of the "object as witness" recalls a theme this book has been following since chapter 1: that the object or monument is a "testimonial" of sorts. Gabus designed and specified the vitrines for the FESMAN, which were constructed in Zurich and shipped and assembled in Dakar. Lit from within, standing tall in the space, they offered a place from which African citizens could deambulate around objects that had always in some sense looked at them from the other side of the vitrine, aptly witnessed from the gallery above. A documentary film made by the US Information Agency about the Festival even made an explicit homage to Resnais and Marker: it opened with a sequence of shot-counter-shots of a Nok sculpture, then a Ugandian statuette, then a manuscript, and other African-made human figures, until this montage of faces was revealed to be taking place in the Dynamic Museum, where the faces of famous black visitors, jazz musician

Figure 4.10 Exhibition "Art Nègre" at the Musée Dynamique in Dakar, 1966. Photo: Maya Bracher © Musée Dynamique Neufchâtel.

Duke Ellington among them, examined these objects in their glowing vitrines.[67] The Musée Dynamique became the setting for a massive postcolonial "looking back."

But the greatest impact of Gabus's dynamic museography as a tool for decolonization lay beyond the museum walls. In 1972, UNESCO held a seminar for museum directors in Livingston where Senegalese cultural official Abdoulaye Diop announced a continent-wide shift in interest from the "museum-building" to the "museum complex."[68] If the colonial museum had been static; its postcolonial successor would be dynamic, which meant thinking in terms of the "open-air." Several tribal compounds had already functioned as museums since the early twentieth century, as Anne Gaugue has put it, "places where one teaches Africans their own culture."[69] Diop's preferred example was the recent National Museum of Niamey: an open-air compound whose plan outline was in the shape of the national territory of Niger, and which contained full-scale mock-ups of its regional building types. Its Portuguese director, Pablo Toucet, vaunted that it "might have been established in any city on the African continent, or in the world." This statement recalls the logic of what Carol Duncan and Alan Wallach call "the universal survey museum," with its claim that it "could be anywhere in the Western world."[70] But its location was in fact tied very literally to the backyard of colonialism: it had been established in the parking lot behind the local offices of the IFAN (Institut Francais d'Afrique Noire) in 1958, two years before the French colony had become the Republic of Niger.[71]

UNESCO's missions encouraged this practice of creating open-air museums out of tribal compounds. But rather than shaping the grounds in an image of the national territory as Toucet had, they inserted a formal-material abstraction into the geometry and materiality of buildings. For example, as part of UNESCO's contribution to the Festival, Gabus and his team toured the former French colony of Dahomey for two days in 1964, spending one at the Royal Palaces of Abomey, which had been burned in a scorched earth campaign by the departing chief.[72] The French colonial authorities had partially restored it, vaunting it as the first African museum to be "housed in buildings stylistically suitable for the contents."[73] But Gabus went further, calling for more architectural missions to make objects out of the buildings themselves. The architect Jean Crozet followed two years later, in a mission where he performed a documentary procedure that took data from the site and built it into its restored materials (figure 4.11). First, he secured a hand-drawn plan of one of the ruined palace buildings from remaining members of the Agoli Agbo tribal family. This single-line annotated sketch was reproduced as a document in the UNESCO report. Then, in a "hypothetical reconstruction," he transformed this sketch into a set of construction drawings, complete with instructions specifying where "traditional technique (TT)" was to be used (for example, replacing sheet-metal roofs with thatch) and where "adapted modern technique (TMA)" would do (for example, new floors throughout the interior).[74] As formal and material finishes were applied to its buildings, the open-air museum became a collection of things. And since the know-how to build this architecture was disappearing, Gabus also recommended "fixing the current state" of the architecture, "without interpretation," *in a model* to be displayed in the central room of the main house.[75] When Crozet followed up, he raised this room by three steps, to make an architectural pedestal for the model, taking advantage of the fact that the French government was already re-planking the floor. The building, effectively, became a vitrine for itself.

In this manner, and under UNESCO's watch, the open-air museum also became one of the birthplaces of the distinction between tangible (artistic) and intangible (folkloric) categories of heritage. Interest in the intangible had been percolating during the planning of the FESMAN, as it became clear that most of the objects on display would be on loan from the West, and the "participation of African states" would be performative.[76] Tribal ritual, also, began to count as heritage: Gabus insisted that objects he collected for the Festival

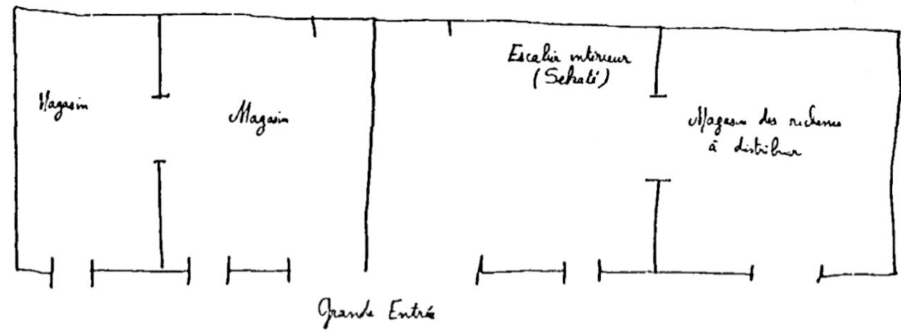

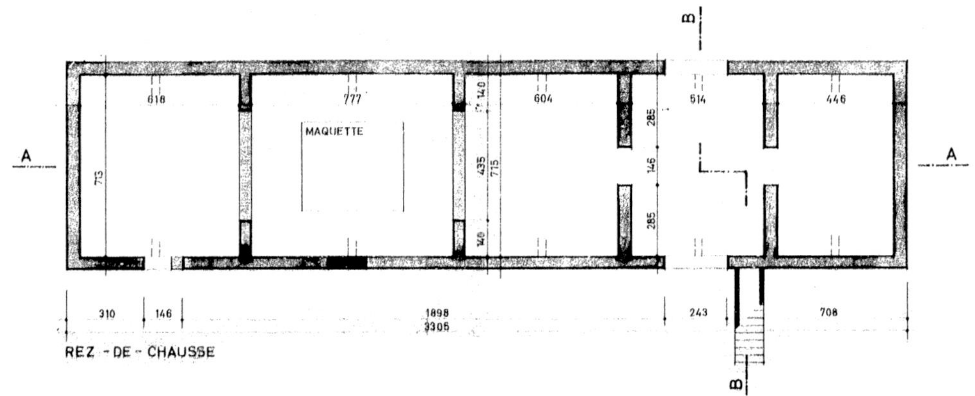

Figure 4.11 The palace of Abomey in Dahomey: a. Sketch plan of one building by a member of the tribal family, and plan drawing of the same building, showing a model room second from left. From Jean Crozet, *Dahomey: Étude de la restauration et de la mise en valeur des palais royaux d'Abomey* (Paris: UNESCO, July 1968). UNESCO 640/BMS.RD/CLT. b. Palace of King Guézo photographed by Jean Gabus during the roof's replacement. © Musée Dynamique de Neuchâtel.

were "functional treasures" which would "recover their ritual function and power" when they were returned to a chiefdom.[77] In the aftermath of the Dakar Festival, UNESCO recommended that wherever objects were to be conserved for posterity, crafts were to be performed on demand. Architecturally too: the modernizations of museum interiors usually brought with them new buildings for "workshops" to house "artisans" who made and sold so-called traditional objects, including replicas of those on display in the museum. As Anne Doquet has suggested, the bringing of commercialized crafts into an art market had the effect of stultifying innovation in both realms.[78] More to the point, these newly built artisanal workshops offered the visitor an experience of what a colonial museum had been (before independence): a small, usually one-room space, cramped with shelves full of objects that were unlabeled and accessible to touch.

Senghor and the other leaders of the FESMAN worked hard to convince their audience that the division of tasks within the nascent cultural diplomacy was willful: the European, a born classifier, would take care of objects; the African was a born performer in charge of "intangible" things. But in fact, it is more accurate to say that modern African objects became international heritage by being authorized by *two kinds* of immaterial practices: those of artisans, priests, and tribal leaders, who "performed" various rituals that certified their authenticity, and those of internationalist experts, whose equally ritualized visits were allowed to leave paperwork behind.

Despite its apparent bureaucratic dryness, UNESCO's notational style of architectural design—hatching, single-line drawing, coding of details—brought radical changes to sites across Africa. There was some debate about whether such inscriptions and annotations could be legible in architectural objects themselves. In 1968 Crozet followed in Gabus's footsteps on a visit to the Palace of Foumban in Cameroun, where tribal chief Njoya had built a palace in what was described as an "eclectic European style"[79] (figure 4.12). The palace had suffered major sagging, and Gabus and Crozet recommended a number of "consolidations" to "restore its initial appearance."[80] Ignoring ad hoc repairs (an added buttress, some concrete patching), they recommended an entirely new structural system for the upper floor. Rather than resting upon the elegant arches below, the second floor would be *cantilevered* off the healthy part of the building. This new, hidden, and definitely modern structural feat paradoxically enabled a far-reaching re-vernacularization of the palace on its exterior, through the "restoration" of decorative details that had been removed to lighten the building's load on its sagging foundations: re-flooring and re-planking of ceilings, standardization of balconies and railings with solid wood, and replacement of the corrugated sheet metal roof with tile.

Crozet's design made the internal structure modern, so the outward details could remain vernacular. But the king, Njoya, who was himself well-versed in the art of conserving crucial elements of his rule while transforming others,

Figure 4.12 a. King Njoya in the Foumban Palace. Photo by Ana Rein-Wuhrmann. Used with permission from Défap-Service protestant de mission, Paris. b. André Lézine drawing of new ceiling finish. From *Afghanistan: Conservation et restauration des monuments historiques* (Paris: UNESCO, January 1964). UNESCO WS/1263–25 BMS.

countered with his own scriptural and modernization practices. He authored two documents that were entered into the historical record as appendices to UNESCO reports. One of them was an architectural history of the compound, explaining that despite its "European style" it was an authentic tribal object, made with local labor and materials.[81] He also recorded this history in mural paintings across the compound. So where Gabus made an architectural model to arrest time, and Crozet used style to preempt architectural evolution, Njoya thought of monuments *as* documents of his rule.

The concept of the open-air museum, where air is the encasing material, did not eliminate the need for a science of materials and of chemistry. The tacit debate that had been born of vitrines and objects—where should the boundary between modernity and tradition be located, and should the visitor see it?—was reconfigured, as the line was increasingly *built in* to material artifacts. This debate unfolded in the background of many other UNESCO missions, and not always between local rulers and international visitors. Consider a UNESCO mission to Afghanistan—a nation that had been coursed through by a network of archaeologists since independence in 1919—to consolidate the state's control of cultural property. André Lézine, the French expert sent by UNESCO, brought with him a preference for reconstituting all monuments as legible objects.[82] After a one-month tour of over 20 sites, he made far-reaching recommendations in a report that included two or three architectural drawings per site. At Mosa-ee Logar he designed the wood formwork to be used in the reconstruction of the dome; in Herat he drew corner details that would give back to the Ghoride Gate at the Great Mosque its sharp edges; at the Bamyian Buddhas, he drew a typical section to smooth the brick profile of the niches. And, to publicize this work, he also proposed to transform the entrance hall of the Kabul National Museum into a "museum of historic monuments," where vitrines built into the piers would display images of the transformation of the nation into a field of crisply legible (and camera-friendly) monumental objects.[83]

Everywhere Lézine traveled, he condescendingly recorded local conservation practices, and recommended alternatives. But he reserved his greatest scorn for the work of an Italian architect, Andrea Bruno, who had traveled independently with the Istituto Italiano del Medio Oriente (ISMEO) and who aimed specifically to leave traces of his conservation work behind.[84] For example, in restoring some mausoleums whose piers were compromised, Bruno had worked with local craftsmen to create new bricks from new, more durable materials, specifying that these should be a different color, so that the resulting piers showed a visible line between old bricks and new (figure 4.13).

Essentially, Lézine and Bruno deployed similar tools for vastly different ends. Bruno designed frames that would appear alternatively or disappear from different vantage points; Lézine in contrast insisted on the crispness of the building's outer edge, a kind of built-in "frame." Compare the drawings each made when they visited the large Buddha at Bamyian. Lézine drew a

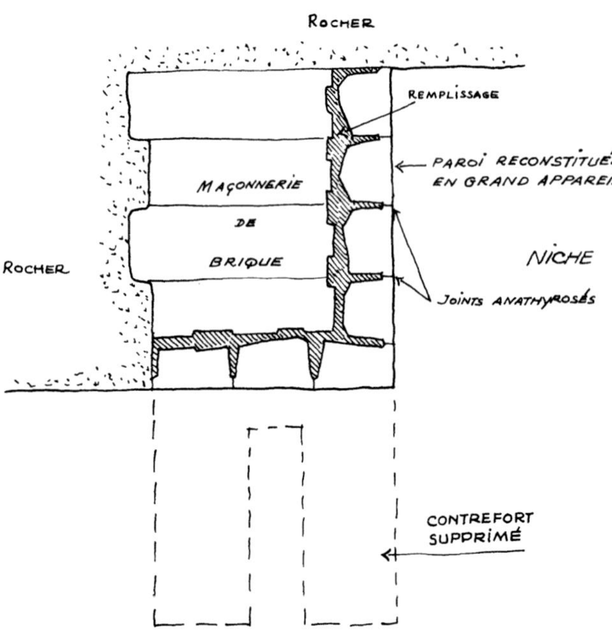

Figure 4.13 Two approaches to detailing masonry in Afghanistan. a. André Lézine, Detail for the niche of the small Buddha at Bamiyan, UNESCO, *Afghanistan: Conservation et restauration des monuments historiques* (January 1964). b. Andrea Bruno, Photograph of new brick work at Rhazni Rausa, 1960. *East and West* 13, no. 2–3 (June–September 1962). © Andrea Bruno.

section through the niche that showed how the stone would get progressively finer towards the outer edge. Bruno, on the other hand, designed an invisible museum to be sunk underground in the valley facing the Buddhas. In a clever design involving a tapered viewing oculus, Bruno's building framed a circular view of the colossus's head, visually cutting off the middle ground. From the outside, this museum was barely visible, and allowed the view of the valley from the top of the Buddah's head, a view that had been recorded innumerable times in photographs since 1926, to remain untouched. The intervention would be invisible from the canonical vantage point, but from slightly different angles, the museum would become visible to the eye. Thus, even when the "open air" was a deserted, featureless landscape, it was conceived as a frame created by changing material conditions (figure 4.14). This debate about whether the modern restorer was allowed to leave visible traces became even more complicated in the design of wholly new museum buildings with conditioned interiors. Here, the question of locating old and new was intersected with the issue of creating physical boundaries for security and for air conditioning.

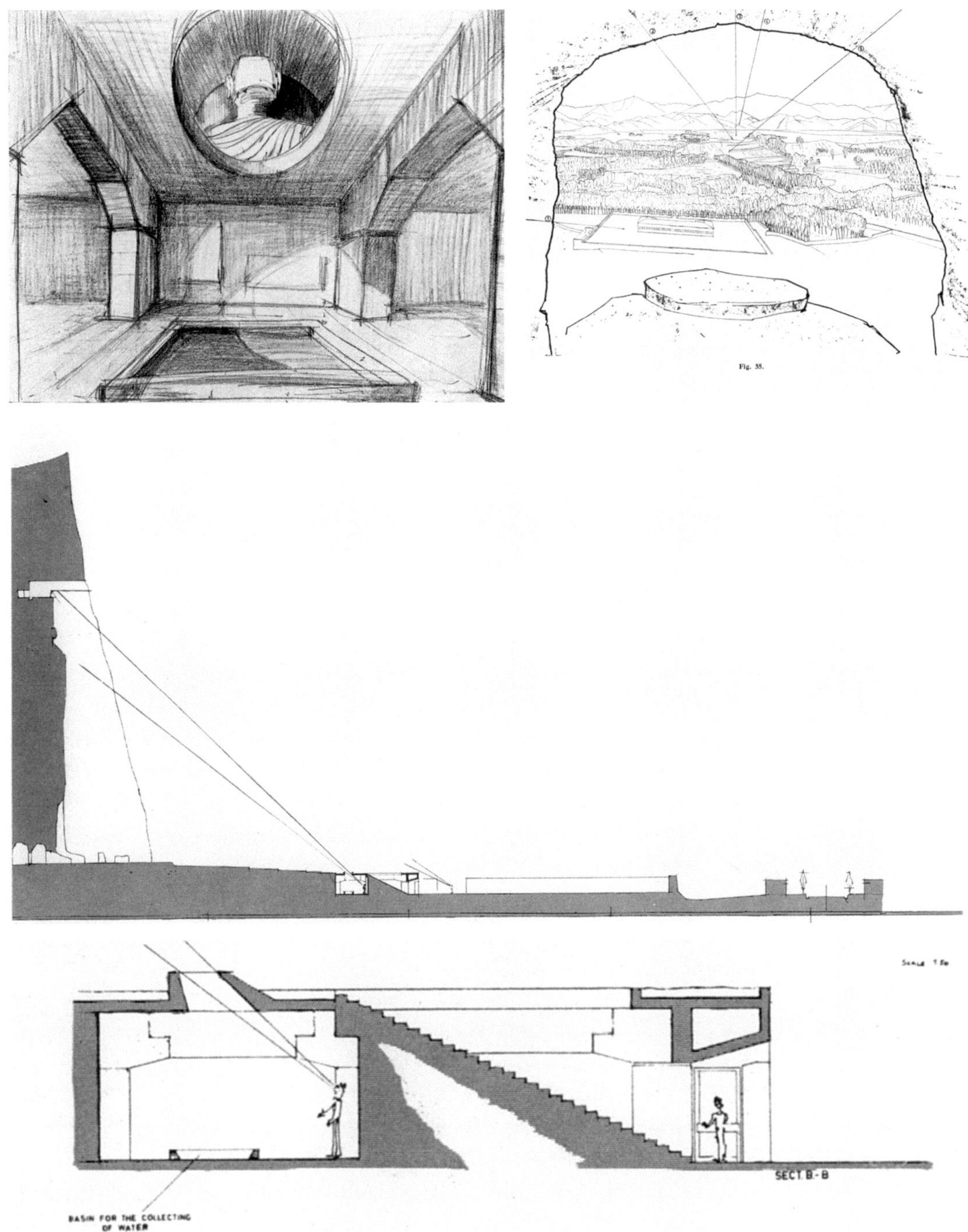

Figure 4.14 Andrea Bruno, Drawings for the Bamiyan site, including views of (and from) the large Buddha's head; site section; and building section of the underground museum. © Andrea Bruno.

The Minimum Museum

When helping states build new museums, the primary effect that UNESCO's architects sought to achieve was continuity. "There is a grave danger," one manual of museum architecture explained, "of breaking the continuity between the traditional cultures and the new ones," and therefore museums could help show "in concrete form the transition between the old and the new."[85]

An ambitious spatial and architectural program grew out of this concern for orchestrating historical continuity in space. All objects were to be displayed in chronological sequence and while no period of history would be omitted, the viewer was encouraged, literally, to move on.[86] The development of this architecture of continuity began in the late 1940s, when Rivière argued that UNESCO should invest in the exhibition as an international "educational medium" and provided a systematic 10-part taxonomy of exhibition types.[87] By 1962, he had replaced "exhibition" with "museum" and republished this inventory, conveying a will to institutionalize, and architecturalize.[88] His exhaustive catalog of museum types showed the manifold educational uses of museums: a central museum could be a "window onto the world," an art museum was a "gallery of world art," an ethnographic museum could "overcome prejudice," the technology museum assist in "interpreting industrial civilization," and so forth.[89] These new museums would achieve an institutional permanence but also needed to maintain the flexibility and ephemerality of the exhibition. For that, Rivière turned to modernism, asking that every UNESCO mission be accompanied by an architect with modern credentials. Echoing the discourse of Tropical Architecture, he forbade the "imitation of traditional styles" that would "cheapen the conception of cultural heritage," but allowed "lessons of tradition" to be learned for adapting architecture to "geographic and climatic conditions."[90]

The desire for a standard, international, flexible museum plan had already emerged in ICOM in the 1940s, continuing from prewar publications and conferences of the Office International des Musées.[91] In 1947 André Léveillé, the ICOM vice-president, and director of the French National Science Museum, proposed two versions ("minimum" and "maximum") of the same museum plan. Both were meant as a revision of the "Museum of Tomorrow" proposed by American architect Clarence Stein in 1934: a concentric plan with a "public's museum for appreciation" in a central rotunda, and a "scholar's museum for investigation" in its outer ring[92] (figure 4.15). In 1947, Léveillé adapted this scheme. The "maximum" museum became a polyhedral plan of galleries, each devoted to one scientific collection. With the rotunda gone, each discipline was internally organized around a circular display, and then laterally connected to others. This plan announced a decentralization and a freeing of museum space from both shape and enclosure. The "minimal" version, then, condensed the same sequence in one small oblong room. Only a faint trace of the complex circulatory diagram remained, in two angled panels at the back

a

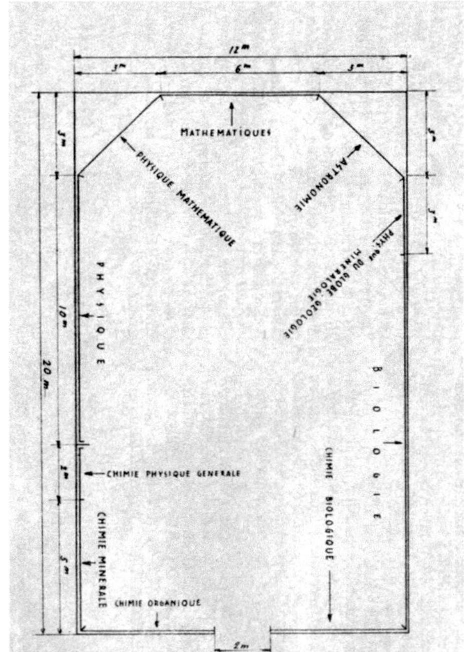

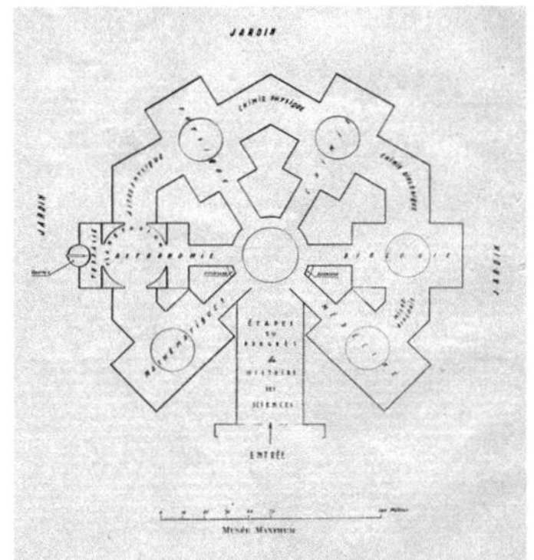

b

c

d

Figure 4.15 Museum plans published by the OIM and ICOM between 1934 and 1963. a. Clarence Stein, "Museum of Tomorrow" (1934); b. André Léveillé, "Maximum Museum" (1948) c. André Léveillé "Minimum Museum" (1948) d. United Nations Museobus, closed and opened (1963).

corners—a single detail that carried the architectural typology's totalizing ambition.[93]

The impulse to curate a maximum of information in a miminum of architecture drove UNESCO's and ICOM's architectural recommendations for much of the 1950s, and into the 1960s. The 1953 manual *Travelling and Temporary Exhibitions*, for instance, depicted numerous placeless and rootless interiors with every display element either mounted on legs or suspended from the ceiling[94] (figure 4.16). The largest uninterrupted plane was that of the floor; contact with the existing walls was kept to a minimum. Cruciform vitrines with arms extended practically delineated room-sized spatial units. Flat media such as carpets and photography were suspended from dowels or struts spanning from floor to ceiling. Whether through a high-design product or

Figure 4.16 UNESCO's first traveling exhibition ("Yugoslav Folk Art"), shown here at the Royal Scottish Museum in Edinburgh. Published in UNESCO, *The Organization of Museums* (Paris: UNESCO, 1960), plate 76. Photographer unknown.

improvised with local materials, a skeleton of display allowed the nation *itself* to be objectified, as a cultural artifact, and floated at eye-height (figure 4.17).

In UNESCO's hands, these skeletal exhibition systems were publicized as means to achieve peaceful political transition.[95] A 1956 mission report for a new science museum in Pakistan, for example, cautioned against premature building, because "a museum is not a building but an organization. Temporary quarters afford the best opportunity for natural growth up to the point where there is stability."[96] This new nomadic model of display was supported by UNESCO-sponsored exhibitions that recommended flat-packing maps of countries, cut out along national borders. International museum space could also be seeded through the *museobus*, a bus retrofitted as a traveling exhibition.[97] Inspired by the bookmobile, it uncoiled impressively from a diminutive footprint into a circuit that oriented the visitor by diagonal shifts much as in Léveillé's Minimum design.[98]

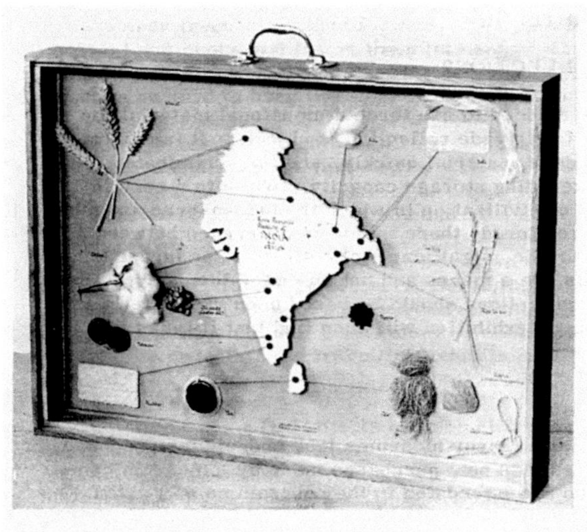
a

b

Figure 4.17 Displaying the nation as an object. a. "A simple suit-case type of exhibit." b. Hanging from dowels at the Museo do Indio, Rio de Janeiro, Brazil, *Museum* 8, no. 1. Photographer unknown.

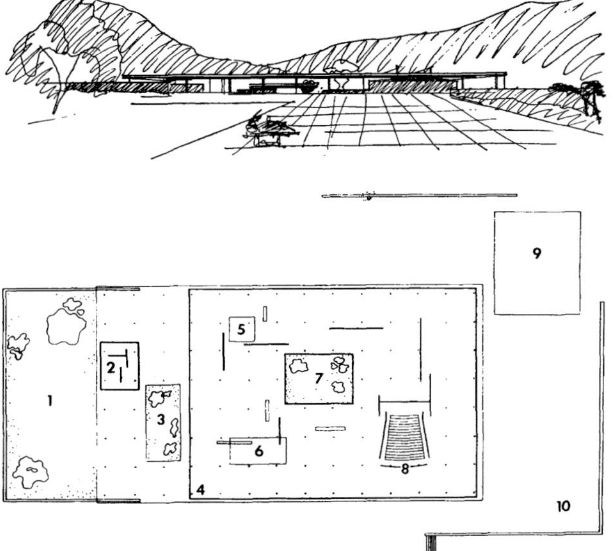

Figure 4.18 Mies van der Rohe, Museum for a Small City, 1942, redrawn for publication in UNESCO, *The Organization of Museums, Practical Advice* (Paris: UNESCO, 1960), fig. 7.

As the decade progressed, modernist architectural examples of full-fledged museum buildings began to appear in the literature. A 1960 reference manual titled *The Organization of Museums* offered a few Bauhaus-inflected modernist museum plans: Mies van der Rohe's 1942 Museum for a Small City, for instance, was captioned as an illustration of "the continuity of interior and exterior spaces," and Max Bill's 1952 Swiss Pavilion as an example of "the absence of architecture"[99] (figure 4.18). But when this minimal architecture of "absence" became a global template in the 1960s, it was wholly transformed through its encounter with the materialist ethos of conservation, which defined buildings as dynamics rather than forms.

The Monoblock

The closest UNESCO ever came to producing a prototype for a new national museum in a Tropical nation, came from its involvement in commissioning the Italian architect Franco Minissi to design an addition to the national museum in Accra, the capital of Ghana, in 1964.[100] Minissi had established an architectural practice in Rome, and built museums, restored monuments, and rearranged archaeological sites. Like other Italian postwar architects, he had gotten several projects by working within a new collaborative alliance of art historians, cultural administrators, and museum curators.[101] He even taught a class on museography at the ICR and the university of Rome, where he defined museums as cultural instruments, whose interiors were "signifying systems" that conveyed meanings by arranging objects in space.[102] This outlook and experience made him a UNESCO-ready expert, though not one with any expertise in sub-Saharan Africa.

The commission asked for an addition to a museum built in 1957 by the British firm of Fry, Drew, and Lasdun, leading designers and theorists in the Tropical Architecture movement. But in many ways this building was atypical of the Tropical genre: composed around a circular dome-covered exhibition interior, with a clerestory and *brise-soleils* all around. As Marc Crinson has argued, the building belongs in a split lineage of late-imperial circular exhibition spaces that reveal a deep ambiguity about the capacity of such circularity to convey political meanings and especially to perform a new global inclusiveness.[103] The museum had been inaugurated with great fanfare as an emblem of Ghana's national independence. But already in 1963 officials complained about the circular shape. "The Museum building being circular in shape," they wrote in a report to ICCROM, "it has not been easy to display specimens strictly according to their type or their country of origin, nor has it been very pleasant for the visitor to know where to start or end looking round the Museum."[104] By 1964, the lack of any spaces for administration, storage, and conservation led them to call for a new wing.

Minissi proposed a two-story mat building addition that dwarfed the original. The new building was to be a square and multistoried complex, with expansive exhibition space (figure 4.19). In accordance with recommendations written by Rivière in 1953, the building offered "carefully studied transitions" between departments through subtle sectional modulations, a few steps up or down at a time.[105]

The Accra museum can be seen as a version of what Minissi called, in his courses, the "monoblock" (*monoblocco*) museum: a cubic form and gridded organization that allowed the architect to make small variations in plan and section.[106] In Accra, Minissi argued that "free planning" gave "maximum flexibility" but visitors could still be controlled along prescribed "circuits" that originated in the lobby, a kind of "switchboard"[107] (color plate 5). Despite this *au courant* cybernetic language, a dual typological legacy was played out in the scheme. On the one hand, Minissi was inspired by UNESCO's recent adap-

Figure 4.19 Franco Minissi, model of a proposed expansion for the National Museum of Ghana, Accra, 1964. © Archivio Centrale dello Stato (ACS).

tion of the "exhibitionary complex" in the form of traveling exhibitions. On the other, the Accra scheme belongs in the architectural lineage of Duncan and Wallach's "Universal Survey Museum." Developed in the aftermath of the French Revolution, in the retrofitted European palaces and Beaux-Arts buildings in America, these museums delivered the political history of the state to its public through art, first allegorized as art history, and then sublimated as ritual.[108] The Accra scheme built on this "civilizational ritual" by reframing the museum's contents as universal, then national, patrimony.

While the universal survey museum was primarily a plan concept, Minissi deployed it in three dimensions. The ground floor had a "Gallery of World Art" and the upper floor would teach "the history of African civilizations." The whole experience was organized around several courtyards through a sectional delamination of floors, ramps, and balconies that ensured visual interpenetration. Minissi had originally worked out this sectional device in his renovation of the Villa Giulia in Rome, where he had built a new interior that appeared to float inside the mannerist shell of a sixteenth-century Italian villa (figure 4.20). A sectional perspective had been published in *Museum* of this "unbroken succession of all the exhibition rooms"—which is to say, an enfilade—where object and subject faced each-other as if in empty space, while around them an intense architectural apparatus worked to let the encounter unfold.[109] The Accra museum was similarly organized through walkways, stairs, balustrades, balconies, vitrines on stilts. But while in Italy the effect was to isolate the object, in Ghana what was displayed was encasement itself. Objects entered into the Villa Giulia to be experienced as such, in a vacuum, acquiring an aura. In Accra, objects were lodged into an architectural dynamic where the crossing of boundaries was productive of space. Once associated with Miesian "absence" and Bauhaus "transparency," the modernist grid was transformed into a checkerboard of meaning and materiality.

Figure 4.20 a. Franco Minissi. Section of the Museo Nazionale di Villa Giulia in Rome. b. Franco Minissi, Expansion of the National Museum of Ghana: view of large hall. © ACS.

Consider the building's envelope. Minissi emphasized that he had made "maximum use of exterior surfaces," but most of these exteriors faced internal courtyards filled with tropical gardens. The interior was a place to protect from the harsh exterior and also to reproduce it. Indeed, checkerboarding continued on the outside (figure 4.21). Lacking a found architectural palace, Minissi designed an eclectic outer shell, mimetic and consumptive of Accra. It was shaped like the rooflines of surrounding vernacular architecture, and entirely clad in "African Rosewood." Even Tropical modernism was ingested, as Minissi rendered the Fry, Drew & Lasdun dome as an oversized thatched hut. Although Minissi went out of his way to specify architectural materials that would be anti-corrosive (resistant to decay), in his perspective renderings, all boundaries were shown as decaying anyways. In one, a stainless steel grille has been carefully erased to get a clear view of the garden, where European visitors are sitting on a parapet, while Ghanian citizens de-ambulate in the garden. On the inside, this division holds again: African subjects stand-statue-like, speaking to one-another in the gallery, while white visitors look into a vitrine. Minissi also felt compelled to airbrush any piece of paper that might otherwise be left blank, as if to convey that no white space was possible in the tropics.

Despite its high modernist pedigree, and its specificity to Minissi's oeuvre, we can detect a kind of monoblock planning at play in other UNESCO projects of this period. Three-dimensional gridding proved surprisingly useful for the restoration of existing structures. The pressure for UNESCO to create museums through the adaptive reuse of existing buildings, whether they were origi-

Figure 4.21 Franco Minissi, Expansion of National Museum of Ghana: view of garden and gallery. © ACS.

nally classified as colonial, traditional, or vernacular, in various urban and rural contexts, only grew as the 1960s progressed. More than a typology, the monoblock was an architecturalization of the nesting of scales we have been following since the beginning of this chapter. It was a method for infiltrating these buildings—by "rationalizing" the plan and section first, updating and consolidating structural conditions, and policing the detailing to create a visual homogeneity throughout the interior space.

For example, in 1968 Jean Gabus visited several West African nations. In the Ivory Coast, he recommended inventing a new building type to house the National Museum, by combining building typologies from Abidjan's surrounding urban fabric: a horizontal wall-house [*maison-mur*] for exhibitions and a vertical tower-house [*maison-tour*] for storage.[110] He also diagrammed a checker-boarding principle, for a project that would alternate interior spaces and exterior microcosms: "the forest," "the bush," "birds."[111] Similarly, in nearby Dahomey, he recommended reconstructing the ruin of a traditional two-story hut [*singho,* or *case à étage*] to house a collection of tribal objects, specifying the stacking with which we are now familiar: general exhibition space on the ground, specialized galleries above.[112] Two years later the transformation of this typology into a minimal monoblock was completed when Swiss architect Walter Ruegg returned. And as the next section will show, the idea of a three-dimensional gridding was even applicable to sprawling monumental complexes.

The Complex

UNESCO experts who traveled to Southeast Asia to investigate the development of tourism in the late 1960s visited many sites but spent little time in each. With time for little more than a sketch and a page of typed notes, the gesture of establishing a uniform museographic "ground," by "leveling" and "re-planting" became an especially expedient recommendation. In 1966, the French archaeologist Raoul Curiel led a one-month mission throughout Pakistan whose report recommended "levelling the ground" of entire monumental structures where he spent one afternoon. For example, Curiel listed four buildings under the heading *Forts in the neighborhood of Dacca*, each with its succinct prescription:

> Sonakanda: Leveling of the interior to eliminate the accumulation in the lower areas.
> [...]
> Hajjigani: Here too, leveling the interior and the structure restored.[113]

Curiel's traveling companion, the architect R. M. H. Magnée, drew a sketch of the Dacca gardens as a stepped landscape, "reconstructed with tank and canals, brick-paved paths, lawns and some trees in groups at several spots."[114]

As the next chapter of this book will show, this re-plinthing became an important step in some of the most spectacular of UNESCO monuments projects in the 1970s, transforming building's apparently natural grounds into artificial topographies: at Abu Simbel, a cliff replaced with a dome; at Borobudur, a mound replaced by a dam; at Anghor Wat, a new "platform" for technical training.[115] But in the decade preceding these heroic campaigns, the dichotomy between natural and artificial ground was less clear-cut, and modernization was presented more as a malleable process that could gently conquer a continuum of social and material conditions—including ones that housed entire communities. Indeed, modern architecture receded as the privileged technology, but modernist ideals of flexibility and continuity were adapted to a particularly tangled set of "live" sociopolitical conditions on the ground.

The increasing number of requests for UNESCO to intervene in monumental sites that were occupied by religious communities began to throw into doubt the norms of conservation science as early as 1969. For example, after returning from the Hindu temple complex of Srirangam in Southern India, the Australian archaeologist Mick Wright opened his 1969 report by openly expressing skepticism towards UNESCO's universalism. "It is not evident," wrote Wright, "that the current ideas and ideals expressed in Western conservation and restoration of ancient monuments are necessarily applicable to Hindu temples in South India which are still living centres of religion."[116] Wright was only one in an ongoing chain of experts sent by UNESCO in the wake of the British Archaeological Survey, a system of colonial tutelage that originally was developed in India and eventually spread to the surrounding region.[117] Indeed, imperial conservators had been able to test "culture-keeping as state action" in India whereas in Britain, there was no such centralized authority over monuments.[118] Still, the Survey did not control what it called "live" monuments: buildings still occupied and controlled by active religious communities.[119] At these sites, alternative maintenance practices, often mixed with religious ritual, were allowed to continue, and state-sanctioned authorities offered only a most general oversight.[120] Intervening more gingerly in Southeast Asia than in Africa, UNESCO allowed local operation and religious use of monumental sites, but often asked that the local arrangements be standardized in a UN-sponsored administration, to receive aid.[121]

Wright had been sent on this 1969 mission—the one where he expressed doubt about UNESCO's suitability—in part to resolve a conflict between the recommendations made by a Bristish conservation architect, Patrick Faulkner, in 1966, and the work that was completed in 1968 by the Hindu temple authorities.[122] This "temple-city" progressed through a set of concentric walls, from a secular periphery (a modern town, built up to the brim with single-story houses and managed by the municipality) to a highly sacred core (a shrine inaccessible to non-Hindus and subject to conservation by religious leaders).

Faulkner had already described the segregated condition of the Srirangam temple and prescribed adding a "separate tourist approach" to pass through them all.[123] This approach would proceed through the modern town, and terminate in a new destination designed for non-Hindus who had no access to the inner-most sanctum. Here, between the fourth and third walls, the tourist could deambulate between interior and exterior spaces—permeable porticos, informal gardens, paved paths, and even one temple interior which was accessible to all. This was to be the terminus but also a space of transition, both in the sense that it unified adjoining visual heterogeneities and that it was a place from which to experience modernity through spatial continuity. As with all retrofitted architectural work, the patterning of the floor was the secret design weapon; it offered visitors "intimate contact" with the architecture.[124] Faulkner produced only one drawing for all of his recommendations: a partial plan with "Suggested pavings, Etc" that came in three patterns: "random" to encourage deambulation; "diagonal" to give directionality; and "sand" to suggest stasis (figure 4.22).

Figure 4.22 Patrick Faulkner, Annotated plan with suggested patterns for paving the Srirangam temple. From *India: The Renovation and Conservation of Temples in South India* (Paris: UNESCO, March 1966). UNESCO Archives.

Two years later, Wright went further. An Australian architect-archaeologist who had worked in the Middle East, Wright would earn the unusual title of "field architect" by making orthographic drawings not only of archaeological finds but also the architectural contexts in which they were found, and, eventually, directing their reconstitution as coherent "sites."[125] He brought this view from above to the Srirangam temple, where he argued that architectural unity was undermined by the diversity of regimes of life inside it.

First, he rephrased the proposal. What "was originally a 'temple-town'" had now "become a temple and a town," he wrote, and might "in future be triply divided into a temple, a town and an ancient monument."[126] Wright also called this solution "a compromise involving 'partition,'" in a clear echo of the political "partitioning" of India and Pakistan. It is worth noting that the "ancient monument" was the third term that had been *created* by the split.

Second, he deployed the same rationalization techniques we have seen in *monoblock* museums and retrofitted tribal palaces: complementing plan continuity with clear sectional striation (figure 4.23). Indeed, Faulkner's visit, and his floor-based approach, had failed to curtail the ritual re-painting of walls that temple authorities considered to be a kind of maintenance. So Wright began by recommending that any painting be visually contained within the features of South Hindu temple architecture, this architecture being understood as 3-part "style." Thus any paint that crossed the "structural divisions of base, shaft, and capital" was to be removed.[127] He also found other opportunities to manipulate the horizontal datum that would satisfy a tourist sightline. In a remarkable passage, he described how a sculpture gallery had come to be "by accident" in a courtyard outside the Venugolapa Temple: the ground had been gradually raised by the accretion of earth, producing a place for "very convenient viewing" where the statues in the wall's niches were located at "modern eye level."[128] Temple authorities had already capitalized on this condition by pouring a concrete floor on top of it (to provide a better viewing platform), and also rendered it more permanent by clearing the earth fill away from the

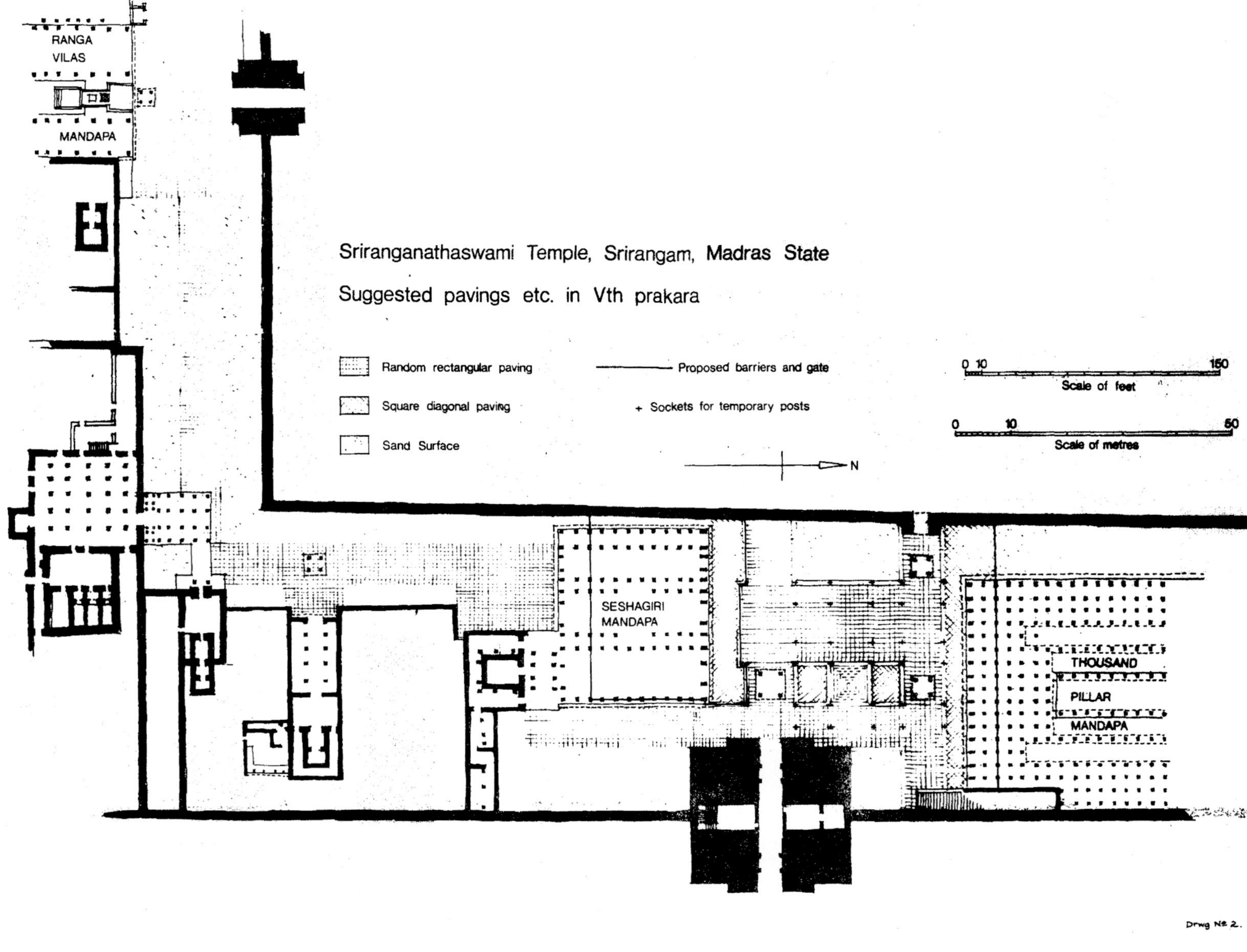
Sriranganathaswami Temple, Srirangam, Madras State
Suggested pavings etc. in Vth prakara
Random rectangular paving
Square diagonal paving
Sand Surface
Proposed barriers and gate
+ Sockets for temporary posts
N
0 10 150
Scale of feet
0 10 50
Scale of metres
RANGA
VILAS
MANDAPA
SESHAGIRI
MANDAPA
THOUSAND
PILLAR
MANDAPA
Drwg Nº 2.

wall (to protect it from dampness). Incredibly, Wright recommended not only removing this makeshift floor and its associated dirt mound, but then *reproducing* this felicitous viewing condition by building a light metal gangway that would place visitors, again, at eye-height with the statues, this time with a larger gap separating people from the sculptures. Effectively, he proposed to replace a mound with a platform.

This project demonstrates how strongly spatial flexibility appealed to internationalists as a tool of cultural governance. This principle appeared inherently liberal—since the overall political allegory of state-making implied that diversifying viewpoints in museums and monuments would have a liberalizing effect on the nation as a whole. Wright was undeniably one of the most self-aware of UNESCO experts and was attuned to the gap between the expectations of internationalists and those of local authorities. Like Eyo in Senegal, he often emphasized the process of restoration over the result.[129] But he ultimately drew the line at legibility. His open-mindedness seemed to end exactly where aesthetic license began. Wright repeatedly chided local artisans for combining Western scientific norms and artisanal craft and for making visible the scientific procedures that UNESCO intended to remain hidden. At the Perumal Temple, local authorities had tried to appropriate Western restoration methods:

Figure 4.23 G. R. H. Wright, Photographs of the "Second Corridor of Rameswaram," before demolition and during rebuilding. From Wright's mission report, *India: Proposal for Restoration Work at Rameswaram Temple* (Paris: UNESCO, February 1971). Images courtesy of the Australian Institute of Archaeology, G. R. H. Wright Archive.

> The stone prakara walls have been extensively repaired by the excellent means of numbering each stone, dismantling and re-erecting. Unfortunately . . . [t]he identifying numbers were painted on the faces of the stones in large black letters and these remain boldly on display as a proud memorial of this activity.[130]

For Wright, the craftsmen had created a strange object that revealed bureaucracy. As with Lézine's critique of Andrea Bruno in Afganistan, Wright objected to rendering visible—let alone "memorializing"—Western conservation norms. He similarly objected to the use of "wide pointing," intended to thoroughly seal all the joints but which gave an image of decay rather than newness:

> This has given the work the appearance of village rubble masonry, and has completely destroyed the noble aspect of the finely jointed ancient masonry—the preservation of which was one of the goals of the labor of recording, dismantling and re-erection.

As a last resort, he recommended using the enchanting powers of science to combat religious sanction. Acknowledging that regularly cleaning the walls would be considered "in some measure 'desanctifying'" them, he recommended that such cleaning be "given the mystique of a 'scientific' operation under 'expert direction,'" turning conservation into a struggle between religious inscription and scientific erasure, a battle of intangibilities.[131]

The Detail

As I have argued throughout this chapter, one of the main features of the material turn in international architectural conservation was its constructive quality. Its legacy is present in innumerable architectural details and design features of museums and monuments, often hidden in plain sight. After a decade of UNESCO-ICCROM missions, a simple architectural detail could structure an entire national style. Consider the sequence of missions that were sent to Thailand. A nation-state since the middle of the nineteenth century, it had developed an important National Museum in its capital city, and begun an extensive regional museum building campaign in the 1940s. When Paul Coremans traveled in 1961 to inspect mural paintings for UNESCO, he included *one* drawing in his entire 1962 report, which combined two aspects of Thai architecture that contributed to the deteriorated state of mural paintings across the territory. This section showed that the traditional plastering of walls had "prevented the monuments from decaying" to such a successful extent that Coremans declared that even "the best modern and costly chemicals" would be "unable to offer the same protection"[132] (figure 4.24). In contrast, another signature feature of Thai architecture, the "pluri-sectioned roof," was highly impractical from a conservation standpoint since it allowed water to drip into the murals below. Here, then, Coremans recommended a synthetic shield,

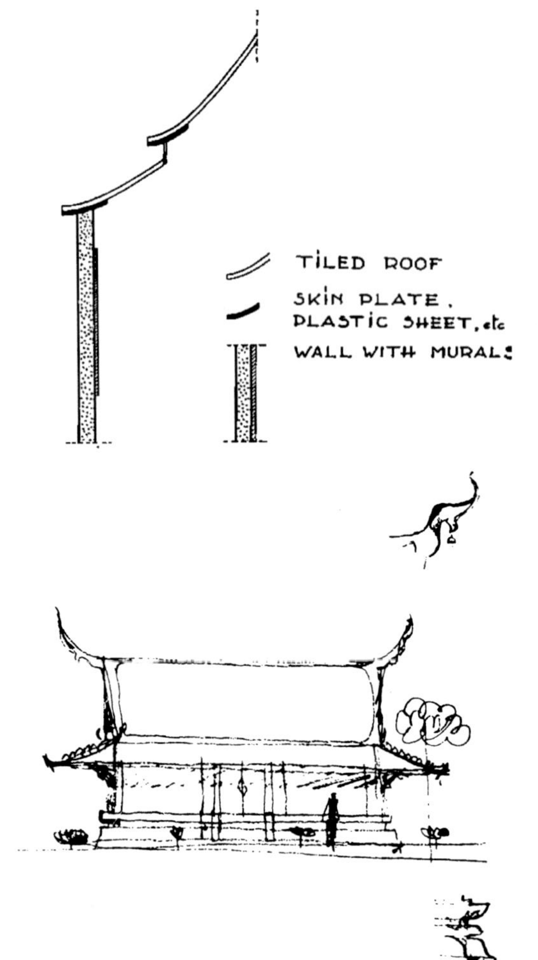

Figure 4.24 Imagery from UNESCO mission reports to Thailand. a. Paul Coremans, "General Remedy" for the protection of mural paintings in Thailand (1963); b. T. T. Barrow, "Suggested General Style of Architecture in Thailand," a project for a national science museum (December 3–29, 1966); c. Photograph of the National Museum in Bangkok. New lower Gallery below "storage floor" placed between ground floor and roof. Grace Morley, *Thailand: Museums and Development* (Paris: UNESCO, 1967). UNESCO Archives.

targeting the chemical weakness of the traditional architecture by inserting "Skin plates, plastic sheets, agglomerate, etc" where roof and wall met. In every subsequent conservation project, the feasibility of this detail became the deciding factor on whether a mural should be conserved in situ, or removed to the National Museum in Bangkok, which was promptly outfitted with a conservation laboratory, and staffed with two conservators trained by Coremans in Brussels.[133]

As Thailand's conservation laboratory grew, this architectural detail, conceived to protect historic architecture, was incorporated into the design of new museum buildings. At the National Science Museum, for example, a shifting cast of UNESCO experts made recommendations for the building's architecture and program. At one point, an international mission included sketch drawings for an "adaptation of traditional Thai features"—including high Wat style walls, and a plurisectioned roof.[134] In 1968 one Canadian expert, Grace McCann Morley, went to investigate a complaint that the new museum's buildings were ill-suited, "far too lofty for the scale of the objects to be exhibited."[135] Morley confirmed that one of the additions (the South) was "indeed very high," but gladly reported that the defect had been addressed when the second addition was built (the North) because "an additional floor [had been] inserted close to the line where the sloping roof meets the walls" and used for storage. This was in the same tectonic meeting point of roof and wall, where Coremans had recommended an insulating detail. Where Coremans placed a synthetic barrier, the museum had inserted a whole new room. This improved the exhibition space below—giving it low and horizontal proportions and thus modernizing the interior while keeping the exterior taller and more "traditional." In this manner, architectural detailing became essential to the material turn in heritage thinking and practice, spanning old and new in less than a decade.

Conclusion

The projects I have examined in this chapter ultimately played a transitional role in the birthing of postcolonial national heritage institutions. For a short decade and a half, UNESCO proposed a scientifically enhanced architecture to help nation-states achieve a spatial cohesion, where none was available historically or socially.[136] But the idea of furnishing every postcolonial city with a museum and laboratory was unrealistic, to say the least, especially given UNESCO's meager budgets. Most proposals remained unbuilt. Not a single corrugated metal roof was replaced *back* with thatch. Furthermore, a new environmental agenda began take hold in the international community, in the early 1970s, provoking a conflation of nature and culture into a new idea of "heritage." Still, as Perrin Selcer has shown, UNESCO's work in the social and natural sciences in this period already re-described the nation as an experimental "field" and contributed to a growing ecological mentality that would not fully emerge until later.[137]

Once a conceptual framework, UNESCO's museum apparatus became another decaying inheritance. The British ethnomusicologist Merrick Posnansky, reminiscing in the 1990s, felt that UNESCO had "taken a wrong turn"—by which he meant that its specialists had chosen to "safeguard concepts" rather than concentrate on material culture. He invoked idle sentinels to make the point: while "museum curators were attending international gatherings," he wrote, "labels fell off and cockroaches ate the numbers from objects."[138] And it is tempting to read these projects as remnants of a bygone bureaucratic ideal. Certainly some of UNESCO's projects produced evocative ruins. Minissi's architectural legacy in Accra, for example, consists of unfinished concrete piers with mangled reinforcing bars jutting out. Abandoned when the government was overthrown in 1966, these walls are as overgrown as the "monuments in peril" that they were meant to protect (color plate 6).

Postcolonial scholars have recently theorized the poisonous legacy of colonialism as a species of ruination. Inspired in part by Franz Fanon's seminal diagnosis in the 1950s of the "germs of rot" that imperialism leaves behind in the mental and physical landscapes of colonized people, they describe the ruin as an "imperial effect" with varying degrees of historical metaphor.[139] The goal of these critiques is to deconstruct the *naturalizations* performed by the imperial episteme. It would be possible to inscribe UNESCO within this lineage. But by focusing on the heritage experts who used the strangely productive nature of physical rot, I have sought to show that, even as ruins, architectural monuments in the post-colony functioned as instruments of *culturalization* too. Some of the protocols of architectural design and monument conservation were borrowed from the crafts, others from the natural sciences—but all helped to intertwine cultural value with physical ruination.

Consider for instance the mud huts of the Jos Museum compound, where UNESCO trainees had originally been lodged. They had been built by craftsmen under Fagg's supervision in the 1950s. In 1974, an inspector recommended that the students should be housed in modern buildings instead, because "the initial romantic period during which the Centre had to find authenticity in concrete African art and culture has now passed."[140] But far from being destroyed or decommissioned, the huts *joined* the museum's collections, becoming a "model village" to be visited by tourists. An obsolete governing structure, masquerading as a vernacular building type.

Art and architectural heritage played a specific role in the political economy of decolonization. UNESCO used museums to make an analogy between the political freedom of the state and the freedom of the artist (the analogy on which Western aesthetic discourse was founded) and in turn between the state and the museum. But the process by which the post-colony entered the international system was different from the way European states had become nations first, then come together to create an international order. The colony had always already been featured inside empire, albeit labeled as "timeless" and "unfree." In order for the contents of these colonial museums to be converted into economic capital, then, art chemistry and the fiction of climate together supplied a productive mechanism. In this mechanism, we find an inversion of artistic making: it is the already-made artifact that produces cultural value for its maker, not the other way around. The next chapter moves on to an episode where this process of value-extraction, and the financialization of the risks faced by material objects, was amplified and spectacularized to a hitherto unconceivable scale.

Conservation in the tropical post-colony was a ritualized and regressive dynamic, where the realization of state independence was performed as a leaving behind. What was produced was a new class of museum conservators who watched over matter, lest it come alive again. Cultural heritage was left behind *and* surveilled, watched like a border whose political legality has faded but whose guards continue to show up for work.

5 Integrities

THE SALVAGE OF ABU SIMBEL, 1960–1980

In 1965, the British architectural historian Reyner Banham responded to a letter from a preservationist who had asked him to intervene against the demolition of the Reliance Building in Chicago. "The day you find me speaking up for the preservation of any building whatsoever," Banham wrote, "send flowers, the next stage will be the general paralysis of the insane." Banham refused to engage in what he called "idiotic preservationist panics" for fear of being subjected to similar requests from "every crackpot period group and broken-down country-house owner in England."[1] But he could also have aimed his sarcasm at preservationists with tastes much closer to his own. 1965 is, after all, the year that Le Corbusier's Villa Savoye, one of the most iconic buildings of "machine age" International Style designed in 1924, was declared a national historic monument in France, thanks in part to an international advocacy campaign by modern architects and historians, including Siegfried Giedion.[2]

Indeed, in the mid-1960s a wave of activism swept up architects and architectural historians of every allegiance across the Western world, apparently unifying architectural modernism and historicism through a common political cause. In 1963, modern architects (including Philip Johnson) joined urban activists (including Jane Jacobs) to protest the demolition of New York's Penn Station. In 1964, a group of architects and archaeologists from sixteen countries coauthored the Venice Charter, the first international document to call for the protection of both monuments and historic sites. A year later, the phrase "World Heritage" was coined at a 1965 White House Conference.[3] This three-year period is bracketed on either side by major acts of legislation that extended the legal protection of historic buildings in the West to entire urban districts: the 1962 Loi Malraux in France and the 1966 National Historic Preservation Act in the United States.

So where Banham saw "idiotic panics," others saw political empowerment. The timeline I have just sketched out is rapidly being historicized as the start of a dramatic rise in the political power of preservationists, coincident with a global shift from conserving individual monuments to preserving entire environments. According to this new historiography, the 1960s saw an enlargement of preservation's domain and a concurrent expansion of its political effectiveness worldwide. The British preservationist Alan Powers has even identified 1965–1985 as the "heroic period of conservation."[4] Like many other national narratives, this story has international implications, whereby local heroism helped to ignite a global movement, which then followed the example of national pressure groups.[5] Thus in an accumulating number of histories, the globalization of preservation is ascribed to a convergence of political will along four axes: an alliance between modern architects and historic preservation activists; a shift of media attention from object-buildings to urban ensembles and vernacular milieus; a joining of forces between nature conservationists and architectural preservationists; and a concerted effort of scholars to diversify the architectural canon and the demand for its protection. And so (the narrative goes) the protective boundary of preservation was progressive enlarged, by sheer force of activism, to include ever-larger sectors of the built environment. "In the span of ten years," wrote the Italian architect Piero Gazzola in 1978, "we have gone from punctual protection to global protection."[6]

The trouble with this narrative of progressive enlargement is that it assumes that architectural monuments stayed the same, while around them mentalities changed. As previous chapters of this book have shown, throughout the midcentury architectural conservation, which was once conceived as a historical accumulation of buildings in time, became a spatial practice that lays a claim to entire environments. But new values and new criteria had to be invented to sustain this expanded political charge. Indeed, one of the sources of preservation's spatial expansion lay in its unwitting alliance with various destructive tools and agents. Several historical analyses have critiqued preservationists' triumphalist self-image by pointing to the social, legal, and technological forms of mediation that intervened to expand their power. Already in the 1970s, the German art historian Willibald Sauerländer commented on the growing consensus that there had been an "extension of heritage," but expressed skepticism that the process had been purely additive. "To conserve is not only to preserve historical evidence but also to mediate it," he wrote. Instead he hypothesized that there had been a shift from quantity to quality, and hinted that public demand for expanding the boundary of protection did not necessarily empower the people who found themselves inside that boundary.[7] The expansion of preservation, he implied, was due not only to an increase in preservationists' power, but also to the fact that power found new ways to circulate through architecture and the built environment.

Building on this insight, in this final chapter, I address the radical change that occurred in international preservation in the mid-1960s by telling the story of one episode when the expansion of preservation's domain "from the punctual to the global" was the subject of an international engineering competition. The objects of the competition were the temples of Abu Simbel: two massive pharaonic shrines fronted by eight colossal figures carved out of a sandstone cliff on the banks of the Nile in the twelfth century BC, under the rule of Rameses II. Between 1960 and 1968, the temple complex was salvaged from drowning, by being moved 208 meters over and 65 meters up from its

original site, in a highly publicized international campaign led by UNESCO (figure 5.1). The salvage remains a famous world-historical event today and an important marker in the history of preservation. These monuments were so large and monolithic that they blurred the boundaries between an architectural object and its site. Their salvage was also a part of a regional plan, which exemplified preservation's expanded scale of operation. Yet because the temples were so remote and had no local constituency advocating on their behalf, the question of what kind of technical and political mediation was required for their salvage—whether tools and techniques, or laws and social norms—was brought into particular relief.[8] They also offer a unique case study of the role technology played in making historic preservation a global field of expertise. In short, the salvage of Abu Simbel exemplifies the new model of monumentality that was catalyzed when new approaches to preservation mixed with geopolitical ambitions and experimental engineering.

Figure 5.1 Large temple of Abu Simbel (Egypt), built ca. 1264–1244 BCE, reconstructed 1960–1968 CE, photographed here on re-inauguration day September 22, 1968. © Torgny Säve-Södeberg.

This chapter focuses on technology not only because the international preservation movement coalesced against a perceived acceleration of technological progress—although it is certainly true that the proliferation of public works and engineering projects throughout the 1960s served as a rallying cry for both environmental and architectural activists. Nor is it simply that technological obsolescence became the dominant criterion, in this period, for determining what qualified as historic architecture to be preserved, though it is true that many of the cases that turned modernists into preservationists involved buildings built around newly-old industrial technologies, such as Penn

Station and the Euston Arch.[9] Architects' attitudes toward technology were crucial in determining where they stood in the debates about the historical self-image of modernism, and the fate of its most famous buildings. No doubt Reyner Banham's real objection to preservation was technological: for him, to be modern was "to keep pace with a technological situation," not to conserve and memorialize past architectural technologies.[10] Yet as I propose to show, like many other architectural practitioners in this period, preservationists tried to "keep pace" with history by adopting and adapting the technologies against which they were fighting. I focus on technology, then, because changing conceptions of history, including architectural history, must be thought in relation to changing technologies, and particularly to those building technologies that translated notions of historical progress, of development, of teleology—in short, of time—into space.

Monument and/as Infrastructure

On January 14, 1964, the *New York Times* published a photograph of Soviet president Nikita Khrushchev and Egyptian president Gamal Nasser "hurling rocks" into the Nile to inaugurate the construction of the Aswan High Dam (figure 5.2). Originally designed in 1946 by an international consortium led by a German-American engineer, the dam was to be one of the largest rock-fill dams ever built, its size commensurate with its impressive multipurpose task: to retain water in a gigantic reservoir lake, generating enough energy to electrify the Nile Valley all the way to the delta, and permanently irrigate much of Egypt along the way (figure 5.3). It was also to become the object of an intense and prolonged geopolitical tug-of-war. As soon as Nasser came to power in 1952, he made the project central to his plan for jump-starting the country's development and achieving agricultural self-sufficiency. Large infrastructural projects were frequently used by non-aligned leaders like Nasser to leverage their strategic position with both sides of the Cold War's East-West divide. In 1956 Nasser approached the West, and received an immediate offer to fund the dam from the World Bank, the US, and the UK. But after it became clear that this economic debt would not dictate Egypt's political allegiance, this Western consortium withdrew its offer. Defiant, Nasser nationalized the Suez Canal to raise funds for the dam—sparking a crisis that would shake up the Middle East for decades—and turned to the Eastern block for further support. By 1964, the dam was being built largely with Soviet money and expertise.[11] In this context, Khrushchev and Nasser's act of "hurling rocks" stands out as a raw and triumphant demonstration of techno-politics: a delegation, by sheer force of gravity, of an immense amount of political power to an enormous machine.

This inaugural photograph was disseminated in the West as a cautionary tale. Suspended in mid-air, the stones of the Aswan Dam were carriers of a political force that could divert not only the flow of the Nile, but also Western channels of influence in the Middle East. There was no shortage of infrastructural metaphors to make the point: Khrushchev himself used his Egyptian trip

Figure 5.2 Egyptian, Soviet, and Yemeni presidents Gamal Abdel Nasser, Nikita Khrushchev, and Abdullah as-Sallal "hurling rocks" into the gap to divert the Nile for the construction of the Aswan High Dam on January 14, 1964. Photo: UPI.

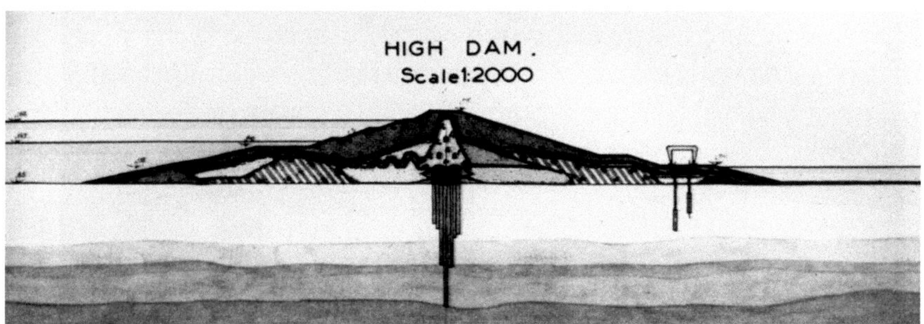

Figure 5.3 Egyptian Ministry of Information. Section through the High Dam at Aswan, 1959.

to declare his intentions to "drown capitalism on the African continent," and another photo-opportunity the next day showed the leaders pushing a button, in unison, to detonate the first explosion that would demolish temporary construction digs. Western commentators witnessing this political theater responded by attacking the monumental qualities of the High Dam: calling it "Nasser's pyramid," and an "Egyptian monopolization of the Nile."[12] But not to be outdone in monumental rhetoric, Nasser's Ministry of Information spent much of the early 1960s comparing the Aswan Dam to the monuments of pharaonic Egypt. One pamphlet, aptly titled *Aswan: A City Whose Public Works Are More Grandiose than Obelisks and Pyramids*, computed that the dam would require "enough stone to build 26 ancient pyramids," a comparison made easier by the fact that the dam was, itself, "in the form of a collapsed pyramid."[13] But the Ministry also emphasized the dam's absolute modernity: whereas the pyramids were "monstrous architectural conceptions" that had wasted material and exploited labor for the memory of only a "few powerful men," the Aswan Dam was a new kind of monument, "larger and more human," because it would remain active, in the service of all Egyptians, in hydrological perpetuity.

This contention between two kinds of monumentality (the one ancient and static, the other modern and dynamic) was no mere metaphor. The 6 trillion cubic foot lake created by the dam was projected to flood dozens of ancient temples and archaeological sites that sat along the banks of the Nile, in Nubia. So by 1964 the High Dam became a veritable iron curtain, which divided the Nile Valley neatly between Eastern and Western blocks, each side running a large-scale engineering project. Downstream, over 800 Russian engineers built the dam and its associated power stations; upstream, Nubia was crowded with Western archaeologists and engineers brought by UNESCO to survey and salvage hundreds of monuments and sites.

The temples of Abu Simbel were the largest and most impressive of the temples, and they were understood from the start of the project as counter-monuments to the dam. Like the dam, they represented engineering projects of massive scale, and also like the dam, their salvage would require unprecedented international cooperation. But unlike the dam, which *generated* power, the colossi of Abu Simbel appeared to *absorb* the immense effort that was invested into them. For instance, in 1960, UNESCO put the temples on the cover of the *Courier* to publicize its appeal to "Save the Treasures of Nubia"; four years later, an almost identical cover image proclaimed that "Victory in Nubia" had been achieved. Nowhere was the human agency required to achieve this victory in evidence; the temples sat unchanged, impassibly facing the Nile. The Soviet publication commemorating Nikita Khrushchev's visit depicted hydroelectricity as a source of political empowerment, proudly claiming that "Russian-Egyptian friendship" had built the dam. In contrast, UNESCO made use of what Bruno Latour has called its "sociological Esperanto" to describe the work of preservation: according to the organization's publicity material, it was "the world" that "saved Abu Simbel."[14]

What does it mean for UNESCO to say that "the world saved Abu Simbel"? One place to start decoding this abstract language is the final engineering report for the salvage of the temples, whose preface further broke down "the world" into six collective nouns:

> The EGYPTIAN PEOPLE, through their GOVERNMENT, have shouldered the greatest part of the burden of this noble enterprise.
>
> UNESCO called on nations and people all over the world and urged them to make generous contributions.
>
> The ARCHAEOLOGIST, represented by specialists from Egypt as well as from other countries, outlined the fundamental conditions for the Salvage Operation.
>
> The CONTRACTOR, in the form of a Joint Venture composed of companies from Egypt, Italy, France, Germany and Sweden, executed the gigantic works involved.
>
> The CONSULTING ENGINEER planned and prepared the whole project and supervised the works. He also submitted this Report.[15]

This disembodied chain of human agency actually describes a very specific set of actors who participated not only in saving Abu Simbel but also in the entire campaign to salvage the twenty-four other temples of Nubia (figure 5.4). Each plural noun represents a human network whose presence in Nubia was carefully orchestrated: from Egyptian workers, to foreign archaeologists

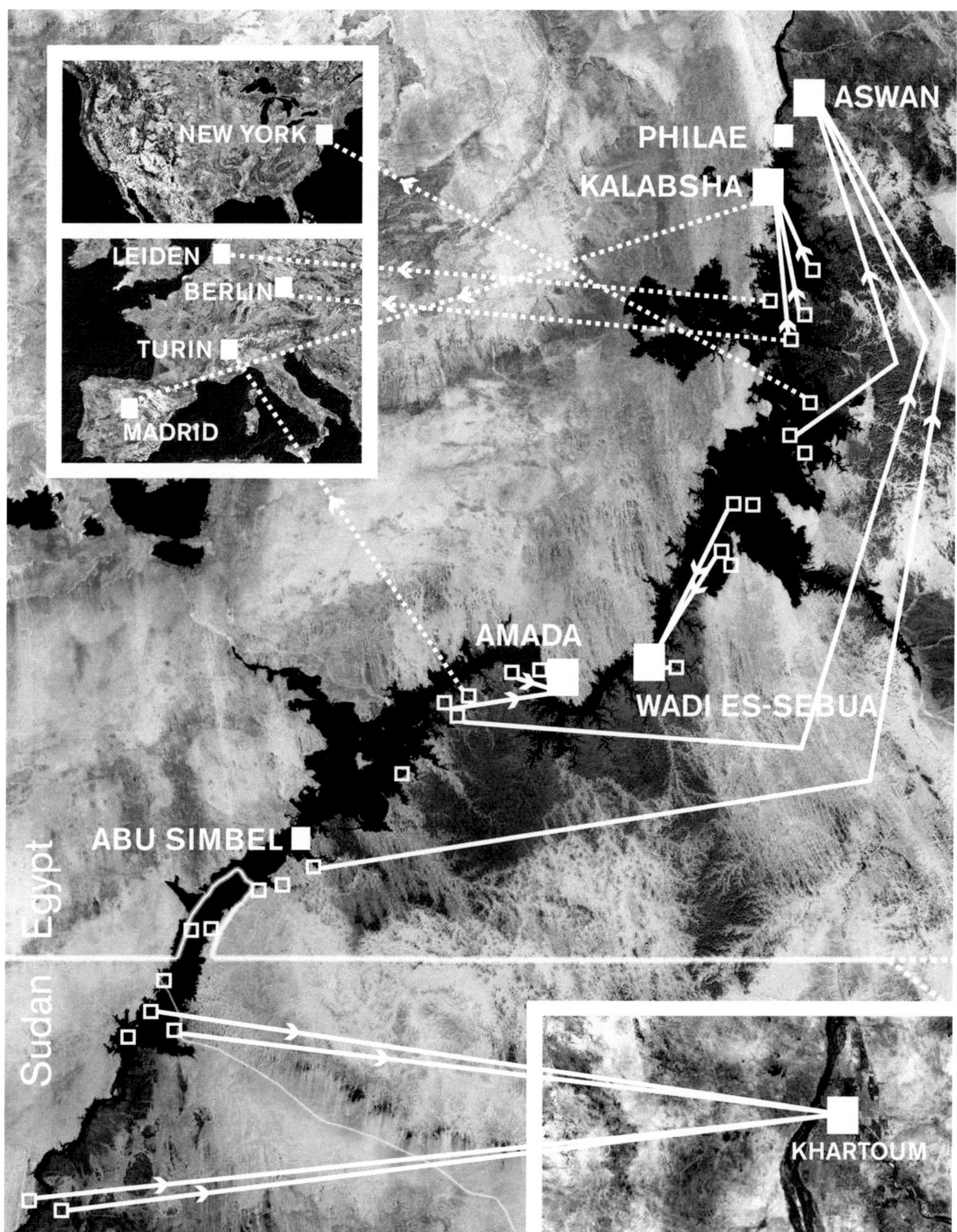

Figure 5.4 Lucia Allais, Relocation of twenty-four temples to four oases along the Nile, and five Western museums, during UNESCO's Campaign to Salvage the Temples of Nubia, 1960–1980. © Lucia Allais.

and engineers, and international bureaucrats. Elsewhere, I have described how this delicate orchestration can be understood as a massive design project, which reconfigured the Nubian desert into a new kind of cultural space.[16] Here it might suffice to note that this design was tacitly regulated by a logic of concentration and dissemination. Beginning in 1959, UNESCO assigned a priority to each temple, designating some as of "first" or "second importance," deeming the rest un-salvageable, and vetting proposals for new sites. Over the next twenty years, some temples were consolidated in four oases along the new lake, while others were dispersed individually in Western museums as "ambassadors of Egyptian culture." To legitimate this work, UNESCO invented an entirely new legal and bureaucratic framework for cultural exchange. But despite UNESCO's guarantee of scientific and political neutrality, the overall effect of the temple movement was to optimize the number of tourists to the temples. In a sense, this redesign of the desert literalized what Gazzola called the passage "from the punctual to the global." Once a sequence of points on a map, the monuments of Nubia became part of a global network where they retained their Nubian identity despite being dispersed across temporal and spatial discontinuities. So although the Abu Simbel temples were technically salvaged in situ—they were not, conceptually, relocated—they were fundamentally transformed by their movement, becoming the crowning moment of this new experiential complex—a new monumental infrastructure for a new nation-state.

Integrities

The actual task of salvaging Abu Simbel was never declared an international competition, but unfolded as a series of alternative schemes that were proposed by national delegations and assessed by UNESCO. For the organization's cultural officers, the project offered an opportunity to codify emerging international criteria for preservation, especially the concept of "integrity." Borrowed from ecological discourse, the idea of integrity appeared especially promising to conservationists eager to expand their activities beyond the walls of individual monuments, because it implied that a matrix of relationships exists between all the elements of a given site.[17] But as in ecological thinking, the notion of integrity also provoked a constant slippage between ethical and scientific discourses. When it came to the moving of monuments, the term integrity came to designate alternatively the morphology of a site, the material properties of an object to be moved, and the moral fiber of the person (or entity) doing the moving.

UNESCO's judging committees were composed of a variety of disciplinary representatives, and each national team making proposals was also an experiment in collaboration. Most teams were led by engineers (who were likely to understand integrity as a structural notion), but also included architects (for whom integrity was a site-planning strategy) and sometimes preservationists (focused on the material integrity of objects). This intricate division of tasks—

between engineers and architects, individuals and institutions, nation-states and international organizations—was further complicated by an underlying debate over whether any modern human gesture should be legible in the desert at all. Here "integrity," as a term applicable to environmental systems, became entwined with "integration," an aesthetic notion developed by European art and architectural conservators since 1945.[18] And while each team's proposal can be read for its contribution to this new international discourse on integrity and integration, the rhetoric surrounding each scheme also reveals a preservation mentality strongly influenced by national traditions. These national discourses can be recalled along with the various schemes—not in order to caricature them, but, on the contrary, to show how invisible these intellectual legacies had become at home, and how incongruous and incompatible they suddenly seemed when forced to compete on an international stage. One irony of preservation history is that while preservation discourse became properly international as early as the mid-nineteenth century, many of its practices and values remained nationally bounded well into the twentieth century, in part because the profession of preservation is largely administered by national state institutions.[19]

Damming, Lifting, Flooding, Floating

The first scheme to salvage Abu Simbel was proposed by the French engineering firm of Coyne et Bellier in summer of 1960: to preserve the monument in situ, by building a rock-fill dam—in some ways a copy of the High Dam—in front of the temples[20] (figure 5.5). This scheme would re-integrate the monuments into the desert, by using the same technologies that radically transformed it. Coyne et Bellier were specialists in thin-shell concrete dams, but they left the design of the dam to French architect Albert Laprade, who sought to maintain what he called "the extraordinary harmony between the elements of this unique site."[21] Laprade devised an intricate choreography where visitors arrived by water at the level of the lake, descended along a sinuous scenic route to circumvent a shallow pool in front of the temples, and finally found themselves aligned with an axis that corresponded with the angle taken by the rising sun during a once-a-year illumination with the inner-most shrine of the large temple.

Laprade felt no qualms about leaving a legible human gesture in the sand—as long as it was a gesture he found to be aesthetically continuous with the original setting. In this sense, he engaged in the French practice of "restoration" as it had been pioneered by Viollet-le-Duc and continued to be followed, in spirit, well into twentieth-century France: the act of "re-instating a monument in a condition of completeness which could never have existed at any given time."[22] This "condition of completeness" had long been the French answer to the question of integrity and Laprade evoked it when he called the site a "timeless landscape." Yet completeness did not mean ideality; having spent much of his career drawing and designing neo-orientalist buildings in an explicit

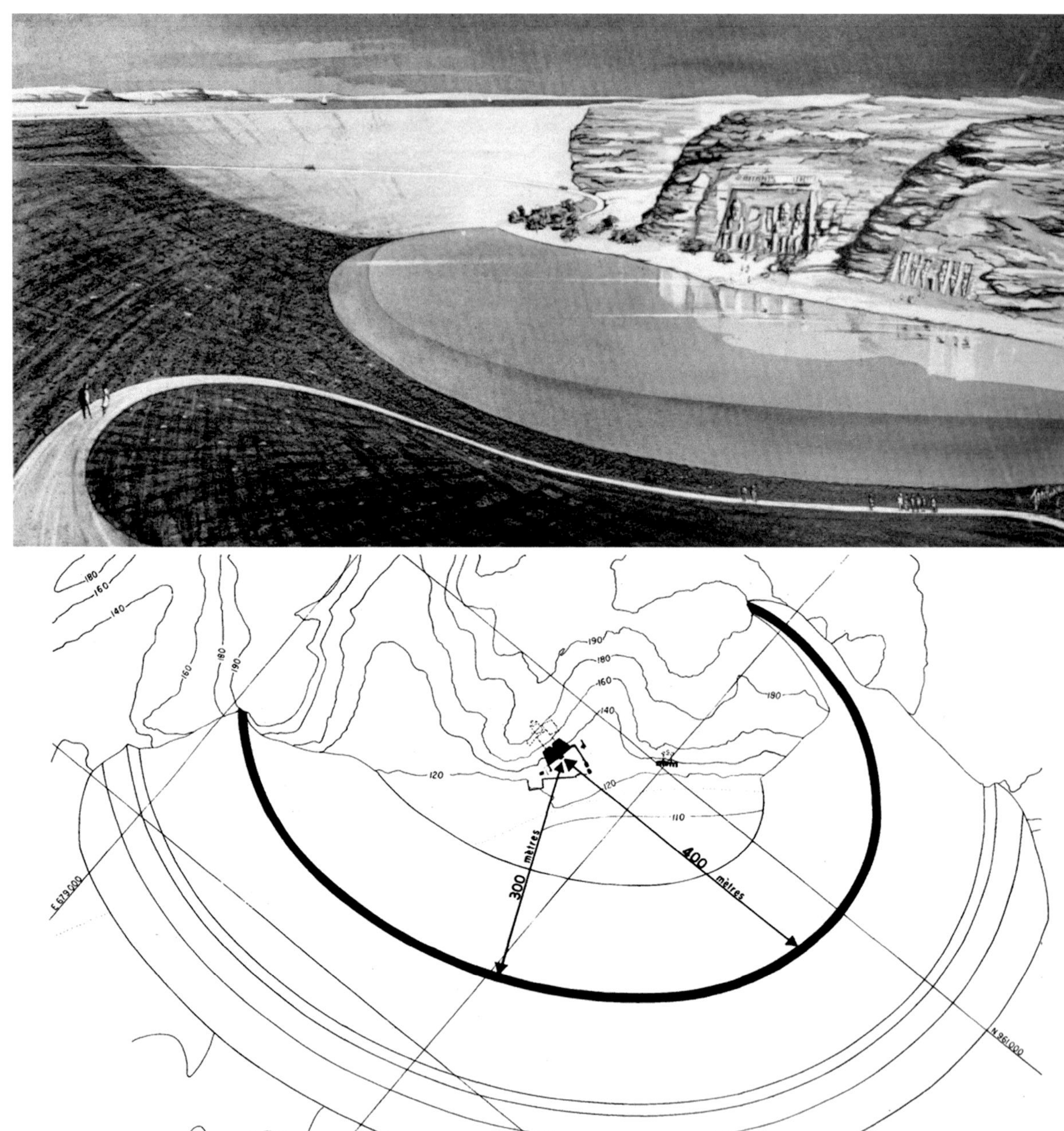

Figure 5.5 Coyne & Bellier with Albert Laprade, Plan and rendering of the "dam" scheme to protect the temples of Abu Simbel, 1960. © Coyne et Bellier, Ingénieurs Conseils.

rebellion against classicism, Laprade rejected circular geometry as "too majestic," favoring instead an elliptical gesture that he argued created "a jewel-case" around the temples, "fusing" his work "into the landscape." Found nature took the place of past architecture in this redefinition of restoration, as the new site was now defined as having an "almost natural appearance."

But the architectural legibility of this "dam" scheme only concealed its weakness as an engineering proposal. As UNESCO's chief archaeologist soon realized, "unfortunately, dams are made to go across streams not to protect something on the side of the stream."[23] A pumping station, located far from view behind the temples, would in fact perform most of the work of preservation. Financing this pumping would have been prohibitively expensive. Faced with the prospect of indefinite maintenance, within a few months UNESCO decided to pursue an alternative plan, which had been proposed by Piero Gazzola—the same Italian preservationist referenced above—during UNESCO's first fact-finding mission in October 1959.[24]

Gazzola was the first to propose "liberating" the temples of Abu Simbel from the mountain, in order to "preserve the integrity of the temple by lifting it whole."[25] Influenced by an Italian tradition of painting restoration, which made a distinction between the *epiderme* and the *struttura* (the skin and the structure) of any work of art, Gazzola transformed the monolithic site into a building with a façade, a structure, and a site—or, as he put it, "the rock, the block and the box."[26] This preliminary sketch idea was further developed and officially presented to UNESCO in October 1960: the temples would be severed from the cliff with three extended cuts into the rock, then encased in a gigantic concrete box, and lifted up about sixty meters, one centimeter at a time, by a grid of hydraulic jacks (figure 5.6). This too implied a certain notion of integrity, very similar to the one theorized by Cesare Brandi in his 1963 *Theory of Restoration*: the idea of preserving "the material wholeness of the work of art."[27] The difference between Italian wholeness and French completeness was that while Laprade had posited a timeless environment, Brandi identified a precise moment in time: restoration occurred at "the methodological moment in which the work of art is appreciated in its material form." Restoration, in other words, was a reenactment of aesthetic value.

One advantage of the theory of reenactment is that it allowed for modern technology to be exposed in preservation. Riccardo Morandi, the structural engineer who joined the Italian team, often contributed to preservation projects by designing modern structures for ancient monuments—most notably, in his entry to the 1965 competition for the Tower of Pisa, where he proposed to build a scaffold around the tower, giving the medieval monument a visible modern crutch against which to lean. Similarly, in Nubia Morandi would reenact the "wholeness" of Abu Simbel through the design of the concrete box to be poured around the temples to secure them during lifting. The box was designed in collaboration with the mathematician Gustavo Colonnetti so that the elasticity of the concrete—its ability to absorb mechanical forces—was continuous with that of the sandstone.[28] The elegance of the scheme lay in

Figure 5.6 Piero Gazzola with Riccardo Morandi, Gustavo Colonetti, and Italconsult, General view of Italian "lifting" scheme to relocate the temples. © Italconsult.

this momentary replacement of integrity by a calculated continuity between old and new materials. After all, this was the first scheme to propose a violation of integrity—a cut, along three planes, that effectively severed the relationships between building and site.

It is difficult to overstate the technological heroism that permeated both the Italian team's rhetoric and the publicity that UNESCO derived from this scheme. Every component was experimental. Morandi drew dramatic sketches of the salvage, which were circulated worldwide for fund-raising. But these renderings did surprisingly little to dramatize the process of lifting. In the most famous view, hydraulic jacks were barely visible—the concrete box dwarfed them. Enframing the seated figures, the box appeared to be a Brutalist monument in its own right, similar to Morandi's own concrete architecture (figure 5.6). The only other perspective view submitted by Morandi didn't even show the temples, instead featuring the "tunnels" dug below the monument, occupied by two Nubian children (figure 5.7). Undoubtedly they were drawn to demonstrate the monumental scale of the hydraulic jacks, but, as the only humans in the whole scheme, they also served an allegorical purpose of inhabiting "the cut" between the old and the new. Despite—or perhaps because of—the utopian resonances of these drawings, this scheme never attracted enough funds for UNESCO to begin construction. By the middle of 1963, as the flooding grew near and fund-raising stalled, other nations volunteered their schemes.[29]

Figure 5.7 Piero Gazzola with Riccardo Morandi, Gustavo Colonetti, and Italconsult, Rendering of the space under the Abu Simbel temples during their "lifting." © Italconsult.

Figure 5.8 William MacQuitty, Jane Drew and Maxwell Fry, with Edmund Happold, "Underwater" scheme to purify the water around the temples, sketch of the large temple's shrine interior by Drew and Fry Architects. Used with permission from the *Architects' Journal.*

Of these, the most fantastic was a British proposal to leave the temples underwater. Based on the assumption that it was not water itself that would disintegrate the temples, but rather the chemical composition in the Nile, the British team proposed to build a concrete dam not to *retain* water, but to *purify* it. The scheme was designed by the young structural engineer Edmund "Ted" Happold, later to become one of the best known among the postwar engineering avant-garde, then still working for Ove Arup. Architects Jane Drew and Max Fry, who had worked with Le Corbusier and Pierre Jeanneret in Chandigarh, joined him. They proposed to delegate the work of maintaining the integrity of the site to one architectural element: a single, thin, reinforced concrete membrane. In plan, this membrane appeared as a rigid curtain, folded for stability.[30] The ingenuity of this solution lay in the thinness of this interface between object, subject, and site. It was not the monument but the *visitor* that was encased: in bubbles, tunnels, and shafts that left undisturbed the harmonious continuum of elements. Visitors were shown casually strolling the underwater realm in their leisure clothes—as if the ordinary city dweller or museum-goer had been transposed into this nomadic underwater condition (figure 5.8).

Here too the scheme can be seen as a critical take on a longstanding British tradition of conservation—although much had changed since John Ruskin famously defined restoration in negative terms as "the most total destruction which a building can suffer."[31] Ruskin preferred that buildings be left to the forces of "universal decay," and his follower William Morris later founded Britain's first Preservation Society, devoted to ensuring that British monuments would be subjected only to minimal intervention, leaving visible only traces of "parasitical sublimity." In the twentieth century, this Morrisian tradition had turned into a careful technical practice, one that maintained old buildings through a combination of material science and picturesque planning. The British scheme at Abu Simbel echoes this tradition and its contradictions by apparently combining willful ruination, minimal intervention, high-tech chemistry, and picturesque enjoyment. Certainly the circulation route around this fantastical underwater scheme was episodic: from a restaurant at the top of the dam, visitors proceeded down an elevator, to access three levels of curved pathways, where circular windows and bubbles of glass offered glimpses of the colossi, or worm's eye views of the inner shrine.

Architecturally, this scheme was the most eclectic. The folded surface recalls contemporaneous structural experiments at Ove Arup, the bubbles of glass echo the plug-in sensibilities of an Archigram-infused British avant-garde, while the nautical windows are a throwback to the first machine age. This eclecticism might be explained by the fact that the original idea had been proposed not by an architect but by a film producer, Bill MacQuitty, who sold the scheme as "a cool modern miracle at a relatively low cost." An avid scuba diver with a theory of underwater perception, MacQuitty intended his visitor to swim around the monuments. He also added an environmentalist's prediction: that nuclear power would replace hydroelectricity, that the dam would become obsolete, the reservoir would be drained, and the temples rediscovered.[32] Perhaps it goes without saying, then, that although this underwater scheme captured the public imagination, it was far more radical than anything UNESCO was willing to imagine. In her memoir, Jane Drew commented that Egypt would probably have refused any plan proposed by Britain anyway.[33]

In contrast to the British scheme's notoriety, a second French scheme was officially proposed in April 1963, but it never gained publicity. Designed by the French military engineer Albert Caquot, the proposal was to "float" the temples to a new site in synchronicity with the rising of the Nile. Caquot had invented various aeronautical devices for military and civilian uses and the circular steel floaters he designed for Abu Simbel were inspired by ship-building technology, "the only procedure being practically used today to lift vertically, and transfer horizontally, any mass weighing thousands of tons."[34] Modern hydraulics were therefore combined with an appeal to the ancient Egyptian tradition of Nile water transport. But the elegance of this solution did not compensate for its incompletion, and for the awkwardness of some of its architectural choices—such as cutting the temples in a triangular shape to maintain their horizontality. The question of water infiltration during lifting was also left unaddressed. In fact, this scheme had only been proposed as a last-minute attempt at a "wet" scheme before "dry" thinking was brought to its dreaded logical conclusion.

Not one of these four schemes was implemented. Instead, the temples were cut into blocks—seven thousand and forty-seven blocks, which were sawed by hand, numbered, removed to a storage area, and then reconstituted on a hill, about two hundred meters behind their original site.

Hand—Sand—Lens

The "cutting" scheme was developed by the Swedish geological engineering firm VBB beginning in September 1962 at the request of the Egyptian government. It was three times cheaper than all preceding ones, and only adopted *in extremis* in June 1963, after it became evident that cutting was the only alternative to flooding, and the United States secretly offered a guarantee of funding[35] (figure 5.9). The cutting was also violently opposed by some of UNESCO's own experts. As late as April 1963, a Control Committee wrote that they were "immensely repulsed at the thought of recommending a project that leads to the cutting or fragmenting of these precious monuments in any way possible, even if they can be reconstituted in another site."[36] Yet within a year, this fragmentation was approved and publicized as a victory. In a complete reversal of the rhetoric of integrity that had been building momentum around the French, Italian, and British schemes, a political logic ultimately seemed to take precedence over any coherent preservation theory.

Yet we should be careful not to equate the failure of the four architectural schemes with a failure of integrity. Instead, we should ask, what definition of integrity was validated in the way the salvage eventually unfolded? After all, integrity stands as an accepted norm today, and nobody—not preservationists, not heritage historians, and least of all UNESCO—dares to speak of the Abu Simbel temples as if they had not remained authentically themselves.[37] I would like to suggest that a theory of integrity lies latent in this Swedish cutting scheme, a theory found not in the doctrinal pronouncements of conservationists, but rather in the salvage apparatus that they were forced to use—the technologies for surveying, cutting, moving, and reconstructing the temples, which formed a complicated assemblage of humans and nonhumans, ancient materials and modern machines.

We can begin to locate this assemblage in the film version of *The World Saves Abu Simbel*, an hour-long publicity film produced by UNESCO in 1967[38]

Figure 5.9
Vattenbyggnadsbryån (VBB). "Cutting" scheme to relocate the temples of Abu Simbel, 1963. Elevation of large temple façade. © SWECO. Used with permission.

(figure 5.10). Set against a free jazz soundtrack, the film documents the cutting process with frightening bluntness. Unlike most films in this genre, it does not open with a dramatization of the drowning of Nubia. Instead the title sequence shows a rapid montage of men at work, cutting away at the face of Rameses against the rhythms of an upbeat xylophone. Men at work dominate the rest of the documentary—despite the many machines in play, the human hand emerges as the most salient architectural technology. The film features an overwhelming display of human labor, as the camera cuts to different workers performing individual parts of this vast enterprise, zooming in on their hands as if to certify the monument's tactility. In the voice-over commentary, much is made of the fact that the most delicate parts of the temples were sawed continuously through the night, so changes in temperature would not affect the size of the seams. And everywhere there is a human hand there is also a lot of sand. Any cutting is followed by the pouring of sand. Any hole is filled with sand. Any block is stored on a bed of sand. Sand is ubiquitous, and its role is to mitigate the impact of various foreign intrusions onto the temple blocks. This alliance between the hand, the sand, and the camera lens produces more than just a propagandist montage. These three technologies also bind together the three aspects of this salvage scheme that made it politically realizable—three aspects I will designate as calculability, aggregation, and spectacularization.

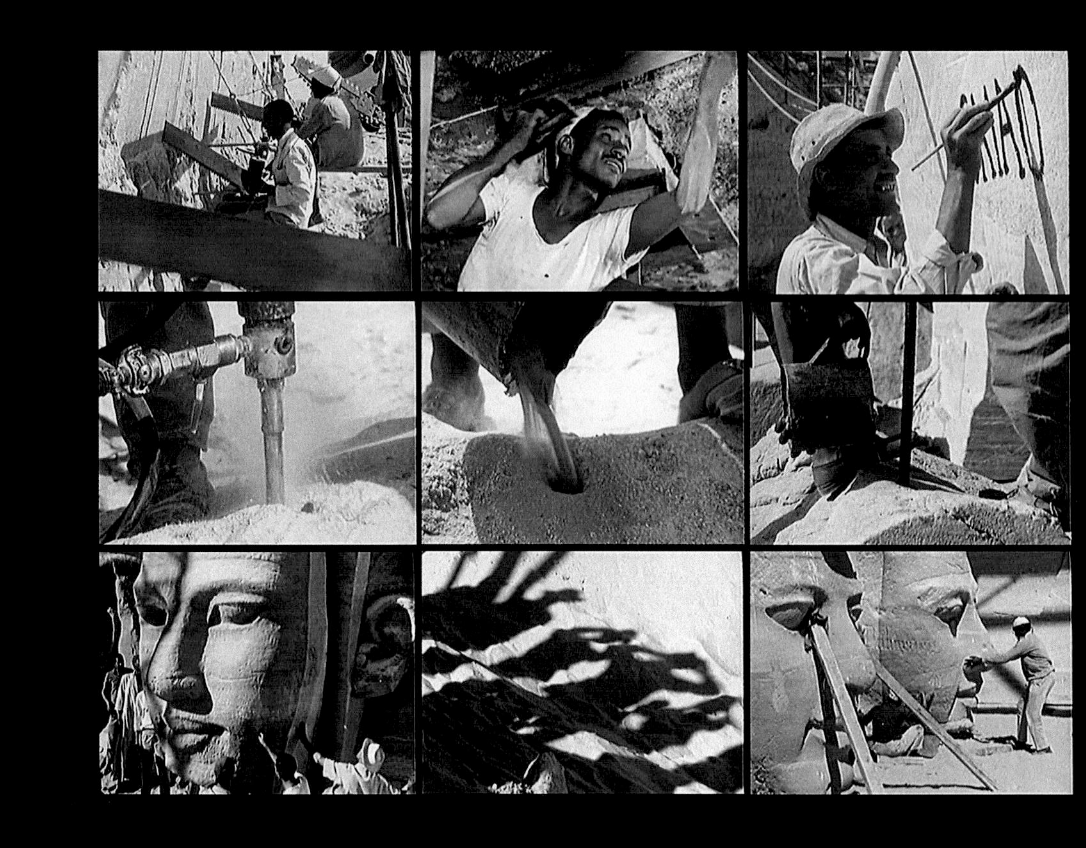

Figure 5.10 Stills from Hubert Frank, *The World Saves Abu Simbel* (Paris: UNESCO 1968).

Calculability

By calculability, I mean the potential of an architectural project to be incorporated into a project of economic development.[39] From the point of view of calculability, cutting had one advantage over all other salvage methods: it requires a lot of labor, which could be paid in local currency—Egyptian pounds—and local currency is what the US was looking to spend in Egypt. The US held large amounts of Egyptian pounds, derived from the sale to Egypt of agricultural surpluses such as wheat and cotton, under the terms of the Food for Peace program established in 1955. If the idea that one country gives its excess food to feed the hungry of another seems simple, almost philanthropic, in fact this "gift" was twice mediated by economic transactions: the US government bought wheat from its farmers, then sold it to the Egyptian government, earning a local purchasing power. The "aid" consisted in the discount that made an American commodity affordable to a poorer nation, but this affordability came with obligations for both sides: a crucial component of the program's "peaceful" ideology was that funds should be spent on projects of national economic development, agreed upon by both governments. This kind of aid, known to

Congress as Public Law (PL) 480 funds, allowed the US government to transform surplus production at home into increased political power abroad.[40] But as diplomatic tensions with Nasser rose in the early 1960s, negotiations on how to spend PL 480 funds lagged. By the time UNESCO's fund-raising campaign for Abu Simbel got underway, US-owned Egyptian pounds were accumulating in Cairo, unspent, under a threat of devaluation. A cultural project like the salvage seemed an expedient and, in the words of one cultural attaché, "non-controversial" way to expend these funds.[41] Thus the Egyptian food-for-peace program became, for a few years in the mid-1960s, a program of monuments-for-peace.

The choice of the cutting scheme was a direct result of this American foreign policy: cutting is labor-intensive, and laborers, to reiterate, could be paid in Egyptian pounds, whereas more experimental technologies (such as the hydraulic jacks, floaters, and pumping stations of the previous schemes) had to be imported with convertible dollars. Against the unmistakably Western character of preceding schemes, the image of so many Egyptian laborers in direct contact with the monuments of Nubia promoted cutting as if it were a native building method. Yet even as local labor appeared to lend cultural authenticity to architecture, its real function was to grant the monuments their international value, to act as a technological bridge between two countries at a time when their diplomatic ties were strained.

The particular economic structure of the food-for-peace program gave American officials the power to dictate not only how, but also whether, the salvage of Abu Simbel would be performed. When John F. Kennedy committed to covering about 30% of the total cost of the salvage (in accordance with a long-standing policy that the United States contribute no more than a third of all expenses in any given international project), calculability became the deciding factor in determining whether the temples would be saved at all.[42]

But it is not only that cutting was cheaper. Calculability also introduced a qualitative logic, subjecting architecture to a procedure where incommensurable values–such as agricultural commodities and temples—were somehow made commensurate. However quantifiable engineering and its technologies were at one end of the equation, an intangible value had to emerge at the other end. The importance of this intangible, "surplus" cultural value for all the nations involved can be detected in the way the Egypt government tabulated the International Fund to Salvage Abu Simbel. Whereas UNESCO tallied the financial contributions of every nation in dollars in a single chart, in contrast Egypt's official records devoted two separate columns to pounds and dollars, separating out the few nations who were able to make local contributions from the others.[43] Those few nations, as it turns out, consisted mostly of the US and the four other Western nations who eventually received a small temple as a "grant-in-return." Despite the complicated financial procedure that rendered these buildings exportable, these temples were conceived essentially as architectural gifts, surplus objects bearing a properly cultural value.

How then did the logic of calculability map onto the architecture of the temples? It is clear that the concept of integrity that emerged from the cutting scheme had less to do with the temples as architectural objects and more with their ability to absorb and redistribute economic value. In fact, the financial feasibility of the salvage provoked a complete rethinking of the notion of objecthood, not only for Abu Simbel, but also for the other Nubian temples. It is significant for instance that American officials originally hoped to devote American aid exclusively to rescuing the entire island of Philae—the so-called Pearl of Egypt, whose eclectic collection of temples the officials felt could become a symbol of America's own cultural pluralism.[44] But a different link between architecture and finance was realized instead. First, Egypt used the American aid to dismantle as many temples as possible, and store them on the island of Elephantine. This act of mass disaggregation had the double effect of distributing funds across the 24 temples and disseminating architectural matter across the desert. Then, Egypt encouraged individual nations to pay for individual reconstructions, and required that any nation hoping to receive the "gift" of a temple contribute to the salvage of one or both of the "big temples," Philae and Abu Simbel. In other words, from a financial perspective, the UNESCO campaign was an elaborate procedure for investing value in two sites (at the big temples) in order to redistribute it, creating a cultural "surplus" in several others (at each Nubian oasis, and in foreign museums).[45] It was the specificity of Nubia's pharaonic architecture—the fact that individual temples could be disaggregated from the desert and then reconstituted in heterogeneous museum environments—that made possible this translation from money to matter.

As the value of Abu Simbel became calculable, and its stone divisible, geological engineering became the dominant techno-scientific discourse surrounding the project. VBB was a large engineering firm with a portfolio of international projects, including a new electric power plant built in Aswan in 1959 to harness the power that would be created by the new High Dam.[46] As managing director Nils Berg later recalled, it was through their direct contacts with the Egyptian government that the firm became involved in the Abu Simbel project, in 1961, when an Egyptian official casually mentioned to Berg that a geological consultant was needed for the Italian lifting scheme.[47] VBB was hired as subcontractors to Italconsult, an Italian consortium that was heading the lifting project. It was only after having engineered the three "cuts" required for the lifting that VBB was eventually asked to develop an alternate scheme where the "cut" became systematic. In other words, calculability travels in expert networks that are not necessarily bound by the rise and fall of diplomatic alliances—in this case, through the hydro-geological specialization of Swedish engineers. More to the point, VBB's changed position from supporting role to center-stage of the salvage operation indexes a shift of attention provoked by the cutting scheme: from the architecture of the temples, to their aggregability.

Aggregation

As specialists in soil mechanics, VBB redefined "integrity" in geological terms, replacing an architectural notion based on the legibility of a "block" with a geological notion based on the mechanics of sand, soil, and stone. This process began when VBB were still acting as consultants to the Italian scheme. Describing the monuments scientifically as an aggregate system, they drew detailed elevations of the fissures in the temple rock, shaded the plan along the likely fault lines that ran across the temples, and constructed a plexiglass model that abstracted these fault lines as diagonal planes.[48] Next came the plans for cutting, which mandated different saws and a sliding scale of stone sizes. Here too prescription arose directly from description: the same nomenclature used to illustrate the results of stress tests eventually became the design tool for a temple reconstruction that would occur in three, sometimes four, different layers of aggregate. Eventually, once the cutting was adopted, no less than three different surface "treatments" were prescribed to replicate different types of rock finish (figure 5.11). The cliff would be cut roughly and into large blocks, whereas sculptures and reliefs would be cut with fine saws, and in pieces calibrated so that seams would least disturb their figuration.

That the integrity of the temples lay in their nature as a stone aggregate is perhaps best evidenced in VBB's final report, which concludes with the triumphant claim that "Every piece of ancient stone still does exist!"[49] What this phrase cleverly avoids mentioning is that the stone was not originally in pieces—and that most of VBB's energies were devoted precisely to designing, then filling, the space *between* the stones, both at the architectural and molecular level. To begin with, a new building material had to be invented and added: a mortar made of local Nubian sand, to join blocks together after they were reassembled. Secondly, copious volumes of epoxy were also injected into the temples, to "consolidate" the outer sculptural layer that soon came to be called the "façade" of the temples. If mortar joined together the stone *blocks*

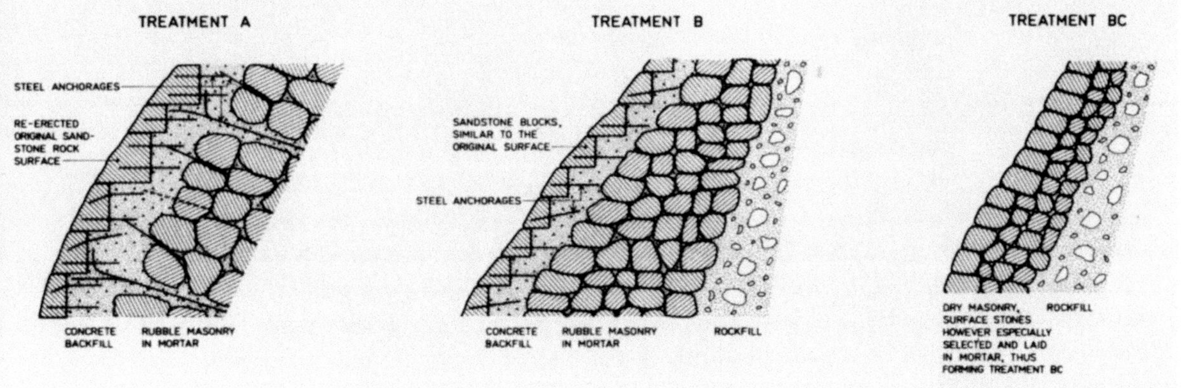

Figure 5.11 Vattenbyggnadsbryån (VBB), Details of aggregate layers for "Façade treatments" to reconstruct the large temples of Abu Simbel. © SWECO. Used with permission.

to dissimulate the cuts, epoxy on the other hand performed a much more pervasive role, intervening in the space between stone *granules* to ensure that the stone did not crumble during cutting, moving, and reassembly. Epoxy was injected three times: before the temples were cut, as the blocks were fastened to their moving anchors, and after the entire complex was reassembled (figure 5.12). VBB was familiar with epoxy as a waterproofing agent in hydrological works; but here they retooled the substance so that it worked, simply put, as glue. In strictly structural terms it was this epoxy glue that performed the "integrity" of the temples, not the "pieces of stone." But soil mechanics is a science fundamentally unconcerned with outward form. Geologists and soil engineers deal with a certain amount of aggregate, and ask how tightly this aggregate is packed, in order to compute the amount of pressure that any pile, including a sculpted one, can withstand. From this molecular perspective, it is true that "every piece of stone" of Abu Simbel remained; it is the voids between these pieces that were dramatically transformed.

Through geological science, VBB redefined the concept of material integrity at an infinitely small scale. As a result, the sand of the Nubian desert became the smallest element in a related family of building materials. VBB made extensive use of sand: as a building material, as protective coating, for shock absorption, to buffer direct contact between metal and stone, and to prevent the collapse of cavities old and new. Every time a stone was severed from the monoliths it was directly put into contact with matter drawn from around the site. By inscribing monument-movement in an intricate system of sand-displacement, VBB maintained Abu Simbel's image as a monolith while actually cutting it into increasingly smaller pieces. In the hands of the Swedish engineers, the sandstone of Nubia was a chameleonic architectural substance: sometimes a solid mass susceptible to stereometry, sometimes a loose substance that could be molded, and, throughout the salvage, a building technology akin to the crane and the saw.

By focusing on sand, VBB also created a direct connection with archaeology. Perhaps most memorably, the entire temple-fronts were covered with a gigantic pile of sand to minimize damage to the sculpted figures, creating an image a half-buried Rameses that became for a time iconic of the entire salvage.[50] As a clever engineering solution, the pile of sand was intended to shield the temples from rocks that might come detached and fall while the "mountain" above them was dismantled (color plate 7). The new plateau created by the pile also served as an elevated ground for the cranes to reach the rocks above, and, eventually, as a scaffolding for the archaeologists cutting the temple faces. This piling technique was inspired by ancient Egyptian artists and engravers, who filled temples with sand in order to work on the upper portions of their walls, then gradually removed the sand in layers as they worked their way down the surfaces.[51] Yet there is more to this striking image of a buried Rameses than the revival of an archaic building technique; the sand cover also rehearsed the *modern* act of archaeological discovery. Ever since its

Figure 5.12 Epoxy being injected into the temple-front of the large temple of Abu Simbel to consolidate it before or after cutting, ca. 1965. © Georg Gerster. Used with permission.

Figure 5.13 Sune Lindström, Alf Bydén, and Rodger Waters (for VBB), Proposals for sculpting the surroundings of the Abu Simbel temples, 1962. © SWECO. Used with permission

rediscovery by a Swiss explorer under a mountain of sand in 1813, Abu Simbel spent much of the nineteenth century being repeatedly dug in and out of sand (including by such famous tourists as Gustave Flaubert and Maxime du Camp). This history of repeated uncovering had even earned the temples a place above the couch in the office of Sigmund Freud, where a David Roberts rendering of the temples was hung to trigger a patient's psycho-archaeological introspection. By capitalizing on this history of excavation, the Swedish scheme highlighted the modern nature of the temples as *discovered*, rather than their ancient nature as *sculpted*.

The aesthetic potential of this archaeo-geological viewpoint was not lost on VBB, especially on its in-house architects, Sune Lindström and Alf Bydén. In 1962—while still working as consultants to the Italian scheme, and entrusted only with the "reconstruction of the site"—they made proposals that took striking formal liberties with the design of the site. The architects offered three options to UNESCO. At one extreme, they proposed to "preserve the setting and appearance of the temples as closely as possible" by reconstructing the rock exactly as in the original site. At the other extreme, they proposed to mold the rock around the temples into a "characteristic silhouette in an otherwise featureless landscape," thereby creating a "new work"[52] (figure 5.13). The mountain around the seated figures would be sculpted into a chain of reinforced concrete splines, faced with sandstone and dramatically extruded to a point of absolute thinness. VBB justified this elastic geometry by talking of "a synthesis of the original conditions and the new" and a need to create "a monument with fresh values, still in the spirit of the ancient Egyptians" but also "embodying present day technology and philosophy." The horizontal plane of approach in front of the temples would also be "shaped," and again Lindström and Bydén offered several options: to geometricize the optimal angles for arrival by boat, or to create a floating pier that could rise and recede with the tide. Both options, however, expanded the futuristic idiom of the elevations, using convex geometry to redesign the new site.

Clearly the architects of VBB were motivated by the same impulse as Albert Laprade, who wanted to inscribe a new elliptical dam in the desert. Within a decade, Lindström and Bydén produced iconic buildings in the Middle East that took up Laprade's orientalizing legacy and brought it to new heights of postmodern regionalism—one famous example being the Water Towers of Kuwait City. Already in their 1962 proposal for the Abu Simbel site, this direction was glimpsed in their unsolicited design for a "floating hotel" shaped as an oval peninsula. Striped so as to disappear in the desert, the hotel would dock itself to the floating platform in front of the temples, offering tourists direct access from the water to the shrine.

UNESCO reacted to these bold sculptural proposals by promptly instituting a rule that "architectural shapes should be avoided" in the reconstruction of the site.[53] Evidently VBB had mistaken building for site, and vice versa. In the final instance, the rock face and water approach were made to look exactly like the original site. Yet a closer look at a section through the temples as built shows that, even without sculptural bravura, the plastic "synthesis" VBB advocated ultimately prevailed in the architectonic logic of the new whole. But rather than being outwardly expressed, this synthesis was turned inward. A new massive concrete dome was built to support the artificial hill in back of the seated figures—a dome whose futuristic interior, worthy of James Bond, is usually excluded from the definition of the monument *as such* (figure 5.14). In fact, this domed space was but the largest void created by a thin layer of reinforced concrete that lined the whole monumental complex. Concrete was the main shaping agent of the work: it supported the interior walls of the shrine, provided a backing for the reconstructed sculptural fronts, and also supported a new rear façade with its a gentle pyramidal form.[54] From an architectural standpoint, the Swedish scheme completely transformed the temples into a new kind of building (figure 5.15). Once a shrine with a single, thick façade, each temple became a façade system wrapped around two inhabitable spaces: a shrine, and a dome. Yet because the scheme was only ever described in geological terms,

Figure 5.14
Vattenbyggnadsbryån (VBB), Section for the reconstruction of the large temple of Abu Simbel, showing reinforced concrete dome and façade backing, 1965. © SWECO. Used with permission.

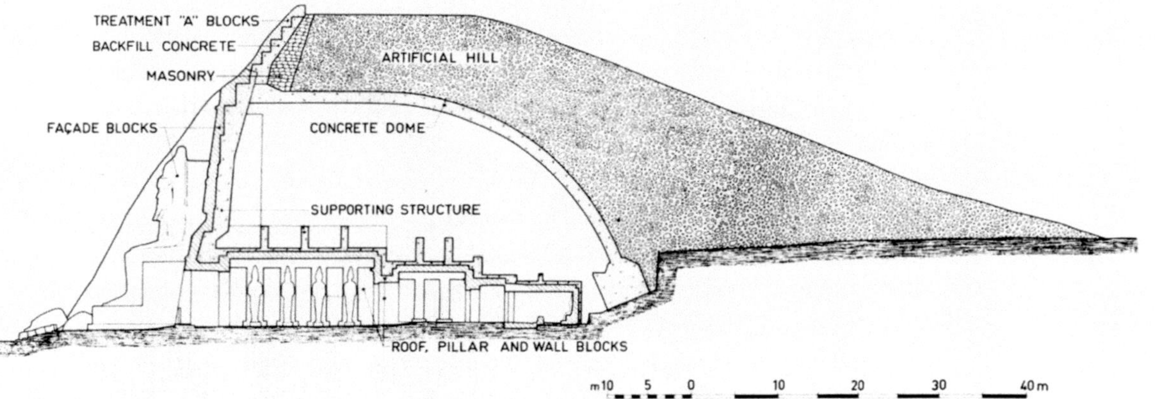

Figure 5.15 Abu Simbel reconstruction showing the building of the dome. © SWECO. Used with permission.

no such architectural overview was ever provided. Instead modern architectural technologies were hidden from view, in a gesture that brings us to the last aspect of the hand-sand-lens alliance—visibility, and its instrument, the eye.

Spectacularization

There is a distinct continuity between the reconceptualization of these temples as geological and financial aggregates and the spectacularization of their movement. This awkward word, "spectacularization," helps to thematize a pattern already encountered, whereby every aspect of the temples' movement was not only visually recorded, but also enhanced, annotated, presented and re-presented, narrated, edited, and dramatized, in order to be showcased across the world. This intense effort to publicize an event taking place deep in the desert of Nubia confirms Guy Debord's 1967 pronouncement that "modern society has invested the surface of every continent—even where the material basis of economic exploitation is still lacking—by spectacular means."[55] And in the case of Abu Simbel, spectacularization also means something more specific: the incorporation of optical technologies into the apparatus that certified and reproduced the integrity of the temples. In order to be saved, the temples had to be validated by experts, technically described by engineers, and, in this third step, popularized to a worldwide public. A crucial component of each of these tasks was performed not by strictly architectural technologies, but by media of visualization that focused on seeing elements of the temples up close (and in pieces) rather than depicting the monumental complex as a whole. In other words, new modes of seeing came to the rescue of the monument, as well.

Throughout the entire salvage, camera crews recorded the movement of every stone. This ever-present lens attested to the integrity of the work, by showing that salvage workers were behaving ethically and that architectural matter was treated authentically. Indeed, filming the movement of stones became standard practice in Nubian salvage work, as evidenced by photographs of the most recent temple reassemblies, which show blocks being lifted while surmounted by an engineer *and* a cameraman.[56] But aside from documenting the work, the filming process also contributed its own mechanics of cutting and editing to the staging of the salvage. As we have already seen in *The World Saves Abu Simbel*, optical montage (of film) and physical assemblage (of blocks) became conjoined, so that cutting between film shots helped to hide the fundamental violence of cutting the stone into blocks.

Another type of mechanical vision also became instrumental at the other end of the process, where reconstruction was aided by the use of a sophisticated apparatus of photogrammetry. The French National Geographic Institute originally used photogrammetry to record the temples as a set of topographic elevations in 1959—indeed the word "salvage" originally designated *only* this process of recording temples before they disappeared—when it was thought they would inevitably be flooded, and that the three-dimensional information of photogrammetry was all that could be "preserved."[57] Once the temple movement actually began, however, these topographic drawings became guarantors of originality, used to check the reconstructed profile. The Institute also produced a film, *Nubia '64*, which showcased photogrammetric technology as a modern wonder, and paused on every component of the machinery as if it were the product of an evolution in visual accuracy[58] (color plate 7). One sequence, in particular, proceeded through a chain of specialized viewing agents: beginning with archaeologists hunched over Egyptian reliefs, continuing with geographers standing upright pointing their cameras at the temples, and culminating with a prolonged sequence about a "machine operator" who is prosthetically attached to a stereometric vision machine through eyes, hands, and feet. The film decomposes the act of seeing into discreet actions, so that the eye is focused on individual lines and points, rather than on the monument as a whole. Conversely, each point on the visible surface of the temples is subjected to intense and close-up examination by the stereometric camera. The eye and the body of the machine operator perform a reenactment of these reference points, and the task of reconstituting the visual whole is then delegated to a "plotting machine."

These optical technologies reconstructed a new image for the temples of Abu Simbel, in the same manner as experimental building technologies reconstituted a new architecture for the temple. Just as cutting and injecting were two ways to intervene directly into the fabric of the stone, so filming and photogrammetry allowed a mechanical reenactment of the visual experience of the monument, even after it could no longer be apprehended as an aesthetic whole. In this manner the perceiving eye was subjected to a logic of disassembly, placing the temples in what Walter Benjamin called the "age of mechanical reproducibility." Indeed, the pairing of architectural and visual technologies at Abu Simbel recalls Benjamin's famous analogy between scalpel and camera with remarkable accuracy—the idea that "the camera operator is like a surgeon, in that he intervenes mechanically in the assemblage of the work of art."[59] Taking Benjamin's cue, we can further specify the hand-sand-lens alliance by imagining that technologies that "penetrated" the stone and those that "scanned" its surface were in fact paired off: the eye and the blade, the syringe and the camera, the block of stone and the reel of film.

The significance of this pairing of visual and surgical technologies is that it was systematically used to perform a delicate balancing act, between truthfully rendering the features of Egyptian architecture, and giving them a newly modern aesthetic significance. Consider the three characteristics of Egyptian art that were theorized by art historians in the twentieth century: first, its nature as an art-form "conceived for strictly near viewing," to use Alois Riegl's words; second, the shallowness of Egyptian representation, its strict adherence to the rules of what Adolf Hildebrand called "relief space"; and third, the representation of body parts as disconnected components, what Erwin Panofsky called its "mechanical," rather than "organic," arrangement of parts.[60] Each one of these formal properties was enhanced and manipulated in the cutting performance. Because Egyptian art is an art with no built-in foreshortening, it was possible to film pieces of the temple in an extreme close-up without exposing any optical distortions. In fact, since the three salvage techniques—cutting, injecting, and photogrammetry—required an extreme proximity of the eye to the sculpted form, they reenacted Riegl's near-view. Similarly, because Egyptian art's planarity bears the memory of the block from which it was carved, it was not shocking to see blocks with elements of relief being carried away from the site—they simply looked like the unfinished Egyptian sculptures that were known from museum collections throughout the world. And finally, because Egyptian artists proportioned each part of the body independently—rather than modifying their shape and size in relation to the whole body—it was possible for parts of the temple to lay exposed in amputated form (as happened with the legs famously photographed without Rameses's torso), without provoking in the viewer repulsion at human dismemberment, producing instead a mild longing for the other limbs, which all retained their idealized proportions on their own. Indeed, perhaps the most important part of the cutting apparatus to aid in the visual reconstruction of the whole was the cutting grid itself. Again Panofsky provides a clue in his description of the Egyptian theory of proportions as a theory that made no difference between viewing and producing. Panofsky emphasized that Egyptian artists worked "not by prospectus (view) but in geometric plan," using a finely meshed grid to subdivide the block of stone and lay out the position of each part.[61] For Panofsky the use of this grid meant that Egyptian art was an art of reconstruction, not imitation—and in light of this, the imposition of a cutting grid onto the temple fronts of Abu Simbel appears no longer as a gesture of deconstruction, but rather of reconstruction: a reenactment of the grid that must have been a part of the temple's original making.

Whereas the original artists of Abu Simbel needed only a grid to convey a normative proportional system to the beholder, in reconstituting Abu Simbel as a modern work of art, the cutting grid was complemented by a proliferation of media. All the views, renderings, drawings, films and photographs gave the modern viewer a simultaneous and separate rendering of multiple projections, narrativizing them over time into a story of "preservation." Consider for instance the most dramatic sequence of *The World Saves Abu Simbel*, when the "face" of Rameses is severed from the body. The camera begins with a wide shot from below (a modern monumentalizing view par excellence), that shows the block of one of Rameses' heads, the crane lifting it, and the men around it. As soon as the face is detached and begins to rise, the camera zooms in on the hands of the archaeologists who take hold of the block to keep it from rotating off axis, inserting their fingers into a hole that has been bored in the face. After this moment of tactility, the camera adopts and maintains the normal view—an axis perpendicular to the surface—following the face of Rameses in a full frontal close-up as it is carried to its new site, and cutting to a counter-shot of what Rameses sees as the voice-over narrates: "King Rameses gives one last majestic look" at his former abode.

More than an added propaganda dimension, this careful re-imaging of the formal qualities of the temples was integral to their material salvage, and their eventual status as international objects. To modernize the temples was to integrate contemporary spectacular values into Egyptian form. And insofar as this effort of spectacularization was done for the sake of preserving the integrity of the temples, "integrity" was redefined as an alignment, across millennia, of ancient modes of construction with modern modes of perception.

Sculpted in Quadriplicate

From the moment its survival was in doubt, the legitimacy of the Abu Simbel complex as a suitable international monument was a matter of contention, especially in the American and international press between 1960 and 1963. Because PL 480 funds were "public" and had to be appropriated by Congress, the temples became the object of a sustained debate, in congress itself and in a constant stream of op-eds, feature articles, first-hand reports, travelogues, radio specials, and museum exhibitions. To be sure, these debates amount to a debased form of criticism, derivative of more sophisticated discourses. (In one notorious episode, it was reported that a presiding congressman reacted to an archaeologist's presentation by "asking the prize question, who is Abu Simbel?" His mistake was quickly rectified: "Mr. Chairman, Abu Simbel refers to a geographical location."[62]) But in this discourse, and especially in the words of detractors who argued *against* any salvage, we find a cohesive new definition of preservation as a practice of mediation.

The first argument against saving the temples was that the sculpted figures were crudely made, that they were not particularly fine examples of Egyptian architecture—not unique enough to be saved. "Look at the thick knees," one critic wrote.[63] This critique echoed the judgment of many architectural historians, among them Sigfried Giedion, who visited Abu Simbel in 1958 and found them too small to be monumental, but too gigantic to be refined. For Giedion, and a whole generation of architects fascinated with pyramids as "space-emanating objects," the Abu Simbel temples were merely colossal—symptoms of decline and mannerism in Egyptian art.[64] A related argument, developed by art critics, was that by drawing attention to Abu Simbel as a "unique work of art" UNESCO had encouraged a confusion between spectacle and art. The temples were valuable only as part of a unique sequence of sun, sand, and Nile, and UNESCO used film and photography to artificially inflate this scenographic value, effectively fabricating a tourist attraction in advance. Certainly the involvement of André Malraux rendered the entire enterprise suspect in some scholarly circles. In 1959 Malraux had taken part in UNESCO's inaugural ceremony, comparing Nubia in a famous speech to his "museum without walls," where sculpture is given new life by photographic reproduction.[65] According to Malraux, ancient art could be reinvigorated by modern media, which granted even secondary works a "spurious" (though positive) "modernism" by blowing up their details to colossal scale.[66] It was through Malraux's rhetoric that many readers of UNESCO's literature first heard of the temples of Abu Simbel, and when Malraux visited the temples in 1966 he was photographed staring down one of Rameses's delaminated faces, undoubtedly testing this "spuriousness" firsthand. But more traditional art scholars found spuriousness not in the works themselves, but rather in the motivation of popularizers such as Malraux and UNESCO, who tried to replace their exacting value judgments (that Abu Simbel was a secondary work) with the seductive value of modern spectacle (that Abu Simbel was photogenic).

The blindness of American cultural officials to these critiques only fed the controversy, especially abroad. For many British Egyptologists, America cared less about Egyptian monumentality than about its own, and the entire project was simply a way for the United States to achieve a colossal presence in the world. The European intelligentsia, well-versed in arguments made by art historians such as Willhelm Wörringer about the "Americanist immoderation" of Egyptian art, came to consider Abu Simbel cynically as a fitting emblem of American arrogance.[67] And even at home, some skeptical pre-historians and politicians were quick to point out that Rameses was not a particularly important pharaoh, but a megalomaniac, a "fanatical builder" obsessed with reproducing himself.[68] To preserve Abu Simbel meant to preserve a monument to a despot, and a not particularly good one. Rameses II's only historical achievement was the creation of an arts industry for the mass production of effigies, reliefs, and statues of himself.[69] Ironically, increased quantity led to a decline in quality, and this repetition rendered any sculpture Rameses commissioned less valuable, including those at Abu Simbel. So at worst the temples of Abu Simbel were emblems of a hollow, narcissistic, imperial power. At best they were simply a site where, as one journalist put it, "Rameses foresightedly had himself sculpted in quadriplicate."[70]

Crude execution, cheap spectacle, questionable politics, showy repetition—none of these attacks put a stop to the salvage effort, because they merely pointed out that the temples of Abu Simbel were already mass-produced objects. In a sense, the lack of originality in their making only facilitated their ability to be reproduced as a modern monument. In the light of these debates, the salvage of Abu Simbel appears as a solution not to the problem of preserving existing cultural value, but the problem of creating a new one. Ultimately the temples of Abu Simbel were saved not *in spite* of the fact that they were cut into blocks, but rather *because* they could be cut into blocks while remaining more or less authentically themselves.

Preservation as a Medium

What does this episode tell us about the expansion of preservation's domain in the 1960s, pithily expressed by Piero Gazzola as "we have gone from punctual to global protection"? To reiterate, the phrase is usually interpreted to mean that monuments in this period became smaller and more vernacular, while the protective environment around them became larger. But in the case of Abu Simbel, a monolith that was literally injected with boundaries, it is the protective norms and forms that became increasingly finer, more "punctual" one might say, while the monument emerged as more "global." It is also clear that while the project offered preservationists unprecedented access to political power, the architectural object itself eventually appeared to take on more power than any of the human actors, none of whom could claim to have control of the project entirely. So while the story is undoubtedly "heroic," we cannot speak, with Alan Powers, of a narrative of local empowerment. Yet it is not enough to say that Abu Simbel is therefore a narcissistic mirage, a symptom of human passivity in the face of tourist machinery.

Some heritage historians have detected in the "heritage inflation" of the last third of the twentieth century a strain of narcissism. Françoise Choay concluded her authoritative 1992 history of patrimony with a chapter on new technologies—of mass communication and transportation–which she blamed for turning heritage into an instrument of "hidden mediation" that only fueled a "cult of passive self-contemplation" worldwide.[71] But if we are to take seriously the claim that preservation's "expansion" diffused architectural values to the point that they mediate social bonds, for good and for ill, then preservation must be taken as a legitimate space-making practice too.

Paying closer attention to technologies of preservation alerts us to the fact that the debate about agency and passivity that has animated preservation circles since the 1960s is really a debate about the emergence of a new architectural medium. By "new architectural medium" I don't mean that preservationists experimented with new materials, such as sand and epoxy, or new crafts, such as cutting and reassembling. Nor do I mean that architectural heritage is a kind of machine for producing images, akin to a camera or a television, although this argument has been convincingly made.[72] Rather, I mean "medium" in the expanded sense of a socio-technical apparatus, whose emergence Raymond Williams recounted in 1972, when he talked about the reification since the nineteenth century of the "properties of the medium" and the "material consciousness" of artistic makers into a set of social, aesthetic, and often commercial institutions.[73]

The apparatus that I have been describing—the hand-sand-lens alliance, its associated financing and engineering structures, and all the networks that made them possible–was one that placed architecture under a logic of media. The logic of moving monuments was allied with the logic of moving images. The logic of storing stones was allied with the logic of storing photographs. And the logic of repeated hand-cutting was allied with the logic of image-reproduction. Throughout these repetitions and translations, the object of preservation was fundamentally transformed. In this sense preservation functioned as a mode of cultural production and communication that incorporated the characteristics of another other mode of production, architecture. Could we not, then, see architectural preservation as a medium, whose content is architecture?

This proposition seems particularly promising for dealing with the historical asynchronies of the history of preservation—the fact that preservation always implies thinking of historical change at two speeds. "Advances" in preservation technology subject architecture to a double axis of progress, and preservationists take seriously the task of mediating between these two tempos. Sometimes they achieve perfect alignment; sometimes syncopation is all they can manage. But even when two speeds of history align, something is always rendered invisible—as in films where the spokes of a rotating wheel appear to us stand still, because the frame frequency of the camera has conspired with the rhythm of the wheel's revolution to fool the eye. For the historian trying to make sense of this mediating act, consulting media theorists may prove helpful. Consider for instance a central axiom of Marshall McLuhan's theory of media, that new media manifest themselves in new environments, and that new environments are usually invisible, serving instead to "make visible the preceding environment" that is their content.[74] Without endorsing McLuhan's particularly teleological history, we can learn from his insight. What should ultimately strike us about the architectural technologies that were used to dismantle Abu Simbel is how unremarkable they were. Cranes, jackhammers, steel bars, flatbed trucks, bulldozers, and thousands of workers—these were the same machines that appeared in projects of development and modernization across the world.

Their use to cut apart an ancient temple may shock us today, but they were effectively invisible to the international citizen of the 1960s. In contrast, the features of Ramesside architecture, with its camera-friendly gigantism, were rendered newly visible and subjected to intense aesthetic judgment.

One way to approach the history of architectural preservation, then, is to look for places where technologies have aged, rendering visible media environments that were previously invisible. At Abu Simbel, counterintuitively, the "cuts" have withstood the test of time and remain more or less invisible, thanks in part to a maintenance crew which regularly fills them with mortar. As for the very technology that once threatened the temple's existence—electricity—it was soon used to incorporate the temples into established touristic norms. Within a decade the temples were plugged into the power grid that was brought up from Aswan, lighting up the temples through an extensive system of light and sound. It is the injected epoxy that has aged the most. Once invisible, it has over time darkened the overall appearance of the entire temple-front by changing its internal structure. Stone derives its usual color from the light reflecting in the space around each particle, but in a phenomenon aptly called "change in specular reflection," the epoxy has saturated the aggregate entirely, impeding the ability of each stone granule to act as a minuscule mirror.[75] So the Rameses we see today is a stiffer, puffier version of his old self.

This material connection between saturation and visuality should help to dispel the idealist misconception that preservation today always operates through nested frames of historicity, or through two images of architecture, one contemporary and framing, the other historic and enframed. The "environmental" turn in preservation practices is also sometimes mistaken to mean that spatial scale now corresponds to historical distance—that the more modern the viewer, the better his or her perspective. Chemical saturation connotes a different idea: that images appear and disappear through subtle changes in the material composition between adjoining spaces and surfaces. Rather than considering the imageability of architecture as an external product independent of its material presence, we can take saturation to mean that images produced through preservation cannot help but return to, and reside in, the architecture itself, and we can imagine that a semi-magical, perhaps electro-chemical process causes a constant toggling between all of these accumulated images, depending upon the discursive environment that comes to pass. Lastly, the notion of saturation reminds us that there has been a historical tipping point: if international architectural preservation has long been a social and political medium, around the 1960s it became a medium, tout court.

The role played by Abu Simbel in giving autonomy to architectural preservation makes it an apt stopping point for the story of midcentury monument survival. Throughout this book, I have balanced projects and case studies with conferences and debates, to demonstrate that their contributions were interwoven. But by the time the last of the Nubian temples had been salvaged in 1980, this forced marriage of the legal/discursive and the technical/applied branches of international preservation—a marriage we have been following since the first meetings of "intellectual cooperation" in the 1930s—had become an impediment to many international initiatives. Today, it is simply assumed that any project to make a monument international will modify the norms and forms into which the monuments are trying to fit. This feedback mechanism has been naturalized, as a result of preservation's politics from below. But it was in fact made possible by massive and hard-earned intergovernmental investment from above. Abu Simbel stands as a heroic marker of the first time an explicitly international consensus about culture was memorialized in built form. But as the coda will briefly argue, it also turned out to be one of the last.

CODA

Viscosities

Every stone has become ironic to us.

Lewis Mumford (1937)[1]

To salvage is to destroy; to destroy is to save yourself.

Superstudio (1971)[2]

The international design practice that monument survival had become by the middle of the 1970s—part technical medium, part artistic vocation, part political cause—is alive and well today, in the early twenty-first century. There are plenty of architects available to send on missions worldwide, a steady supply of planning projects that require their expertise, and a sprawling bureaucracy to manage their progress. A cogent surrounding discourse has also developed, to periodically rethink the legacy of World Heritage, especially questioning its object-centered view of architecture by devoting more attention to the problem of urban "buffer zones," or to the question of material "reversibility."[3] While many of the episodes recounted in this book were experienced as exceptions to ongoing practice, adventures in the lives and careers of those involved, they have now become canonical. Indeed, internationalist preservation has acquired its own history.[4] Yet architectural design no longer holds a monopoly over heritage protection in the global imagination. There are too many practices competing for the management of risk as an aspect of daily life, too many risks that hover, too many demands for protection, and too many ways of making a world *through* protection.[5] Material endangerment has become an experiential category, which far exceeds the conscripted legibility of architectural intervention.[6]

Architecture's ally in the rise of World Heritage—the intergovernmental organization—has also waned in scope and power, and not only in the cultural sphere. The era of international big government, so to speak, ended almost as soon as it had begun.[7] The oil crisis of 1973 transformed the logic of economic aid, and a wave of neoliberal reforms in national politics cemented those changes, throwing into question the assumption that cultural property, qua property, was best managed as a transnational public good rather than in private hands.[8] The end of the Cold War upended the geopolitical blocks that had structured international diplomacy and made it navigable to cultural actors.[9] Meanwhile, shifting modes of warfare transformed once again the criteria by which military forces calibrate their moral compass—or fail to do so.[10] Ideologically, too, the appeal of humanist culture as a universal cause that could gather disparate constituencies began to fade after 1968, with ecological consciousness gradually taking its place as a cause and a paradigm. And through each of these shifts, architectural monuments as platforms for experimenting with new technologies were completely transformed, because all techno-politics began to be shot through with infrastructure of a more pervasive, computerized kind, acquiring since the 1990s the irrevocably digitized form they assume today.

This is not to say that all the work that midcentury internationalists put into rethinking the monument was for naught. Certainly in architecture, their victories contributed to a massive thaw in the modernist/historicist divide. Postmodernism, as an architectural movement, ascended to global visibility in the 1970s in part by combining highly technical building methods with the creative reuse of forms of the past. As such, it owed a lot to preservation's own consolidation as a transnational discipline in the years prior. Indeed, many of the building practices that postmodern architects rediscovered as "vernacular" or "historic" had survived as ways not of making new buildings but of maintaining old ones. These traditions' openness to structural modernizations, both literal and figural, had been very much predetermined. Conversely, some building cultures, most famously that of Egypt's Nubians, were shored up by international intervention long before they became fodder for postmodern or regionalist discourses. Of course, postmodern architects took many liberties with objecthood, and exploded the "monument" that had been the stable object-referent for international preservation, as this book has chronicled it. Fragmented into so many useable tectonic parts, monumental heritage became a geographically amorphous imaginary where entire oeuvres, or styles, are fully deterritorialized.

In humanistic scholarship also, the monument reappeared in the last third of the twentieth century as an especially fruitful object for thinking across disciplines, in a way that far outperformed Panofsky's already remarkable 1937 claim that "everyone's monument is everyone else's document," which we heard in chapter 2.[11] Post-structuralist theory periodically appealed to monuments: in 1969 Michel Foucault called for an "archaeology of knowledge" in order to undermine the presumed hierarchy between a monument (mute and requiring investigation) and a document (preselected by archivists and passively received by historians).[12] Jacques Le Goff took this oscillation between monument and document as a scholarly method in itself, key to a new materialist historiography.[13] The long-term benefits of these theoretical innovations has been felt in the rise of new subdisciplines that study heritage critically, revealing how historical inequalities are embedded in disciplinary formations and social practices.[14] Older disciplines have also rediscovered the historiographic capaciousness of monumental architecture. Art historians who have rethought the spatio-temporal bases of the history of aesthetics often refer to architecture's stratification in time and space, and anthropologists have described how social meanings organize themselves concentrically around objects—often monumental ones.[15]

More than a happy accident or a postmodern haunt, the forceful return of monuments and memory in the last third of the twentieth century was owed in part to the deliberate material transformations that, as this book has chronicled, were effected in the midcentury to ensure innumerable architectural objects would retain their mnemonic powers. No wonder these ideas found themselves newly applicable to architecture, "after the great divide."[16]

Whither architectural survival, then, today? As a branch of design it thrives in new arenas. Before I spring forward to the present day, I want to span between the 1930s and the 1970s once more, this time through the eyes of the avant-garde, beginning again with Lewis Mumford. When in 1937 he declared the death of the monument, he also quipped that every stone had "become ironic."[17] This seems an untimely observation, given the profoundly un-ironic way the built environment became a target of destruction in the four decades that followed. But a taste for architectural ironies eventually did arise in the 1970s, and played a part in reviving interest in monuments among an international architectural avant-garde that had long dismissed them as irrevocably passé.

Consider *Twelve Italian Cities*, a project of the Italian group Superstudio. It opened with a polemic, "to salvage is to destroy; to destroy is to save yourself," and continued with six proposals to "save" Italian city centers by designing the way they would succumb to a variety of cataclysmic emergencies[18] (figure 6.1). The irony lay in the way each salvage was performed, through one deadpan urban gesture: flood Florence, drain Venice, bury Rome, tilt Pisa, encase Milan, stage Naples. If disasters had become normal events in architectural history, then every stone's demise could be designed, ironically. But the real target of Superstudio's critique was bureaucracy. By subtitling the project *Italia Vostra* (Your Italy), and formatting it as tear sheets from an inventory, Superstudio mimicked the methods of the Italian preservation group *Italia Nostra* (Our Italy) who had mastered the art of provoking bureaucratic action by stoking public outrage. The group had developed a strident visual and rhetorical style, to protect buildings against a wave of demolitions that they blamed on deregulated economic speculation and tourist development.[19] Superstudio called their anti-capitalist bluff, however, showing that, even in a radically ruined or engulfed state, canonical monuments could be optimized for consumption. To add insult to injury, this ultimate commodification came through paper too, in the form of seductive, glossy, realistic, photomontages.[20]

Figure 6.1 Superstudio, Study for the city of Graz (*Un Cubo d'aqua per Graz*), 1971. Photo: Craig Stephens. Used with permission from Drawing Matter Collections. © The artist.

Superstudio's visual technique learned from an ongoing and pervasive conflation of document and monument. After all, the combined materialities of building and paper were key aspects of the special branch of activism that had attracted these Italian radicals to architectural salvage in the first place. They had been students in Florence in 1966 when a spectacular flood engulfed the historic city center and brought thousands of volunteers to salvage the city's cultural treasures, and innumerable international media outlets to watch, as paintings, sculptures, manuscripts, were passed, one by one, down a human chain of "mud angels" (figure 6.2). Their photomontages of city centers, then, sublimated these waterlogged manuscript pages into airbrushed dystopias.

Superstudio was not the first avant-garde to cast a desiring eye on the old-new material apparatus of architectural salvage. Bauhaus master László Moholy-Nagy, who had traveled to Athens to record the activities of the architects of the Congrès internationaux d'architecture moderne (CIAM) in 1933, had already been captivated by Nicolas Balanos's work on the Acropolis—the same work we encountered in chapter 1. In his film documenting the congress, Moholy-Nagy captured the Erechtheion colonnade in an altered tectonic state, with a steel rod between each caryatid, holding up the architrave (figure 6.3). Lingering on this found montage of stones, clouds and steel, Moholy's camera found inspiration for his own photograms.

Figure 6.2 Students helping to salvage volumes from the Florence National Central Library during the flood of Florence, November 4, 1966. © Getty.

Between steel made to act like stone in 1933 and paper airbrushed to look like water in 1971, the salient material property of architectural heritage—that quality that seemed to offer designers an ethic or stance—had shifted: from integrity to viscosity. As a model for aesthetic and political action, salvage was no longer to be guided by an ideal of internal resistance (integrity), but rather by the possibility of permeability and resilience to context (viscosity). No longer a rhythmic chopping of history at two speeds, architectural monuments offered a way of being in history that was a blurry and messy miasma of action and reaction. The Marxist architectural historian Manfredo Tafuri even named "viscosity" as the reason that architecture successfully infitrated, in the late twentieth century, a conservation discourse once dominated by painterly concepts.[21]

This shift provides an apt heuristic for thinking more broadly about how architecture's historical depth—or its capacity as a medium for storing history—has changed in the international imagination since the 1970s. Keeping this notion of viscosity in mind, I want to briefly outline four ways that politics, technology, and aesthetics intersect in global preservation practice today.

First, nongovernmental agencies (NGOs) have taken over for intergovernmental agencies in feeding the global apetite for architectural survival, and they function through a flexible infiltration, rather than a rigid control, of political institutions. Today UNESCO defers largely to the consultancies whose births this book has witnessed—from ICOM to ICCROM and eventually ICOMOS—to set its agenda. This mode of global cultural governance was foreshadowed at the 1965 White House Conference where the phrase "world heritage" was coined, with American volunteer groups as models. As the Committee on Cultural and Intellectual Exchange remarked, "The role of government is different in the US from what it is in Europe." Endorsing this reduced role "of equipping [. . .] private groups and financing," the Committee recommended the creation of "a semi-autonomous foundation."[22] For architects, non-governmentality has meant smaller budgets, less state intervention, and many more negotiating tables. But a nimble activist strand of the architectural profession is periodically activated in the wake of natural disasters and humanitarian crises. Some agencies for applied academic research also deploy architectural tools to create place-based, cartographic, or even juridical critiques of violence—ones where the distinction between historic and functionalist architecture is entirely and productively blurred.[23]

Second, heritage has become a liquid asset. Against the midcentury assumption that cultural property was best managed by public or semi-public agencies, financial and economic agencies have taken over the management of heritage in many local and global arenas. Certainly the World Heritage list has turned out to be operable as a kind of market, in no small part because it owes its existence to an alliance of cultural conservationists with environmental activists, for whom calculating exchanges and offsets is a core competency.[24] Unlike national inventories, World Heritage works by asking sites

Figure 6.3 László Moholy-Nagy, *Architects' Congress*, 1933, film stills showing metal struts that help the Erechtheion caryatids support their load.

to fulfill one or several of ten "criteria" and *then actually names those criteria*. Thus petitioning nation-states pursue opportunities selectively, to build a certain portfolio. UNESCO also uses these criteria to police the scarcity of World Heritage, distinguishing monuments from whatever cultural products seem dangerously abundant at any given moment.[25] Since a "Global Strategy for a Representative, Balanced and Credible World Heritage List" was launched in 1994, for example, the criteria have been periodically revised to account for imbalances, including an excess of "particularisms," a surplus of works authored by "globally significant persons," and an overemphasis on "monumentality."[26]

Third, in the shift from an international to a global imagination, the object of protection has shifted from culture as a social structure to culture as a substance, a glue for cohabitation. Some heritage advocates are looking for ways to leverage intangible categories to earn disenfranchised groups new cultural rights or new visibility, using heritage as a weapon of the weak.[27] In this aspect at least, international institutions retain tremendous power. Even though the idea of a "disaster" as a paradigmatic event is on the rise, the World Heritage Committee has resisted being beholden to a history of events, especially the pressure to designate monuments whose only "criterion" for preservation is that they memorialize violence against, or oppression of, a people.[28] Thus, advocates push the definition of heritage as a language instead, and of "untranslatability" as a value. Here too, the metaphor of fluidity dominates. Contesting the "watertight barriers" between different types of patrimony, they recast cultural practices as far apart as mud-making and ritual dancing as daily expressions, which stay alive through transmedial representation.[29]

Finally, stickiness, not authenticity, is the epistemological quality that cultural heritage is sought for. By this I mean that the role once played by documents and their formatting in authenticating preservation is increasingly played by "data" as something that can be drawn directly from a building. Take the Venice Charter, written in 1964 to do exactly what the Athens Conference could not: to make prescriptions on how to conserve buildings. Almost as soon as they succeeded in creating a binding "document," however, internationalists began to backtrack from many of their prescriptions because they seemed to willful, too fixed.[30] Rather than being the namesake for an important charter, Venice became more regularly invoked as a flooded object, like Florence, and Nubia (color plate 8). Not written documents, but films, radio broadcasts, photographs recording the imperiled state of heritage: these are the media that are extracted from endangered sites.[31] It is not that monuments and heritage have relinquished their documentary power. But today, protocols of witnessing are powered by technologies of data visualization, sensing, and mining, that are concerned with the location of materials themselves, no paper necessary. For example, after Ansar Dine occupied Timbuktu in 2013, destroying its libraries and its shrines, the international reaction was to take on both the digitization of its medieval manuscripts and the rebuilding of its mud architecture. But

Figure 6.4 Office for Metropolitan Architecture / Rem Koolhaas, Il Fondaco dei Tedeschi, carved out terrace, early collage. © OMA.

now that the manuscripts are digitally available, they are likely never to return to be conserved in situ, and will more probably be traded or exhibited to raise capital for sustaining the city's cultural life in other ways.[32]

Gone is the scorn with which the heirs of modern architecture used to regard historic buildings. Gone is the disdain of the historian for the physical monument as inferior to the written archive. And gone also is the irony. Architects dealing with preservation no longer adopt the obligatory self-distancing that the avant-garde and its postmodern successors resorted to when conserving something existing rather than building something new. When the Dutch architect Rem Koolhaas conducted a research project on how to intervene in historic cities in China, and evocatively concluded that "preservation is overtaking us," he was dead serious.[33] His architectural office, OMA-AMO, went on to realize a number of preservation projects that are no more, nor less, polemical than its other designs just because they include protected architecture (figure 6.4). Their early collages for a project to restore the *Fondaco dei Tedeschi* in Venice, for instance, took a cue from Superstudio's radical dystopias. But there is little ironic defamiliarization, whether mournful or gleeful, in the final design; what emerges from the layered and luxurious spatial experience of the interior is a sensitive homage to the Venetian school of *restauro*.[34]

Equally un-ironic are the motivations fueling a group of American and European architectural designers who have tried to reclaim architectural preservation as a profession and turn it into an "experimental" practice. Leveraging "choice" as a gesture inherent to preservation, and projecting a progressive politics into this act of choosing, they replace ironic distance with deliberate engagement.[35] Their model is the international avant-garde, and their nemeses are national conservation establishments. Indeed, city and state governments have begun to use the listing and protection of modernism's own iconic buildings as ways to prove they valorize democratic or progressive ideals.[36]

Finding a new fit between progressive politics and architectural preservation is tempting indeed. But, as this book has shown, a soft and middling cultural politics was built into (and out of) hard architectural materials and permanent monumental structures across the globe in the middle decades of the twentieth century; it will take more than a few projects, or experiments, to undo this forceful link. One of liberalism's greatest promises is that creative production, even within the confines of a culture industry, can be a model for human freedom and volition at large.[37] But if the destructive events of the midcentury gave monuments' keepers powerful new tools for designing aesthetic effects, these designs of destruction only ever gave them the *illusion* of intention. Theirs was an ever-fleeting freedom, and an aleatory kind of architectural power.

Acknowledgments

I owe an immense debt of gratitude to the persons and institutions who have supported this project in its many phases. They are too many to list, and probably to recall precisely. After finishing this book, I had planned to make a starred and annotated list, worthy of an international commission, to convey the complexity of this debt. But I have settled for a more straightforward narrative report, beginning with the many archivists who offered access to and patient guidance through various collections. I want to thank particularly Jens Boel, Maria Mata Caravaca, Nadia de Conciliis, Robin Cookson, Christopher Davey, Pia Gazzola, Bernard Knodel, Muriel Perez, the late Susan von Salis, Natalia Vogeikoff, and Ines Zalduendo.

A number of fellowships have afforded me the time and resources to follow through on the ambition of this project. I was astonishingly fortunate to receive a Behrman-Cotsen Postdoctoral Fellowship at the Princeton University Society of Fellows, where Leonard Barkan, Scott Burnham, Susan Stewart, and Mary Harper created a superb environment for writing and thinking, and continued to be valued mentors long after it was their job to be so. My fellow-fellows On Barak, Eduardo Canedo, Yaacob Dweck, Misha Gabovitch, Amin Ghaziani, Graham Jones, and Ricardo Montez were indispensable as supporters and critics. Later, I was also grateful to receive a Frieda L. Miller Fellowship at the Radcliffe Institute for Advanced Studies, where the project grew under the protective watch of Liz Cohen and Judy Vichniak, and in productive dialogue with its incredibly diverse scholarly community. I still cannot believe my luck at the reading group that assembled there—Caroline Jones, Ewa Lajer-Burcharth, Ruth Mack, Francesca Orsini, and Sophia Roosth—powerhouses all, and each a kindred spirit. At Princeton University, I have been supported by an Arthur H. Scribner Bicentennial Preceptorship, by the University Committee for Research in the Humanities and Social Sciences, and by a subvention from the Barr Ferree Publication Fund that has allowed me to give the book its compelling visual arc.

The Princeton School of Architecture has been a wonderfully lively home for unpacking the implications of my research. I thank the deans Stan Allen, Alejandro Zaera-Polo, and Monica Ponce de Leon for their steadfast support. My faculty colleagues have been eager interlocutors, each sharper than the next, together making up an unmatched disciplinary superego. My colleagues in history and theory (Christine Boyer, Beatriz Colomina, and Spyros Papapetros), as well as Hal Foster and Tom Levin, have been generous with advice. The school's staff provided world-class support, and I especially thank my students, too many to name, who are always my most exacting audience. Expert research and image assistance has come from Philip Denny, Megan Eardley, Justin Fowler, Andreas Kalpakci, Leen Katrib, Anna-Maria Meister, Clelia Pozzi, Paul Ruppert, François Sabourin, Samuel Stewart-Halevy, and Juliet Wolf. Alek Bierig and Michael Faciejew gave thoughtful editorial input.

Portions of this book have greatly benefited from being presented and workshopped in various scholarly venues, including conferences, talks, and series organized by Tim Anstey, Pier Vittorio Aureli, Claire Bishop, Elija Borrero, Peter Christensen, Jean-Louis Cohen, Sheila Levrant de Bretteville, Edward Dimmendberg, Christian Fuhrmeister, David Gissen, Romy Golan, Nikolaus Hirsch, Tom Keenan, Jennifer Leung, Jorge Otero-Pailos, Alina Payne, Eva-Liisa Pelkonen, Peter Probst, Laurent Stalder, Philip Ursprung, Evren Uzer von Busch, and Eyal Weizman. I am grateful for each occasion and conversation, and for the inevitable improvements that followed. At Princeton, conversations with Shel Garon, Michael Gordin, and Alison Isenberg helped me tackle my archival burden and imagine my large-scale narrative.

I am blessed with a constellation of co-conspirators whose voices swirl around my head at all times. They are: the Aggregate Architectural History Collaborative, whose questioning I relish (Danny Abramson, Zeynep Çelik Alexander, Arindam Dutta, Ed Eigen, John Harwood, Timothy Hyde, Pamela Karimi, Jonathan Massey, John May, Ijlal Muzaffar, Michael Osman, Meredith Ten Hoor); my co-editors at *Grey Room* whose critical acumen I envy (Eric de Bruyn, Zeynep Çelik Alexander again, Noam Elcott, Byron Hamman, John Harwood again, and Matthew Hunter); and the evolving brain-trust that is Princeton's iHum, whose rigor I aspire to. I want to acknowledge the teachers and mentors who have pushed me to pursue this project, whether their input was punctual or sustained, whether their chosen medium was enthusiasm or critique: the incomparable Mark Jarzombek, as well as David Friedman, Michael Ann Holly, Rem Koolhaas, Reinhold Martin, Daniel B. Monk, Antoine Picon, Hashim Sarkis, Felicity Scott, Heghnar Wattenpaugh, Sarah Whiting, and Mark Wigley.

The hard work of reading one or several chapters has earned a trusted few a seat in the pantheon of undying gratitude: Danny Abramson, On Barak, Zeynep Çelik Alexander, Noam Elcott, and Lauren Kroiz. I am all the more grateful for feedback from these brilliant persons as they are also cherished friends. Julian Rose's editing talents were a godsend at a moment when the manuscript was particularly overwrought. Thank you also to my friends Heidi Beebe, Janna Israel, Ana Miljacki, Michael Rock, and Stephan Wolohojian, for helping me face the various mental and intellectual obstacles to completion.

Susan Bielstein at the University of Chicago Press has been an undeservedly generous supporter, delivering input with poise and almost surgical precision. I am especially grateful for her patience while I wove a cogent narrative thread through this very heterogeneous material. James Toftness is owed many thanks for helping with reluctant image providers. Mary Corrado was a masterful copy-editor, Kitty Chibnik produced the evocative index. And I thank the Press's anonymous readers for their extensive, illuminating comments.

In the solitary process of researching and writing, I have relied on my family to sometimes unforgivable extent. My sister Paola and her family joyously hosted me during impromptu archival emergencies. I also thank my parents, Anna and Claudio, my siblings Nicola, Letizia, and Luca, their partners and children, as well as my adoptive family Fred, Chris, and Sean, who all withheld their judgment (or at least their tongues) and extended their continued affection during my many writerly moods.

I wish to dedicate the book to Katie Andresen, who suffered the worst of it, and has stuck with me in mind, body, and spirit with unending wit and grace. She has indelibly shaped what is on the page, and more. She shares the credit with Louis Allais-Andresen, who arrived just in time to provide his own spark, and much-needed second opinions.

Acronyms

ACRIM American Committee for the Restoration of Italian Monuments, Inc.
ADHG American Defense-Harvard Group
AMG American Military Government
CIC Committee on Intellectual Cooperation of the League of Nations
ICCROM International Center for the Conservation and Restoration of Cultural Property, Rome
IICI Institut International de Coopération Intellectuelle, Paris
ICOM International Council of Museums, Paris
ICOMOS International Council on Monuments and Sites
ICR Istituto Centrale del Restauro, Rome
LN League of Nations, Geneva
OIM Office International des Musées, Paris
SHAEF Supreme Headquarters Allied Expeditionary Force
UN United Nations, New York
UNESCO United Nations Educational, Scientific and Cultural Organization, Paris
Note: In this book I follow the American convention of naming this Organization with a fully capitalized acronym, rather than follow its internal custom, informed by French usage, of capitalizing only the first letter as if it were a proper noun, Unesco.

Archives

AAA Archives of American Art, Smithsonian Institution.
  EP Erwin Panofsky papers. Microfilm Reels 2108–2128
  WGC William George Constable papers. Microfilm Reels 3060–3089
AAPG Associazione Archivio Piero Gazzola (Verona)
ACS Archivio dello Stato (Rome)
  AABBAA Ministero della Pubblica Istruzione. Direzione Generale Antichità e Belle Arti
  FM Fondo Franco Minissi
  PCM Presidenza del Consiglio dei Ministri
American School of Classical Studies at Athens, Archives.
  WBD William Bell Dinsmoor Papers. Series VIII. American Commission for the Protection and Salvage of Monuments in War Areas.
BDA Bundesdenkmalamt (Vienna)
BMA British Museum Archives (London)
Frick Art Reference Library (New York)
  CC Central Correspondence
  HCF Helen Clay Frick Correspondence
GG Archivio del Centro di Studi per la Storia dell'Architettura Fondo Gustavo Giovannoni
GTA GTA-Archiv ETH
  Papers of Sigfried Giedion
Harvard Art Museum Archives, Harvard Art Museums, Harvard University
  PJS Papers of Paul J. Sachs
Harvard University Archives, Harvard University Libraries
  ADHG Archives of the American Defense-Harvard Group
  JOB Papers of John Otis Brew
  WK Papers of Wilhelm Reinhold Walter Koehler
ICCROM Library and Archives of the Rome Center for Conservation of Cultural Property (Rome)
ICOM Archives of the International Council for Museums (Paris)
JD Archives Jules Destrée, Musée Jules Destrée (Charleroi)
JH Julian Sorrell Huxley Papers, Woodson Research Center, Rice University
KIK-IRPA Institut Royal du Patrimoine Artistique (Brussels)
LN League of Nations Archives (Geneva)
  IICI Institut International de Coopération Intellectuelle
MAE Archives des Affaires Étrangères (Paris)
MH Archives des Monuments Historiques. Médiathèque de l'Architecture et du Patrimoine (Paris)

0080/003 Monuments Historiques pendant les guerres 1914–1918 et 1939–1945
0081/ Restaurations d'Édifices
0082/ Plans d'Édifices

NA National Archives (London)

NARA National Archives and Records Administration (Washington, DC)
RG 165 Civil Affairs Division, Records of the War Department, General and Special Staffs
RG 239 Records of the American Commission for the Protection and Salvage of Artistic and Historic Monuments in War Areas
RG 331 Records of Allied Operational and Occupation HG, WWII (SHAEF)
Entry 55B. Monuments, Fine Arts and Archives Section

NGA National Gallery Archives, Smithsonian Institution, Washington DC
FH RG 28 MFAA D Frederick Hartt Papers
JR RG 28 MFAA J James J. Rorimer Papers

NYPL The New York Public Library. Astor, Lenox, and Tilden Foundations.
JHF John H. Finley papers. Manuscripts and Archives Division. Series 1 "Correspondence". Box 96. "Parthenon."

Princeton University Library. Manuscripts Division, Department of Rare Books and Special Collections
CRM C0511 Charles Rufus Morey Papers
EDW C0420 Ernest Theodore DeWald Papers
PF CO 779 Paul Frankl Papers

Sert Josep Lluis Sert Collection. Frances Loeb Library, Graduate School of Design, Harvard University

SZ Solly Zuckerman Papers, University of East Anglia

UNESCO UNESCO Archives
IICI Institut International de Coopération Intellectuelle
OIM Office International des Musées

Yale University Library. Manuscript and Archives.
SMcC MS 114.4 Papers of Sumner McKnight Crosby

Notes

Introduction

1. Lewis Mumford, "The Death of the Monument," *Circle: International Survey of Constructive Art* (London: Faber and Faber, 1937), 263–270.

2. "Death of the Monument," 264.

3. See Nasser Rabat, "Palmyra and ISIS," *Art Forum* (November 2015) and Max Fisher, "What Obama Really Saw at the Door of No Return," *Washington Post*, June 28, 2013.

4. The evocative phrase "cult of monuments" was invented by Alois Riegl, "The Modern Cult of Monuments" [1903], trans. Kurt W. Forster and Diane Ghirardo, *Oppositions* 25 (Fall 1982): 30–51. On the religious connotations of the phrase, see Margaret Olin, "The Cult Of Monuments as a State Religion in Late 19th Century Austria," *Wiener Jahrbuch für Kunstgeschichte* 38 (1995): 177–198. See also nn73–74 in this chapter. Two case-studies of monuments embroiled in both local and global politics are Daniel B. Monk and Andrew Herscher, "The New Universalism," *Grey Room* 61 (Fall 2015): 66–127 and Mrinalini Rajagopalan, "A Medieval Monument and Its Modern Myths of Iconoclasm," *Reuse Value* (Chicago: University of Chicago Press, 2016), 199–222.

5. Mumford elaborated his theory of technics in *Technics and Civilization* (New York: Harcourt & Brace, 1934).

6. Mumford's use of this phrase departs from Martin Heidegger's 1938 seminal definition of modernity as the age where the "world" is grasped as a picture, notably in that Mumford occasionally uses the plural "world pictures." Martin Heidegger, "The Age of the World Picture," *The Question Concerning Technology and Other Essays*, trans. William Lovitt (New York: Harper and Row, 1977), 115–154. Peter Gordon explicates Heidegger's existential notion of "worldhood" and "its spatial character" in "Realism, Science and the Deworlding of the World," *A Companion to Phenomenology and Existentialism*, ed. H. L. Dreyfus and M. A. Wrathall (London: Blackwell, 2009), 425–444.

7. As Anson Rabinbach puts it, "the twentieth century's man-made catastrophes were to no small extent bound up with a deep propensity to apocalyptic thinking." *Between Shadow and Catastrophe* (Berkeley: University of California Press, 1997), 2. Shruti Kapila argues destruction opened a new global "Archimedean view" in "Global Intellectual History and the Indian Political," *Rethinking Modern Intellectual History*, ed. Darrin McMahon and Samuel Moyn (London: Oxford, 2014), 253–274.

8. On creative destruction in Western cities see Daniel Abramson, *Obsolescence: An Architectural History* (Chicago: University of Chicago Press, 2016); on interwar Europe, Mark Mazower, *Dark Continent* (New York: Knopf, 1999); on the colonial experience of the wars, Heike Liebau, *The World in World Wars* (Leiden, The Netherlands: Brill, 2010); on military destruction in the colonies, Sven Lindqvist, *A History of Bombing* (New York: New Press, 2003).

9. Many who did not experience destruction firsthand were still exposed to its ubiquity in visual culture, especially as pictures of physical damage were often allowed while depictions of human death were suppressed. Joëlle Beurie, "Mapping Visual Violence in Germany, France and Britain, 1914–1918," *Liberal Democracies at War*, ed. Andrew Knapp and Hilary Footitt (London: Bloomsbury, 2013), 19.

10. Cornelia Navari, "The New Diplomacy and the New State," *Internationalism and the State in the Twentieth Century* (London: Routledge, 2000), 252–269.

11. The Convention was for protecting "culture" and "nature," but the text of the law ultimately deals with monuments first, adding natural "sites" only secondly. Francesco Franconi, ed., *The 1972 World Heritage Convention: A Commentary* (London: Oxford, 2008).

12. Max Weber, "Bureaucracy" [1922], trans. H. H. Gerth and C. Wright Mills [1946], *Economy and Society*, vol. 2 (Berkeley: University of California Press, 1978), 956–1005.

13. Martha Finnemore and Michael Barnett, *Rules for the World* (Ithaca: Cornell University Press, 2004).

14. Weber himself described how Ancient Egyptian patrimonialism made possible long-season construction projects in *Economy and Society*, 1044–1045. In architectural history, Siegfried Giedion attributed Egyptian monumental forms to the temperament of various Egyptian rulers and to the hard slave labor available to them in *The Eternal Present* (New York: Bollingen Foundation, 1962–1964).

15. Paul B. Jaskot, *The Architecture of Oppression* (London: Routledge, 2000), 3.

16. Mischa Gabowitsch, "Soviet War Memorials," trans. Bela Shayevich, *Chto Delat? Face to Face with the Monument* 37 (2014): 6–8.

17. Mark Mazower, *Governing the World* (London: Penguin, 2012).

18. New interdisciplinary approaches include: in history, Paul Betts and Corey Ross, *Heritage in the Modern World* (Oxford: Oxford University Press, 2015); in anthropology, Peter Probst, *Osogobo and the Art of Heritage* (Indiana: Indiana University Press, 2011); in literature, Barbara Cassin and Danièle Wozny, eds., *Les Intraduisibles du Patrimoine en Afrique Subsaharienne* (Paris: Demopolis, 2014); in art history, Heghnar Wattenpaugh, "Cultural Heritage and the Arab Spring," *International Journal of Islamic Architecture* 5, no. 2 (June 2016): 245–263; and in museum and heritage studies, Tony Bennett, Fiona Cameron, Nélia Dias, Ben Dibley, Rodney Harrison, Ira Jacknis, and Conal McCarthy, *Collecting, Ordering, Governing* (Durham: Duke University Press, 2017). Architectural historians with transdisciplinary approaches include Thordis Arrhenius, *The Fragile Monument* (London: Black Dog, 2012), Mrinali Rajagopalan, *Building Histories* (University of Chicago Press, 2016), and many authors in the journal *Future Anterior*.

19. Margaret Miles, *Art as Plunder* (Cambridge: Cambridge University Press, 2008). See also Zainab Bahraini, *Rituals of War* (New York: Zone, 2008).

20. On the construction of an architectural public through print see Richard Wittman, *Architecture, Print Culture, and the Public Sphere* (London: Routledge, 2007).

21. Mari Lending, *Plaster Monuments: Architecture and the Power of Reproduction* (Princeton: Princeton University Press, 2016).

22. "Since wars begin in the minds of men, it is in the minds of men that the defenses for peace must be constructed." Archibald MacLeish, Preamble to the Constitution of the United Nations Educational, Scientific and Cultural Organization (Paris: UNESCO, November 16, 1945).

23. Among this literature, see Dario Gamboni, *The Destruction of Art* (New York: Reaktion, 1997); Daniel B. Monk, *An Aesthetic Occupation* (Durham: Duke University Press, 2002); Andrew Herscher, *Violence Taking Place* (Stanford University Press, 2010); Eyal Weizman, *Hollow Land* (London: Verso, 2012) and *The Least of Possible Evils* (London: Verso, 2011); Andreas Huyssen, *Twilight Memories* (New York: Routledge, 1995); Stephen Graham, ed.,

Cities, War, and Terrorism (London: Blackwell, 2004); W. J. T. Mitchell, *What Do Pictures Want?* (Chicago: University of Chicago Press, 2004); Robert Bevan, *The Destruction of Memory* (London: Reaktion, 2006); Bruno Latour and Peter Weibel, *Iconoclash: Beyond the Image-Wars in Science, Religion and Art* (ZKM and MIT Press, 2002). A major reference text is Walter Benjamin, "The Destructive Character" [1931], *Selected Writings*, vol. 2, 1927–1934, trans. Edmund Jephcott, ed. Michael W. Jennings, Howard Eiland, and Gary Smith (Cambridge, MA: Harvard University Press, 1999), 541–542; see also Hal Foster, "Dada Mime," *October* 105 (Summer 2003): 166–176.

24. For Arendt the holocaust and the possibility of nuclear annihilation had thrown into doubt the Enlightenment idea that international solidarity would be based on a common history and/or a shared future. Hannah Arendt, "Karl Jaspers: Citizen of the World," *The Philosophy of Karl Jaspers*, ed. Paul Arthur Schlipp (La Salle: Open Court, 1965), 539–549.

25. On culture as an ideological battleground see Raymond Williams, *Keywords in the 20th Century* (London: Oxford University Press, 1985), 87–93. On its internationalist valences see Fred Halliday, "Three Concepts of Internationalism," *International Affairs* 64, no. 2 (Spring 1988): 187–198. On the UN's operative definition of culture, Akira Iriye, *Cultural Internationalism and World Order* (Baltimore: Johns Hopkins University Press, 1997).

26. Arendt wrote more on survival in *The Human Condition* (Chicago: University of Chicago Press, 1958), for example, 46.

27. Theodor Adorno and Max Horkheimer, "The Culture Industry: Enlightenment as Self Deception," *Dialectic of Enlightenment*, trans. Edmund Jephcott (Stanford: Stanford University Press, 2002), 94.

28. Henry-Russell Hitchcock, *Architecture: 19th and 20th Centuries* (London: Penguin, 1971), 583–584.

29. See Jörn Düwel and Niels Gutschow, eds., *A Blessing in Disguise* (Berlin: Dom, 2013). Already in 1976 French architect Marcel Lods called this "a monstruous opportunity." Marcel Lods, *Le Métier d'Architecte* (Paris: Editions France-Empire, 1976), 25.

30. On the International Style see Annabel Wharton, *Building the Cold War* (Chicago: University of Chicago Press, 2001), and Terence Riley, *The International Style* (New York: Rizzoli, 1992).

31. Histories that identify an international turn in architectural conservation as a discipline, movement, or profession around 1968 include Miles Glendinning's *The Conservation Movement* (London: Routledge, 2013); Jukka Jokilehto, *A History of Architectural Conservation* (Boston: Butterworth-Heinemann, 1999); and John Stubbs, *Time Honored* (New York: John Wiley, 2009). In contrast, Paul Betts and Corey Ross identify an earlier consolidation of conservation practices, writing that "the period since 1914 is often portrayed as a devastating Age of Extremes characterized by war, revolutions, mass death and destruction; yet it was also an age that saw sustained efforts to protect and cherished cultures, objects and landscapes under threat from military conflict and violent social engineering projects of all stripes." *Heritage in the Modern World*, 8.

32. On endangerment see Fernando Vidal and Nélia Dias, *Endangerment, Biodiversity and Culture* (London: Routledge, 2015). On the international avant-garde becoming a bureaucracy, see Eric Mumford, *The CIAM Discourse on Urbanism* (Cambridge: MIT Press, 2000). On architects mobilized during the war, see Jean-Louis Cohen, *Architecture in Uniform* (Montreal: CCA, 2011). On continuities between prewar imperial and postwar postcolonial architecture, Mark Crinson, *Modern Architecture at the End of Empire* (London: Ashgate, 2003).

33. Unless otherwise noted, throughout the book I defer to cited authors and actors when using the terms "preservation," "conservation," "restoration," and "reconstruction." In this introduction, I follow contemporary American usage of "preservation" to designate any ar-

chitectural project whose stated goal is the transformation or maintenance of an existing structure.

34. Abbé Henri Grégoire, *Rapport sur les destructions . . .* [Paris: 1793]. Translation mine. On the French Monuments Service see Dominique Poulot, *Une histoire du patrimoine en occident* (Paris: PUF, 2006), and Jean Pierre Babelon and André Chastel, "La Notion de Patrimoine," *Revue de l'Art* 49 (1980): 5–32.

35. On nineteenth-century European debates see Wim Denslagen, *Architectural Restoration in Western Europe* (Amsterdam: A&N, 194). On India, Tapati Guha-Thakurta, *Monuments, Objects, Histories* (New York: Columbia University Press, 2004).

36. Rudy Koshar, "'What Ought to Be Seen,'" *Journal of Contemporary History* 33, no. 3 (July 1998): 323–340.

37. Between 1890 and 1914 monuments went from "a cause of national and imperial concern to one of international concern." See Melanie Hall, *Towards World Heritage* (London: Ashgate, 2011).

38. Arthur Sambon and George Toudouze, eds., "La protestation des écrivains et des artistes contre la restauration du Parthénon," *Le Musée* 2 (1905): 1–29.

39. On destruction "from above and from below," see Gamboni, 63.

40. David Kennedy, "The Move to Institutions," *Cardozo Law Review* 8 (5): 841–988.

41. "World court of public opinion" was Wilson's expression; see Harold Nicolson, *The Old Diplomacy and the New* (London: Davies Memorial Institute of International Studies, 1961).

42. "The League works in public—that is to say, in the presence of and with the Press." *The League of Nations and the Press* (Geneva: League of Nations, 1928), 7. See also Kaarle Nordenstreng & Tarja Seppä, "The League of Nations and Mass Media" (presented at the XV Conference of the International Association for Mass Communication Research, New Delhi, August 27, 1986).

43. UNESCO was the CIC's successor but also incorporated other agencies, notably the International Bureau of Education. See Jean-Jacques Renoliet, *L'UNESCO Oubliée* (Paris: Sorbonne, 1999); January Kolasa, *International Intellectual Cooperation* (Wroclaw: Travaux de la Société des Sciences et des Lettres, 1962); and T. V. Sathyamurthy, "Changing Concepts of Intellectual Cooperation," *International Review of Education* 9, no. 4 (1963–1964): 386–395.

44. For an early critique see Albert Thibaudet, "Pour la Société des Esprits" (November 21, 1931) and "L'intelligence en cooperation" (February 6, 1932), *Réflexions sur la politique* (Paris: Robert Laffont, 2007), 635–645. In the 1940s, Dell G. Hitchner, "The Failure of the League: A Lesson in Public Relations," *Public Relations Quarterly* 8, no. 1 (Spring 1944): 61–71, and Hans Morgenthau, *Politics among Nations* (New York: Knopf, 1949).

45. *A League of Minds*, an International series of Open Letters I (Paris: IICI, 1933).

46. Paul Valéry, "Politics of the Mind" [1932], in *History and Politics*, trans. Denise Folliot and Jackson Mathews (New York: Pantheon, 1962). See also Annamaria Ducci, "Europe and the Artistic Patrimony of the Interwar Period," in *Europe in Crisis*, ed. Hewitson and D'Aria (New York: Berghahn, 2012), 227–242.

47. Walter Benjamin, "Paul Valéry, on his Sixtieth Birthday" [1931], *Selected Writings*, vol. 2: 1927–1934, ed. Michael Jennings, trans. Rodney Livingston et al. (Cambridge, MA: Belknap /Harvard, 1999), 534. As Jacques Derrida remarked later, Valéry's preferred of mode of intellectual inquiry under these catastrophic conditions was "quasi-political" salvage. Jacques Derrida, *The Other Heading*, trans. Pascale-Anne Brault and Michael B. Naas (Bloomington: Indiana University Press, 1992).

48. Valéry, "Politics of the Mind," 89 . Valéry frequently referred to this 1932 text in the IICI's conversations, for example in *L'Avenir de la culture*, Entretiens (Paris: Société des nations, Institut international de coopération intellectuelle, 1934), 301, and *L'Avenir de l'esprit*

européen, Entretiens (Paris, Société des nations, Institut international de coopération intellectuelle, 1933), 284.

49. Paul Valéry and Henri Focillon, *League of Minds*, 15.

50. On the "failure" of the League see E. H. Carr, *The Twenty Years' Crisis* [1939] (London: Papermac, 1995), and "The Failure of the League of Nations," in *Akehurts's Modern Introduction to International Law* (London: Routledge, 1997), 25. Recent histories have separated this political failure from more "technical" successes. Susan Pedersen, "Back to the League of Nations," *American Historical Review* (October 2007); 1091–1117 and *The Guardians* (London: Oxford, 2015); Mark Mazower, *No Enchanted Palace* (New York: Princeton University Press, 2009), 40.

51. A preparatory committee did convene once in October 1932 and established a "Programme of the International Commission on Historical Monuments." *Bulletin of Intellectual Cooperation* (December 1933–January 1934): 29–35.

52. *La protection des monuments et oeuvres d'art en temps de guerre: Manuel technique et juridique* (Paris: IICI, 1938) [henceforth: *Manuel technique*].

53. Historians of the League's work in art and archaeology highlight how the seemingly apolitical turn to the "technical" favored some nations over others, and reflected values of imperialism, nationalism, and economic liberalism. Pierre Leveau, "Le problème de l'apolitique de la conservation-restauration," *CRBC* 19 (2011): 5–26; Ana Filipa Vrdoljak, *International Law, Museums and the Return of Cultural Objects* (Cambridge: Cambridge University Press, 2006), 112–139.

54. On the "lawyer's diplomacy" see Guillaume Sacriste and Antoine Vauchez, "The Force of International Law," *Law and Social Inquiry* 32, no. 1 (Winter 2007): 88.

55. See for instance Alfredo Fabrizi, "Entente internationale pour la défense des monuments d'art," in *Congrès international d'histoire de l'art* (Paris: Presses Universitaires de France, 1923), 220–226.

56. Murray, cited in José Rénau, "L'organisation de la défense du patrimoine artistique et historique espagnol pendant la guerre civile," *Mouseion* 39–40 (1939): 64. See also Elly Herman, "Le Désarmement moral, facteur dans les relations internationales pendant l'entre-deux guerres," *Revue d'histoire* 156 (October 1989): 23–36.

57. The Roerich Pact movement gathered momentum in the early 1930s with its proposal to protect "cultural or scientific institutions." The League considered it in 1930 and rejected it in 1934. See Yulia Orgutsova, "Le role de Nicholas Roerich dans la sauvegarde du patrimoine en temps de guerre (1930–1940)" (thesis, Université Paris VI, 2007); and Pierre Leveau, "Le souvenir de la Grande Guerre dans les réseaux de conservation de l'Entre-Deux-Guerres," *In Situ* 23 (2014). A parallel proposal, Raphael Lemkin's Genocide Convention, would have protected "cultural rights" as part of "human rights." Dirk Moses, "Raphael Lemkin, Culture, and the Concept of Genocide," *The Oxford Handbook of Genocide Studies*, ed. Donald Bloxham and A. Dirk Moses (Oxford: Oxford University Press, 2010), 19–41.

58. E. Foundoukitis, "L'Office international des musées et la protection des monuments et oeuvres d'art en Espagne," *Mouseion* IX–X (1935–1936), Supplément Mensuel Sept–Oct 1936, 187–200. Jean-Louis Fournel and Isabelle Delpia, eds., "Barbarisation et humanisation de la guerre," *Astérion* 2 (2004): 1–40.

59. Charles de Visscher, "Preliminary draft international convention for the protection of historic buildings and works of art in times of war" (in the original French "historic buildings" was "monuments"), *Manuel Technique*, 180–201.

60. David A. Meyer, "The Hague Convention as Customary Law," *Boston University International Law Journal* 11, no. 2 (1993): 349–390.

61. Charles de Visscher, *Report to the League*, reprinted in *Mouseion* 35–36 (1936). See also "Commentaire du Projet," *Manuel Technique*, 200.

62. On World War I see "Konvolut Kunstzchutz," *Kunshistoriker im Krieg*, ed. Christian Fuhrmeister, Johannes Griebl, Stephan Klingen, and Ralf Peters (Weimar: Böhlau, 2012), 290–315.

63. "Protezione anti-aerea opere d'arte" (Circolare Ministero del 31 Dicembre 1934). ACS AABBAA/Div II/1934–1940, 57.

64. "Mesures Préventives et dispositions à prendre dans les Édifices classés en cas d'hostilités," May 20, 1935. MH Défense Passive 80/3/52.

65. "La Protection des chefs-d'oeuvre de l'esprit," *Nouvelles Littéraires*, July 3, 1937; February 5, 1938; and February 21, 1938.

66. Louis Réau, *Histoire du vandalisme* (Paris: Robert Laffont, 1994).

67. Ugo Ojetti, *Les Monuments Italiens et la guerre*, trans. Maurice Mignon (Milan: Alfieri & Lacroix, 2017); Paul Clemen, *Protection of Art during War* (Leipzig: Seemann, 1919).

68. Latour and Weibel, *Iconoclash*, 14–37. Latour implicitly periodizes this phenomenon by associating it with late-twentieth-century science wars and contemporary art. In *The Destruction of Art*, Dario Gamboni identifies 1973 as a hinge, when modern art relinquished its monopoly over destructive aesthetics, and older forms of vandalism returned to the world stage.

69. Inez and Eyal Weizman, *Before and After* (Moscow: Strelka, 2013).

70. *Mouseion* 39, no. 3 (1937): 13; *Manuel technique*, 123. See also Miguel Caballero, "Protection and Negation," *Cabinet* 54 (Summer 2014); and Josep Adell Argilés, *Salvaguardia y trabajos de emergencia durante la guerra 1936–1939* (Madrid: Munillalería, 1998–99).

71. Direzione generale delle Arti, *La Protezione del patrimonio artistico nazionale dalle offese della guerra aerea* (Firenze: Le Monnier, 1942). See also Raffaella Biscioni, "La Propaganda fotografica dei danni al patrimonio artistico," *Storia e Futuro* 19 (February 2009): 2–31.

72. *Protezione del patrimonio*, 244–245.

73. On Riegl see Henri Zerner, "Aloïs Riegl: Art, Value, Historicism," in *The Vienna School Reader*, ed. Christopher Wood (New York: Zone, 2000), 94–95; Olin, *State Religion*; Margaret Iversen, *Alois Riegl: History and Theory* (Cambridge: MIT Press, 1993); Sandro Scarrocchia, ed., *Alois Riegl: teoria e prassi della conservazione dei monumenti* (Bologna: CLUEB, 1995); Françoise Choay, "Riegl, Freud et les monuments historiques," in *World Art*, ed. Irving Lavin (Washington, DC: ICAH, 1986), 799–807; and Diana Reynolds Cordileone, *Alois Riegl in Vienna 1875–1905* (London: Ashgate, 2014).

74. In Alan Colquhoun's words, "we are still in the period that Riegl defined as dominated by 'age-value,' even though the problems connected with this concept are no longer those that confronted Riegl himself." "Newness and Age Value in Riegl," *Modernity and the Classical Tradition* (Cambridge, MA: MIT Press, 1989), 213–221. Three noteworthy updates are Mark Wigley, "The Architectural Cult of Synchronization," *Journal of Architecture* 4, no. 4 (1999): 409–435; Thordis Arrhenius, "The Cult of Age in Mass Society," *Future Anterior* 1, no. 1 (Spring 2004): 74–80; and Mario Carpo, "The Postmodern Cult of Monuments," *Future Anterior* 4, no. 2 (Winter 2007): 51–60.

75. Froidevaux recalled that he knew from the first moment he visited the "wounded cathedral" that he wanted to "leave it as is," making the sanctuary functional again, "keeping pure" the "new beauty" that had been "born of its destruction" by intervening only minimally, and leaving new walls intentionally blank, in "a prayer for peace." MH 0081.

76. Robert Patry, *St-Lô: La capitale des ruines* (1948); Darren Gribben, "Beckett's Other Revelation," *Irish University Review* 38, no. 2 (2008): 263–273.

77. David Mitrany, "A Working Peace System" [1943], *Functional Theory of Politics* (London: St. Martin's, 1975), 118. See also Cornelia Navari, "Functional Internationalism," *Thinkers of the Twenty Years' Crisis* (Oxford: Clarendon, 1995).

78. Graham Beckel, *Workshops for the World* (New York: Abelard-Schuman, 1954).

79. Supra 22.

80. Julian Huxley, *TVA: Adventure in Planning* (London: Architectural Press, 1943), 94. See also Huxley, *From an Antique Land* (New York: Harper & Row, 1964), 82, and his recommendation that "Town planning and architecture could be an extremely fruitful field for UNESCO." *Report of the Director General on the Activities of the Organization in 1948*, 21. UNESCO/DG/1948.

81. In 1946–47 alone, Walter Gropius and Sigfried Giedion wrote to UNESCO on behalf of CIAM (Congrès internationaux d'architecture moderne) for five different reasons: the choice of an architect for the UN, creating an international town planning agency, reforming architectural education, publishing *Space, Time and Architecture* as a textbook, and preserving "the decaying Villa Savoye." Gropius to Huxley, May 27, 1946, Sert/E003; Giedion to Carter, August 20, 1947, UNESCO/ICMA; Giedion to Sert, November 11, 1952, Sert/CIAM.

82. Geneva and the League of Nations site featured prominently in these debates, with Le Corbusier's "Mundaneum" scheme also a subject of critical distinction between "instruments and monuments." See the texts by Le Corbusier and Karel Teige reintroduced by George Baird, *The Oppositions Reader* (Cambridge: MIT Press, 2000), 586–588.

83. Sigfried Giedion, Josep Lluis Sert, and Fernand Léger, "Nine Points on Monumentality" [1943], Sigfried Giedion, *Architecture, You and Me* (Cambridge: Harvard, 1958), 48–51. See also *New Architecture and City Planning*, ed. Paul Zucker (New York: Philosophical Library, 1944); and Wolfgang Schivelbusch, *Three New Deals* (New York: MacMillan, 2007), 1–16.

84. "Nine Points," 50.

85. Sigfried Giedion, *The Eternal Present* (New York: Bollinger Foundation, 1962–1964) and *Architecture and the Phenomena of Transition* (Cambridge, MA: Harvard University Press, 1971). One deliberate precedent was Gottfried Semper, who distinguished various forms of monumentality in *Style in the Technical and Tectonic Arts* [1860–1871], trans, Harry Francis Mallgrave and Michael Robinson (Santa Monica: Getty Research Institute, 2004). On the Swiss valences of monumentality, Akos Moravanski, "Peter Meyer and the Swiss Discourse on Monumentality," *Future Anterior* 8, no. 1 (Summer 2001) 1–20.

86. In November 1943, Giedion was asked to give names of notable "modern" structures in the north of France. In December he suggested using the map "Paris Moderne 1937" from *l'Architecture d'Aujourd'hui*. GTA 43-K-1943-11-19G. He also supplied a list of "contemporary buildings in the Netherlands." 43-K-1943-11-11 (G):1.

87. Supra 81.

88. Giedion developed the phrase "pseudo-monumentality" in 1946 for a symposium "In Search of a New Monumentality," later published in *Architectural Review* (September 1948), 117–128. Also *Architecture, You and Me*, 25–39. Another obvious reason for this missed connection is the social and professional antagonism between the avant-garde and Beaux-Arts architectural circles.

89. This was point 1. "Nine Points," 48.

90. Giedion, "List of modern buildings in Paris, including the suburbs." Giedion to Crosby, 19 November 1943. GTA 43-K-1943-11-19G.

91. Sigfried Giedion, *Space, Time and Architecture: Growth of a New Tradition* (Cambridge: Harvard University Press, 1946).

92. "Ideology," Huxley wrote, "will have to adapt itself to the new reality." *Report of the DG*, 21.

93. On this, see "Some Considerations on the Meeting of Experts held at UNESCO House 17–21 Oct 1949," *Sites and Monuments* (Paris: UNESCO, 1949), 49. Follow-up confer-

ences are the Congress of International Conservation Architects (Paris, 1957) and the Conference for Monument Conservation (Venice, 1964).

94. On the *Courier* as a photographic publication see Tom Alleneson, "Photographic Diplomacy in the Postwar World," *Modern Intellectual History* 12, no. 2 (August 2015): 383–415.

95. In German media theory the phrase "cultural technique" (*Kulturtechnik*) has been proposed by Bernhardt Siegert, to conceptualize the study of media as a contribution to intellectual history and philosophy. Bernhardt Siegert, *Cultural Techniques*, trans. Geoffrey Winthrop-Young (New York: Fordham University Press, 2015). Applied retroactively to UNESCO, the phrase aptly captures the mood in a period when the organization increasingly used permutations of the words "cultural" and "technical" to describe its mission, rather than searching for a specific message to convey through its media.

96. *The Public Library* (Paris: UNESCO, May 16, 1949) UNESCO/LBA/1/Rev. See also Luther Evans, "UNESCO Work and Method Illustrated by the Library Programs," *Library Quarterly* 24, no. 2 (April 1954): 92–100. Julian Huxley gives a telling anecdote that implicates the logo in this transition and reveals its provincialism, if not orientalism: "After much discussion, we in UNESCO adopted a letterhead in the form of a Greek temple with its pediment supported by the letters UNESCO, elongated to represent pillars. We had never reflected that when the word was translated into Arabic, the letters could no longer be made to serve as supports, but looked like a broken-down jumble of ruins." Huxley, *From an Antique Land*, 82.

97. Technical assistance became a regular part of UNESCO's budget in 1954. On UNESCO's intersection with development institutions, see Richard Jolly, Louis Emmerji, Dharam Ghai, and Frédéric Lapeyre, *UN Contributions to Development Thinking and Practice* (Bloomington: Indiana University Press, 2004), 203–219. More broadly see Frederick Cooper and Randall Packard, eds., *International Development and the Social Sciences* (Berkeley: University of California Press, 1997); "The Rise and Fall of Development Theory," in *The Anthropology of Development and Globalization*, ed. Marc Edelman and Angelique Haugerud (Malden, MA: Blackwell, 2005), 109–125.

98. "UNESCO's Participation in the United Nations Expanded Programme of Technical Assistance." UNESCO 33 EX/29.

99. See Convention (1954), and Convention (1970). *Convention for the Protection of Cultural Property in the Event of Armed Conflict*, UNESCO SHC/MD/1 (1954), and *Convention on the Means of Prohibiting and Preventing the Illicit Import, Export and Transfer of Ownership of Cultural Property*, UNESCO SHC/MD/6 (1970).

100. Henri Lavachery and André Noblecourt, *Les techniques de protection des biens culturels en cas de conflit armé* (Paris: UNESCO, 1954), 156.

101. This very warning was sounded in 1953 by an American delegate to the Hague Convention, who argued the legal text should be short and not technical; that focus should be on setting up "monuments organizations" before war because it was "impossible to account for technical unpredictability" and "changing techniques of warfare." Charles W. Porter III, "Comments on Draft of a Convention Proposed by the Government of Italy for the Protection of Objects of Cultural Value in Case of War." JOB 7.

102. The MonCom saw its task as "watching over the protection of sites and monuments." Establishment of a Permanent International Committee for Monuments and Archaeological Excavations (25 August 1949) UNESCO MUS/Conf.1/2.

103. The task of the "conservation and protection of the world's inheritance of books, works of art and monuments of history and science" was written in Article I of the organization's constitution, and cited at the First Session of the International Committee on Monuments. UNESCO Com.Mon.1.4 Doc. 12 (25 September 1951). See also Museums and Monuments 1 [M&M1], 49.

104. See David Meyer, "The 1954 Hague Cultural Property Convention and Its Emergence into Customary International Law," *BU International Law Journal* 11 (1993): 349.

105. Giedion, *The Eternal Present* (1962–1964); *Architecture and the Phenomena of Transition* (1970).

106. Egypt was the subject of intense scrunity from UNESCO as a non-aligned territory, including as a place to locate a "regional training center" for conservators. Harold Plenderleith, "Some Observations on the Suggestion to Make a Centre for Cultural Property in the UAR and Africa" (Cairo, September 1966). ICCROM Mission Egypte 6/1.

107. Minissi called the building "self-effacing," and avoided anything too "artificially" modern or "mimetically" historicist. Franco Minissi, "Il Museo delle barche di Cheofe presso la grande piramide di Gizah—Cairo," "Gizah, Il Cairo: Museo delle barche faraoniche di Cheofe presso la grande piramide 1957–1962)." ACS FM 9.

108. White House Conference for International Cooperation (November 28 to December 1, 1965), *National Citizens Commission: Report of the Committee on Culture and Intellectual Exchange* (Washington, DC: WHCIC, 1965).

109. Roger Meyer, "Travaux Préparatoires for the UNESCO World Heritage Convention," *Earth Law Journal* (1976): 45–81. The bracketed list is a footnote in the original.

110. *Premier Festival Mondial des Arts Nègres,* Dakar, 1–24 Avril 1966 (Paris: André Rousseau / Bernard Gaulin, 1966): 45; William Greaves, *First World Festival of Negro Arts* (1966) US Information Agency; Léopold Senghor, *The Foundations of Africanité* (Paris: Présence Africaine, 1967).

111. Mark Hinchman, "House and Household in Gorée, Sénégal, 1758–1837" *JSAH* 65, no. 2 (June 2006), 166–187.

112. Hamady Bocoum and Bernard Toulier, "La fabrication du Patrimoine: l'exemple de Gorée (Sénégal)," *In Situ* 20 (2013).

113. A 1974 mission report noted that the island acquired a "Mediterranean" feel when all the roof-terraces that once terminated the houses were replaced by tiles imported from Marseilles. A. Grégoire, *Sénégal: Monuments historiques de l'île de Gorée et de Saint Louis du Sénégal* (UNESCO: May 1974), 5. Also *Sénégal: Rapport Technique* (Paris: UNESCO, 1975) and *Gorée: Island of Memories* (Paris: UNESCO, 1981).

114. Maurice Halbwachs, *On Collective Memory*, trans. Lewis A. Coser (Chicago: University of Chicago Press, 1992). For example, Léon-Gontran Damas received a grant from the *Musée de l'Homme* to travel to America to identify the "survivances" of African culture in American literary production. See F. Bart Miller, "Damas's Confrontation with Colonialism" *Rethinking Négritude through Léon-Gontran Damas* (Amsterdam: Rodopi, 2014).

115. Halbwachs's method was thoroughly topographic: his site was the Holy Land, his primary source was the Bible, and he wished for a second-century pilgrim as a living witness. Maurice Halbwachs, "The Legendary Topography of the Gospels in the Holy Land" [1941], *On Collective Memory*, 193.

116. Pierre Nora, "Between Memory and History: Les Lieux de Mémoire," *Representations* 26 (1989): 7–24 and "Introduction," *Lieux de Mémoire*, vol. 4 (Paris: Gallimard, 1986), 8.

Chapter One

1. *La Conservation des monuments d'art et d'histoire* (Paris: OIM, 1933) [henceforth *CMAH*].

2. The conference conclusions were originally published as *La Conservation des Monuments. Conclusions*. Les Dossiers de l'Office International des Musées No. 1 (Paris: IICI, 1933) [henceforth *Conclusions*]. The earliest mention of this document as a "charter" comes in the 1964 *Venice Charter* (Venice: ICOMOS, 1964). Authors who use the phrase "Athens Charter"

include Jukka Jokilehto, *A History of Architectural Conservation* (Boston: Butterworth-Heinemann, 1999); John Stubbs, *Time Honored* (Hoboken: Wiley, c2009); Miles Glendinning, *The Conservation Movement* (New York: Routledge, 2013); Jean-Yves Andrieux and Fabienne Chevalier, eds., *Le Patrimoine Monumental* (Rennes: PU, 2014), 388. Francoise Choay published a critical edition of excerpts from this volume as *La Conférence d'Athènes* (Paris: Tranches des Villes, 2002). See also Rosa Anna Genovese, "La conferenza di Atene (1931)" in *Note in Materia di Conservazione e Restauro des Monumenti* (Arte Tipografica, 1996), 9–56, and "On heritage charters and conventions," *Getty Conservation Institute Newsletter* 19, no. 2 (2004).

3. François Hartog, *Régimes d'historicité* (Paris: Seuil, 2003), 196–198.

4. This opposition is often conveyed through a comparison with the modernist *Athens Charter* [1933] (New York: Grossman, 1972). See for instance Ignacio Sola-Morales, "Dal contrasto all'analogia," *Lotus International* 46 (1986): 37–46.

5. Nicolas Balanos, *Les monuments de l'Acropole* (Paris: Massin et Lévy, 1935); "Modern Greece Takes Over the Care of the Heritage of the Old," *New York Times*, June 8, 1930.

6. Can Bilsel, *Antiquity on Display* (Oxford: Oxford University Press, 2012), 222.

7. Ben Kafka, *The Demon of Writing* (New York: Zone, 2012).

8. Susan Pedersen, "Back to the League of Nations," *American Historical Review* (October 2007): 1091–1117, and *The Guardians* (London: Oxford University Press, 2015); Mark Mazower, *Governing the World* (London: Penguin, 2012).

9. See Christian Topalov, "Les réformateurs et leurs réseaux," in *Laboratoires du nouveau siècle* (Paris: EHESS, 1999), 11–58. International events where monument conservation was discussed include a special session of the 1889 Exposition Universelle in Paris. Charles Normand, *Congrès international pour la protection des œuvres d'art et des monuments* (Paris: Imprimerie Nationale, 1889), 28; a 1905 discussion of the first International Congress of Archaeology asking "in what spirit and to what extent ancient monuments should be restored," *Comptes rendus du Congrès international d'archéologie*, 1e Session, Athènes (Athens: Hestia, 1905), 63–64. Every meeting of the International Congress of Architects between 1896 and 1911 devoted a session to monuments, debating in 1906 the creation of an International League for the Defense of Monuments. Congrès International des Architectes, Avril 1904, *Comptes rendus* (Madrid: 1906), 281. Monuments became a recurrent theme in the International Town Planning Conferences after the war. See *Town Planning Review* 4, no. 2 (July 1913): 98–117, and *Town Planning Review* 10, no. 4 (February 1924): 248–252. By 1921, the International Conference of Art History openly called for an "International Agreement" for the protection of monuments. Alfredo Fabrizi, "Entente Internationale pour la défense des monuments d'art," in *Actes du congrès d'histoire de l'art* (Paris: PUF, 1923), 220–226.

10. Conférence internationale d'experts pour l'étude des problèmes relatifs à la protection et la conservation des monuments d'art et d'histoire, *Procès-Verbaux*, 6. OIM.4.1932 [henceforth *Athens PV*].

11. "Le discours de M. Jules Destrée," *Le Messager d'Athènes*, October 22, 1931, 3.

12. "Discours de M. Jules Destrée."

13. David Long and Brian Schmidt, *Imperialism and Internationalism in the Discipline of International Relations* (New York: SUNY, 2005), 14.

14. The agenda was published in *Mouseion* 14 (1931): 92–94. Form letter sent by Foundoukitis to OIM delegates, April 20, 1930. OIM.VI.17.

15. On one side of this debate were followers of French rationalist architect Eugène-Emmanuel Viollet-le-Duc, who advocated the "restoration" of historic buildings "to a state that may have never existed." Viollet-le-Duc, "Restauration," *Dictionnaire raisonné de l'architecture française du XIe au XVIe siècle* (1856). In the opposite camp were the heirs of British

romantic art critic John Ruskin, for whom restoration was "the most total destruction which a building can suffer," and who offered a minimal "conservation" instead. John Ruskin, *The Seven Lamps of Architecture,* vol. 1 of *The Complete Works of John Ruskin* (New York: Thomas Y. Cromwell, 1905), 32. Thordis Arrhenius summarizes the debate in *The Fragile Monument* (London: Black Dog, 2012).

16. On the softening of conservation dogmas in Germany, Austria, and Italy in the early 1900s, Marion Wohlleben, *Konservieren oder restaurieren?* (Zurich: Fachvereine, 1989).

17. E. Foundoukitis, Radio Address, 1931. LN/Radio.

18. Otto Fischer, "Die internationale Konferenz für Denkmalpflege in Athen," *Neue Zürcher Zeitung,* December 15, 1931.

19. *CMAH,* 51–59, 70–74.

20. *CMAH,* 448–503.

21. Paul Léon, "La restauration des monuments en France," *CMAH,* 51–59.

22. *Conclusions,* 10–11.

23. As Martha Finnemore and Michael Barnett explain, regulation "manipulates incentives to shape the behavior of another actor" whereas constitutions embody "the ability to create, define and map social reality." *Rules for the World* (Ithaca: Cornell University Press, 2004), 7.

24. The Italian *Carta del Restauro* was published in *Bollettino d'Arte* (January 1932), and later in *Mouseion* as "Une Charte de la Conservation des Monuments en Italie," *Mouseion* 17–18 (1932): 200–204. On the competing charters in prewar Italy see Paolo Nicoloso, "La Carta del Restauro di Giulio Carlo Argan," *Annali di architettura* (1994): 105–115.

25. Léon, *CMAH,* 51.

26. Several sources, including some linked to ICOMOS, mistakenly cite the following text, which appears to be a paraphase of Léon, as being part of the Athens "charter" itself: "Monuments are documents as much as a charter would be and it would not be any more admissible to modify the text of these great archives of stone with corrective marks, with complements or stylistic unity, than it would be to leave them to perish from abandonment." www.icomos.org.

27. Léon, *CMAH.* The bibliography for Léon's massive *Les monuments historiques: conservation, restauration* (Paris: 1917) reads as a chronicle of the all the *traités* on historic buildings emitted in France since the French revolution. See also Michael Hull, "Documents and Bureaucracy," in *Annual Review Anthropology* 41 (2012): 251–267.

28. "Programme of the International Commission on Historical Monuments," *Bulletin of Intellectual Cooperation* (December 1933–January 1934), 29–35. This program was coauthored by Roberto Paribeni (Italy), Ricardo Orueta y Duarte (Spain), Leodegar Petrin (Austria), Ralegh Radford (Great Britain), and Louis Hautecoeur (France).

29. The 1913 French law defines a historic monument as a building "whose conservation is, from the point of view of history or art, in the public interest." "Loi du 31 décembre 1913 sur les monuments historiques," *Journal Officiel de la République Française* (January 4, 1914), 129–132: Art. 1, Ch. 1.

30. "Conclusions de la Conférence," *CMAH,* 405 (French); 450 (English).

31. See Roger O'Keefe, *The Protection of Cultural Property in Armed Conflict* (Cambridge: Cambridge University Press, 2006), 35–91.

32. Nele Matz, "Civilization and the Mandate System under the League of Nations as Origin of Trusteeship," *Max Planck Yearbook of United Nations Law* 9 (2005): 47–95. On the connection between the Mandate system and the notion of "tutelage" in cultural property law at the League, see Ana Filipa Vrdoljak, *International Law, Museums and the Return of Cultural Objects* (Cambridge: Cambridge University Press, 2006), 112–139.

33. Louis Hautecoeur, "Utilité d'une documentation internationale sur les monuments historiques," *CMAH*, 395.

34. Conclusion VII also described monuments as civilizational repositories ("masterpieces in which civilization resides"). *CMAH*, 451.

35. *CMAH*, 451–452; Destrée, "Rapport du Président du Comité de direction de l'Office international des musées sur les travaux de la Conférence d'Athènes," *CMAH*, 11–12; and "Recommendations Adopted by the Assembly of the League of Nations on Oct 10th 1932," *CMAH*, 454–455.

36. Destrée, *Rapport du Président*, 11–12.

37. In the early 1930s the League had tried to initiate textbook reform by asking governments to excise passages that fueled nationalism and xenophobia from pedagogical material. *La révision des manuels scolaires contenant des passages nuisibles à la compréhension mutuelle des peuples* (Paris: IICI, 1932). Given the resistance it had encountered there, education on monuments must have appeared comparatively feasible.

38. "Résolution by the Chairman on the subject of Archaeological Research" (August 4, 1922) CIC "Minutes of the First Session, Geneva Aug 1–5, 1922," 30. IICI ICI C. 570. M. 224. 1922

39. Francesco Ruffini, "Report on an International Understanding for the 'Discovery of Archaeological Monuments and the Publication of the Results,' Submitted to the Committee By Senator F. Ruffini," Annex IV of CIC, *Minutes of the Second Session*, 63. IICI C. 570. M. 224. 1923. XII. William Bell Dinsmoor also voiced this critique in "New Trends in Humanistic Studies," *Columbia University Quarterly* (December 1935): 419.

40. CIC, *Report on scientific property submitted by Senator F. Ruffini and approved by the Committee* (September 1, 1923). LN Doc. A.38 1923 XII. On Ruffini and this movement for intellectual property rights, see Ariel Simon, "Reinventing Discovery," *University of Pennsylvania Law Review*, 157, no. 6 (June 2009): 2175–2232; and David Philip Miller, "Intellectual Property and Narratives of Discovery/Invention," *History of Science* 46 (2008): 299–342.

41. *Report on Scientific Property* § 13 (11).

42. Scientists should be compensated in proportion to the "likelihood of a discovery's obtaining utility," just as artists were compensated for the likely increase in the value of their works over time. *Report on Scientific Property*.

43. Henri Bergson, *Creative Evolution* [1897], trans. Arthur Mitchell (New York: Dover, 1998), 10–11. With statements like "matter is . . . in great part the work of memory," Bergson apparently reversed the usual hierarchy between "image" and "reality." See Bergson, *Matter and Memory* [1908], trans. Nancy Margaret Paul and W. Scott Palmer (New York: Zone, 1991), 182. It should be noted that Bergson's theory is often mentioned in the mix of post-Nietzchean "theories and concepts" at the basis of modern, internationalist conservation practice. See Jokilehto: 213–244; and John H. Stubbs and Emily G. Makkas, *Architectural Conservation* (New York: Wiley, 2011), 55.

44. Max Horkheimer, "On Bergson's Metaphysics of Time" (1934), *Radical Philosophy* 131 (May–June 2005): 11.

45. See Jimena Canales, *The Physicist and the Philosopher* (Princeton: Princeton University Press, 2015); Bruno Latour, *Le débat Bergson/Einstein* (Centre Pompidou, June 21, 2010). On scientific internationalism more generally, Jean-Jacques Salomon, "The Internationale of Science," *Science Studies* (January 1971): 23–42; Brigitte Schroeder-Gudehus, "Probing the Master-Narrative of Scientific Internationalism," *Neutrality in Twentieth-Century Europe* (London: Routledge, 2012), 19–44.

46. Henri Bergson to Oscar Halecki (1924). LN 1924, Coop Int., 13c/33877/33877/IX.

47. On Bergson as diplomat, see Philippe Soulez, "Les philosophes dans la mêlée," in

Vingtième Siècle, 10 (April–June 1986), 122–124, *Bergson Politique* (Paris: PUF, 1989): and George Oprescu, "Bergson-Oprescu: Correspondence Inédite," *Romanian Journal of Sociology* (January–December 1991): 117.

48. Simon, *Reinventing Discovery*.

49. Destrée, *Le messager d'Athènes*, 3. Destrée also called himself a "simple passer-by" in the concluding remarks of the preceding conference in Rome. *Conférence Internationale pour l'étude des méthodes scientifiques appliquées à l'examen et à la conservation des œuvres d'art, Rome 13–17 Octobre 1930: Procès verbal de la séance de clôture*. IICI. (G. 86. 1930).

50. On Destrée see Geneviène Duchenne, "Jules Destrée diplomate, de la Grande guerre à l'idée de l'Europe," *Musée Jules Destrée* (Charleroi: Musée Destrée, 2000); "La pensée Européenne du socialiste Jules Destrée," *Annales d'études européennes de l'Université catholique de Louvain* 5 (2001): 21–45; and Georges-Henri Dumont, *Jules Destrée: le multiple* (Bruxelles: Académie Royale, 1995), 78–106.

51. Jean-Pierre Paulus, *Au prémices de l'humanisme socialiste* (Bruxelles: Labor, 1971); Edmond Picard, *Comment on devient socialiste* (Brussels: Lacomblez, 1895).

52. Edmond Picard, "Pour qui nous possédons des oeuvres d'art," *L'Art Moderne* (January 10, 1897): 9–11.

53. Jules Destrée, *L'art et le socialisme* (Brussels: Propagande Socialiste, 1896), 23.

54. Destrée, *L'art et le socialisme*, 8.

55. Georg Karo, "Tagung für Denkmalpflege in Athen," *Die Denkmalpflege* 34 (1931): 37–40. An earlier comparative survey had been published by G. Baldwin Brown, *The Care of Ancient Monuments* (Cambridge: University Press, 1905).

56. Raymond Weiss, *Athens PV*, 7–8.

57. *CMAH*, 449. What emerged from this comparative survey is that states administered their monuments through pressure from various private interests—religious groups, aristocratic land owners, urban property developers, and volunteer citizens' committees. "La restauration des monuments en France," "La législation des monuments historiques en Italie," *CMAH* 51–59; 105–114. Astrid Swenson summarizes German, French, and British cases in "The Law's Delay?," *Towards World Heritage*, ed. Melanie Hall (London: Ashgate, 2011), 139–154.

58. Destrée, *Athens PV*, 8.

59. Letter from E. Foundoukitis on behalf of Jules Destrée to Greek Minister N. Politis, 20 April 1931. IICI-OIM-VI-17 (1).

60. "The Emergence of International Property Law," *North Carolina Law Review* 90, no. 2 (January 2012): 461–509.

61. Destrée, *Rapport*.

62. See Alois Riegl, "Neue Strömungen in der Denkmalpflege," and Georg Dehio, "Denkmalschutz und Denkmalpflege im neunzehnten Jahrhundert," [1905] in *Konservieren, nicht restaurieren* (Braunschweig/Wiesbaden, 1988).

63. Jules Destrée, *Pour en finir avec la guerre* (Brussels: Églantine, 1930), 9–10.

64. Jules Destrée, *Villes meutries de Belgique: Les villes Wallonnes* (Bruxelles: Van Oest Et Cie, 1917).

65. Destrée, *Pour en finir*, 63.

66. See Alexander Badenoch, "Myths of the European Network," in *Materializing Europe* (London: Palgrave, 2010), 47–77.

67. Peter Burgess, "Coal, Steel and Spirit," in *Europe and the Other and Europe as the Other*, 421.

68. Rudy Koshar, "'What Ought to Be Seen,'" *Journal of Contemporary History*, 33, no. 3 (July 1998): 323–340.

69. *Pour en finir*, 67–70. For example, Destrée supported a Belgian proposal for a "European Electrical Union," which was opposed by Belgium's Monuments Commission because electrical poles and wires "defaced" Belgium's picturesque townscapes. *Bulletin des commissions royales d'art et d'archéologie* (January–June 1932): 81–82.

70. "Aesthetic Enhancement of Ancient Monuments," *CMAH*, 449.

71. On the Denkmalpflege see Wohlleben, *Konservieren oder restaurieren?*, 37–64.

72. Clemen to Foundoukitis, 28 July 1931. IICI-OIM-VI-17(1), 2. Others who complained about time constraints included the Italian minister of culture, who had initiated the conference. See Pellati's comments in OIM, "Réunion du Comité de Direction," Paris, 13–14 Ap 1931, 9. LoN R2227. Several criticized the proportion of time spent in meetings (4 days) and travel (6 days). OIM, "Réunion du Comité de Direction tenue à Athènes" (October 1931). LN R2216. Clemen spoke from authority, having edited a report on the protection of monuments across enemy lines in World War I, *Protection of Art during War* (Leipzig: Seemann, 1919). See also his *Belgische Kunstdenkmaler* (Munchen: Bruckmann, 1923). His nationalism grew in the 1930s, culminating in his 1933 book *Die Deutsche Kunst und die Denkmalpflege*, which was prefaced with a citation from Hitler. On the *Tagung*'s nationalism see Koshar, *Germany's Transient Pasts* (Chapel Hill: UNC Press, c1998), 45.

73. J. Wojcenhowski, "La législation des monuments historiques en Pologne," *CMAH*, 149.

74. Francesco Pellati, "La législation des monuments historiques en Italie," *CMAH*, 30–38.

75. Mazower, "The Standard of Civilization," *Governing the World*, 77.

76. The Pan-European movement was founded by count Coudenhove-Karlegi in 1922, proposing among other things to merge all Europe's colonies into a "field for the release of [Europe's] economic energies." Destrée, "Paneuropa," *Pour en finir*, 11–14.

77. Louis Hautecoeur, "Utilité d'une documentation internationale sur les monuments historiques," *CMAH*, 395.

78. Jules Destrée, "L'Activité de l'Office International des Musées," *Mouseoin* 14: 92–94.

79. On the nationalist rooting of European art history more generally, see Eric Michaud, *Histoire de l'art: une discipline à ses frontières* (Paris: Hazan, 2005).

80. Otto Fischer, "Die internationale Konferenz," Op. cit. Translation mine.

81. Lopez Otero, "La fonction et la nature des matériaux de restauration," *CMAH*, 185–191.

82. See papers given by Torres Balbas, Giovannoni, Lauterpach, Powys, Pellati, Nyns, and Wojciehowski. *CMAH.*

83. Léon situated this period after an "empirical period" and a "doctrinal period." Léon, *CMAH*, 51–59.

84. In Vienna, most buildings needing repair were not medieval churches, but the revivalist buildings of the Ringstrasse. Kieslinger, "Études sur la désagrégation des pierres à bâtir," *CMAH*, 203–219.

85. "La désagrégation des monuments," *CMAH*, 449.

86. Justus Schmidt, "Méthode pratique de conservation des monuments en Autriche," *CMAH*, 222.

87. Lopez Otero, *CMAH*. See also Carlo Anti, *Athens PV*, 11.

88. Luigi Pernier, "La conservation des palais minoens en Crète," *CMAH*, 266–273.

89. See Jean Hendrickx, "La Consolidation et la réfection des monuments d'art," *CMAH*, 89–92.

90. Jean-François Cellerier, "La désagrégation des pierres naturelles et les moyens de préservation," *CMAH*, 210–214. "Humanity has at its disposal a quantity of ancient monu-

ments whose date is sufficiently fixed and agreed upon" to serve as a control group for further experiments. *CMAH*, 211.

91. Hendrickx, *CMAH*, 91.

92. Lopez Otero, *CMAH*.

93. "IV. Restoration Materials," *CMAH*, 449.

94. As an article in *Mouseion* that same year recalled, "the chemical analysis of works of art" had been "first employed with the goal of detecting the technique of the most famous ancient painters." Placido Geraci, "L'analyse chimique appliquée aux oeuvres d'art," *Mouseion* 19 (1932): 47–64.

95. There were presentations on the Pantheon in Rome, the Anvers Cathedral, the Utrecht Cathedral, the Palace of Versailles, the Parthenon in Athens, and San Marco in Venice. *CMAH*, 231–245; 280–296; 352–359.

96. Alois Kieslinger, *Zerstörung an Steinbauten* (Leipzig: Franz Deuticke, 1932). Kieslinger impressed many conference attendees; Giovannoni described his work as a "higher order of research." Giovannoni, "La Conferenza," *Bollettino d'arte* (July 1931): 408–420.

97. Kieslinger, *Zerstörung*, 9.

98. "Letzten Endes sollen sie 'geologisch sehen' lehren." Kieslinger, *Zerstörung*, 9. Kieslinger built on the massive work of German geologist Julius Hirschwald, *Handbuch der Bautechnischen Gesteinsprüfung* (Berlin: Borntraeger, 1912).

99. See also Jorge Otero-Pailos, "The Ambivalence of Smoke," *Grey Room* 44 (Summer 2011): 90–113.

100. Conclusion VI declared that in matters of technique it was "impossible to formulate any general rules," given the limitations of "knowledge at present available." *CMAH*, 445.

101. European volunteer citizens' organizations in the late nineteenth century struggled to be officially recognized. (In Italy the *Associazione della Storia dell'Architettura*, in England "friends of" societies; in France the *Caisse nationale des monuments*.) Attempts to ally in a broader transnational movement created backlash; see Frank C. Sharp, "Exploring the Revolution: The Work of the SPAB outside Britain 1878–1914," *From William Morris*, ed. Chris Miele (New Haven: Yale, 2005), 187–212, and Swanson, *The Law's Delay?*

102. For instance John J. Clarke, "Report of the International Town Planning Conference, New York, 1925," *Town Planning Review* 12, no. 2 (November 1926): 141–144. For an overview see Daniel T. Rodgers, *Atlantic Crossings* (Cambridge: Harvard University Press, 1998), ch. 5.

103. Cecil Harcourt-Smith, "La législation des monuments historiques en Grande-Bretagne," *CMAH*, 101–105.

104. "In the construction of buildings, the character and exterior aspect [*physiognomie*] of the cities in which they are to be erected, especially in the neighborhood [*voisinage*] of historic monuments, the surroundings [*entourage*] should be given special consideration. Even certain groupings [*ensembles*] and certain particularly picturesque perspective treatments should be preserved." Horta, *CMAH*. Monuments now had to compete against more quantifiable urban amenities: commercial surface area, amount of fresh air, or population density. Cecil Harcourt-Smith noted this incommensurability. Harcourt-Smith, *CMAH*, 101–105.

105. Victor Horta, "L'Entourage des monuments—principes généraux," *CMAH*, 149–154.

106. On Art Nouveau as the architecture for a cooperative agenda see Paolo Portoghesi, "Introduzione," *Victor Horta*, ed. Portoghesi and Borsi (New York: Rizzoli, 1991); Alan Colquhoun, *Modern Architecture* (New York: Oxford, 2002), 18–21; on Art Nouveau as a "false start" of modernism, Manfredo Tafuri and Francesco dal Co, *Modern Architecture* (New York: Rizzoli, 1976), 7–13.

107. Planners rushed to gut parts of the city but proceeded only with demolition. See

Alexander Murphy, "Landscapes for Whom?" *Yale French Studies* 102 (2002): 190–206; André de Vries, *Brussels: A Cultural and Literary History* (Oxford: Signal, 2002), 191–206; Werner Oechslin, "Town, Monument and Its Synthesis," *Daidalos* (September 1993).

108. In a 1925 lecture Horta already proposed to regulate the relationship of the buildings to their surrounding fabric by categorizing them in three classes: truly modern, truly historic, and "abnormally modern." Victor Horta, "Etude objective sur les auteurs des Serres du jardin botanique de Bruxelles," [1935], in *Questions d'architecture et d'urbanisme* (Brussels: Académie Royale de Belgique, 1996), 79. Translation mine.

109. According to Barry Bergdoll, the League of Nations competition jury sealed "Horta's reputation as a reactionary." "Review: *Horta: Brussels*," *Burlington Magazine* (February 1997): 136–138. On the headquarters competition see L. Anzivino and E. Godoli, *Ginerva 1927* (Calenzano: Modulo, 1979).

110. Joshua Arthurs, *Excavating Modernity* (Ithaca: Cornell University Press, 2012); Spyro Kostof, "His Majesty the Pick," *Design Quarterly* 118–119 (1982): 32–41; Tim Benton, "Rome Reclaims its Empire," *Art and Power* (London: Thames & Hudson, 1996), 120–129; and Medina Lasansky, *The Renaissance Perfected* (University Park: Penn State Press, 2004).

111. Foundoukitis, Draft of a letter, March 10, 1931. IICI-OIM-VI-17(1).

112. A conference on art conservation planned in the mid-1920s had been shelved for lack of funds. In 1928 the fascist regime had funded a new branch of the CIC devoted to film. See Zoë Druick, "The Rome Institute of Educational Cinematography, Reactionary Modernism, and the Foundation of Film Studies," *Canadian Journal of Film Studies* 16, no. 1 (Spring 2007), 80–97.

113. Giovannoni had just published a massive treatise, *Città vecchie ed edilizia nuova* (Torino: Unione tipografico-editrice torinese, 1931) on how to modernize Italian cities and was at work on an Italian "Charter." He was designated to lead the Athens delegation on June 20,1931. Rocco to Giovannoni 20 June 1931. GG 3.9.1. On Giovannoni see Giovanni Carbonara, "Il restauro 'scientifico' nella prima metà del XX secolo," in *Avvicinamento al restauro* (Napoli: Lugori, 1997), 231–268, and Guido Zucconi, "Gustavo Giovannoni: La naissance de l'architecte intégral en Italie," *Annales de la recherche urbaine* 44–45 (December 1989): 185–194, and "Theory and Practice of Urban Conservation," *Change Over Time* 4, no. 1 (Spring 2014): 76–91.

114. Gustavo Giovannoni, "La Restauration des monuments en Italie," *CMAH,* 60–66. Françoise Choay removed this opening homage to the fascist state in her 2002 edition, *La Conférence d'Athènes*, 57.

115. Giovannoni struggled to strike the proper international tone. Inspired by Destrée he settled on pacifism, with "objects of the past" offering a "refuge" against "waves of violence and greed." "Conferenza Atene," GG 3.9.1. This language made it into two reports he published about the Athens Conference: "La Conferenza," and "Congresso internazionale per il restauro dei monumenti," *Bollettino del Reale istituto di archeologia e storia dell'arte* 5, no. 1–3 (1932): 54–63.

116. Giovannoni, *La Restauration.*

117. Gustavo Giovannoni, "Il miglioramento dei nuclei interni: la teoria del diradamemto," *Vecchie città ed edilizia nuova* (Torino: Unione tipografico-editrice torinese, 1931), 248–280.

118. Gustavo Giovannoni, "Les moyens modernes de construction appliqués à la restauration des monuments," *CMAH*, 179–184.

119. Giovannoni, *La Restauration.*

120. For cogent commentary on the fractured nature of the Italian political architectural scene, Diane Ghirardo, "Italian Architects and Fascist Politics," *JSAH* 39, no. 2 (May

1980): 109–127; Manfredo Tafuri, "Architettura e Storia," *Rivista dei libri* (April 1994): 10.

121. Maristella Casciati, "The Architect as Historian," *JSAH* 62, no. 1 (March 2003): 92–101; Henry Millon, "The Role of History of Architecture in Fascist Italy," *JSAH* 24, no. 1 (March 1965): 53–59.

122. Gustavo Giovannoni, "L'Urbanistica Italiana nel Rinascimento," *L'Architettura del Rinascimento* (Milano: Fratelli Treves, 1935), 267–305.

123. Giorgio Ciucci, *Gli Architetti e il Fascismo* (Torino: Einaudi, 1989), 84; Vanna Fraticelli, *Roma 1914–1929* (Roma: Officina, 1982), 34–61.

124. Giovannoni, *La Restauration.*

125. Horta, "L'entourage des monuments," *CMAH*, 149–154. Giovannoni, cited in Fraticelli, Op. cit., 42.

126. The deliberations were appended to the Conclusions although they were not binding. *CMAH*, 452–453.

127. "Proceedings of the Conference on the Anastylosis of the Acropolitan Monuments," *CMAH*, 450.

128. "ἀναστήλ-ωσις, εως, ἡ, *setting up of a monument,* Ptol.Heph. ap. Phot.*Bibl.*147B." Henry George Liddell and Robert Scott, *A Greek-English Lexicon* (1940). Balanos claimed to have first used it as a "neologism" in 1925: "This principle consists of forbidding any complete restoration of the monument based on its remaining parts; it only allows for the re-erection (*relèvement*) of authentic pieces from the monument which have been found on the ground and placed back in their place according to constructive methods that are appropriate to the Monuments. . . . This neologism was first used in Brussels in my presentation during the Meeting of the Academies in 1925." Balanos, *Les monuments de l'Acropole,* 7 n.1–2.

129. See Arthur Sambon, "La protestation des écrivains et des artistes contre la restauration du Parthénon," and George Toudouze, "Le Parthénon en Danger," *Le Musée* 2 (1905): 1–3, 5–10. See also Georges Toudouze, "L'impiété des restaurations," *Le Musée* 1 (1904): 74–78.

130. The deliberations are summarized in *Athens PV*, 24–25.

131. On the deleterious effects of Balanos's methods upon marble, see Richard Economakis, *Acropolis Restoration: The CCAM Interventions* (London: Academy, 1994), 323–326.

132. They "refrained from expressing their general opinion" on his methods. Proceedings, *CMAH*, 453.

133. *Athens PV*, 25. See also "Doctrines—General Principles," *CMAH*, 448.

134. Kieslinger cited the Vienna Opera house, where stone had been "protected" with concrete. But Balanos discounted the advice of anyone who had experience only in France or Austria. Water was "not to be feared in Greece, where drying occurs very rapidly." Bals also argued, "Greek marble is very crystalline, it does not absorb moisture easily." *Athens PV*, 25–26.

135. Lorraine Daston, "Introduction," *Things that Talk* (New York: Zone, 2004), 12.

136. Jean Capart, "La conservation des monuments et la nécessité d'une collaboration internationale: L'exemple de Philae," *CMAH*, 385–391.

137. Officially Balanos worked for the Archaeology Division of the Greek Department of Education. See E. Korka, ed., *Foreign Archaeological Schools in Greece: 160 Years* (Athens: Hypourgeio Politismou, c2005).

138. Karo claimed that "a majority of experts" approved Balanos's proposal. These recommendations included the following: forbidding restoration as "making of fakes" [*trucage*], demolishing the Frankish Tower, defining anastylosis, and asking for continued "monitoring" of Balanos's work. *Athens PV*, 24–25.

139. Conclusion VII, which referred to the Greek government's history of "accepting

the collaboration of archaeologists and experts from every country" confirms that the OIM looked to these institutes as models of cultural diplomacy. *CMAH*, 449–450.

140. In the months leading up to the conference, organizers went to great lengths to broker an agreement between Greek and British delegations to preempt any mention of the Elgin dispute. British OIM member Cecil Harcourt-Smith was told "no regrettable incidents" would occur and no "inopportune questions" would be raised. Foundoukitis to Harcourt-Smith, undated. OIM.I.6/OIM.VI.17. The OIM leadership was admonished to avoid "delicate questions" when they arrived. OIM Réunion du Comité de Direction (October 1931) 1ere Séance (20 October), 2. OIM.VI.17.

141. Louis P. Cassimatis, *American Influence in Greece: 1917–1929* (Kent, OH: Kent State University Press, 1988), 196.

142. Cass Gilbert summarized his objections: "Distressed at method replacement columns Parthenon very unsatisfactory large unsightly patches concrete and some cases entire drums being built up in concrete advise stopping work." Telegram from Gilbert to Finley, June 9, 1927. JHF/96.

143. William Bell Dinsmoor, "Report on the Restoration of the North Colonnade of the Parthenon," January 7, 1927 . Cited in Fani Mallouchou-Tufano, ed., *Anastelose ton archaion mnemeion ste neotere Hellada* (Atheina: Archaiologikei Hetaireia, 1998), 314–327.

144. As Dinsmoor wrote, Balanos had previously "gotten his concrete from Germany and his moral support from the German institute." Dinsmoor to Finley, January 31, 1928. JHF/96.

145. Finley to Capps, June 12, 1926; "A Fund for Restoring the Parthenon Columns," undated draft of a press release. JHF/96.

146. *New York Times*, August 12, 1926. JHF/96.

147. "Royal Cortissay" to Finley, August 25, 1926. JHF/96.

148. McAndrew to Finley, October 10, 1926. JHF/96.

149. Finley learned from the American architect William Welles Bosworth, that if "complete fragments of a body were found, and no head," then no reconstruction should proceed. Bosworth to Finley, 19 July 1929. JHF/96.

150. Finley to Gilbert, July 9, 1926; Gilbert to Finley, October 20, 1930. JHF/96.

151. John Brown to Finley, August 16, 1926; "Royal Cortissay" to Finley, August 25, 1926. JHF/96.

152. Finley to George W. Wickersham, July 15, 1926; Gilbert to Finley, July 12, 1926. JHF/96.

153. According to Dinsmoor, the Council had requested "column by column" drawings but Balanos never produced them. For Dinsmoor, no drawings meant "no control." Dinsmoor to Finley, June 18, 1928. JHF/96. Balanos did present drawings "used to do the work" to the League group. *Athens PV*, 24. The drawings are published in Balanos, *Relèvement*.

154. "The temple was saved by the pen." Gilbert to Finley, October 20, 1930. JHF/96.

155. Capps to Finley, June 1, 1932. JHF/96.

156. Finley to Capps, March 8, 1933. Finley to Excellency Ch. Simopoulos, September 5, 1933. JHF/96.

157. Stuart Thompson to Finley, February 1, 1929. JHF/96.

158. Rhys Carpenter to Capps, June 8, 1930. JHF/96.

159. Buschor, cited on the use of cement in "Opinions of Archaeologists on the Method being Followed by Dr. Balanos in his reconstruction of the Parthenon under the Auspices of the Archaeological Council of the Ministry of Education." Attachment to Capps to Finley, 26 June 1927. JHF/96.

160. Fragment of a letter used for fundraising (original April 13, 1932). JHF/96.

161. Carpenter to Capps, June 8, 1930. Raymond Fosdick was "prepared to dislike" the project but converted by the sight. Cited in Capps to Finley, March 31, 1933. JHF/96.

162. Fragment.

163. Walter Lippman to John Finley, April 19, 1931. JHF/96 On Murray see Peter Wilson, "Gilbert Murray and International Relations," *Review of International Studies* 37 (2011): 881–909. Murray was traveling with other would-be donors, writer Henry James, journalist Walter Lippman, banker Thomas Lamont, and their wives.

164. Murray was on the board of the British Museum, and a member of the "Elgin Room Subcomittee"; he intervened by letter on May 6, 1931, to say that while he recognized that the Pope design necessarily made "some sort of a shrine" for the marbles, he was willing to accept it. See Elisabeth Kehoe, "Working Hard at Giving It Away," *Historical Research* 77, no. 198 (November 2004): 512.

165. The room was "so magnificent that it dwarfed the marbles," and encouraged a false arrangement that implied the collection was of the whole frieze rather than partial selection. "Elgin Room Subcommittee," *British Museum Standing Committee Notes* (May 8, 1931), 4776. BM.

166. The two models were made by the sculptor R. C. Lucas in 1845. See R. C. Lucas, *Remarks on the Parthenon* (Salisbury: W. B. Brodie, 1845.). The Museum Board began discussing how to discard the "reconstructed" one, which had not been on view for decades, in April 1931. Sale was arranged in 1936. *British Museum Standing Committee Notes* (April 11, 1931), 4765. BM.

167. Finley to Fosdick, September 13, 1933. JHF/96.

168. Bergson, *Matter and Memory*, 182.

Chapter Two

1. Dwight D. Eisenhower, "Letter on Historical Monuments," (December 29, 1943). NARA RG165 CAD000.4(3-25-43)(1).

2. "Discrimination" refers to the idea that war should be aimed at combatants and not civilians; "proportionality" demands that the need to inflict civilian casualties be measured against the ranked importance of military objectives. See Matthew Evangelista, "Introduction," *The American Way of Bombing*, ed. Matthew Evangelista and Henry Shue (Ithaca: Cornell University Press, 2014).

3. Joseph Goebbels, cited in Michael Balfour, *Propaganda in War* (London: Routledge, 1979), 265. On the aerial bombing of civilian populations in European cities see Claudia Baldoli, Andrew Knapp, and Richard Overy, eds., *Bombing, States and People in Western Europe 1940–1945* (New York: Continuum, 2011) and Richard Overy, *The Bombing War: Europe 1939–1945* (London: Allen Lane, 2013).

4. *Report of the American Commission for the Protection and Salvage of Artistic and Historic Monuments in War Areas* (Washington, DC: US Government Printing Office, 1946) [henceforth RC Report].

5. Originally named for Europe, the Commission changed its name to the more inclusive "War Areas" on April 21, 1944. *RC Report*, 3.

6. Case studies with before-and-after maps include Hermann Knell, *To Destroy a City* (Cambridge, MA: Da Capo, 2003), Elena Franchi, *Arte in assetto di Guerra* (Pisa: ETS, 2006); Lorenzo de Stefani and Carlotta Coccoli, eds., *Guerra monumenti ricostruzione* (Venezia: Marsilio, 2011), and Hartwig Beseler and Niels Gutschow's massive collaborative compendium, *Kriegsschicksale Deutscher Architektur* (Neumünster: Wachholtz, 1988).

7. Roger Chickering and Stig Förster, eds., *A World at Total War* (Cambridge: Cambridge University Press, 2005), 1–18.

8. As John R. Gills and Michael Geyer seminally put it in *The Militarization of the Western World* (New Brunswick: Rutgers, 1989), militarization (as distinct from militarism) is "the contradictory and tense social process in which civil society organizes itself for the

production of violence." See also Michael Sherry, *In the Shadow of War* (New Haven: Yale University Press, 1995), xi.

9. Robert Edsel, *Monuments Men* (New York: Center Street, 2009). Memoirs include Lord Methuen, *Normandy Diary* (London: Robert Hale, 1946); John Skilton Jr., *Défense de l'art Européen*, trans. Jacqueline de Gromard (Paris: Editions Internationales, 1948); James Rorimer, *Survival* (New York: Abelard, 1950); Frederick Hartt, *Florentine Art under Fire* (Princeton: Princeton University Press, 1949); and Henry LaFarge, ed., *Lost Treasures of Europe* (New York: Pantheon, 1946). Recent book chapters on the MFAA include Marta Nezzo, "The Defence of Works of Art from Bombing in Italy during the Second World War," in *Bombing, States and People in Western Europe 1940–1945*, ed. Claudia Baldoli, Andrew Knapp, and Richard Overy (London: Continuum, 2011), 99–101. Excerpts of MFAA correspondence in Italy include Roger Absalom, *Gli alleati e la ricostruzione in Toscana (1944–1945)* (Florence: Leo S. Olschiki), 2001.

10. Laurie W. Rush calls the MFAA's ability to mobilize "the highest level" of the army leadership despite its own restricted manpower a "force multiplier." "Cultural Property Protection as a Force Multiplier in Stability Operations," *Military Review* (March–April 2012): 36–43.

11. Nicola Lambourne, *War Damage in Western Europe: The Destruction of Historic Monuments* (Edinburgh: Edinburgh University Press, 2001), 163.

12. Statistics on human casualties are still contested; this summary is from Tony Judt, *Postwar* (New York: Penguin, 2005), 16.

13. On bombing prophecies see Sven Lindqvist, *A History of Bombing*, trans. Linda Haverty Rugg (New York: New Press, 2001); on their connections to the unfolding Allied war, Tami Davis Biddle, *Rhetoric and Reality in Air Warfare* (Princeton: Princeton University Press, 2002).

14. As late as 1943 a British study titled *Is Bombing Decisive?* addressed how the ongoing war was correcting bombing-theoretical discourse. F. O. Miksche, *Is Bombing Decisive?* (New York: Norton, 1943).

15. Giulio Douhet, *The Command of the Air*, trans. Dino Ferrari, [1928] (Washington, DC: Office of Air Force History, 1983), 196. On the dissemination of Douhet's ideas see Biddle, *Rhetoric and Reality*; Stephen Garret, *Ethics and Airpower in World War II* (New York: St. Martin's, 1993), 8; Baldoli et al., *Bombing, States and People*; and "Air Power in Theory and Reality," *Journal of Strategic Studies* 18, no. 1 (1995).

16. Douhet, 6–7.

17. Frances Kamm distinguishes between "military" and "political" aspects of bombing in "Types of Terror Bombing," in *Action, Ethics, Responsibility* (Cambridge, MA: MIT Press, 2010).

18. Official orders to target civilians came in the first half of 1942: from the Allies, in a February order to attack "the morale of the civilian population," Alan Levine, *The Strategic Bombing of Germany, 1940–1945* (London: Praeger, 1992), 6; from the Axis, in an order for a terror attack on April 14, 1942, Niall Rothnie, *The Baedeker Blitz* (Shepperton: Ian Alan, 1992), 11.

19. On bombing as political bargaining, see George Quester, "Bargaining and Bombing during World War II in Europe," *World Politics* 15, no. 3 (April 1963): 417–437.

20. Roger O'Keefe argues that "There was little difference in legal terms" between Allied and Axis bombings, and argues "the uncharacteristic restraint on the Nazis' part . . . was for reasons more pragmatic than principled: they feared retaliation by the more powerful RAF." Roger O'Keefe, *The Protection of Cultural Property in Armed Conflict* (Cambridge: Cambridge University Press, 2006), 62n129.

21. Sheldon Garon gives a comparative analysis of the "homefronts" in Japan, the UK,

and Germany, "Defending Civilians against Aerial Bombardment," *Asia-Pacific Journal* 14, no. 23/2 (December 1, 2016).

22. See H. W. Koch, "The Strategic Air Offensive against Germany: The Early Phase, May-Sep 1940," *Historical Journal* 34, no. 1 (1991): 117–141.

23. Sir Arthur Harris, *Despatch on War Operations* [1946] (London: Frank Cass, 1995), 38.

24. *United States Strategic Bombing Survey, Overall Report: European War* (Washington, DC: September 30, 1945). In the few months immediately following the end of war, analysts concluded that "bombing succeeded in lowering psychological morale but its effects upon behavior was less decisive." Later studies confirmed this; see Irving Janis, *Air War and Emotional Stress* (New York: McGraw-Hill, 1951), 132. The Survey was in fact already started in late 1944, and kept separate from British studies, producing a division between the study of the effects of "AAF and RAF bombs" that still organizes the literature today.

25. See Rothnie, *The Baedeker Blitz* for a timeline. Susanne Müller explains the World War II manipulations of the Baedeker format by arguing it is an "empty basket" for "any kind of content or meaning." *Die Welt des Baedekers* (Frankfurt: Campus, 2012) , 251.

26. Thomas Mann, *Listen Germany!* (New York: Knopf, 1943), 85.

27. Cited in A. C. Grayling, *Among the Dead Cities* (London: Bloomsbury, 2006), 51. German strategists did not actually use Baedeker guides, but coined the phrase *post facto*. Rothnie, 130–134, and Charles Whiting, *The Three-Star Blitz* (London: Leo Cooper, 1987).

28. Lambourne, 52.

29. Josef Böröcz, "Travel Capitalism and Europe," *Comparative Studies in Society and History* 34, no. 4 (October 1992): 708–741.

30. James Buzard, "A Continent of Pictures," *PMLA* 108, no. 1 (January 1993): 30–44.

31. Rudy Koshar, "What Ought to Be Seen," *Journal of Contemporary History* 33, no. 3 (1998): 323–340; James Buzard, *The Beaten Track* (Oxford: Clarendon Press, 1993); Edward Mendelson, "Baedeker's Universe," *Yale Review of Books* 74, no. 3 (April 1985): 391.

32. "Protection of Monuments: A Proposal for Consideration during War and Rehabilitation" [undated] draft, and W. G. Constable, "Works of Art During and After the War," December 21, 1942, both attached to a letter from Constable to Perry, December 31, 1942. ADHG/72. Letter likely coauthored by George Stout, and cosigned by George Chase (Dean of the University) and Paul Sachs, directed to Francis Taylor (AAM), Dinsmoor (head of AIA) and Coleman (Museums Association), and Waldo Leland (ACLS). The ACLS memo names Herbert Lehman, who had just been appointed as the head of the new Office of Postwar Rehabilitation, and became a part of the Roberts Commission. WGC/3077.

33. "Memorandum for Submission to the President of the United States," November 21, 1942, likely authored by Francis Henry Taylor with chief Justice Stone and cosigned by the heads of several national scholarly associations. Accompanied by William Bell Dismoor, "Proposal regarding protection of European monuments," and "Outline for the functions and organization of the American Committee on Historic Monuments in Europe." A note from January 1, 1943, indicates that "the president is studying the proposal." WBD III/1.

34. Robinson to Dinsmoor, April 23, 1943, WBD I/2; Constable to Wildenstein and Conant, WGC/3077; McCaff to Dinsmoor, February 13, 1945, WBD VI/17.

35. W. G. Constable, "Karl Baedeker." Lecture at Smith College (1953). WGC/3077.

36. W. G. Constable, "Art: Its Place in a Changing World." Lecture (November 1942). WGC/3071. For a British audience, he used London instead of Washington and called it a "reasonable utopia." W. G. Constable, *Art History and Conoisseurship* (Cambridge: Cambridge University Press, 1938).

37. W. G. Constable, "Works of Art During and After the War." Lecture draft (December 21, 1942). WGC/3077.

38. Constable, Op. Cit.

39. *The Bomber's Baedeker: A Guide to the Economic Importance of Cities and Towns*. London: 1944. See Uta Hohn, "The Bomber's Baedeker," *GeoJournal 34, no.* 2 (October 1994): 213–230.

40. "The Economic Appraisal," *The Strategic Air Offensive against Germany 1939–1945*, vol. 1 (London: HMSO, 1961), 467–469.

41. "Economic Appraisal," 469.

42. Peter Galison, "The Ontology of the Enemy," *Critical Inquiry* 21, no. 1 (Autumn 1994): 228–266.

43. Peter Galison, "War Against the Center," *Grey Room* 4 (Summer 2001): 8. Charles W. McArthur, *Operations analysis in the U.S. Army Eighth Air Force in World War II, Part 790*, American Mathematical Society (1990); Robert Ehlers and Robert A. Donnelly Jr., *Targeting the Third Reich* (Lawrence: University Press of Kansas, 2009).

44. Franklin D. Roosevelt, "Joint Press Conference with Prime Minister Churchill at Casablanca," January 24, 1943. See also Churchill's statement on July 26, 1943, that "the supreme aim" was "the destruction of Hitler, Hitlerism, and Nazi Germany." Allan Winkler, *The Politics of Propaganda* (New Haven: Yale, 1978), 97.

45. Precision appealed to the operational minimalism of military strategists, to political leaders through economic efficiency, and to the general public by promising to keep the war at an apparently safe technological distance. Sean Malloy, "Liberal Democracy and the Lure of Bombing," Bruce Schulman, ed., *Making the American Century* (London: Oxford, 2014), 109–123. Also Stephen L. MacFarland, *America's Pursuit of Precision Bombing, 1910–1945* (Washington, DC: Smithsonian Institution, 1995).

46. Dwight D. Eisenhower, *Crusade in Europe* (New York: Garden City, 1952), 4.

47. Harry L. Coles and Albert K. Weinberg, *Civil Affairs: Soldiers Become Governors* (Washington, DC: Center of Military History, 2004).

48. "Prepare to Occupy," *Fortune* 27, no. 2 (February 1943): 90–214; Col. Joseph Harris, "Selection and training of Civil Affairs Officers," *Public Opinion Quarterly* 7, no. 4 (Winter 1943): 694–706. On how Casablanca set the stage for Project Paperclip, that "grandiose technology transfer that was soon to mark the international postwar order" transferring a whole sector of German industry to the United States, see Friedrich Kittler, "Unconditional Surrender" in *Materialities of Communications*, ed. Hans Ulrich Gumbrecht and K. Ludwig Pfeiffer (Stanford: Stanford University Press, 1994), 326.

49. Shoemaker to Perry, on May 14, 1943. ADHG/73.

50. Eisenhower, *Letter to Commanders*.

51. Dwight Eisenhower, Letter on Preservation of Historical Monuments, May 26, 1944. NARA SHAEF/G5/751. [Henceforth, *Preservation*].

52. "In some circumstances the success of the military operation may be prejudiced in our reluctance to destroy these revered objects. Then, as at Cassino, where the enemy relied on our emotional attachment to shield his defense, the lives of our men are paramount. So, where military necessity dictates, commanders may order the required action even though it involves destruction of some honored site." Eisenhower, *Preservation*.

53. Eisenhower, *Preservation*.

54. This first draft was coauthored by Sir Leonard Woolley. See Dinsmoor, "First Weekly Report Sunday Apr 23, 1944." WBD III/3.

55. See Fred I. Greenstein, *The Hidden Hand Presidency* (New York: Basic, 1982), and Martin Medhurts, *Dwight D. Eisenhower: Strategic Communicator* (London: Greenwood, 1993).

56. He continued: "One of the most important characteristics of the successful officer today is his ability to continue changing his methods, almost even his mental processes, in

order to keep abreast of the constant change that modern science ... brings to the battlefield." Eisenhower, *Crusade in Europe*, 235.

57. On wartime collaborations' impact on postwar social science see Joseph Tobin's "The HRAF as Radical Text?" *Cultural Anthropology* 5, no. 4, (November 1990): 473–487, and Ellen Herman, *The Romance of American Psychology* (Berkeley: University of California Press, 1995).

58. Stout to Constable, March 30, 1945, WGC/3077.

59. ADHG, *Final Report*, 14. AHDG/73.

60. Sachs to Dinsmoor May 18, 1943. WBD III/2.

61. See Craig Hugh Smyth and Peter Lukchart, *The Early Years of Art History in the United States* (Princeton: Princeton University Press, 1993), 6. Many historians have credited the arrival of European émigrés for lifting the goals of a discipline that was "sporadic and provincial." John Coolidge says they "unified the practice" in "Walter Friedlander," *Art Journal* (1967): 260. Walter Cook recollected "the spontaneous efflorescence of the history of art in the United States," in Panofsky, "Three Decades of Art History in the United States," *Meaning in the Visual Arts* (New York: Penguin, 1955), 376. See also: Kathryn Brush, "German *Kunstwissenschaft* and the Practice of Art History," *Marburger Jahrbuch für Kunstwissenschaft* (1999): 7–36; and Thomas Crow, "The Practice of Art History in America," *Daedalus* 135, no. 2 (Spring 2006): 70–90.

62. Colin Eisler, "*Kunstgeschichte* American Style," in *The Intellectual Migration: Europe and America, 1930–1960*, ed. Fleming and Bailyn (Cambridge, MA: Harvard University Press, 1969), 559.

63. On list-making in the *longue-durée* of art historiography see Donald Preziosi, *Rethinking Art History* (New Haven: Yale University Press, 1989).

64. This three-part distinction is given by James Ackerman and Rhys Carpenter, *Art and Archaeology* (Princeton: Princeton University Press, 1963), 141. Eisler (supra 62) also divided the field into three: historians interested in "ideas," in "stones," and in "facts."

65. Charles Rufus Morey, "Value of Art as an Academic Subject" *Parnassus* 1, no. 3 (Mar 15, 1929), 7, quoted in Constable, "The Arts in Education," 1929, WGC/3071.

66. Wartime issues of the *College Art Journal* published many MFAA officers' reports side by side with discussions of the discipline's future. See for instance "Statement on the Place of the History of Art in the Liberal Arts Curriculum," *College Art Journal* (March 1944): 82–87. The Society of Architectural Historians (SAH) also branched off the CAA in 1941 with a preservationist clause in its mission statement. See "Round Table Discussion on the Preservation of Historic Architectural Monuments," *JSAH* 1, no. 2 (1941).

67. See for instance Lennox Grey's defensive introduction to Patricia Beesly's influential *The Revival of the Humanities* (New York: Columbia University Press, 1940) and W. Edward Farrison, "Humanities vs. War," *Phylon* (1944): 334–338. A historical overview is Steven Markus, "From Classics to Cultural Studies," *Daidalos: On the Humanities* (Spring 2006): 15–21.

68. Ralph Barton Perry, *In the Spirit of William James* (New Haven: Yale University Press, 1938), 129.

69. Ralph Barton Perry, "A Definition of the Humanities," in *The Meaning of the Humanities*, ed. T. M. Greene (Princeton: Princeton University Press, 1938), 9. See also Ralph Barton Perry, "Philosophy," lecture outline, March 3, 1938. CRM 10/G. Constable cited "Perry's conception of freedom for enlightened choice" as opposed to "an anarchical freedom" in "Art, Its Place in a Changing World." WGC/3071.

70. American Defense-Harvard Group, "Circular of December 18, 1940," and *Final Report: June 1940-June 1945*: 5; 19; 39–40. ADHG/73.

71. "Why Colleges Are Preferable to Army Posts for CA Training," *Soldiers Become Governors*, 81.

72. Shoemaker to Perry, March 18, 1943. ADHG/73. They avoided Harvard's inquisitive delegate of the State Department's Cultural Relations Division, Ralph Turner, whose goals were what they called "broader." Shoemaker to Perry, April 19, 1943. WGC/3077.

73. The ACLS was founded as liaison between American academics and the League of Nations, via national associations. William Bell Dinsmoor, "New Trends in Humanistic Study," *Columbia University Quarterly* (December 1935): 415–426.

74. "I find it hard to believe that any machinery could be set up to carry out" the suggested program. Clark to Constable, February 25, 1943; "I doubt that there is anything that art historians like ourselves can do in times of war," MacLagan to Constable, February 27, 1943. WGC/3077.

75. The project initially was geared at all buildings in "vulnerable areas" and switched to more explicitly monumental sites that might be targeted for historic importance after the Baedeker Raids. "Report Concerning Bibliography on War Damage in the British Isles" [May 1945?]. SMcC I/ 4.

76. Ralph Barton Perry, *A General Theory of Value* (Harvard University Press, 1926), 115f.

77. Perry, *A Definition*, 33.

78. "The Safeguarding of Works of Art and of Monuments of Cultural Importance in Occupied Countries." Sent by Perry to Shoemaker in multiple copies and received on April 7, 1943. ADHG/73.

79. Perry, *General Theory*.

80. Stout, *The Safeguarding*, n77.

81. Memo from Shoemaker for Dr. William Longer, Chairman, Board of Analysts, Office of Strategic Studies. Forwarded to Perry. March 30, 1943. WGC/3077.

82. Shoemaker to Perry, April 7, 1943. ADHG/73.

83. By April, Shoemaker had outlined to Perry "three functions" that the art historians' material was to fulfill in the Army's hands. Shoemaker to Perry, April 19, 1943. ADHG/Shoemaker.

84. Shoemaker to Hencken, June 15, 1943. ADHG/Shoemaker.

85. Shoemaker to Perry, June 11, 1943. ADHG/Shoemaker.

86. Form letter sent to all contributors, for example Hencken to Doro Levi, April 3, 1943. ADHG/ Levi.

87. Hans Huth, "Observations Concerning the Conservation of Monuments in Europe and America" (Document 118727), Washington, DC: National Park Service, 1940. See also Huth's "The Evolution of Preservationism in Europe," *JSAH* 1, no. 3–4 (July–October 1941): 5–12.

88. "Lecture on the Protection of Cultural Treasures," WBD IX/2.

89. "The Protection of a Cultural Heritage," *Rockefeller Foundation, Annual Report*, 1943, 34. WBD XI/3.

90. On the humanities see Snyder, "The Humanities in Education," *College English* 15, no. 2 (November 1953): 119 and Gerald Graf, "General Education and the Pedagogy of Criticism: 1930-1950," in *Professing Literature: An Institutional History* (Chicago: University of Chicago Press, 1987), 133. On the classics see Steven Markus, "From Classics to Cultural Studies," *Daidalos*: *On the Humanities*, 15–21; "Classics and Commercials," *The Making of Middlebrow Culture* (Durham: UNC Press, 1992), 148–208.

91. Erwin Panofsky, "The History of Art as a Humanistic Discipline," *The Meaning of the Humanities*, 91–118. Panofsky's lecture has become a landmark of art historiography for what Thomas Crow has called its "degree-zero definition" of a work of art, as "an object that demands to be experienced aesthetically." Thomas Crow, "The Practice of Art History," 73.

92. Erwin Panofsky, "Art and Archaeology," lecture outline, February 24, 1938, CRM 10/G. See also Erwin Panofsky, "Proposed Amendments to Draft of Circular to the Mem-

bers of the College Art Association." Attached to a letter to Sumner Crosby, June 10, 1941. AAA EP /2111.

93. As Michael-Ann Holly has pointed out, Panofsky borrowed this distinction between physical and mental sciences from Wilhelm Dilthey. *Panofsky and the Foundations of Art History* (Ithaca: Cornell University Press, 1984), 38; 20.

94. Huth, *Observations*, 1.

95. March 17, "Memorandum of Telephone Conversation with Lt-Col James H. Shoemaker," appended to Letter from Shoemaker to Perry, March 18, 1943. ADHG/73.

96. Shoemaker to Sachs, April 4, 1943. Sachs to contributors, May 24, 1943. ADHG/73.

97. On the rise of a new American collecting class see David Watkin, *The Rise of Architectural History* (London: Architectural, 1980), 36. On conservation at the Fogg, Francesca Bewer, *A Laboratory For Art* (New Haven: Yale University Press, 2010).

98. Kantor, *Alfred H. Barr Jr and the Intellectual Foundations of the Museum of Modern Art* (Cambridge, MA: MIT Press, 2002), 171.

99. Constable cited Berenson's definition of "the work of art itself as the event of art history," to distinguish between the connoisseur, who narrates this event, and the art historian, who collects it in four steps. W. G. Constable, *Art History and Conoisseurship* (Cambridge: Cambridge University Press, 1938), 10.

100. "Talk by Mr. WG Constable" in *Fine Arts 15a "Museum work and Museum Problems"* 30th Meeting, Mar 16, 1931, Shady Hill, Paul J. Sachs, *Paul J Sachs Museums Course* 142c.

101. The aphorism is from Voltaire. Constable, "Works of Art in Wartime," January–March 1944. WGC/3077.

102. Sachs to contributors, May 24, 1943. ADHG/73.

103. Levi to Hencken, July 8, 1943. ADHG/73.

104. Constable to Hencken, August 11, 1943. ADHG, "List of Protected Monuments, France." ADHG/Hencken.

105. See Appendix "C-6" to Report 20345/0/MFAA and "Sample page from 'Lists of Protected Monuments, Italy,'" *Final Report, General* (January 1, 1946). NGA/FH2-11.

106. Pierre Bourdieu, *Distinction: A Social Critique of the Judgement of Taste* [1979], trans. Richard Nice, (Cambridge: Harvard University Press, 1994), 8.

107. W. G. Constable, "Museum Ethics," 14. WGC/3073. In a lecture titled "Ethics for Museum Men" on March 11, 1940, he also enunciated, "one function of a museum is to provide standards of taste and judgement." WGC/3072, 218.

108. Constable, "Works of Art in Wartime."

109. [Sigrid Unset], "Introduction," *Civil Affairs Handbook, Norway*, Section 17: Cultural Institutions (M350-17: 19 July 1944). ADHG/76. [Jakob Rosenberg], "Introduction," *Civil Affairs Handbook, Belgium*, Section 17: Cultural Institutions (M361-17, 13 May 1944). ADHG/74 [Ernst Kitzinger], "Introduction," *Civil Affairs Handbook, Netherlands*, Section 17: Cultural Institutions (M357-17: 13 May 1944). ADHG/77. [George Wildenstein and Kenneth Conant], "Introduction," *Civil Affairs Handbook, France*, Section 17B: Cultural Institutions (M352-17B, 3 June 1944), vii. [Margaret Ames], "Introduction," *List of Protected Monuments in Hungary by Margaret Ames*. ADHG/75. [Doro Levi], "Introduction," *Civil Affairs Handbook, Italy*, Section 17A: Cultural Institutions (M353-17A, 6 July 1944), vii. [Otto Benesch], "Introduction," *List of Protected Monuments in Austria by Otto Benesch*. ADHG/74.

110. Erwin Panofsky, *Three Decades*, 376.

111. The donation of the estate to Harvard had been Sachs's doing. Goodwin, 59. Berta Segall, "The Dumbarton Oaks Collection," *American Journal of Archaeology* (January–Mar 1941): 7.

112. Urgent requests came on April 24, 1943: Hencken requested "whatever material you have already assembled dealing with material of artistic and cultural importance in Tunisia,

Germany, Belgium, Luxembourg, Hungary, and the Balkans. This should be marked, 'Preliminary draft—incomplete—subject to revision'." Hencken to Koehler, April 24, 1943. ADHG/72. "Home Center" is from an undated memo from Koehler to Hencken, summarizing a discussion with Sachs the week prior. ADHG/72.

113. Koehler to Sachs, May 26, 1943; "Minutes of the Administrative Committee for Dumbarton Oaks." ADHG/72.

114. Constable to Hencken, June 23, 1943. WGC/3077 and Constable, *Ethics for Museum Men* (1940) WGC/3072.

115. The list opened thus: "Among the monuments the Mohammedan buildings are particularly important because of their religious significance. The religious fanaticism of the Mohammedans is notorious." *Lists of Monuments for Tunisia* ADHG/76. Koehler's "preliminary draft" had left a space empty for an introduction preceding this paragraph; it was the Harvard editors that made it the opening statement.

116. "Introduction," *Civil Affairs Handbook, Japan*, Section 17: Cultural Institutions M354-17 (July 24, 1944).

117. Hencken gave Koehler credit for the formatting. ADHG/72.

118. Koehler delivered the Lists for Central and South Central Italy in person to Shoemaker on August 4, 1943, for instance. ADHG/73.

119. Hencken to Koehler, September 11, 1943. ADHG/72.

120. Undated draft of an Introduction for the German List, of which page 1 is missing. Koehler's critique of the Nazi regime was likely contained in the missing first page. This draft can be found in WBD V/1 and as "Germany" in Koehler's handwritten notes ADHG/72. In this first draft Koehler referred to the "two generations of German art historians" who had "worked impartially towards compiling comprehensive inventories of monuments in publications such as the "*Bau- und Kunst-denkmäler*." Koehler, "The German Organization in charge of the Conservation of monuments." ADHG/72.

121. Koehler had been in contact with Max Dvorák and Wilhelm Böde when the German *Kunstschutz* was founded, and thought of the Roberts Commission as a parallel effort. See Koehler to Sachs, February 5, 1943. PJS/49. On the *Kunstschutz* see Christian Fuhrmeister, ed., *Kunsthistoriker im Krieg* (Cologne: Böhlau; Vienna: Weimar, c2012.). Clemen was recorded as "Nationalist. Definitely anti-nazi but very old" in the American Commission's files. (NARA M1944 108). On Clemen's ambivalent legacy see Antoine Fleury, "Le Kunstschutz entre mémoire et histoire," and Christina Kott, *Préserver l'art de l'ennemi?* (Bruxelles: Peter Lang, 2006).

122. In this draft, Koehler struggled to work out a definition of the monument, by starting with buildings. "Throughout this introduction the word 'monument' ~~designates not only buildings, but refers to~~ is used in its most general sense, [. . .] including works of art of all kinds, materials, techniques and size." Koehler, Germany—Introduction. ADHG/72.

123. Constable's rewritten draft reads: "Whether included here or not, every one of [Germany's treasures] is representative of the civilization which is ours. As such they must, so far as war allows, receive consideration and respect." ADHG/76.

124. Dinsmoor to Shoemaker, October 9, 1943. WBD I/6.

125. Dinsmoor, "Frick Reference Library Status, Jan 4, 1944." WBD I/8. In September 1944, after the atlases had been compiled, this entire card file was sent to the OSS. Dinsmoor to Constable, September 21, 1944. WGC.

126. This decision was taken at the first meeting of the ACLS Committee on June 25, 1943.

127. Lee to Hencken, September 2, 1943. ADHG/ Lee.

128. In May, Perry had urged Koehler to opt for "a relaxation of one's scholarly standards and scruples" and promised that there would be "plenty of time to edit the lists." Perry

to Koehler, May 10, 1943. ADHG/Koehler. The cajoling for adding stars is in Hencken to Koehler, undated, probably June 1943. ADHG/72.

129. On June 10 Milton Anastsos also wrote that "looking back over the Greek list" he was "a little troubled by the asterisks (both when present and absent)." Anastos to Koehler, June 10, 1943. ADHG/72. Constable found this drive to perfection misplaced: "the main job is to get something helpful in the hands of the War Department, as quickly as possible, not perfect."

130. Koehler to Shoemaker, November 2, 1943. ADHG/ Koehler II. Emphasis in the original.

131. "American militarization took place without fanfare and with little of the militaristic rhetoric that was typical of interwar Europe. While . . . the old militarism glorified war but often failed to prepare for it, the emerging militarization process intensified the preparation while concealing its purposes and obscuring its consequences." John Gillis, *The Militarization of the Western World* (New Brunswick: Rutgers University Press, c1989), 7.

132. In response, Koehler received a notice that his list had already left the Commission's hands. Hencken to Koehler, November 5, 1943. ADHG/72.

133. Cited by Angeliki E. Laiou, "Dumbarton Oaks Conference, 1944–1994: Remarks from the Opening Session," *The Dumbarton Oaks Conversations and the United Nations 1944–1994*, ed. Ernest May and Angeliki Laiou (Cambridge: Harvard University Press, 1998), ix.

134. Ames's list had divided Tunisia into regions, following the French military maps, and offered a lexicon of different kinds of "Mahommedan" building types. Ames, "Tunisia-Introduction."

135. On the building of these urban amenities across the Maghreb and Middle East, see Zeynep Çelik, *Empire, Architecture and the City* (Seattle: University of Washington Press, 2008). Other instances when destroyed infrastructure was confused for a religious building in Tunisia include the Bizerte train station, dramatically fragmented and fallen to the ground, taken for a mosque. "First Day in Bizerte," *Life*, December 27, 1943, 67.

136. Lisa Gitelman, *Paper Knowledge* (Durham: Duke University Press, 2014).

137. "Memorandum: Lecture to British Officers and NCOs" [Undated, ca. February 1944]. NARA RG 331 324/Lectures.

138. WGC/1272.

139. New lists for Belgium and Netherlands were issued February 20, 1945. *Soldiers Become Governors*, 873.

140. Woolley, *A Record of the Work*, 41. See also General Board, *CA and MG Activities*: "Considerable difficulty was encountered in the collection of monuments. Many world famous and universally accepted buildings and museums were of course to be listed, but there were also a number of lesser monuments, not so spectacular but equally important from the cultural point of view, between which the choice was not so portent"; 14.

141. The meeting is described in E. H. J. Maxse, "Air Mission" Memo 3. NARA RG331/10000/145/259. The list itself begins with "Rome," then gives a numbered list starting with "1. Florence, 2.Venice, 3. Siena" ending with "45. Aquila" followed by three "cities on the Dalmatian coast." Baillie Reynolds to Zuckerman, October 8, 1943. NARA RG331/AFHQ/Roll30.

142. E. H. J. Maxse, "Air Mission" Memo 4. NARA RG 331/10000/145/259.

143. Bourdieu, supra 106.

144. Hammond to Webb, May 31, 1944. NARA RG331/SHAEF/Air Staff.

145. See also Woolley's description of the incident in Sir Leonard Woolley, *A Record of the Work*, 41, and in Lord Methuen, *Normandy Diary* (London: Robert Hale, 1946), xvii.

146. "Decision as to discrimination was to be made by the officer in the field." See also: "Some internal dissension arose regarding the nature of these lists . . . the discretion of the

MFAA officers as a solution to this problem." General Board, *Civil Affairs and Military Government Activities*, 14.

147. C. P. Cabell, "Protection of Historical Monuments and Civilian Populations," January 12, 1945. From "Bombing Restriction," NARA RG 331/AFHQ/ MAAF HQ Operations / roll 32H.

148. In a lengthy and remarkable footnote to this text, Panofsky addressed the Rieglian definition of monuments as objects that hold "intentional" value as well as "age-value," but bracketed the latter as "accidental" to aesthetic value. Panofsky, "History of Art as Humanistic Discipline," 14–15n11.

149. All the scholars were asked to make lists of persons and separate them from those of places. Paul Sachs made a list titled "Paul J. Sachs European List (Personal Acquaintances)" subtitled "All Museums, Libraries, etc in separate books." NARA. RG 331/M1944/Roll60. "White" and "Black List" of Nazi-sympathizers in the German art world were submitted to the OSS. On November 1, 1944, Lee wrote Crosby, "Bill Burke tells me you know about the Panofsky black and white lists." SMcC I/3. A letter from Hammond on 6 October 1944 refers to the existence of "grey" lists. NARA RG331/55B/331 Panosfky also "checked" the maps of Hamburg, Hanover, Münster, Paderborn, Sardt, Marburg, Dortmund, Wiesbaden and "such part of Lübeck as had erroneously been listed under Hamburg." Crosby to Panofsky, May 21, 1944, and March 13, 1944. WBD V/1.

150. Erwin Panofsky, "List of Libraries in Which I have studied" [undated, ca. March 1944]. WBD V/8.

151. Frankl had been suggested as a potential collaborator by Koehler on May 19, 1943. ADHG /72.

152. Paul Frankl, "*Weltregierung*: English Translation (draft)," 193. PF/4. This is a never-published English translation of *Weltregierung* (Leiden: Stenferd Uitgevers, 1948), 288–289. English edited for clarity.

153. Francis Taylor, *Babel's Tower* (New York: Columbia University Press, 1945), 7. As Meyer Schapiro pointed out, Taylor supported this dubious jab at Panofsky with an inchoate and conspiratorial view of the reciprocal ties between intellectual and political histories of Germany, Italy, and the United States. Meyer Schapiro, *The Art Bulletin*, 27, no. 4 (December 1945): 272–276.

154. Francis Taylor, "The Rape of Europa," *Atlantic Monthly* (January 1945): 52–58.

155. Stout to Sachs [30 Mar 1945?] WGC/3077. Stout wrote several other times to Sachs to complain about Taylor and "the attitude of these art-political characters." Stout to Constable November 29, 1943 WGC3077; Stout to Sachs, 19 January 1945. PJS/48. Other MFAA officers also complained about Taylor's visits. Hammond to Newton, 16 December 1944, *Military Affairs* (April 1988), 67.

156. Stout to Sachs [March 30, 1945?]. WGC/3077.

157. At war's end, even Leonard Woolley conceded that knowledge may have been the only product of the MFAA's work: "The clear task of the MFAA Sub-Commission was to ensure that at least no part of this destruction should be wrought through ignorance of the existence of individual monuments." Leonard Woolley, *A Record of the Work Done by the Military Authorities for the Protection of the Treasures of Art and History in War Areas* (London: MHSO, 1947), 28.

158. In this commentary on Goethe's novella, *Elective Affinities*, Benjamin distinguished real choice from the "false sense of freedom felt by those who only choose, but never decide." Walter Benjamin, "On Goethe's Elective Affinities," *Selected Writings*, vol. 1, 1913–1926, ed. Marcus Bullock and Michael W. Jennings (Cambridge, MA: Belknap /Harvard, 2002), 297. N. K. Leacock, "Narrative, Silence and the Novel: On Goethe's *Elective Affinities*," *Narrative* 10, no. 3 (2002): 277–306.

Chapter Three

1. On the Rome raid's planning see Richard Overy, *The Bombing War* (London: Penguin, 2013), 522–528. On its reception, Cesare de Simone, *Venti angeli sopra Roma* (Milano: Mursia, 1993).

2. They gathered intelligence about damage in part to use as counter-propaganda against the inevitable accusations of "profanatory vandalism." Cited in Giuseppe Vedovato, *La città aperta nella seconda guerra mondiale* (Florence: Biblioteca della Rivista di studi Politici Internazionali, 2002), 95. As Overy (supra 1) points out, ultimately American public opinion was much harsher than the Italian.

3. Letter Richard Krautheimer, Helen Franc, and John Phillips Coolidge, to Alexander Wetmore, July 19, 1943. WBD I/3.

4. On Krautheimer see Ulrike Wendland, *Biographisches Handbuch deutschsprachiger Kunsthistoriker im Exil 1* (Munchen: Saud, 1999), 377–385, and Richard Krautheimer, "And Gladly Did He Learn and Did He Teach," Canadian International Art History Center, *Rome: Tradition, Innovation and Renewal* (Montreal: CCA, 1997), 93–96.

5. Executive Board of the Visiting Comitttee of the Department of Art and Archaeology, Princeton. Meeting on November 26, 1943. Frick CC. Similarly, by 1945 Francis Taylor claimed that pilots had taken "desperate risks in pinpointing bombing in order to spare a cathedral or famous palace." Taylor, "The Rape of Europa," *Atlantic Monthly* (Jan 1945), 53.

6. "Rome: Precision Bombing Problem Was What to Hit and Also What Not to Hit," *Impact: A Confidential Picture History of World War II*, 1, no. 6 (September 1943), 42–49.

7. Norton Wise gives a useful preliminary description of precision as a criterion that operates within an established numeric range, different from accuracy in that it allows "straying." Wise offers the illuminating example of a rifle aimed at a target, which reliably fires a "tightly grouped set of holes in the target" even if the group "lies some distance from the center of the target," to describe that the rifle is "precise" despite its being relatively "inaccurate." Norton Wise, *The Values of Precision* (New York: Princeton University Press, 1997), 7–8.

8. "If definite instances of the intentional targeting of historic monuments are rare, indisputable cases of intentional avoidance of those buildings are equally elusive"; "in the absence of a positive stated Allied policy of bombarding buildings of historic and cultural importance . . . the strongest impression given is more that of a lack of interest in avoiding them." Nicola Lambourne, *War Damage in Western Europe* (Edinburgh: Edinburgh University Press, 2001), 163. See also Jeffry Diefendorf's review in *Journal of Military History* (October 2001): 1151–1152.

9. Peter Galison, "Ontology of the Enemy," *Critical Inquiry* 21 (Autumn 1994): 228–266; Samuel Weber, *Targets of Opportunity* (New York: Fordham Press, 2002); Manuel De Landa, *War in the Age of Intelligent Machines* (New York: Zone, 2001); John Harwood, "Danger Zones," *Grey Room* 54: 80–106.

10. Dinsmoor, "Frick Reference Library Status, Jan 4, 1944." The card file was sent to the OSS in September. Dinsmoor to Constable, September 21, 1944. WBD I/8.

11. "We should probably not be allowed to work directly" on target maps "under any circumstances." Dinsmoor to McLeish, August 19, 1943, WBD I/4.

12. John A. Gilmore, "Text for a Proposed Press Release," December 1943. NARA RG 331/M1944/Roll16.

13. Stratton Hammon, "Memoir of the Ranking Monuments, Fine Arts and Archives Officer in the ETO during World War II, in *Military Affairs* (April 1988), 62. When the MFAA map-making was moved to the west of England, some of the maps issued by the British Geographic Section, General Staff (GSGS) were used as base, with insets featuring the mon-

uments of German cities in three-dimensional, extruded axonometric. (25 November 1944) SMcC 1/3.

14. Geoffrey Webb, "Jun 1944 Report to CofS," cited in Harry L. Coles and Albert K. Weinberg, eds., *Civil Affairs: Soldiers Become Governors* (Washington, DC: Center of Military History, 2004), 861–862.

15. "The primary purpose of the cultural maps is for the briefing of our bomber crews in efforts to avoid the bombing of those structures. In the ground forces they are supposed to be used by the artillery commanders of the division corps, army and separate artillery groups." Newton to Webb, April 20, 1944, WGC/3077. "We carried purposely prepared maps with the town map in gray and the important buildings in black." Hammon, *Memoir*, 62.

16. Executive Board, supra 5.

17. *Civil Affairs Handbook, Germany*. Supplement 17. *Atlas on Churches, Museums, Libraries and Other Cultural Institutions in Germany* (March 1944).

18. *Soldiers Become Governors*, 415.

19. Roberts Commission Special Meeting, Friday, October 1943, WGC/3077.

20. Zuckerman to MacGregor, November 18, 1943. NARA RG331/M1944/30H. Zuckerman had originally been enlisted in RE to study the concussive effects of bombing in civilians. See W. W. Rostow, *Pre-Invasion Bombing and Strategy* (Austin: University of Texas Press, 1981), 7–14.

21. E. H. J. Maxse, "Air Mission" Memo 3. NARA RG331/10000/145/259. This memo depicts Zuckerman as interested and cooperative, although in his memoirs, he records that he "did not have enough faith in the bombing accuracy of the aircrews to believe that [the maps] could be of any real value." Solly Zuckerman, *From Apes to Warlords* (New York: Harper and Rowe, 1978), 211. In London he also approached Kenneth Clark at the National Gallery, who repeated what he had already conveyed to W. G. Constable almost a year earlier. See chapter 2.

22. Philip O'Brien, *How the War Was Won* (Cambridge: Cambridge University Press, 2014), 325.

23. Constable continued to dismiss the Frick Atlases as "a kind of Emily Post's guide to good behavior when bombing enemy cities," presenting them as "valuable punctual supplements to the Harvard Lists." W. G. Constable, "Works of Art in Wartime," 38. WGC/3077.

24. Charles Rufus Morey and William Bell Dinsmoor, "Text for a Lecture on Cultural Monuments, Final Draft," 1. WBD IX/ 2.

25. Crosby traveled to Europe in October–December 1944, and again February–July 1945. SMcC I/4. Leonard Woolley, *Digging up the Past* (Middlesex: Penguin, 1937). The British granted Woolley grade in part because the American MFAA had too little authority. Woolley, *A Record of the Work Done by the Military Authorities for the Protection of the Treasures of Art and History in War Areas*. (London: His Majesty's Stationery Office, 1947), 6.

26. Dinsmoor, "First Weekly Report: Sunday April 23, 1944," 29. WBD III/3. See also "A large part of damage by troops occurred between the time when the combat troops moved forward and when reserved and administrative units moved into an area." Joseph M. Scammel, "The Duties of Monuments, Fine Arts, and Archives Officers" (29 December 1944), 8. WBD IX/2.

27. Dinsmoor to Roberts, October 25, 1943. WBD I/6. Roberts responded that they "reached the affected areas at the earliest practicable moment," given they were "not trained for combat work."

28. Dinsmoor, "Lecture on the Preservation of Monuments." Delivered at the symposium "Europe's Monuments as Affected by the War" organized by the Archaeological Institute of America at the Metropolitan Museum of Art, on December 29, 1944. WBD IX/2.

29. William Bell Dinsmoor, *The Architecture of Ancient Greece* (New York: Scribner, 1927), xvii.

30. He continued citing the French news report: "the maps handed over to the liberating bombardiers have been of remarkable efficacy." Dinsmoor, *Lecture on the Preservation.*

31. Jean Verrier noted that this system created an "all too dry but, alas, all too eloquent" visual record of the war. The scale was: [0] destroyed; [1] very severely damaged; [2] severely damaged ; [3] moderately damaged; [4] lightly damaged. Jean Verrier, "Les dommages de guerre aux édifices classés parmi les monuments historiques et inscrits à l'inventaire supplémentaire," *Bulletin Monumental* (1946): 207. See also *Bulletin Monumental* (1940): 241–258.

32. Memoirs and secondary sources have inherited this language of relative success, e.g., Lord Methuen, *Normandy Diary* (London: Hale, 1946), Appendix A, 200. Sometimes this is effective; e.g., "The General effect of the Blitz on London's historic monuments might be described as 'a little damage to a lot of monuments'." Lambourne, 50.

33. Sir Leonard Woolley, "The Preservation of Historical Architecture in the War Zones," *Journal of the RIBA* (December 1945): 38.

34. James Doolittle and Carroll V. Glines, *I Could Never Be So Lucky Again* (New York: Bantam, 1991), 333.

35. John S. Taylor, "Rome Raid," *Bombs Away!* (New York: Doubleday, 1971), 199–201.

36. Eisenhower, *Crusade in Europe*, 195. See also Marshall to Eisenhower, October 14, 1943, *Soldiers Become Governors*, 415. For a study of leaflets see Claudia Baldoli and Marco Fincardi, "Italian Society under Anglo-American Bombs," *Historical Journal* (December 2009): 1017–1038.

37. Stewart Halsey Ross, *Strategic Bombing by the United States in World War II* (Jefferson, NC: MacFarland, 2003), 129.

38. "Operations of Norden Mark 15/M-Series Bombsight." Stephen McFarland, *America's Pursuit of Precision* (Washington, DC: Smithsonian, 1995), 230.

39. Manuel De Landa notes that "Human qualities of trust and morale had to flow at all levels of the man-machine assemblage." De Landa, 61, 78.

40. On Doolittle see Ronald Schaffer, *Wings of Judgment* (New York: Oxford, 1985), 9–10; Lowell J. Thomas and Edward Jablonski, *Doolittle* (New York: Doubleday, 1976).

41. Cited in Bill Yenne, *Hit the Target* (London: Penguin, 2015), 214.

42. Eisenhower, *Crusade in Europe*, 169.

43. Thomas and Jablonski, 246.

44. Doolittle and Glines, 333.

45. For the palace, Doolittle later specifically recalled this as a choice, or decision: "I could have made the palace a target . . . but I decisively didn't." Doolittle and Glines, 264.

46. Vincent Orange, *Tedder: Quietly in Command* (London: Cass, 2004).

47. Churchill, cited in Orange, *Tedder*, 254.

48. The first encounter was between Maxse and a Maj. Thompson on October 13, 1943.

49. Executive Board, supra 5.

50. Baillie-Reynolds to Zuckerman, October 8, 1943. NARA RG331/M1944/30H.

51. Having been "unofficially informed" that US pilots already in the Mediterranean had brought with them "lists of buildings, area, etc., of religious or historic interest should not be bombed," the leadership in Whitehall inquired with Tedder: "Is this so? And if so, is the list used of value in briefing? We are asked whether RAF would be willing to accept such a list and brief crews accordingly, subject of course to all military exigencies. What is your opinion on this? Would it help you to receive marked town plans from us or would American list meet all needs?" Letter from Whitehall to HQ of MAAF Command, November 22, 1943. NARA 331/M1944/30H.

52. To Tedder about Pompeii, November 12, 1943 . NARA 331/M1944/30H.

53. Lauris Norstad, Appendix C-5, Report 20345/O/MFAA. NARA 331/HQMAAF. See also a letter on March 19, 1944, about the distribution of this "atlas" and "Military Report 1943–1946: Final Report." NGA/FH.

54. A letter from Eisenhower to the War Department on October 22, 1943, indicates the "policy is already in effect," asking to "avoid destruction of immovable works of art insofar as possible without handicapping military operations." *Soldiers Become Governors*, 415.

55. "The Handbooks . . . cannot be compared with an aerial photograph clipped upon the operational clipboard in the hands of the pilot as he drops into the bomb run." Col. Newton, the ranking MFAA officer on the ground. Cited in Woolley, *Record of the Works*, 29.

56. The Air Force magazine *Impact* even published a composite aerial photograph showing railyards to be "hit" (labeled with letters) and cultural sites to be "missed" (labeled in numbers). *Florence: How to Miss*, supra 1.

57. Lauris Norstad, "Special maps showing the principal monuments of historical, cultural and religious importance." NARA 331/M1944/30H.

58. E. Christopher Norris, "Preservation of Italian Works of Art. Rough survey of historic monuments and collected art treasures north of Capua–Termoli line" 12 November 1944. NARA RG331/M1944/30H. Use of the maps became mandatory on March 9. This document was in the hands of MAAF photo-intelligence as late as February 25, 1944.

59. "Category I. Quintessential creations of world famed importance including either high treasured items [. . .] Category II. Towns, monuments (either in main fabric or in ornament) essential in the quality of their contribution to the main body of Italian Art as a whole." Norris, *Preservation of Italian Works*.

60. Norstad, *Special Maps*.

61. Norstad, *Special Maps*.

62. C. Vlad, "A Historical Approach to the Use of Military Specialized Terminology," *Linguistic and Philosophical Investigations* 13 (2014): 701–707. As Vlad notes this value was determined "through the radius of the circle around a target inside of which it is expected to be dropped 50% of the missiles aimed to it." On the use of CEP in Spaatz's records see MacFarland, 179.

63. Ross, *Strategic Bombing*, 129. See also "Attitudes and Perceptions among American Airmen" in Conrad C. Crane, *Bombs, Cities, and Civilians* (Lawrence: University Press of Kansas, 1993), 48–62. More likely, and especially given worsening European weather, choices in these less-than-optimal situations were made entirely "blindly." *Bombs Away!*, 306. A conference on accuracy convened in 1945 established that much of the bombing since Mar 1944 "had been blind bombing." Richard Overy, *The Bombers and the Bombed*, 204. There was also blindness due to flak. See "Last Mission," *Bombs Away!*, 299–304.

64. P. Cabell, "Protection of Historical Monuments and Civilian Populations." January 12, 1945. NARA 331/HQ MAAF/Operations/32H.

65. Sean Malloy, "The Rules of Civilized Warfare," *Journal of Strategic Studies* 30, no. 3 (June 2007): 475–512; David Fedman and Cary Karacas, "A Cartographic Fade to Black," *Journal of Historical Geography* 38 (2012): 306–328.

66. *United States Strategic Bombing Survey*, 21–38. See also W. Hay Parks, "Precision and Area Bombing: Who Did Which, and When?" *Journal of Strategic Studies* 18, no. 1 (1995): 145–174.

67. Josef Konvitz, "Représentations urbaines et bombardements stratégiques, 1914–1945," *Annales ESC* (July–August 1989): 823–847.

68. The plan would "run like a thread through all the operations up to the end of the war."

Tedder, 256. The Allies would devote both air forces to "concentration against one common system, both day and night." *How the War Was Won*, 530.

69. Eisenhower, *Crusade*, 256.

70. "Larger targets" were "often large enough to contain the whole bombing pattern of an attacking force." W. W. Rostow, *Pre-Invasion Planning and Strategy* (Austin: University of Texas Press, 1971), 11.

71. *How the War Was Won*, 325

72. Among national case studies are Marco Giovannini and Giulio Massobrio, "La lotta della Bellezza contro la guerra," in *Bombardate l'Italia* (Milano: Rizzoli, 2006), 415–433; Philippe Tanchoux, "La Protection Monumentale en 1939–1945," in *Guerre et patrimoine artistique à l'époque contemporaine* ed. Philippe Nivet (Amiens: Encrage, 2013), 345–365.

73. Eisenhower, *Crusade*, 230.

74. George C. S. Benson and Maurice Neufeld, "American Military Government in Italy," in *American Experiences in Military Government in World War II*, ed. Carl J. Friedrich and Associates (New York: Reinhart, 1948), 122. On the US policy of "stabilization" in Italy see James Edward Miller, *The United States and Italy 1940–1950* (Chapel Hill: UNC Press, 1986). For an extensive collection of documents on this reconstruction in Tuscany, see Roger Absalom, ed., *Gli alleati e la ricostruzione in Toscana (1944–1945)* (Florence: Olschki, 2001).

75. Marta Nezzo, "La protezione delle città d'arte," in *I bombardamenti aeri sull'Italia*, ed. Nicola Lablanca (Bologna: Il Mulino, 2012), 195–212.

76. US Army General Mark Clark, cited in Ilaria Dagnini Brey, *The Venus Fixers* (London: MacMillan, 2012), 109.

77. The USSBS called this "cumulative damage." *USSBS*, vol. 5 (New York: Garland, 1976), 55.

78. "Note on Italian Domestic Architecture: Summary." SZ.OEMU.50.8.4.

79. See Martin Blumenson, *Salerno to Cassino* (Washington, DC: Office of Military History, 1969): David Richardson and David Hapgood, *Monte Cassino* (New York: Congdon & Weed, 1984); E. Grossetti and M. Matronola, *Il bombardamento di Montecassino: Diario di Guerra* (Montecassino: 1997); Gustavo Giovannoni, *L'Abbazzia di Montecassino* (Milano: Electa, 1945).

80. Bombing: Special Operations: Cassino, "The Bombardment of Cassino" (15 Mar 1944). NARA/331/30.

81. See Hugh Cave, *We Build, We Fight!* (New York: Harper & Brothers) and more generally Francesca Ammon, *Bulldozer* (Yale University Press, 2016).

82. *First Aid Protection for Art Treasures and Monuments.* WBD VIII/11.

83. "Instructions for Restoration of Buildings," *First Aid*, 7.

84. Deane Keller, cited in Theodor Sizer, *A Walpolean at War* (Walpole Society, c1947), 3–27.

85. Frederick Hartt, "Final Report on Emilia" (August 1945), 1. NGA/FH2-15.

86. *Verzeichniss und Karte Durch den Bevollmächtigten General der Deutschen Wehrmacht in Italien Geschützten Baudenkmäler.* NGA/FH2. On the Kunstschutz, see Christina Kott, "Le Kunstschutz en 1939–1945"; Nivet, *Guerre et patrimoine artistique*, and Christian Führmeister, Johannes Griebel, Stephan Klingen, and Ralph Peters, eds, *Kunsthistoriker im Krieg* (Cologne: Behlau, 2012).

87. James Rorimer, *Report* 16 August 1944. NGA/JR1–1

88. A pamphlet, *Per i monumenti d'arte danneggiati dalla Guerra della Campania*, was coauthored by Paul Gardner and the Italian Superintendent of Galleries (Napoli: 1944) NGA/FH1–23.

89. Amedeo Maiuri, *A Companion to the Visit of Pompeii* (Pompeii: Sicignano, 1944); and *A Companion to the Visit of Herculaeum* (Pompeii: Sicignano, 1944). *A Soldier's Guide to Florence* (prepared by Morale Services Section, NATOUSA) NGA/FH2-3; *What to See in Florence* (compiled by AMG, Eighth Army for Education, Eight Army); *Masterpieces of Sienese Art*, Held at Regia Pinacotea (18 December 1944). WBD V/5.

90. See "Suggestions for Using the Material in the Commission File." NARA RG331/ M1944/154.

91. Pompeii was bombed by the Allies September 13–26, 1943. The Montecassino Abbey was flattened on February 15, 1944. The two sites were tied because Maiuri had deposited some of the movable objects from the Naples museum there. See Benedetta Gentile and Francesco Bianchini, *I misteri dell'Abbazia* (Florence: Le Lettere, 2014).

92. Amedeo Maiuri, *Taccuino Napoletano* (Napoli: Vajro, 1956), 165; "Restauri di Guerra a Pompeii," *Vie d'Italia* (1947): 215–21.

93. Sizer, *Walpolean at War.*

94. See Luca Goldoni, Aldo Ferrari, and Gianni Leoni, eds., *I Giorni di Bologna-Kaputt* (Bologna: Giornalisti Associati, 1980), 117.

95. DeWald to Sachs, September 24, 1944. WGC/3077.

96. On the *sventramenti* see Medina Lasantzky, *The Renaissance Perfected* (University Park: Penn State University Press, 2004), and chapter 1 of this book.

97. Ben Shepard, "Becoming Planning Minded," *Journal of Contemporary History* (July 2008): 405–409.

98. Hartt to Cook, November 24, 1944, WGC/3077.

99. Hartt, "Eleventh Monthly Report, For September 1944," October 13, 1944. NGA/ FH3-10. On Pisa see Elena Franchi, *Arte in assetto di guerra* (Pisa: Edizioni ETS, 2006).

100. Four separate exhibitions traveled to US cities from October 18, 1946 to June of 1947. Millard Meiss, "Report to the members of ACRIM, December 15, 1946." PJS/49. *War's Toll of Italian Art* (New York: Metropolitan Museum of Art, 1946). Ranuccio Bianchi-Badinelli, "Foreword," *Fifty War-Damaged Monuments of Italy*, trans. Sara T. Morey (Istituto Poligrafico dello Stato: Roma, 1946). See also Associazione Nazionale per il Restauro dei Monumenti Danneggiati dalla Guerra, *Mostra d'Arte Italiana a Palazzo Venezia* (Roma, 1945). Richard Krautheimer gives one of the earliest references for organizing this group in a letter to Crosby, March 5, 1946. SMcC 5.

101. "Report given by Frederick Hartt to the members of ACRIM, November 1946." WGC/3078.

102. "The primary criterion in choice should be artistic and historic importance and [. . .], subject to these overriding criteria, considerations of geographical distribution, American interest, and urgency of repair should be taken into account." Report to the members of ACRIM, December 15, 1946. PJS/49. The region around Naples was excluded. Digest of the Minutes of the Meeting of the Directors of ACRIM, April 1, 1948. PJS/50.

103. "The word 'monuments' in the Committee's name was bound to mislead the larger public, and the Chairman added that 'restoration' was equally objectionable. It was agreed to emphasize in all statements made by the Committee, its concern with the 'preservation of Italian art.'" ACRIM, Minutes of meeting of Directors held at 2 east 82nd street, January 30, 1947. PJS50.

104. Postal Vote by the Members of Subcommittee on Monuments to which immediate assistance should be given, March 15, 1947. PJS/50.

105. Roberto Pane, *La Ricostruzione del patrimonio artistico Italiano* (Roma: Libreria dello Stato, 1950), 12. See also "Il restauro dei monumenti e la sistemazione delle zone monumentali e ambientali," Istituto Nazionale di Urbanistica, *Urbanistica ed Edilizia in Italia* (Roma: 1948), 137–166; Carlo Perogalli, ed., *Architettura e restauro* (Milano: Görlich, 1955);

Difendiamo il patrimonio artistico, Ulisse: 11, no. 5 (Fall–Winter 1957); and de Stefani and Coccoli, *Guerra monumenti.*

106. Letter from Mayor Corrado Capezzuolo, December 4, 1947, "Tempio Malatesta." ACS/AABBAA/II/55. See also "Restauro del Tempio Malatestiano," *Bollettino d'arte* 4, no. 2 (April–June 1950): 176–184; Angelo Turchini, *Il Tempio distrutto* (Cesena: Ponte Vecchio, c. 1998); and Pane, *La Ricostruzione*, 102.

107. Letters from Morey and Meiss describing the Kress donation. ACS/AABBAA/II/55.

108. *Sites and Monuments: Problems of Today* (Paris: UNESCO, 1953), 72–76.

109. See *Concorso per la ricostruzione del coperto della Basilica di Vicenza*, NGA/FH1–9, and Damiana Lucia Paterno, *Palladio nel tempo* (Saonara: Il Prato, 2015), 167–218.

110. In the postwar period this regionalism was confirmed by the establishment of an international scholarly center for his work, The "Centro Internazionale di Studi d'architettura Andrea Palladio" was tasked with "salvaging the Palladian patrimony... not only of the Vicentino but of the entire Veneto." See Paterno, 196–218.

111. *Soldiers Become Governors*, 862.

112. In contrast, in the Pacific theater the more expedient way to house troops was to build barracks on beaches, in jungles, or in the desert. See *We Build, We Fight!*

113. On the lengthy process of decision see Overy, *Bombing War*. Neither British nor American Air Force leaders were in favor of this plan, convinced that this was a misuse of their forces.

114. *Report of the American Commission for the Protection and Salvage of Artistic and Historic Monuments in War Areas* (Washington, DC: US Government Printing Office, 1946) [henceforth RC Report].

115. "Committee Resolution: Carpet Bombing and the Vaucher Commission." Minutes from a Special Meeting of the American Commission for the Protection and Salvage of Artistic and Historic Monuments in Europe held July 27, 1944. WBD III/2.

116. Professor Paul Vaucher (Chairman) and "Monsieur d'Orange" and Lieut. (de Vasseau) Gilloux, French delegates to the (inter-allied) Commission for the Protection and Restitution of Cultural Material—created by the Conference of Allied Ministers of Education. "The areas marked in green crayon, of course, represent the approximate areas occupied by the Allied Expeditionary Forces up to today, and may be extended with the course of events. But it will be noted that, as of today, only five (nos. 43A, 46, 47, 58, 60) of the 23 sites lie within the areas yet occupied by Allied forces, though others are very close to the present line." William Bell Dinsmoor, WBD III/2.

117. Preservation of French Historic Monuments (25 August 1944). NARA RG331/SHAEF/324, MFAA Corrdespondence.

118. See for example Brutails's influential 1919 guide, *Pour comprendre les monuments de la France* (Paris: Hachette, 1918).

119. On the extensive debates with British command leading up to D-Day, see Rostow; *Tedder*, 530–543.

120. "Bombing operations in Support of Overlord" (3 June 1944). NARA RG 331/262/1.

121. The list was sent by Major Mitchell, SHAEF. NARA RG 331/MAAF/2611000B.

122. See Jean-Claude Valla, *La France sous les bombes Américaines 1942–1945* (Paris: Sede, 2001).

123. See Merritt Y. Hughes, "Civil Affairs in France," in *American Experiences*, ed. Friedrich, 148–168.

124. Methuen, *Normandy Diary*, xix.

125. Eddy Florentin, *Quand les Alliés bombardaient la France* (Paris: Perrin, 1997); Robert Brichet, "Une Restauration Originale: Notre Dame de Saint-Lô," *Construction Moderne* 81, no. 2 (1965): 57; Robert Hérin and Rémi Rouault, eds., *De la ville perdue à la ville retrouvée, la*

ville en devenir (Caen: PU, 2008); Patrice Facon, "Les bombardements alliés sur la France," in *Villes en Guerre*, ed. Philippe Chassaigne and Jean-Marc Largeaud (Paris: Armand Colin, 2004), 75–85; André Prothin, "Administrative Factors of Metropolitan Planning in Western Europe," *Planning of Metropolitan Areas and New Towns* (New York: UN, 1967), 65–69; Jean-Yves Andrieux et Fabienne Chevallier, *Quand les monuments construisaient la nation* (Rennes: Presses Universitaires de Rennes, 2014), 368–372.

126. Fedman and Karacas.

127. When new lists were made in England, the breakdown of monuments was as follows: France: 1643 / Belgium: 463 / The Netherlands: 224 / Luxembourg: 30 / Germany: 1055. United States Forces, Europe Theater: General Board. *Civil Affairs and Military Government Activities in Connection with Monuments, Fine Arts and Archives.* NARA 14–15.

128. *List of Monuments for Germany—by Wilhelm Köhler.* NARA RG 331/M1944/Roll47.

129. Geoffrey Webb to Marvin Ross (or Lafarge), June 24, 1944. NARA RG331/55B/331.

130. "The total destruction of this city would achieve immeasurable results in reducing the industrial capacity of the enemy's war machine." Arthur Harris, May 1943, cited in Ross, *Strategic Bombing*, 177. On the debates preceding the raid see Randall T. Wakelam, *The Science of Bombing* (Toronto: Toronto University Press, 2009), 139–156.

131. Ministry of Home Security, Research and Experiments Department, *German Domestic Architecture*. SZ.OEMU.50.8.2. See also Mike Davis, *Dead Cities* (New York: New Press, 2002) and Enrique Walker, "Erich Mendelsohn at War," *Perspecta* 41 (2008): 83–91.

132. Robert E. Dickinson, "The Development and Distribution of the Medieval German Town: I. The West German Lands," *Geography* (March 1942): 9–21.

133. Olivier Dumoulin, "A Comparative Approach to Newsreels and Bombing in the Second World War: Britain, France, Germany," in *Bombing, States, and People*, ed. Claudia Baldoli, Andrew Knapp, and Richard Overy (London: Continuum, 2011), 298–314, and 11.

134. Hans Erich Nossack, *The End* [1943], trans. Joel Agee (Chicago: University of Chicago Press, 2004), 39.

135. *Apes to Warlords*, 321–322. W. G. Sebald, "A Natural History of Destruction," *New Yorker*, November 4, 2002.

136. Walter Hancock, cited in *RC Report*.

137. James Rorimer, "Seventeenth Report (First for Germany) MFAA 15 April-31 May 1945. NGA/JR2. "Owing to the great destruction of monuments on the SHAEF Official List of Protected Monuments, Germany, it was agreed that first aid and reporting called for in various directives were secondary considerations at the present time."

138. Earl F. Ziemke, *The U.S. Army in the Occupation of Germany 1944–1946* (Army Historical Series), 54.

139. Alternate plans for "Scorched and unscorched conditions," were made by US and British respectively. This means that in planning the scope of administrative and financial involvement it was predicted that retreating German forces would not burn down everything in their wake. See *Soldiers Become Governors*, 112, 681.

140. Ibid., 54.

141. David Irving, *The Destruction of Dresden* (New York: Ballantine, 1963).

142. Overy, *Bombing War*, 393.

143. The disappearance of archives would mean that "thousands . . . would have to search through public records for evidence that will be legally acceptable as to their very identity." Solomon Buck to Archibald MacLeish, October 1, 1943. WBD I/6

144. On the continuing legacy of Dresden's peculiar status as an erased city in its rebuilding, see Mark Jarzombek, "Disguised Visibilities: Dresden/ 'Dresden'," in *Memory and Architecture*, ed. Eleni Bastea (Albuquerque: University of New Mexico Press, 2004), 49–78 and *Urban Heterology: Dresden and the Dialectics of Post-Traumatic History* (Lund: Lund University School of Architecture, 2001).

145. Some also complained that MFAA soldiers should have had architectural or engineering training, rather than "Knowledge of the fine arts, as such," which "proved on the whole to be not entirely necessary." *Soldiers Become Governors*, 876.

146. Charles Kunzelman, "Some Trials, Tribulations, and Successes of the Monuments, Fine Arts and Archives Teams in the European Theater During WWII," *Military Affairs* (April 1988): 57.

147. *RC Report*, 140, 151.

148. Webb, cited in Woolley, *Final Report*, 52.

149. *RC Report*, 147.

150. "Chapter XIV: "The Plunder of Art Treasures." In the Office of the United States Counsel for Prosecution of Axis Criminality, *Nazi Conspiracy and Aggression*, vol. 1 (Washington, DC: US Government Printing Office, 1946), 109.

151. W. G. Constable, for one, served as the museum and monument advisor to cultural reconstruction in Germany in 1947–1948.

152. Johanna Blokker, "Reconstructing Identity: World War II and the Reconstruction of Cologne's Destroyed Romanesque Churches" (PhD diss., NYU, 2011).

153. Pane, supra 106.

154. Already in a November 1943 meeting, the Roberts Commission established the areas which would be omitted from the listing and mapping. WGC/1272. The Final Commission Report of Activities to November 1943, described the exceptions as follows: "A. the Italian colonies in Africa, the British being already in occupation / B. Burma and Malaysia, because of hesitation to compete with the specialized British knowledge of these areas / C. any area of presumed Russian interest: the occupied parts of the Soviet Union, Finland, the Baltic states and Poland / D. the Philippines, and other islands of the pacific." ADHG, *Report*, 6.

155. Archibald MacLeish, Preamble to the Constitution of the United Nations Educational, Scientific and Cultural Organization (Paris: UNESCO, November 16, 1945).

156. "Comments by Former MFAA officers on the Draft Convention," SMcC 1/3.

157. H. Noblecourt and Lavachery, *Les techniques de protection des biens culturels en cas de conflit armé.* (Paris: UNESCO, 1954); "Notiziario," *Bollettino ICR* 21–22 (1955): 80–91.

Bridge

1. "If UNESCO has not yet gripped the public imagination in the simple way as has FAO or WHO, the primary reason is that its aims are not so simple." Julian Huxley, *Report of the Director-General*, presented to the Third Session of the General Conference (UNESCO: November–December 1948), 25.

2. James P. Sewell, *UNESCO and World Politics* (Princeton: Princeton University Press, 1975), 180. Before he was Director, Evans already opposed the idea of a Monuments Committee.

3. George Kubler, *Cuzco* (Paris: UNESCO, 1951); Ferdinando Forlati, Cesare Brandi, and Yves Froideaux, *Saint Sophia of Ochrida* (Paris: UNESCO, 1951); Paul Collard, Emir Maurice Chéhab, and Armando Dillon, *Lebanon* (Paris: UNESCO, 1954); Paul Collart, Selim Abdul-Hak, and Armando Dillon, *Syria* (Paris: UNESCO, 1954).

4. The mission to Lebanon was planned at the MonCom's first meeting in October 1949, and likely originated in Julian Huxley's own interest in building new infrastructure in the Middle East after having traveled there in 1947. UNESCO MonCom/069/569.3.

5. For a history of this design process see Lucia Allais, "The Architecture of Mediocracy," in *Marcel Breuer: Building Global Institutions*, ed. Barry Bergdoll and Jonathan Massey (New York: Lars Mueller, 2018). See also Katrin Schwarz, *Bauen für die Welt-Gemeinschaft* (Berlin: DeGuyter, 2014), and Christopher Pearson, *Designing UNESCO* (London: Ashgate, 2010). On the analogy between design and diplomacy see Henri Stierlin, "Les organizations

internationales et l'architecture: un grand espoir,"*Werk* 7, no. 74: 821–867; Stanislas van Moos, "Kasino der Nationen," *Werk-Archithese* 23–24, 32–36; George Dudley, *A Workshop for Peace* (Cambridge: MIT Press, 1994); and Victoria Newhouse, "The Battle of Designs," *Wallace K. Harrison, Architect* (New York: Rizzoli, 1989).

6. See for instance "Three Pointed Star Rises in Paris,"*UNESCO Courier* (November 1958).

7. *Let's Visit UNESCO House* (Paris: UNESCO, 1948).

8. On Le Corbusier's *Plan Voisin* see Thordis Arrhenius, *The Fragile Monument: On Conservation and Modernity* (London: Artifice, 2012), 112–137; on Le Corbusier in Paris see Pierre Joly, *Le Corbusier à Paris* (Paris: La Manufacture, 1987), 111–164.

9. Luther Evans, "Preface," *UNESCO Headquarters in Paris* (New York: Frederick A. Praeger, 1958), and "Le Siège de l'UNESCO, Paris," *l'Architecture d'Aujourd'hui* 29, no. 81: 2–33.

10. Photographer Lucien Hervé was hired to document the construction. The images are published in Françoise Choay, *Le Siège de l'UNESCO à Paris*. Photographs by Lucien Hervé (Paris: Fréal, 1958).

11. "Preserved and protected" is quoted in "Annex III," *UNESCO, Avant Projet, Place Fontenoy, Paris, 2 avril 1953*, by Marcel Breuer, Bernard Zehrfuss, Pier Luigi Nervi (Paris: UNESCO, 1953). "Hidden treasure" is from Lewis Mumford, who wrote a whole separate review of the Assembly Hall, "UNESCO House II: The Hidden Treasure," *New Yorker*, November 19, 1960, 213–220.

Chapter Four

1. René Sneyers, "Stones Also Die," *UNESCO Courier* 18 (January 1965): 26–32.

2. Chris Marker, commentary for *Les statues meurent aussi* (1953), in André Cornand, "Les statues meurent aussi," *La revue du cinema* 233 (March 1969): 193–201. See also Emma Wilson, *Alain Resnais* (Manchester: Manchester University Press, 2006).

3. Jean Rouch, "The Awakening of African Cinema," *UNESCO Courier* 3 (March 1962): 10–15.

4. Martha Finnemore, "International Organizations as Teachers of Norms," *International Organization* (Autumn 1993): 565–597.

5. Frederick Cooper, *Africa Since 1940* (Cambridge: Cambridge University Press, 2002), 7. Pierre Englebert calls this the "patrimonial theory" of Africa; "Pre-colonial institutions, Post-colonial states, and Economic Development in Tropical Africa,"*Political Research Quarterly* 53, no. 1 (March 2000). Mahmood Mamdani argues that "the institutional part of the colonial legacy remains more or less intact," in *Citizen and Subject* (Princeton: Princeton University Press, 1996), 4.

6. Frederick Cooper and Randall Packard, eds., *International Development and the Social Sciences* (Berkeley: UC Press, 1997). See also "The Rise and Fall of Development Theory," in *The Anthropology of Development and Globalization*, ed. Marc Edelman and Angelique Haugerud (Malden, MA: Blackwell, 2005), 109–125, and Richard Jolly, Louis Emmerji, Dharam Ghai, and Frédéric Lapeyre, *UN Contributions to Development Thinking and Practice* (Bloomington: Indiana University Press, 2004), 203–219.

7. *The Problems of Museums in Countries Undergoing Rapid Change* (Paris: UNESCO, 1964), 38. See also *Hague Convention for the Protection of Cultural Property in the Event of Armed Conflict* (Paris: UNESCO, 1954).

8. Rudolf Salat, "Cultural Values and International Cooperation," *UNESCO Chronicle* 6, no. 11 (1961): 416.

9. "African countries, having undergone different and drastic political and administrative change within the last century, cannot formulate their policy without looking into their

glorious past." T. A. Fasuyi, "Introduction," *Cultural Policy in Nigeria* (Paris: UNESCO, 1973). "The re-discovery of cultural heritage is one of the fundamental aspects of national development." *L'Avenir de l'enseignement supérieur en Afrique* (Paris: UNESCO, 1963), 54. See also Paul Coremans, "Organization of a National Service," *The Conservation of Cultural Property, With Special Reference to Tropical Conditions*, Museums and Monuments 11 [M&M11] (Paris: UNESCO, 1968), 71–79.

10. The phrase was coined by Tony Bennett in a Foucaultian take on the massive expansion of museums in the modern era. It was re-theorized to its full orientalist and technopolitical extent by Timothy Mitchell. "Orientalism and the Exhibitionary Order," in *Colonialism and Culture*, ed. Nicholas B. Dirks (Ann Arbor: University of Michigan Press, 1995), 289–318. For an architectural analysis, see Patricia Morton, *Hybrid Modernities* (Cambridge, MA: MIT Press, 2000).

11. On "object-focus" see Craig Forrest, *International Law and the Protection of Cultural Heritage*, 12; on "immateriality" see Naomi Mezey, "The Paradoxes of Cultural Property," *Columbia Law Review* (2007): 2004–2046; for an earlier argument that architectural conservation should take "space" as its "raw material" see Carlos Chanfon Olmos, *The Training Center at Churubusco, Mexico and Its Concept of Restoration* (Laval: Presses Universitaires du Québec, 1981).

12. Hiroshi Daifuku, "The Significance of Cultural Property," M&M11, 19–26; J. J. H. Szent-Ivany, "Identification and Control of Insect Pests," M&M11, 57–66.

13. Suman Seth, "Putting Knowledge in Its Place," *Postcolonial Studies* 12, no. 4 (2009): 373–388; Timothy Mitchell, *Rules of Experts* (Berkeley: University of California Press, 2002), 27.

14. Sheila Jasanoff, ed., *States of Knowledge* (London: Routledge, 2004).

15. Lucile H. Brockway, "Science and Colonial Expansion," in *The Postcolonial Science and Technology Studies Reader*, ed. Sandra Harding (Durham: Duke University Press, 2011), 127–139.

16. Constant Houlbert, *Les insectes ennemis des livres* (Paris: Alphonse Picard & Fls, Éditeurs, 1903), 11; Édouard Rouveyre, *Connaissances nécessaires à un bibliophile* (Paris: Édouard Rouveyre Éditeur, 1899), 1–46.

17. "Causes of Damage to Museum Objects," M&M11, 39.

18. On the hut as a unit of fumigation, F. Kuhlow, "Field Experiments on the Behaviour of Malaria Vectors in an Unsprayed Hut and in a Hut Sprayed with DDT in Northern Nigeria," *Bulletin of the World Health Organization* 26, no. 1 (1962): 93–102. On malaria see Amy L. Staples, *The Birth of Development* (Kent: Kent State University Press, 2006), 161–180, and David Kinkela, *DDT and the American Century* (Chapel Hill: University of North Carolina Press, 2011).

19. B. de Meillon, "Killer Insects of the World," *UNESCO Courier* 9 (April 1956): 5–8.

20. Maxwell Fry and Jane Drew, *Tropical Architecture in the Dry and Humid Zones* [1956] (New York: Reinhold, 1964). See also Arthur M. Foyle, "Traditional Materials and Construction," and Fello Atkinson, "Style and Tropical Architecture," in *Conference on Tropical Architecture*, ed. Arthur M. Foyle (London: Allen & Unwin, 1953), 71–79; 83–89. And Vandana Baweja, "Otto Königsberger and the Tropicalization of British Architecture," in *Third World Modernism*, ed. Duanfang Lu (London: Routledge, 2011), 236–254.

21. Paul Coremans, "Climate and Microclimate," M&M11, 31, 54. A lineage of architectural books that begin with this climate chart includes the following: B. M. Holmes's *Weathering in the Tropics* ([Melbourne]: C.S.I.R.O., Division of Building Research, 1951) and Robert A. Kennedy's *Conservation in the Wet Tropics* ([Kampala]: Museums Association of Middle Africa, 1959). Holmes used a map from Bernhard Haurwitz and James M. Austin's *Climatology* (New York: McGraw-Hill, 1944); Kennedy used Jane Drew and Maxwell Fry's map from their 1956 *Tropical Architecture*. See also Jiat-Hwee Chang, "Thermal Comfort and Climatic

Design in the Tropics: An Historical Critique," *Journal of Architecture* 21, no. 8 (2016): 1171–1202.

22. Harold Plenderleith, *The Conservation of Antiquities and Works of Art* (London: Oxford University Press, 1956), 7. On Plenderleith see Andrew Oddy and Sandra Smith, eds., *Past Practice—Future Prospects* (London: British Museum, 2001), and Harold Plenderleith, "A History of Conservation," *Studies in Conservation* 43 (1998): 129–143.

23. Paul Coremans, "The Museum Laboratory," *The Organization of Museums* (UNESCO: Paris, 1960), 96. On Coremans see Harold Plenderleith, "Paul Coremans 1908–1965," and Hiroshi Daifuku, "Paul Coremans and UNESCO," *Bulletin de l'Institut Royal du Patrimoine Artistique* (1975). Coremans died in 1965; René Sneyers succeeded him at IRPA. Liliane Masschelein-Kleiner and Pierre Colman, "René Sneyers," *Bulletin of the IRPA* (1975).

24. René Lefève, *Final Report, Consultant Mission, Pilot Program for training of museum technicians*, from 4.4 to 30.5.1964 (Paris: UNESCO, 1965).

25. On "synthetic" materials see Plenderleith, "Reminiscences from the Laboratory," *Iraq* 22, *Ur in Retrospect* (Spring–Autumn 1960): 20–22. On the passage from "passive to active" see Oddy and Smith. See also Mary M. Brooks, "Decay, Conservation and the Making of Meaning through Museum Objects," *Ways of Making and Knowing* (Ann Arbor: University of Michigan Press, 2014), 377–404.

26. See Sheldon Keck, "Some Picture Cleaning Controversies: Past and Present," *Issues in the Conservation of Painting*, ed. David Bomford and Mark Leonard (Santa Monica: Getty Conservation Institute, 2004), 347. Also see Cesare Brandi, "The Cleaning of Pictures in Relation to Patina, Varnish and Glazes," *Burlington Magazine* 16 (July 1949): 183. This exhibition became a model for more international ones: a 1975 show on "Science in Conservation of Cultural Property" in New Delhi, began with images of objects from its National Museum, then showed images of their decay, and finally, the scientific tools used to restore them. O. P. Agrawal and Smita J. Baxi, "Science in Conservation of Cultural Property: Exhibition," *Museum* 27, no. 2 (1975): 91–93.

27. Paul Coremans, "Cleaning and Restoration of Old Paintings: The Point of View of a Physical and Chemical Laboratory," *The Cleaning of Pictures*, Museums and Monuments 2 (Paris: UNESCO, 1951), 111.

28. ICOM, *Problems of Conservation in Museums* (Paris: Eyrolles, 1969), 14.

29. On sentinels see "Sentinel Devices," issue *Limn* 03 (limn.it/issue/03/) and especially Frederick Keck and Andrew Lakoff, "Figures of Warning."

30. Lefève, *Final Report*.

31. Hiroshi Daifuku, "Paul Coremans and UNESCO," *Bulletin de l'Institut Royal du Patrimoine Artistique* 15 (1975): 95–96.

32. Bruno Latour, *The Pasteurization of France*, trans. Alan Sheridan and John Law (Cambridge, MA: Harvard University Press, 1988), and K. Knorr and M. Mulkay, "Give Me a Laboratory and I Will Raise the World," *Science Observed* (1983): 141–170.

33. "The Central Laboratory for Indian Museums as Locus for the Regional Training Centre." Paul Coremans and Harold Plenderleith, *India: Conservation of Cultural Property* (1965), Participation Programme: UNESCO/PP/IND/CUA.

34. Brussels, where Coremans's own Institute was located, was the other serious contender, although Switzerland also made an early offer. Rome was chosen primarily for financial reasons, but a distinction was also made between Brussels's focus on basic science research versus Rome's more "practical focus" as a "clinic." Rome already acted as a hub for the decentralized system of other Italian laboratories and also "attracted more students from the southern countries." "Location of the International Centre for the Study of the Preservation and Restoration of Cultural Property: Supplementary Report," UNESCO 42

Ex/19 (Paris: September 20, 1955). JoB 7 Rome Center. See also Hiroshi Daifuku, "The First Decade," *ICCROM Comes of Age* (Rome: ICCROM, 1979). And "AG 1/3. *Rapport Moral du Conseil Provisoire* (1 mars 1959 au 30 Juin 1960)." ICCROM ODG/1-1.

35. Mario Micheli, "L'attivita del ICR all'estero negli anni 50," *Omaggio a Cesare Brandi*, ed. Caterina Bon Valsassina (Firenze: Edifir Edizioni, 2008), 181–187.

36. "Conservation philosophy at the center is . . . approached from the more universal standpoint of understanding the nature and behavior of materials of which cultural property is composed. ICCROM Training Brochure, Corrected Draft, April 12 and 19 [1974?] Amended by Mrss. Angle, Garvey, Morton & Philippot. Training Brochure, 1974[?] ICCROM CR-47

37. Lefève, *Final Report*, Annex 1: Syllabus.

38. Coremans, "The Museum Laboratory," 93; Coremans, "Museums in Tropical Africa," *Museum* 18 (1965).

39. "How can one hope to deal," he asked, "with a monument carved in crumbling laterite, exposed in a monsoon climate to alternatives of fierce heat and torrential rains? We can do some calculated guess-work," he wrote "which, in the scientific field, is often the precursor of the pilot-experiment that leads to an eventual solution." Plenderleith, "The New Science of Conservation," 18.

40. The designation of laterite triggered a "circular reasoning" where a building material was the result of geological formation *and* disintegration. See T. R. Paton and M. A. J. Williams, "The Concept of Laterite,"*Annals of the Association of American Geographers* 62, no. 1 (March 1972): 42–56. On laterite as a pre-weathered building material for housing, "Estimation of reserves of laterites in regions especially where they are utilised for building," (1963) UNESCO/NS/HT/120. R. Maignien, *Review of Research on Laterites* (UNESCO: 1966).

41. Paul Coremans, "Climate and Microclimate," 30.

42. "The main characteristic of a professional restorer is his integrity, his honesty of purpose in aiming to conserve all that is authentic [. . .] The key word to all good modern restoration is "integrity." Plenderleith, M&M11, 125.

43. Paul Coremans, *Museum* 26, no. 3/4 (1974). Robert P. Grifig Jr., "Nature et Portée d'un stage d'étude," *The Development of Museums: UNESCO Regional Seminar* (New Delhi, 1966), 212.

44. Richard Nunoo, "Perspectives for African Museums," *Journal of World History* (1972): 137–149.

45. On museum-building in colonial Jos, see Amanda Hellman, "The Grounds for Museological Experiments," *Journal of Curatorial Studies* 3, no. 1 (2014): 74–96. On Jos's training center see Emmanuel Nnakenyi Arinze, "Training in African Museums: The Role of the Center for Museum Studies, Jos," *Museum* 39, no. 4 (January/December 1987): 278–280. On museum training in general see UNESCO, *Meeting of Experts in the Field of Training of Museum Specialists* (Rome: 26 to 30 April 1976) SHC/76/Conf.643/I.

46. On AMAT-MATA, see Mallan Liman Ciroma, "Formation of the Museums Association of Tropical Africa," *Man* 61 (August 1961): 142–143 and Robert A. Kennedy, "Conservation in the Humid Tropical Zone," *Museum News* 38, no. 7 (March 1960): 16–20.

47. *Report on the Regional Training Centre for the Preservation of Cultural and Natural Heritage at Jos*, Nigeria (JIU/REP/74/8), 1974, 98 EX/7: 10. This report also complained that "most of the trainees" had trouble "assimilating somewhat abstract, although simple scientific arguments."

48. An amateur potter, she spent over half a century in Nigeria, first as the director of a finishing school for African girls, and then as a volunteer in the new Jos Museum, where she was still an intermittent presence and teacher in the 1950s–1960s. Sylvia Leith-Ross,

Stepping Stones: Memoirs of Colonial Nigeria 1907–1960, ed. Michael Crowder (London: Peter Owen, 1983), 152.

49. On Fagg's encounter with objects brought to him from the mines see Hellman. On Fagg see also Ekpo Eyo, "Obituary: Bernard Fagg," *Anthropology Today* 4, no. 1 (February 1988), and Frank Willett, "To Bernard Fagg on his Seventieth Birthday," *African Arts* 19, no. 3 (May 1986): 73–74.

50. Ekpo Eyo, "The Protection of Africa's Artistic Heritage." In "Africa and the African Genius," *UNESCO Courier* 20, no. 6 (1967): 17–18. William Fagg had a theory of insect-enabled creative destruction: "The continuity of African art is owed to the high rate at which termites eat up carvings as soon as they are made, so creating the need to produce new ones." He also described working "under Negro command" as atonement for the colonial past, a "freeing from 'imperialist' taint." William Fagg, "Africa and the Modern World," *Premier Festival mondial des Arts nègres*, Dakar: 1–24 Avril 1966 (Paris: André Rousseau / Bernard Gaulin, 1966), 45. On Eyo, see Caleb Adebayo Folorunso, "Ekpo Okpo Eyo (1931–2011)," *Azania: Archaeological Research in Africa* 46, no. 3 (2011): 363–364.

51. Eyo, *Protection*, 18.

52. *Museum Techniques in Fundamental Education*, Educational Studies and Documents 17 (Paris: UNESCO, 1954), 6.

53. Histories of this phenomenon include Enid Schildkrout and Curtis A. Keim, eds., *The Scramble for Art in Central Africa* (Cambridge: Cambridge University Press, 1998). On the legacy of this license to "plunder" today see Peter R. Schmidt and Roderick J. McIntosh, eds., *Plundering Africa's Past* (Bloomington: Indiana University Press, 1996).

54. On Dakar-Djibouti, see Jean Jamin, "Aux origines du Musée de l'Homme: la mission ethnographique et linguistique Dakar-Djibouti," *Cahiers Ethnologiques* 5 (1984) : 7–86; Michel Leiris, *Afrique Fantôme* (Paris: Gallimard, 1934); and Philip L. Ravenhill, "The Passive Object and the Tribal Paradigm," in *African Material Culture*, ed. Mary Jo Arnoldi and Kris L. Hardin (Bloomington: Indiana University Press, 1996), 265–282. On Christian missions as internationalist see Mazower, *Governing the World*, 31–64.

55. Daniel T. Sherman, *French Primitivism and the Ends of Empire, 1945–1975* (Chicago: University of Chicago Press, 2011).

56. James Clifford, *The Predicament of Culture: Twentieth Century Ethnography, Literature, and Art* (Cambridge, MA: Harvard University Press, 1988), 127.

57. "The object is no less than a witness, which must be considered as a function of the information it brings on a certain civilization, and not for its aesthetic value." Marcel Griaule, Mission Dakar-Djibouti, *Instructions sommaires pour les collecteurs d'objets ethnographiques.* Clifford, *The Predicament of Culture*, 49–63; Fabrice Grognet, "Objets de musée, n'avez-vous donc qu'une vie?" *Gradhiva* 2 (2005): 49–63; Anne Doquet, "Les Masques Dogon: de l'objet au Musée de l'Homme à l'homme objet de musée," *Cahiers d'études africaines* 39, no. 3–4 (1999): 617–634.

58. Georges-Henri Rivière and Paul Rivet, "La Mission éthnographique et linguistique de Dakar-Djibouti," *Minautore* 1, no. 2 (1933): 3–6; Nina Gorgus, *Le magicien des vitrines* (Paris: Editions de la Maison des Sciences de l'Homme, 2003). While his travel as an international consultant gradually took the place of any fieldwork collecting French vernacular objects, Rivière also sought to build a museum of French Popular Arts and Traditions in Paris. Martine Segalen, *Vie d'un musée 1937–2005* (Paris: Editions Stock, 2005).

59. George-Henri Rivière, *Regional Seminar on the Educational Rôle of Museums*, Rio de Janeiro, Brazil, 7–30 September, 1958: Report. Educational Studies and Documents 38 (Paris: UNESCO, 1958).

60. On institutional segregation see Mamdani, *Citizen and Subject*, 62–108.

61. Merrick Posnansky, "The Uganda Museum," *Museum* 16, no. 3 (1963): 149–152.

62. On acculturation as "deculturation" see Lamine Dakhaté, "Le processus d'acculturation en Afrique Noire," *Présence Africaine* 56 (1965): 68–81.

63. *L'Art Nègre: Sources Évolution Expansion* (Dakar, 1966).

64. Senghor, *The Foundations of Africanité* (Paris: Présence Africaine, 1967).

65. Ousmane Sow Huchard, "The Musée Dynamique,"*Anthology of Contemporary Fine Arts in Senegal*, ed. Friedrich Axt and El Hadji Moussa Babacar Sy (Frankfurt: Museum für Völkerkunde, 1989), 57–59.

66. Jean Gabus, "The Arrangement of Space or the Basic Data of an Exhibition," and "Human Contacts—Aesthetic Principles and General Planning of Educational Exhibitions," *Museum* 18, no. 1 (1965). Horizontally, Gabus rearranged his museum floor for every new exhibition, pitching tents on elongated plinths to echo the Saharan desert, while also making abstract checkerboard patterns with pedestals. Jean Gabus, *Au Sahara* (Neuchâtel: Les Éditions de la Baconnière, 1954).

67. William Greaces, *First World Festival of Negro Arts* (US Information Agency, 1966).

68. Abdoulaye Sokhna Guèye Diop, "Museological Activity: Its Role and Purpose," *Museum* 26, no. 4 (1973): 250–255.

69. F. T. Masao, curator of the National Museum of Tanzania, argued that the "private collection of various objects" held by various "African kings" should themselves be considered museums, despite the fact that they weren't public. "Quotations from Communications Made at the Livingstone Seminar, 1972," *Museum* 25, no. 4 (1973): 255. Anne Gaugue has argued precisely that the continued private use of these objects by kings should exempt these palaces from being designated museums. Gaugue, *Les États Africains et leurs musées* (Paris: L'Harmattan, 1997), 121.

70. Carol Duncan and Alan Wallach, "The Universal Survey Museum," *Art History* 3, no. 4 (December 1980): 466. Daniel J. Sherman, *Worthy Monuments* (Cambridge, MA: Harvard University Press, 1989); Andrew McClellan, *Inventing the Louvre: Art, Politics and the Origins of the Modern Museum in Eighteenth-Century Paris* (Berkeley: University of California Press, 1994); Patricia Falguières, "La Société des objets," in *Les Cabinets d'art et de merveilles de la renaissance tardive*, ed. Julius von Schlosser (Paris: Macula, 2012), 7–54.

71. Pablo Toucet, "The Museum of Niamey and Its Environment,"*Museum* 24 (1972): 204. On this museum in general see Julien Bondaz, "La Fabrique de la Nation," in *L'exposition postcoloniale: Musées et zoos en Afrique de l'Ouest (Niger, Mali, Burkina Faso)* (Paris: L'Harmattan, 2014), 45–83.

72. Jean Gabus, *Rapport de la Mission Jean Gabus 21 mars au 11 avril 1964*. WS/1064.112. The mission spent 5 days in Cameroon and 2 days in Dahomey.

73. Eva L. R. Meyerowitz, "The Museum in the Royal Palaces at Abomey, Dahomey," *Burlington Magazine* 84, no. 495 (June 1944): 146–149. For a longer history of this museum as part of the French colonial museum network see Agbenyega Adedze, "Symbols of Triumph: IFAN and the Colonial Museum Complex in French West Africa (1938-1960)," *Museum Anthropology* 25, no. 2: 50–60.

74. Jean Crozet, *Étude de la restauration et de la mise en value des palais royaux d'Abomey*, Février-Mars 1968, 640/BMS.RD/CLT (Paris: UNESCO, July 1968).

75. Gabus, *Rapport de la mission Jean Gabus*, 5. By "fixing the current state [*fixer l'état actuel*]" of the building Gabus meant immortalizing it, not repairing it.

76. Engelbert Mveng, "Mission en Afrique Centrale et Orientale pour la préparation du Premier Festival Mondial des Arts Nègres," 10 mars–26 avril 1965 (Paris: UNESCO, [1966]), 42.

77. Gabus, *Rapport de la mission Jean Gabus*, 1–2.

78. Anne Doquet, "Les Masques Dogon,"*Cahiers d'études africaines* 39, no. 3–4 (1999): 617–634.

79. Crozet reported that French structuralist anthropologist Claude Tardits was on site and advocated for the preservation of the palace. Tardits's thesis argued that the Foumban were an example of a state structure that developed out of family kinship, rather than to its detriment, as had been assumed by political theorists since Engels. Philippe Laburthe-Tolra, "Claude Tardits (1921–2007)," *L'Homme* 184 (2007): 221–226. Claude Tardits, *Le royaume Bamoun* (Paris: Armand Colin, 1980) and *Histoire Singulière du Royaume Bamoun* (Paris: Maisonneuve & Larose, 2004). Also Christraud Geary, *Things of the Palace* (Wiesbaden: Steiner, 1983) and on architecture, Itohan Osayimwese, "Architecture and the Myth of Authenticity during the German Colonial Period," *TDSR* 224, no. 11 (2013): 11–22.

80. Jean Crozet, *Cameroun: Etude de la restauration et de la mise en valeur du Palais de Foumban* (UNESCO, February–March 1968).

81. The second was a "Document describing the old palace of the Sultan Njoya." "Annexe IV" and "Annexe V," Jean Gabus, *Rapport de la Mission Jean Gabus, 21 mars au 11 avril 1964*. WS/1064.112.

82. André Lézine, *Afghanistan: Conservation et restauration des monuments historiques* (Paris: UNESCO, January 1964). UNESCO / RP/ AFG/1.

83. Lézine, *Afghanistan*, 4.

84. Andrea Bruno, "The Planned and Executed Restoration of Some Monuments of Archaeological and Artistic Interest in Afghanistan," *East and West* 13, no. 2–3 (June–September 1962): 99–185.

85. Hiroshi Daifuku, "The Museum and the Visitor," M&M9, 78. See also Hiroshi Daifuku, "Exhibitions in the Technically Underdeveloped Countries," M&M10, 44.

86. Paul Coremans, "Organization of a National Service," M&M11, 71.

87. George Henri Rivière, *The Museum and Adult Education* (10 June 1949). UNESCO/Ed/Conf.4/20. Reprinted as "The Organization and Functions of the Museum," *Museum* 4 (1949): 206–226. For a brief overview of the history of international museums associations see Kenneth Hudson, *Museums of Influence* (Cambridge: Cambridge University Press, 1987), 14–16.

88. George-Henri Rivière, "Types of Museums," *Rapid Change*, 52–75. The new list had seven categories.

89. Rivière, *Rapid Change,* 36. Such typologizing always began with the assertion that the dominance of "art" museums in the West was challenged by the need for "scientific" ones in the South. This turn from art to science had been prepared before UNESCO's arrival, as colonial museums in the midcentury began to be attached to universities and scientific research institutes. On the British Institute of Archaeology and History in East Africa, see Jonathan R. Katz, "An Interview with Merrit Posnansky,"*African Archaeological Review* 27 (2010): 177–210. On the colonial origins of this differentiation in the British Empire see Vinita Damodaran, "Natural Heritage and Colonial Legacies: India in the Nineteenth Century," *Studies in History* 20, no. 1 (2013): 1–20. On the French IFAN created in 1938, see Adedze, supra 73 and Gaugue, supra 69.

90. Rivière, *Rapid Change*, 36.

91. Coremans, "Organization of a National Service," M&M11, 71.

92. Clarence Stein, "The Art Museum of Tomorrow," *Architects' Journal* (January 1930): 5–12. This plan was presented at the League of Nations conference on museum architecture in 1934 and published in OIM, *Muséographie* I (Paris: IICI, 1934), 23.

93. André Léveillé, *Scientific, Technical, Health Museums, Planetaria and the Popularization of Science* (Paris: ICOM, 1948).

94. Elodie Osborn, *Manual of Travelling Exhibitions* Museums and Monuments 5 [henceforth M&M5] (Paris: UNESCO, 1953) revised as UNESCO: *Temporary and Travelling Exhibitions* (Paris: UNESCO, 1963) [henceforth M&M10].

95. A preference for Modernism was conveyed through a recommendation for "simple and effective" presentation, with "clean lines," and also promotion of the work of known designers such as George Nelson and Herbert Bayer. *Museum Techniques in Fundamental Education*, Educational Studies and Documents 17 (Paris: UNESCO, 1954), 26–27. See also Herbert Bayer, "Aspects of Design of Exhibitions and Museums," *Curator* 4, no. 9 (1961): 257–287. On the preference for modern art in UNESCO's archive of color reproductions, see Rachel Perry, "Immutable Mobiles: UNESCO's Archives of Color Reproductions," *The Art Bulletin* (June 2017): 355–375.

96. Robert T. Hatt, *Proposal for the Development of Science Museums in Pakistan* (Paris: UNESCO, December 27, 1956), 10. This was in fact a 1939 quotation by Laurence Vale, director of the American Museums Association. See Paul Di Maggio, "Cultural Entrepreneurship in Nineteenth Century Boston," *Media Culture and Society* 4 (1982): 33–50.

97. Hiroshi Daifuku, "An Experimental Mobile Museum for Tropical Africa," *Museum* 18 (1965); Abraham Beer, "Expandable Mobile Museum for Arid Zones," *Museum* 7 (1954).

98. Robert Gessain, "Museums in Tropical Africa," *Museum* 18 (1965). The *museobus* turned out to be ill-suited to the tropics, where seasonal rains made many roads unusable for all but for three months of the year. Jean Gabus, *Report of Mission: Jos (Nigeria)*, 28 March 1965–4 April 1965 (Paris: UNESCO, [1965]), 5.

99. Bruno Molajoli, "Modern Architecture," M&M9, 146–185.

100. For an overview of this commission see Beatrice A. Assunto Vivio, *Franco Minissi: Musei e Restauri* (Rome: Gangemi, 2010).

101. Italian monument reconstructions were featured as examples in UNESCO's first Museums and Monuments manual in 1951, and the "reorganization" of Italian museums showcased at the Genoa meeting of ICOM in 1953. On ICCROM see Jukka Jokilehto, *ICCROM and the Conservation of Cultural Heritage* (Rome: ICCROM, 2011).

102. Cited respectively in Franco Minissi, *Corso di Museografia*, Universita degli Studi di Roma (1965–1966). ICCROM Library IIIa21 [unpaginated] and Dante Bernini, *Colloqui con Franco Minissi sul museo* (Roma: Edizioni de Luca, 1998), 9.

103. Marc Crinson, *Modern Architecture and the End of Empire* (London: Ashgate, 2003), 100–156. See also Arianna Fogelman, "Colonial Legacy in African Museology: The Ghana National Museum," *Museum Anthropology* 31, no. 1 (2008): 19–26, and Mark Crinson, "Nation-Building, Collecting and the Politics of Display," *Journal of the History of Collections* 13, no. 2 (01/2001).

104. Ghana Museum and Monuments Board, Ghana Museum and Monuments Board Report to the International Centre for the Study of the Preservation and Restoration of Cultural Property. Second Session. Rome, April, 1963. ICCROM Library.

105. Rivière, *Rapid Change*, 61.

106. Minissi, *Corso*.

107. Franco Minissi, "The New National Museum of Ghana, Accra," *Museum* 18, no. 3 (1965), 161.

108. "The museum's final claim is that the universal is embodied in the state." Carol Duncan and Alan Wallach, "The Universal Survey Museum," 463.

109. Franco Minissi, "The National Museum of the Villa Giulia in Rome," *Museum* 9, no. 2 (1956), 124–132.

110. Jean Gabus, "Conclusions," *Ivory Coast: Report Abidjan Museum,* (Paris: UNESCO, 1967):, 24.

111. Jean Gabus, *Ivory Coast: Report*, 25.

112. Jean Gabus, *Rapport de la Mission Jean Gabus, 21 Mars au 11 avril 1964* [Cameroun et Dahomey] (UNESCO, 1964); Jacques Crozet, *Dahomey: Etude de la restauration et de la mise en valeur des palais royaux d'Abomey* (UNESCO, 1968); and Walter Ruegg, *Dahomey: Mission M. Jean Gabus. Rapport de l'architecte* (UNESCO, [1965]). See also Jean Gabus, "Monuments historiques du Dahomey et du Cameroun: projets de restauration," *Museum* 20, no. 2 (1967): 131.

113. Raoul Curiel, *Pakistan: Preservation of Historic Sites with a View to Cultural Tourism* (Paris: UNESCO, 1966), 11.

114. R. M. H. Magnée, *Pakistan: Architectural Presentation of Historic Cities, Sites and Monuments with a View to Cultural Tourism* (Paris: UNESCO, November–December 1966), 10.

115. Angkor Wat also appeared in Snyers, "Stones Also Die," 28, and in Louis Malleret, "La restauration des monuments d'Angkor et ses Problèmes," *Studies in Conservation* 4, no. 3 (May 1959) : 60. On Borobudur see *The Restoration of Borobudur* (Paris: UNESCO, 2005), and Marieke Bloembergen and Martijn Eickhoff, "Save Borobudur!" in *Cultural Heritage as Civilizing Mission*, ed. M. Falser (Zurich: Springer, 2015).

116. G. R. H. Wright, *India: Proposals for Restoration Work at Srirangam Temple* (Paris: UNESCO, May 1969).

117. Various legislative models for heritage management had already migrated across the Indian Ocean during colonial expansion and late imperial rule, and UNESCO leveraged this legacy of exchange between sub-Saharan Africa and Southeast Asia. In the 1890s, India had already been the site of an ambitious new form of institutionalized conservation that cast "the whole territory as an open-air museum." Tapati Guha-Thakurta, *Monuments, Objects, Histories: Institutions of Art in Colonial and Post-Colonial India* (New York: Columbia University Press, 2004), 61. See also Dilip Chakrabarti, *Archaeology in the Third World* (New Delhi: DK Printworld, 2003), 161–208.

118. Indra Sengupta, "Culture-Keeping as State Action," ed. Paul Betts and Corey Ross, *Heritage in the Modern World* (Oxford: Oxford University Press, 2015), 153–177.

119. The section titled "Living Monuments" of John Marshall's 1923 *Conservation Manual* for India read: "In the case of 'living' monuments (by which is meant those monuments which are still in use for the purpose for which they were originally designed) it is sometimes necessary to restore them to greater extent than would be desirable on purely archaeological grounds." The following section explained that "It is the policy of Government to abstain as far as possible from any interference with the management or repair of religious buildings." John Marshall, *Conservation Manual* [1923] (Delhi: Caxton, 2006), 11. See also Nayanjot Lahiri, "Destruction or Conservation? Aspects of Monument Policy in British India 1899–1905," in *Destruction and Conservation of Cultural Property*, ed. Robert Layton, Peter G. Stone, and Julian Thomas (New York: Routledge, 2001), 264–275.

120. For a site-based historiography of heritage in Southeast Asia, see Marieke Bloembergen and Martijn Eickhoff, "Save Borobudur!" and "Conserving the Past, Mobilizing the Indonesian Future," *Bijdragen tot de Taal—, Land—en Volkenkunde* 167, no. 4 (2011): 405–436.

121. On portability see Donna C. Mehos and Suzanne M. Moon, "The Uses of Portability," in *Entangled Geographies*, ed. Gabrielle Hecht (Cambridge: MIT Press, 2011); Paul Basu and Vinita Damordaran, "Colonial Histories of Heritage," in *Heritage in the Modern World*, 241–271.

122. Patrick A. Faulkner, *India: The Renovation and Conservation of Temples in South India with Particular Reference to the Temple of Sri Ranganathaswam Srirangam, Madras*. Mission Report of 1966 (Paris: UNESCO, March 1967).

123. Faulkner, *Srirangam*, 16.

124. "The common man seems unaware that the floor possesses any character at all," Wright wrote, reinforcing a comment Faulkner had already made three years earlier, that the floor had a "wider import than might appear at first sight." Both recommended undoing recent "repaving" by local priests. Wright, 27; Faulkner, 11.

125. Christopher Davey, "G. R. H. (Mick) Wright: A Remarkable Australian Archaeological Architect," *Buried History* 49 (2013): 37–52. Wright also spent time in Nubia with the UNESCO-sponsored German team that relocated the temple of Kalabsha. G. R. H. Wright, *Kalabsha* (Berlin: Mann, 1972).

126. Wright, *Srirangam*, 43.

127. On the Srirangam temple in nineteenth-century canonization of Hindu architecture as a "style," see Tapati Guha-Thakurta, *Monuments, Objects, Histories*, 55.

128. Wright, *Srirangam*, 35–36.

129. "The efforts made to restore the temple of Rameswaram," he wrote, "will be more important in themselves than the results achieved." G. R. H. Wright, *India: Proposal for Restoration Work at Rameswaram Temple*, November–December 1970, 2325/RMS.RS/CP (Paris: UNESCO, February 1971), 19.

130. Wright, *Srirangam*, 54; See also G. R. H. Wright, *A Background to Restoration of Monuments in Southern India* (Tamilnadu State Department of Archaeology, 1969).

131. Wright, *Srirangam*, 30.

132. Paul Coremans, *UNESCO Mission to Thailand*, 10 April–1 May 1961 (Brussels: Institut Royal du Patrimoine, 1961), 8. Coremans approved of this plastering method after having acknowledged that it would never become agreed-upon by conservators "starting from aesthetic theories."

133. O. P. Agrawal, *Thailand: Conservation of Cultural Property*, 15 February–26 May 1967 (Paris: UNESCO, 1967), 2. 18/1. BMS. RD/CLT.

134. J. W. Evans, *Proposals for the Establishment and Development of a Natural History Museum in Bangkok, Thailand* (Paris: UNESCO, November 1961), WS/1261.111; and *Report No.2*. On the mural painting see Agrawal, *Thailand,* 2. T. T. Barrows, *Thailand: A Project for a National Science Museum, 3–29 1966* (Paris: UNESCO, January 1967), WS/0167.144 CLT: 3.

135. G. L. McCann Morley, *Thailand: Museums and Museum Development* (May–June 1967) (Paris: UNESCO, June 1968), 3. UNESCO 628/BMS. RD/CLT.

136. John Comaroff, "Governmentality, Materiality, Legality, Modernity," *Perspectives on African Modernities*, ed. J.-G. Deutsch, P. Probst, and H. Schmidt (London: James Currey, 2002), 122.

137. Already at the turn of the 1970s, UNESCO's Cultural Affairs Division changed its focus "from museum techniques to wider problems of preserving the cultural and natural heritage." Perrin Selcer, "Patterns of Science: Developing Knowledge for a World Community at UNESCO" (PhD diss., University of Pennsylvania, 2011). Publicly accessible Penn Dissertations. Paper 323.

138. Merrick Posnansky, *Africa and Archaeology* (London: Radcliffe, 2009): 129–130. See also Merrick Posnansky, "Coping with Collapse in the 1990s," in *Plundering Africa's Past*, ed. Peter Schmidt and Roderick McIntosh (Bloomington: Indiana University Press, 1996), 143–163, and Jonathan R. Walz, "An Interview with Merrick Posnansky,"*African Archaeological Review* 27, no. 3 (2010): 177–210.

139. See Ann Laura Stoler, "'The Rot Remains': From Ruins to Ruination," in *Imperial Debris*, ed. Stoler (Durham: Duke University Press, 2013), 1–38; for Fanon's original mention "germes de pourriture", sometimes translated as "germs" or "seeds" of "rot" or "decay," see Franz Fanon, *Les damnés de la terre* [1961] (Paris: La Découverte & Syros, 2002), 210 and 239.

140. *Jos Report*.

Chapter Five

1. Reyner Banham to Thomas Stauffer, January 20, 1965, cited in Daniel Bluestone, "Academics in Tennis Shoes," *JSAH* 58, no. 3 (September 1999): 300–307.

2. Kevin D. Murphy, "The Villa Savoye and the Modernist Historic Monument," *JSAH* 61, no. 1 (March 2002): 68–89; Panayotis Tournikiotis, "Le Corbusier, Giedion, and the Villa Savoye," *Future Anterior* 4, no. 4 (Winter 2007).

3. A proposal for "world heritage" was made at the White House Conference for International Cooperation convened (November 28 to December 1, 1965) by the Sub-Committee on Natural Resources Conservation and Development. Issues of preservation were also the focus of the Sub-Committee on Architecture, chaired by Scully. The issue made it to the front of the overall report, according to which "the spread of international culture has reactivated interest and pride in local cultural heritages." White House Conference on International Cooperation, *National Citizens Commission: Report of the Committee on Culture and Intellectual Exchange* [Washington, DC: The Conference, 1965].

4. "The parallel progress of voluntary association and legislative and administrative action, combined with media pressure" triggered a politics of expansion that aimed to establish "the place of conservation in life as a whole." Alan Power, *The Heroic Period of Conservation*, Twentieth Century Architecture 7, ed. Elain Harwood and Alan Powers (London: Twentieth Century Society, 2004), 7–18. Powers borrowed the phrase from Alison and Peter Smithsons' 1965 "The Heroic Period of Modern Architecture 1917–1937,"*Architectural Design* 35 (December 1965)—eventually a book, Alison Smithson, *The Heroic Period of Architecture* (New York: Rizzoli, 1985).

5. On the convergence of counterculture and heritage in Scandinavia, Thordis Arrhenius, "Preservation and Protest," *Future Anterior* 7, no. 2 (Winter 2010): 106–123.

6. Gazzola also warned against thinking that this "diffusion of criteria" had created a blanket of control. "Total protection can lead to non-protection." Piero Gazzola, "L'evoluzione del concetto del restauro prima e dopo la Carta di Venezia,"*Bollettino del Centro Internazionale di Studi di Architettura Andrea Palladio* 20 (1978): 243. Translation mine.

7. Willibald Sauerländer, "Erweiterung des Denkmalbegriffs?"*Deutsche Kunst und Denkmalpflege* 33 (1975): 117–130. Translation mine. Sauerländer used *Erweiterung* to mean "extension" and *Vermittlung* to mean "mediation."

8. The term "local population" was used during the salvage to denote the Nubian villagers who cohabitated with the temples, but it would be an understatement to say that they were disempowered. Not only did they have no say over the fate of the monuments, they also had little control over their own, and were eventually relocated by Egyptian and Sudanese governments to distant new towns completely removed from the Nile. For a brief account of this forced relocation in relation to the history of architectural mobility see Lucia Allais, "Global Agoraphobia,"in *Global Design History,* ed. Glenn Adamson, Giorgio Riello, and Sarah Teasley (London: Routledge, 2011), 174–179.

9. The Smithsons eulogized the Euston Arch in *The Euston Arch and the Growth of the London, Midland & Scottish Railway* (London: Thames & Hudson, 1968).

10. In his own eulogy for the first machine age, Banham explained that "architecture moving with its times will always seem 'difficult'" because "modern architecture . . . represents an ancient craft trying to keep pace with a technological situation." Reyner Banham, *The Age of the Masters* (London: Architectural Press, 1962), 3.

11. The dam designer, Karl Tarzhegi, is known as the founder of soil mechanics; he eventually resigned from the international oversight in protest against the Soviet implementation of his design. For a political history of the Dam see John Waterbury, *Hydropolitics of the*

Nile Valley (Syracuse: Syracuse University Press, 1979); for its devastating environmental effects see Timothy Mitchell, "Para-Sites of Capitalism," *Rule of Experts* (Berkley: University of California Press, 2002), 19–122; for an in-depth investigation of the relationship between economics, technology, and politics see Ahmad Shokr, "Hydropolitics, Economy, and the Aswan High Dam in Mid-Century Egypt," *Arab Studies Journal* (Spring 2009): 10–31.

12. "Nasser's Pyramid" was the expression used by Herbert Addison in *Sun and Shadow at Aswan* (London: Chapman & Hall, 1959), 122. The "Egyptian monopolization of the Nile" is from Morris Llewellyn Cooke, *Nasser's Aswan High Dam* (Washington, DC: Public Affairs Institute, 1956), 19. In "The Technological Aspects of Decision Making," *World Politics* (October 1980), 57, Robert W. Rycrift and Joseph Szyliowicz conclude that within Egypt "other hydrological approaches were actively discouraged," and "only the High Dam gained access to the political agenda" of the Nasser regime. John Waterbury summarized that "whether a triumph of Soviet-Egyptian solidarity or a triumph of the Egyptian people, the diplomatic history of the dam dictated that it be a triumph of some sort," and the dam was "consecrated [as a] massive monument, built by the Soviets." Waterbury, *Hydropolitics*, 114–115.

13. United Arab Republic, *Assouan: La ville des nouvelles réalisations plus grandioses que les obélisques et les pyramides* (Cairo: Administration de l'information, 1961), 18. Translation mine. Reporter Max Freedman returning from a visit to the construction site in 1963 noted that "everywhere one hears about the contrast between the dam and the Pyramids." "The Aswan Dam," *Washington Post*, February 23, 1963.

14. The soviet text is Pravda, *Asuan—simvol sovetsko-arabsko-fi druzhby* [Aswan, Symbol of Egyptian-Soviet Friendship] (Moskva: Politicheskaialit-ry, 1964), the UNESCO book is Christiane Desroches Noblecourt and Georg Gerster, *The World Saves Abu Simbel* (Vienna: Koska, 1968). During a 2004 discussion of "cosmopolitics" Latour accused Ulrich Beck of "believing in a UNESCO koine, a sociological Esperanto." Bruno Latour, "Whose Cosmos, Which Cosmopolitics? Comments on the Peace Terms of Ulrich Beck," *Common Knowledge* 10, no. 3 (2004): 450–462.

15. Vattenbyggnadsbyran [VBB], *The Salvage of the Abu Simbel Temples: Concluding Report* (Cairo: Arab Republic of Egypt Ministry of Culture, 1971), 5.

16. See Lucia Allais, "The Design of the Nubian Desert: Monuments, Mobility, and the Space of Global Culture,"Aggregate, *Governing by Design: Architecture, Economy and Politics in the 20th Century* (Pittsburgh: University of Pittsburgh Press, 2012), 179–215. To sum up each actor: "the Egyptian People" were in fact 120,000 Nubian villagers whose homes disappeared under the new lake; "the Archaeologist" was composed of over sixty archaeological teams from all over the world; "the Contractor" was a multinational consortium created to allow foreign developers to operate in Egypt. As for UNESCO, while the engineering report cited here emphasizes the universalism of its appeal to "nations and people all over the world," in fact mapping the number of responses to this appeal on a geographical dial reveals the dominance of Western experts.

17. The American environmental thinker Holmes Rolston argued in *Conserving Natural Values* (New York: Columbia University Press, 1994) that integrity became "the law of the land" in American nature conservation after 1949. Catherine Howett gives an overview of how the term was enlarged from ecological to cultural usage in "Integrity as a Value in Cultural Landscape Preservation," *Preserving Cultural Landscapes in America* (Baltimore: Johns Hopkins University Press, 2000), 187–207. In architecture the term was popularized by the *Venice Charter*, where Article 14 mandates that "sites of monuments must be the object of special care in order to safeguard their integrity." By 1968 UNESCO arrived at a definition, in a document relating to the last of the Nubian temple complexes to be saved, the island of Philae: "By the phrase *integrity of monuments* is meant the preservation of the

original geographic, architectural and cultural position and ambiance of the monument including not only the position of various buildings vis-à-vis each other, but also their original relationship with surrounding physiographic and cultural features in the area." UNESCO/S/NUBIA15 (1968).

18. The aesthetic concept of "integration" and "re-integration" gained popularity during the postwar European experience with fragments and lacunae, as an alternative to "reconstruction," which had continued to hold negative connotations since the nineteenth century. Both terms describe a modern intervention, but whereas reconstruction implies that the new imitates the old, re-integration is focused on creating a aesthetic "whole" that is visually apprehensible, while not allowing confusion between old and new. The authoritative text, which connects the practice to a Kantian aesthetic vision, is Giovanni Carbonara's *Reintegrazione dell'Immagine* (Roma: Bulzoni, 1976). Some earlier texts, which are representative of the way the term became popular during the heated international debates about painting restoration in the 1950s, are collected in the "Reintegration of Losses" section of *Historical and Philosophical Issues in the Conservation of Cultural Heritage*, ed. Nicholas S. Price, M. Kirby Talley Jr., and Alessandra M. Vaccaro (Los Angeles: Getty Conservation Institute, 1996), 326–363.

19. The famous "scrape / anti-scrape" debates of the nineteenth century were international; for an overview see Price, Talley, and Vaccaro, *Historical and Philosophical Issues*; on the internationalism of preservationists at the turn of the twentieth century see Melanie Hall, ed., *Towards World Heritage* (London: Ashgate, 2011).

20. Coyne et Bellier were specifically commissioned to design a "rock-fill dam." The UNESCO commission also considered three other options: "lifting the temples and surrounding rocks above the levels of the surrounding waters; construction of a concrete dam in front of each temple; construction of a vaulted concrete dam, protecting the temples from up close." The commission mandated that the dam be "approximately 700 meters wide, in such a manner that the rock mounds in which the temples have been hewn are respected in their totality" and that "the distance between the façade of the great temple and the crest of the dam would be around 300 meters." UNESCO/55 EX/7 Annexe 1: "Réunion d'Experts Internationaux pour la sauvegarde des sites et monuments de Nubie menacés," Cairo, October 1–11, 1959, *Rapport*, 6.

21. Albert Laprade, "Esthétique," Bureau d'études André Coyne et Jean Bellier, *Avant-Projet des Ouvrages de Protection des Temples d'Abou Simbel.* Vol. 1: Rapport. (Paris, 1960).

22. Viollet-le-Duc, *On Restoration*, trans. Charles Wethered, (London: Sampson, Low, Marttson, Low and Sparce, 1875).

23. Brew to Barney (December 20, 1962.) JOB/10. Brew was the chairman of UNESCO's committee comparing these schemes.

24. This meeting consisted of representatives of archaeology, engineering, architecture, and cultural ministries, who traveled down the Nile by boat to visit each threatened temple. *Meeting of International Experts on the Safeguarding of the Sites and Monuments of Ancient Nubia* (Cairo, November 12, 1959). UNESCO/SN/R.EXP/SR.

25. Piero Gazzola, *Transfert des temples et autres monuments et ruines: considérations de caractère architectural et archéologique*. Rapport de M. Piero Gazzola (Cairo, September 28, 1959), 3. Translation mine. UNESCO/SN/R.EXP/6.

26. Italconsult, *Saving the Temples of Abu Simbel* (Rome, November 1960). ICCROM Library.

27. Cesare Brandi, "The Concept of Restoration," in *A Theory of Restoration*, trans. Cythia Rockwell (Rome: Nardini/ Istituto Centrale per il Restauro, 2005), 52. "Restoration should aim to re-establish the potential oneness of the work of art."

28. Gustavo Colonnetti, "Il Progetto italiano per il salvataggio dei templi di Abu-Simbel," in *Problemi attuali di scienza e di cultura* (Roma: Accademia Nazionale dei Lincei, 1961), 3–12.

29. In December 1962 the UNESCO General Conference decided not to compel all of its member states to make contributions to the Abu Simbel salvage and instead set the deadline of March 31, 1963, for receiving "voluntary contributions" for the Italian scheme, planning a pledging conference for March 20 of the same year. In the meantime the price for the lifting was evaluated at $60 million. By the time the deadline passed, only $7.5 million of hard currency had been raised.

30. Edmund Happold, "The Scheme Explained," *Architects' Journal* (March 20, 1963).

31. John Ruskin, "The Lamp of Memory," *The Seven Lamps of Architecture* (New York: Farrar, Straus and Giroux, 1988), 178.

32. William MacQuitty, "Khartoum to Abu Simbel," in *A Life to Remember* (London: Quartet, 1991), 341. In "New Scheme to Save Abu Simbel Temples," *Architects' Journal* (March 20, 1963), 610, MacQuitty is cited as predicting that "[w]ithin the next hundred years the high dam itself will be outdated by atomic power bringing new methods of irrigation and electricity. And if that happened the Nile water would return to its original level, and the temples of Abu Simbel could be restored to their present state." See also "The Author's Scheme," Bill MacQuitty, *Abu Simbel* (New York: Putnam's, 1965), 182.

33. Jane Drew, unpublished memoir, Collections of the Canadian Center for Architecture, Montreal.

34. Albert Caquot, *Les Temples d'Abou Simbel: Avant-Projet de leur Déplacement Complet* (Paris: Simecsol, 1963), 8.

35. A "Preliminary Report on the Project of Dismantling, Moving and Re-erecting the Abu Simbel Temples" was produced by VBB for the Egyptian Government in September 1962 and marked "confidential"; it is cited in a report, "Report on Visit of Wendell E. Johnson to Egypt Re Abu Simbel Temples," April 1962. JOB. Johnson, Chief of the Engineering Division of the US Army Corps of Engineers, was sent to Egypt on a "fact-finding mission." He wrote approvingly of "the 'dismantling and re-erection'" plan of VBB, calling it "entirely feasible" and recommending it "based on engineering considerations, and subject to appropriate considerations of the archaeological, geological, financing and policy aspects." In April 1963, after refusing to pledge funds for the Italian scheme, the US Department of State communicated a message to the UAR offering "the cooperation of the US toward the development of an alternative that would be technically and financially feasible." Max McCullough to Brew, May 1, 1963. JOB.

36. UNESCO/Nubia/4.

37. Another scheme to "reproduce the temples completely as replicas," by using photogrammetric information and casting reinforced concrete copies of the temple-fronts, was discussed in correspondence from Jo Brew to Edmund White, of the American Consulting Commission, in 1960, JOB X. Its very existence confirms that preserving the original stone material, even in pieces, was enough to make the new temples authentic.

38. *The World Saves Abu Simbel* (Paris: UNESCO, 1967).

39. Timothy Mitchell extracts this term from Georg Simmel in "The Character of Calculability," *Rule of Experts*, 80–118.

40. On how PL 480 tied domestic politics and foreign affairs, see Lisa Martin, *Democratic Commitments* (Princeton: Princeton University Press, 2000). For a history of the Food for Peace program see Harriet Friedmann, "The Political Economy of Food: The Rise and Fall of the Postwar International Food Order," *American Journal of Sociology*, 88 Supplement (1982): S251.

41. See "Statement by John A. Wilson," *Mutual Security Act of 1960: Hearings before the Committee on Foreign Relations*, S. 3058 (Washington, DC: US Government Printing Office, 1960), 576.

42. John F. Kennedy, *Letter from the President to the President of the Senate and the Speaker of the House*, April 6, 1961. Reprinted as *Press Release PR(61)5*, April 7, 1961. The funds ($12 million) were originally devoted to the Philae Temples, but since Abu Simbel was further upstream, the United States eventually accepted to have this amount transferred to Abu Simbel. The one-third proportional requirement remained, however, making possible only a project of roughly $36 million. The cutting project was priced at $32 million. It eventually cost $42 million, of which $21.47 million was provided by an "international fund," within which the US's $12 million constituted 56%. It was Egypt who provided the remaining half.

43. UNESCO's final accounting is published in an appendix in *Temples and Tombs of Ancient Nubia*, ed. Torgny Säve-Söderbergh (London: Thames & Hudson, 1987). The Egyptian financial report was included in a book published by the Ministry of Information as "Rameses Crowned by Modern Man," and marked as being printed "through the PL 480 Program." Tharwat 'Ukashah, Insan al-'asr yuttawiju Ramsis. (al-Qahirah: al-Hay'ah al-Misriyah al-'Amah lil-Ta'lif wa-al-Nashr, 1971).

44. See note 42 above.

45. For a more explicit theorization of the entire UNESCO campaign as an example of a gift economy applied to a new regime of cultural "surplus" invented by UNESCO, see Lucia Allais, "The Design of the Nubian Desert," *Governing by Design*.

46. The powerplant is described by Walter Furuskog and Geoffrey Kennedy, "The Aswan Hydro-Electric Scheme," *Proceedings of the Institution of Civil Engineers* 17 (1960): 201. See also abstract no. 3514 of the *Institution of Electrical Engineers* (February 1961), where a note informs us that "For his part in the design of the project and the co-ordination of the engineering services, Mr. Kennedy was awarded the Order of Merit, First Class, by President Nasser." These texts constitute evidence that an American-Egyptian-Swedish working relationship existed as early as 1958. On the international networks of geology, see Evan Schofer, "The Global Institutionalization of Geological Science, 1800 to 1990," *American Sociological Review* 68, no. 5 (October 2003): 730–759.

47. "At a conference in Rome in 1961, I ran into an Egyptian minister whom I knew from the dam project. 'Do you want to be consultant on the Abu Simbel project?' he asked. 'Certainly,' I told him." Cited in "Europe's Top A-E Makes It on Work Underground and Abroad," *Engineering News Record*, July 27, 1972, 16–17.

48. Nils Hast, *A Study of the Internal Stress Distribution in the Abu Simbel Rock and Temples: The Occurrence of Horizontal Rock Pressure*. Preliminary Report (August 1962). ICCROM Library.

49. VBB, *Final Report*.

50. This image made the cover of *Life* magazine on October 23, 1965.

51. VBB, *Final Report*, 62–65.

52. VBB, *Abu Simbel: Salvage of the Temples, Landscaping and General Layout* (January 1962), ICCROM Library.

53. "Meeting of a Group of Experts on the Consolidation of the Façades and Interior of the Abu Simbel Temples and the Reconstitution of the Site: Report of the Group" (March 30, 1962), 6–7. UNESCO Nubia/2 CE/8.

54. See "The Role of Concrete in the Abu Simbel Project," *Concrete* (November 1971): 343–347.

55. Guy Debord, *The Society of the Spectacle* [1967], trans. Donald Nicholson-Smith (New York: Zone, 1994), 37.

56. See for example the re-erection of the Kiosk of Kertassi and the temple of Beit el Wali on the "new island of Kalabsha" in 2001. Zahi Hawass, *The Island of Kalabsha* (Cairo: Supreme Council of Antiquities/American University in Cairo Press, 2004).

57. The earliest plans for this recording operation date from 1956, when UNESCO's Monuments Committee suggested an expert mission be sent to Nubia. The first UNESCO presence in Nubia was established in 1958 with the *Centre d'étude et de documentation sur l'ancienne Égypte* (C.E.D.A.E.) headed by Louvre Egyptologist Christiane Desroches Noblecourt, which paired with the National Geographic Institute to publish surveys of each temple as early as 1958.

58. Robert Genot, *Nubie 64: Quelques aspects de la coopération internationale à la sauvegarde des monuments de la Nubie égyptienne* (Paris: Institut géographique national, 1968).

59. Walter Benjamin, "The Work of Art in the Age of Technological Reproducibility," republished in *The Work of Art in the Age of Technological Reproducibility and Other Writings on Media*, ed. Michael W. Jennings, Brigid Doherty, and Thomas Y. Levin, trans. Edmund Jephcott (Cambridge: Harvard University Press, 2008).

60. "Anyone who carefully examines Egyptian images will recognize that they were conceived from strictly near viewing," otherwise "they become like flat mirages." Alois Riegl, *Historical Grammar of the Visual Arts* [first version,1897–1898], trans. Jacqueline E. Jung (New York: Zone, 2004), 191. Adolf Hilderbrand, *The Problem of Form in Painting and Sculpture* [first version, 1893] trans. Max Meyer and Robert Morris-Odgen (New York: Stechert, 1907), 125. "The movements of the figures are not organic but mechanical, i.e. they consist of local changes in the positions of specific members, changes affecting neither the form nor the dimensions of the rest of the body." Erwin Panofsky, "The History of the Theory of Human Proportions as a Reflection of the History of Styles" [orig. 1921], in *Meaning in the Visual Arts* (Chicago: University of Chicago Press, 1955), 57.

61. Panofsky, 60–62.

62. Drew Pearson, "Aid for Historic Treasures Denied," *Los Angeles Times*, June 3, 1964.

63. Letter from Emma Swan Hall, "Abu Simbel as Art: Preserving Temples Threatened by Dam Waters Questioned," *New York Times*, April 28, 1963, 185. See also "Just Browsing: Ramses' Monuments," *Chicago Tribune*, July 12, 1964, where columnist Barbara Watz asserts the temples are "not one of the most beautiful in the world," and refused to use the adjective "beautiful" at all.

64. Abu Simbel appears in Siegfried Giedion's *The Eternal Present* (New York: Bollingen Foundation, 1962–1964) several times, most notably in an unfavorable comparison with the Sphinx of Giza, where Abu Simbel is an example of Ramesside colossal statuary that "never attained the mystic power that still emanates from the Sphinx despite its mutilated features." Giedion, 73.

65. André Malraux, "Speech delivered at the launch of the International Campaign for the Salvage of the Monuments of Nubia, UNESCO House, Mar 8, 1960," *UNESCO Courier* (May 1960): 8. For more on Malraux's specific role, see Allais, *The Design of the Nubian Desert*.

66. André Malraux, *Museum Without Walls*, trans. Stuart Gilbert and Francis Price (New York: Doubleday, 1967), 160.

67. In 1928 Wörringer famously compared Egyptian architecture and the architecture of the American grain silos, "alike their over-estimation of the colossal." Wilhelm Wörringer, *Egyptian Art*, trans. Bernard Rackham (London: Putnam, 1928).

68. The *New York Times* even opined that "[i]f Rameses II were alive today he would probably be recognized as one of the world's most boring and dangerous characters, though he would have competition." *New York Times*, January 24, 1960, E10.

69. See for instance Edwards' "Foreword," MacQuitty, *Abu Simbel*, 9–11.

70. Jay Walz, "Cairo Seeks to Save Temples above Aswan," *New York Times*, January 23, 1960, 3.

71. "Heritage today seems to play the role of a vast mirror in which we . . . contemplate our own image." Francoise Choay, *L'Allégorie du Patrimoine* (Paris: Seuil, 1992), 198. Translation mine.

72. Peter Probst has written evocatively about heritage as an image-generating machine. Peter Probst, "An African Journey," *RES* 52 (Autumn 2007): 153–160.

73. Raymond Williams, "From Medium to Social Practice," *Marxism and Literature* [1977] (Oxford: Oxford University Press, 1988), 158–164.

74. McLuhan's theory was that every medium's content is another medium, and that this chain literally established the basic pattern for a technologically driven, progressive history of media; see "The Medium Is the Message," *Understanding Media: The Extensions of Man* [1964] (Cambridge: MIT Press, 1999), 8. The point about containment still holds without this teleology, however, especially in his spatialized version of the argument, offered in an architectural journal, "The Invisible Environment: The Future of an Erosion," *Perspecta* 11 (1967): 161–167, where historical causality seems less important than spatial replacement.

75. "The darkening of the surface of a porous stone following treatment with an epoxy resin solution is an optical effect." See also William S. Ginell & Richard Coffman, "Epoxy Resin-Consolidated Stone: Appearance Change on Aging," *Studies in Conservation*, 43, no. 4 (1998): 242. Epoxy has since become controversial, and Abu Simbel was one of the earliest examples of epoxy used to reinforce not the joints between stone blocks but the actual fabric of a monument. For retrospective histories of the use of the material, see Lal Gauri, "Efficiency of Epoxy Resins as Stone Preservatives," *Studies in Conservation* (May 1974): 100–101; P. Kotlík, P. Justa, and J. Zelinger, "The Application of Epoxy Resins for the Consolidation of Porous Stone," *Studies in Conservation* (May1983): 75–79; and Nicholas L. Gianopulos, "Doubts about Epoxy Article," *APT Bulletin*, 21, no. 1. (1989): 2–3. For two conflicting account of the post-darkening experience, see Stephen Marks, "Abu Simbel, Egypt: A Revealing Experience," and Shawn Kholucy, "More Thoughts on Abu Simbel," *Transactions of the Society for the Conservation of Ancient Buildings* 17 (1992), 56–60; 88.

Coda

1. Lewis Mumford, "The Death of the Monument," *Circle: International Survey of Constructive Art* (London: Faber and Faber, 1937), 263–270.

2. Superstudio, "Salvataggi di centri storici italiani," *IN: Argomenti e immagini di design* (May–June 1972): 4–13. Translated by Lucia Allais, "Salvages of Italian Historic Centers," *Log* 22 (Spring/Summer 2011): 114–124.

3. See Francesco Bandarin and Ron van Oers, eds., *Reconnecting the City: The Historic Urban Landscape Approach and the Future of Urban Heritage* (Chichester: Wiley Blackwell, 2015), and A. Mahmsen-Milan, "Energy Restoration and Retrofitting," *Journal of Cultural Heritage* 14, no. 3 (2013): E41–E44.

4. Synthetic histories include Paul Betts and Corey Ross, *Heritage in the Modern World* (Oxford: Oxford University Press, 2015); Miles Glendinning's *The Conservation Movement* (London: Routledge, 2013); Jukka Jokilehto, *A History of Architectural Conservation* (London: IIC,1999); and John Stubbs, *Time Honored: A Global View of Conservation* (New York: Wiley, 2009).

5. Ulrich Beck, *World at Risk*, trans. Ciaran Cronin (Cambridge: Polity, 2002).

6. Fernando Vidal and Nélia Dias, *Endangerment, Biodiversity and Culture* (London: Routledge, 2015).

7. On "the twilight of internationalism" and its link to environmental politics see Mark Mazower, *Governing the World* (New York: Penguin, 2012).

8. This change is pervasive but is especially acute in the British case. See Robert Hewison, *The Heritage Industry* (London: Methuen, 1987); Jordann Bailkin, *The Culture of Property: The Crisis of Liberalism in Modern Britain* (Chicago: University of Chicago Press, 2004); and Dan Brockington and Rosaleen Duffy, "Revisiting Neoliberal Conservation," *Capitalism and Conservation* (New York: Wiley, 2011). On neoliberal reform in Ireland and Sweden, see Elene Negussie, "Implications of Neo-liberalism for Built Heritage Management," *Urban Studies* 43, no. 10 (2006): 1803–1824.

9. UNESCO always thought non-aligned countries were fertile ground to bring together the Eastern and Western blocks culturally, but non-aligned governments often used internationalist missions to pit the two sides against one another.

10. The failure to secure the Iraq National Museum is rightly seen as an instance where the American military jettisoned its World War II legacy. See *Catastrophe! The Looting and Destruction of Iraq's Past*, ed. Geoff Emberling and Katharyn Hanson (Chicago: Oriental Institute Museum of the University of Chicago, 2008). On renewed efforts to train troops see Laurie W. Rush's contribution to "Preservation of War," *Future Anterior* 14, no. 1 (Summer 2018).

11. Erwin Panofsky, "Art and Archaeology," lecture outline, February 24, 1938, CRM 10/G. See also supra, chapter 2, note 92.

12. Michel Foucault, *The Archaeology of Knowledge* [1969], trans. Sheridan Smith (New York: Pantheon, 1972), 7.

13. Jacques Le Goff, "Monumento / Documento," *Enciclopedia Einaudi*, vol. 5 (Torino: Einaudi, 1984), 38–48.

14. One recent work is Tony Bennett, Fiona Cameron, Nélia Dias, Ben Dibley, Rodney Harrison, Ira Jacknis, and Conal McCarthy, *Collecting, Ordering, Governing* (Durham: Duke University Press, 2017).

15. In the humanities, works that have resituated the monument include: on the temporal aspect of built forms, Christopher Wood and Alexander Nagel, *Anachronic Renaissance* (New York: Zone, 2010); on the concentricity of meaning, Alfred Gell, *Art and Agency* (New York: Clarendon, 1998); and on expansion and limitation in Classics, Brooke Holmes and Constanze Guthenke, "Inside and Outside the Canon," *Marginality, Canonicity, Passion*, Classical Presences, ed. M. Formisano and C. Kraus (Oxford: Oxford University Press, 2018), 2.

16. Andreas Huyssens, *After the Great Divide* (Bloomington: Indiana University Press, 1987).

17. Mumford, supra 1.

18. Superstudio, *Salvataggi*. Here I draw from my introduction, "Disaster as Experiment: Superstudio's Radical Preservation," *Log* 22 (Spring/Summer 2011): 125–129.

19. Italia Nostra, *Art and Landscape of Italy: Too Late to Be Saved?* (Florence: Centro Di, 1972), 81–92. The group was based in Rome and headed by senator-for-life and meridionalista Umberto Zanotti-Bianco. See also the editorials in *Burlington Magazine*: "The Future of Venice" (January 1963): 3; "An Italia Nostra Exhibition" (January 1969): 3–5; and "A Future for Naples?" (November 1984): 667.

20. The conservation movement in Italy was in fact politically split, and Superstudio significantly did not propose to intervene in Bologna, where a communist government was already working with preservationists to create an affordable historic city center. See Paolo Scrivano and Filippo De Pieri, "Representing the 'Historical Centre' of Bologna," *Urban History Review* 33, no. 1 (2004): 34–45.

21. Manfredo Tafuri, "Storia, conservazione, restauro," Interview with Chiara Baglione and Bruno Pedretti, *Il Progetto del passato* (Milano: Bruno Mondadori, 1997): 90.

22. Protecting the neutrality of the expert was given as rationale for taking this nongovernmental route. Being semi-independent would avoid "being exposed to charges of political or economic opportunism." The Committee on Cultural and Int ellectual Exchange,

"Role of Government," in The White House Conference on International Cooperation: National Citizens' Commision Report on the Committee on Cultural and Intellectual Exchange (Washington, DC: November 28–December 1, 1965), Doc/28 (Final draft), 11.

23. On field survey methods applied to heritage destruction see Andras Riedlmayer and Andrew Herscher with Donna Viscuglia, *The Destruction of Cultural Heritage in Kosovo, 1998–1999: A Postwar Survey* (Cambridge, MA: Kosovo Cultural Heritage Project, 2001); on cartographic methods see Laura Kurgan's work in Aleppo, *Conflict Urbanism*, http://c4sr.columbia.edu/conflict-urbanism-aleppo/; on architectural skills applied to juridical ends see the work of Eyal Weizman, ed., *Forensis: The Architecture of Public Truth* (Berlin: Sternberg, c2014). A recent polemical proposal is to use heritage designation to spark debate about the rights of refugees: "Refugee Heritage," at http://www.decolonizing.ps/site/.

24. For the ways the rise of NGOs was tied not only to ecological events but also to institutionalization, see David John Frank, Ann Hironaka, John W. Meyer, Evan Schofer, and Nancy Brandon Tuma, "The Rationalization and Organization of Nature in World Culture," in *Constructing World Culture*, ed. John Bolu and George M. Thomas (Stanford: Stanford University Press, 1999), 81–99.

25. See Lucia Allais, "This Criterion Should Preferably Be Used in Conjunction with Other Criteria," in *Grey Room* 61 (Fall 2015): 92–01.

26. See Abduquail Yussuf, "Article I: Definition of Cultural Heritage," *The 1972 World Heritage Convention: A Commentary*, ed. Francesco Francioni (Oxford: Oxford University Press, 2008), 23–50.

27. See Valdimar Tr. Hafstein, "Protection as Dispossession: Government in the Vernacular," in *Cultural Heritage in Transit: Intangible Rights as Human Rights*, ed. Deborah Kapchan (Philadelphia: Penn Press, 2014). I borrow the expression "weapon of the weak" from James C. Scott, *Weapons of the Weak* (New Haven: Yale University Press, c1985).

28. Most recently the Committee debated whether to change the language of criterion (vi), which is the only one that allows a site to be inscribed for its association with an "event." Supra 25.

29. "Heritage Untranslatables in Sub-Saharan Africa" in Barbara Cassin and Danièle Wozny, *Les intraduisibles du patrimoine en Afrique Sub-Saharienne* (Paris: Demopolis, 2014), 101–105.

30. On the legacy of the Venice Charter, see Michael Petzet, "Principles of Monument Conservation," *International Charters for Conservation and Restoration* (Munich: ICOMOS, 2004), 7–29.

31. An "International Campaign for Venice and Florence" was launched on December 2, 1966. See "Florence, Venice: UNESCO Opens World Campaign," *UNESCO Courier* (January 1967). Indeed, in 1966 Rex Keating made six recordings *from Florence* that were rebroadcast on UNESCO Radio to raise awareness. Rex Keating, "Florence: A series of six programmes based on recordings made in Florence in connection with the flood." UNESCO PI/R/47.

32. See Lucia Allais, "Amplified Humanity and the Architectural Criminal," in "Preservation and War," *Future Anterior* 14, no. 1 (Summer 2018).

33. Rem Koolhaas, "Preservation Is Overtaking Us," *Future Anterior* 1, no. 2 (Fall 2004).

34. On *restauro critico* see for example Giovanni Carbonara, "Il restauro critico," *Il progetto di Restauro, interpretazione critica del testo architettonico*, ed. Nullo Pirazzoli (Trento: Comitato Giuseppe Gerola, 1988), 27 and Miles Glendinning, *The Conservation Movement* (London: Routledge, 2013), 264.

35. "Experimental preservationists choose objects in order to test their capacity as heritage." Jorge Otero Pailos, ed., *Experimental Preservation* (New York: Lars Müller, 2016), 11–39.

36. Two examples are the recent listing and protection of Le Corbusier's Weissenhof-Siedlung houses and of Patrick Geddes's plan for Tel Aviv.

37. Immanuel Kant, *The Critique of Judgement* [1784] (Trans. Meredith Oxford, 2007): §6–14; Theodor Adorno and Max Horkheimer, *Dialectic of Enlightenment*, trans. Edmund Jephcott (Stanford: Stanford University Press, 2002).

Index

Page numbers in italics refer to illustrations.